Volume IX 1871–1881

Volumes VIII and IX are supplementary, with every item keyed to the original edition by volume, page, and line number. Of the 473 letters in Volume IX only 116 are by George Eliot. While she was writing *Middlemarch* and *Daniel Deronda,* Lewes conducted all her business correspondence and, as always, shielded her from seekers of autographs and photographs. In 1868 he gave up journalism to devote himself to *Problems of Life and Mind,* an ambitious attempt to formulate a science of psychology, based on physiology with no metaphysical assumptions. Their letters refer increasingly to ill health. Besides the psychomatic ailments troubling most writers, George Eliot suffered in 1874 the first attacks of kidney stone that afflicted her until her death.

As her fame increased, the Sunday afternoon gatherings at the Priory grew larger and more distinguished. In the summers the Leweses took long holidays on the Continent or rented some country house where they could work quietly. In 1877 after much searching they bought the Heights at Witley. George Eliot returned no calls and accepted few invitations.

One exception was the family of Mrs. William Cross at Weybridge, whose hearty hospitality offered the Leweses a pleasant refuge from London life. Mrs. Cross's son John, a banker, invested for George Eliot the large sums earned by her novels. After Lewes's death in 1878 she turned to John, who was twenty years younger, for the affection she could not live without. They were married in 188   dding trip in a fit of me jumped into the Ca recovered. They ret moving into a new where three weeks The most intimate details or n.. come from the curious autobiography of Edith Simcox, which is quoted extensively in this volume.

Times

THE YALE EDITION

of the

GEORGE ELIOT LETTERS

IX

THE

George Eliot Letters

EDITED BY Gordon S. Haight

Professor Emeritus of English, Yale University

VOLUME IX

1871–1881

New Haven and London, YALE UNIVERSITY PRESS

1 9 7 8

Published with assistance from
the Louis Effingham deForest Memorial Fund.

Library of Congress catalog card number: 52–12063
International standard book number: 0–300–02235–2

Set in Monophoto Baskerville by
Asco Trade Typesetting Limited, Hong Kong.
Printed in the United States of America by
The Vail-Ballou Press, Binghamton, N.Y.

Published in Great Britain, Europe, Africa, and Asia (except
Japan) by Yale University Press, Ltd., London. Distributed in
Australia and New Zealand by Book & Film Services,
Artarmon, N.S.W., Australia; and in Japan by Harper & Row,
Publishers, Tokyo Office.

CONTENTS OF VOLUME IX

LETTERS 1871–1881

Shottermill

V, 131:1 GE TO EMILY DAVIES, LONDON, 2 JANUARY 1871

MS: Girton College. *Envelope:* Miss Emily Davies | 17 Cunningham Place | N.W.
Postmark: ST JOHNS WOOD SO | N.W | JA 2 | 71.

The Priory | 21 North Bank | January 2. 1871.

My dear Miss Davies

If you have not made up your mind as to the person who ought to be Chief Secretary to the Educational Board, will you turn your attention to the claims of Mr. Nassau Senior?

I am interested in him for the sake of his wife—one of the best women I know. But the best of wives is not a good reason for a man's election to an important office, and I am far from undertaking to recommend Mr. Senior to you as the fittest candidate, since I know nothing of his rivals. Of his own qualifications I only know that he was Secretary of Commissions under three Lord Chancellors, and that he appears to me, from my own slight observation and the more experienced testimony of others, to have some qualities which would make him a good public servant and fellow-workman.

But my utmost intention in troubling you with this note, is to give some emphasis to his name as a candidate supposing that you have any attention to spare for them.

Always yours sincerely
M. E. Lewes.

V, 133:6 GE TO THOMAS HENRY HUXLEY, LONDON, 2 JANUARY 1871

MS: Imperial College of Science, London.

The Priory | 21 North Bank
January 2. 71.

Dear Mr. Huxley

I trouble you with this letter for the sake of a very good, sweet woman —Mrs. Nassau Senior.[9] It is true that her goodness is not a sufficient reason for her husband's appointment to the chief secretaryship of the Educational Board. But you, I imagine, are especially bound to regard it as a

---

9. Mrs. Jane Elizabeth Hughes Senior (1828–77), wife of Nassau John Senior (1822–91). The appointment went to George Hector Croad.

5

presumption in a man's favour, and a becoming background to his other advantages, that he has chosen an excellent wife. So far as real qualifications for the post in question are concerned, I only know that Mr. Senior has had all the experience implied in having been Secretary of Commissions for four years under three Chancellors, and I have reason—chiefly in the unsought indirect testimony of those who know him intimately—to believe that he has some of the moral qualities which help to make a good public servant and fellow-worker.

If your judgment is already satisfied as to the person who ought to be appointed, you will, I trust, pardon this ignorant letter of mine. It is not intended as more than a pencil-mark by the side of a name in a list of candidates, on the supposition that you may be looking at such a list with a mind not yet decided. Such a mark, from whatever hand it might come, would give a little emphasis to your attention. I feel sure that you will not suspect me of presuming further. I remain,

Yours sincerely
M. E. Lewes.

V, 133:6 GHL TO ROBERT LYTTON, LONDON, 4 JANUARY 1871

MS: Lady Hermione Cobbold.

4th January 1871.

Dear Lytton

Your pleasant welcome greeted us on our return from the Isle of Wight where we had spent Christmas with some friends in an intensely ritualistic house (lent to our friends) where a scourge was hanging up in the study—I hope more for show than use—and where there was not (in an extensive collection of books) a Shakspeare or any other profane author except Haydn's Dict[ionary] of Dates, Crockford's Clerical Directory, and Scott and Liddell's Lexicon! It was quite an experience to have seen the inside of such a place.

Thank you both (from both) for your kindly thoughts of us and believe in their return.

Morier's paper[1] interested us greatly—I advise you by all means to send your Voltaire[2] to the Fortnightly as *the* best vehicle. How well the review keeps up!

1. Unidentified.
2. Lytton's paper on Voltaire did not appear in the *Fortnightly*.

What you tell me of your children is not so pleasant as what you tell me of your fables. *Tallow the noses* of the one, and polish the verses of the other and remember that for both *tonics* are indispensable. You ought to do something with those fables! What you will do with your children—or what they will do with you—is less certain!

I must tell you that we both think that photo of your wife a horrid perversion of her sweet face—we decline to show it to any one—and therefore petition for a more representative one. Also for one of you, which we have not.

Mrs. Lewes is pretty well but has been shaky all the year. However she is now at work again. I have been unusually well this last few months; have just finished my History, and recur with delight to my 'Problems.'

Tell Villers[3] that we are both grateful to him for holding us in remembrance and that he is often spoken of by us.

Our souls are sick of this war!

With affectionate greetings from both to both, believe me

Yours ever
G. H. L.

V, 133:6 GHL TO MME EUGÈNE BODICHON, [LONDON, 6 JANUARY 1871]

MS: Yale.

Friday.

Dear Barbara

I went yesterday to see dear old Owen[4] and found him better, but still lumbaginous. This weather Hastings must be delightful and I hope you will paint "much sea" and "much well."

Polly is ailing and rheumatic. Your's truly was upset by the small crossing and has had two days headache in consequence but is jolly again and hard at work on his "Problems."

How I should enjoy broaching some of the conclusions of those Problems at a serious tea such as Miss Edwards describes! Talk of a scourge! Imagine the virtuous faces elongated and paled beyond recovery from Souchong, and the vaticinations as to my future prospect (especially *temperature*).

3. Ludwig Victor, Marquis Villers (1810–81), whom the Leweses met at Vienna in 1870. See v, 89, n. 8.

4. "Called on Owen Jones and smoked cigar with him." (GHL Diary, 5 January 1871.)

Bessy[5] came and sat some time with Polly on Saturday. I did not put in an appearance. Tuesday we lunched with the Howards[6] who expressed great pleasure at the idea of meeting Daubigny—so bear it in mind.

Polly would send her love if she knew I was writing.

Ever yours faithfully
G. H. L.

V, 134:11   GE TO MME EUGÈNE BODICHON, [LONDON, 24 JANUARY 1871]

MS: Berg Collection, New York Public Library.

Monday.[7]

Dear B.

For a bit of effective writing on the *one* subject, *vide* Col. Hamley's letter in this morning's Times.

It is the only thoroughly good bit I have yet seen. I was afraid you might by some chance miss it, if you did not know Col. Hamley's name well enough to be drawn by it at once. I have written to thank him and beg him to go on.

My head is very bad still.

M. E. L.

V, 134:11   GE TO FRANÇOIS D'ALBERT DURADE, LONDON, 27 JANUARY 1871

MS: Yale. *Partly published*, v, 134–135.

The Priory, | 21 North Bank, | Regents Park.

January 27. 1871.

My dear Friend

I had a great longing to hear from you, and I confess that I had almost suspected you of having ceased to think of me. That was an unworthy

---

5. Bessie Parkes Belloc came 31 December 1870. GHL was not too ill to "look over a house in St. John's Wood Park" that day.

6. George James Howard (1843–1911), later 9th Earl of Carlisle, married (1864) Rosalind Frances, youngest daughter of the 2d Baron Stanley of Al-derley. The Howards were at the Priory 22 January 1871, when Mme Bodichon brought Charles François Daubigny to lunch.

7. GE mistakes the day; E. B. Hamley's letter appeared on Tuesday, 24 January 1871, protesting Prussian ruthlessness. See v, 134, n. 1.

suspicion, for since I had not ceased to think of you, I had the best reason for trusting in your faithful kindness as greater than my own. The heart-crushing miseries of our fellowmen which have been growing and growing ever since July last, have made me cling all the more to those with whom I am in any bonds of affection or even of more distant regard, and it is unspeakably sweet to me to have some intimation of what you and dear Madame d'Albert have been feeling and doing in these late months. I fear that the erysipelas in the head from which dear Maman has been suffering must have been a most trying illness for I once witnessed that complaint in a relative of my own. Seventy-one! I imagine how beautifully venerable she must look now. Is it not nearly ten years since I saw her with her fine figure as firm and upright as ever? I bless her from my heart. She is one of the sweet memories of my life.

This war has been a personal sorrow to every human creature with any sympathy who has been within reach of hearing about it; still more to those who have gone out to see and help the sufferers. Several of our friends have been among these latter.[8] But even we who have stayed at home have seen as well as heard the effects of the great calamity, for the French who are among us are many of them half or wholly ruined. Last Sunday we had the eminent paysagiste D'Aubigny[9] to see us, a grave, amiable simple-mannered man. His house on the Loire, full of his own painting on such objects as his daughter's bedstead and all such family memorials, has been completely destroyed. He is now living with his family in small lodgings at Kensington. This is but a mild sample of the myriad sorrows produced by the regression of Barbarism from that historical tomb where we thought it so picturesquely buried—if indeed one ought not to beg pardon of Barbarism, which had no weapons for making eight wounds at once in one body, and rather call the present warfare that of the Devil and all his legions. Enough! I like better to think how Madame d'Albert would exert herself in all helpfulness as long as she had strength to do so.

I did not know of your change of residence. I have a remembrance of M. Lombard's[1] bureau, and trust that the new position, being under the same roof as Monsieur Covelle,[2] is an advantage to you in every way. It would be a great joy to me to see you again, and we are not without hope of paying a visit to Geneva, under brighter skies and happier auspices than these wintry times are affording us. Mr. Lewes's aged mother is now gone to her rest, and we are without ties that oblige us to keep at home.

Our health is unhappily variable and rarely good. This winter has

8. See v, 134, n. 2.
9. See v, 134, n. 3.

1. Henri Clermond Lombard.
2. Mme D' Albert's brother-in-law.

passed very heavily for me personally from unusually incapacitating weakness. I suffer from the want of sunshine and country scenery, and since our return from the country in the autumn, I have been constantly good-fornothing. Mr. Lewes was remarkably well for a few months, but he too has broken down again, and has his old symptoms of frequent dyspepsia and exhaustion. If it were not for these drawbacks our happiness would be perfect; and as it is, we have more than our share of good in this world of difficulty. Writing does not go on quickly under bodily depression, but Mr. Lewes has lately prepared a new edition of his History of Philosophy, with many changes and additions, and carries on at his leisure his favourite work on physiological psychology. That is his sole occupation now, and he has long given up all other forms of writing.

I think my affections grow more intense and my interest in such studies increases rather than diminishes, but physically I feel old, and Death seems to me very near. The idea of dying has no melancholy for me, except in the parting and the leaving behind which Love makes so hard to contemplate.

Goodbye, dear Friend. I trust we shall see each other again. But I hope you will not let so long an interval pass again before you send me news of Madame d'Albert and yourself. How vividly I remember the excellent M. Heyer[3] and M. de Ferney of whom you speak! God bless both of you, and let me sometimes be assured that you believe in me as

Your affectionate friend
M. E. Lewes.

Our son Charles is well and happy, his wife delicate in health after a second miscarriage. Our last news of Herbert, the son who is in South Africa, was the very good news that he was engaged to be married to a young lady of good education, the daughter of a long-established colonist.

V, 135:18   GHL TO CHARLES EDWARD APPLETON, LONDON, [6 FEBRUARY 1871]

MS: Mr. J.H. Appleton. *Endorsed:* Lewes. Feb. 6 1871.

21 North Bank | Monday.

My dear Sir

I have availed myself of almost all your suggestions—quoted some of your criticisms and modified the passages to meet others.[4] One or two

3. Théophile Heyer. See IV, 465, n. 5.

4. Charles Edward Cutts Birch Appleton (1841–79), founder and editor of the *Academy*, was a lecturer in philosophy at St. John's College, Oxford. "The metaphysics of Hegel, considered from a

points are left untouched because to discuss them would have led too far. Many thanks to you for the trouble you have taken.

May I suggest to you the desirability of your not only completing your translation of the Propädeutik but rendering it available to English readers by numerous annotations of an explanatory kind? It is a work for which you are peculiarly fitted and would be a real service to the public. Stirling's book is even less intelligible than Hegel; but you have the power of re-thinking in English what Hegel has thought—and that is what is most wanted.

I am very much disgusted with the result of my labors now I see them in proof. What is clear enough in my own mind does not stand out clearly in my exposition. I ought to have begun by an exposition of the Phenomenology, and passed onward from that. But it is now too late.

Ever yours truly
G. H. Lewes.

C. Appleton Esq.

V, 137:1   GE TO MME EUGÈNE BODICHON, [LONDON, 14 MARCH 1871]

MS: Berg Collection, New York Public Library.

Tuesday Evening.

My dear Barbara

I thoroughly understood that the painful question about E. B.[5] was not to be mentioned. Be sure that it will remain unuttered by me.

We have been to Weybridge today and I am come back tired.[6] It was

theological (and almost an Anglican) standpoint, was the special branch of learning to which he was himself inclined; but his sympathies were wide enough to comprise everything that a German includes under 'Wissenschaft.' " (*DNB.*) He read the proof of GHL's chapter on Hegel in the 4th ed. of the *History of Philosophy*, 1871, in which GHL wrote: "A friend, to whose revision this chapter is much indebted, urges, in defence of Hegel, 'that it is not the business of Philosophy to discover empirical facts, but to investigate the general relation between the Cosmos and the thinking mind.' " (II, 598.)

5. Possibly the unfortunate experience of Dr. Elizabeth Blackwell, who had returned to England in 1869 and lived for a time with Mme Bodichon. She engaged medical consultation rooms "in an apparently respectable house in York Place" and had her name put on the door. "I soon found, however, that my doctor's sign was intended to conceal the dubious character of the occupier of the house, and I had unconsciously walked into a trap!" (Elizabeth Blackwell, *Pioneer Work*, 1895, p. 246.)

6. They went to see a cottage the Crosses had told them of. (GHL Diary, 14 March 1871.)

better for me not to see more than that one sketch of reeds and moonlight
—I have carried away so vivid a remembrance of that.

The damsel will not be wanted until the late autumn, I think.

Ever thine
Marian.

I did not speak strongly enough to you of the pleasure I had in your large
picture at the Dudley.[7]

V, 138:1   GHL TO JULIUS V. CARUS,[8]
LONDON, [27 MARCH 1871]

MS: Frankfurter Goethemuseum, Frankfurt-am-Main.

The Priory 21 North Bank | Regents Park.

My dear Carus

Our friend Miss Edwards[9] proposes to stay some weeks in Leipzig, and
if you can help to make her stay pleasant and profitable I am sure you will
do so. You are perhaps too busy a man to have read her novels, but you will
not be too busy to enjoy her acquaintance.

I think she would be pleased to go over your Museum in your company.
Perhaps also you could make her acquainted with Czermak,[1] to whom
give my remembrances, and tell him I sent him a number of 'Nature' with
a slight notice of his 'Studien.'[2] This is a long time ago, but perhaps he
didn't receive it.

By the time you receive this I hope your war labours will be happily
over. A friend to whom I gave a letter for you ⟨the⟩ last summer told me
you had joined the army.

Ever yours faithfully
G. H. Lewes.

7. GE and GHL went to the Dudley
Gallery 7 March 1871 and saw "some
fine landscapes." (GHL Diary.)

8. Julius Viktor Carus (1823–1903),
German zoologist, was Custodian of the
Museum of Comparative Anatomy at
Oxford 1849–1851 before becoming
Professor of Comparative Anatomy at
Leipzig in 1853. GHL had known him
there in 1858; in 1861 he translated
GHL's *Physiology of Common Life* into
German.

9. Matilda Betham-Edwards, who
was at Ryde with GHL and GE at
Christmas 1870, called at the Priory 27
March 1871. GHL wrote also to Tauchnitz urging the reprint of her novels on
the Continent. (M. Betham-Edwards,
Mid-Victorian Memories, 1919, p. 52.)

1. Johann Nepomuk Czermak (1828
–1873), Bohemian physiologist, introduced the use of the laryngoscope.

2. "Popular Lectures on Physiology," *Nature*, 2 (3 February 1870), 353,
a review of Czermak's *Populäre Physio-
logische Vorträge gehalten in Akademischen
Rosensaale zu Jena*, Vienna, 1869.

V, 139:1   GE TO GEORGE JAMES HOWARD, LONDON, 4 APRIL 1871

MS: Mr. George Howard.

21 North Bank, | April 4. 1871.

My dear Mr. Howard

I am grateful to you for sending me word at once of Baby's safe arrival.[3] It always cheers me to know that I have friends who trust in my regard and believe that their good is also mine. Generally, there is not half enough care for those exquisite charities of life which have nothing to do with material help. Friendship is not taken seriously enough.

Please give my love to Mrs. Howard—which means, that I think of her new happiness with a sort of grandmotherly pleasure. My last vision of her was a very pretty one, one Sunday when she came by herself.[4] She looked so well that we condescended to approve of Nature's Selection in making her a mother.

I am interested to know how your picture came out in its completed state.[5] But I have been so feeble lately, with a state of head that will not let me bend over my desk and that obliges me to sit bolt upright with my paper on my knees! Sometimes I think that I shall not be able to stay in town long enough to see the Exhibition. At present, however, we mean to try and stay over the beginning of May.

Always yours sincerely
M. E. Lewes.

V, 145:1   GE TO [?], LONDON, 29 APRIL [1871]

Text: Maggs Brothers Catalogue 312 (July–August 1913), 2278.

Regents Park.

Dear Friend

All yesterday was taken up by a cruel headache and a visitor[6]. . . . And now we go away early on Tuesday, so that my farewell must be said in this note.

3. Herbert George Lyulph Howard (8 April 1871–September 1898).
4. On Sunday 12 March 1871. (GHL Diary.)

5. GE may have seen it when she and GHL lunched with the Howards 3 January 1871. (GHL Diary.)
6. "Lunch with the Congreves and

Imagine me in the country at the extremity of Surrey (near Haslemere), and be sure that I carry you with me as part of my treasury of memory.

V, 145:1   GHL TO ROBERT LYTTON, LONDON, 29 APRIL 1871

MS: Lady Hermione Cobbold.

The Priory, | 21. North Bank, | Regents Park.
29 April 1871.

My dear Lytton

Just as we are packing up for the country your welcome letter arrives, and I suspend the hateful work of stooping for the pleasant work of chatting with you both.

We are somewhat puzzled by the contradictory statements you make as to your condition. You first 'can't afford' Carlsbad—then you are 'fortunately this year independent of all vile pecuniary considerations'—and further you give up your house at the end of the summer—How reconcile this, Master Brook?[7] As we are anxious on the material question pray enlighten us when next you write. It is horrible to think of you as perplexed with money matters.

I am glad to hear that the 'Fables' will put in an appearance. Polly has a poem about to appear in Macmillan's (July) a copy of which will be sent you. She is also at work on a novel and we go into the solitudes of Surrey, away from London with its oppression of peeresses, poets, philosophers, and indiscriminate Christians, who make our Sundays in the season very exhausting. In our country cottage far away from all distraction we hope to get on with our work—how people do work who live in society is a mystery—but perhaps the mystery is simply that *they don't*! We have taken an artist's cottage[8] for the summer with option of continuing it as yearly tenants. There I shall dig, and dig, and dig at the foundations of philosophy, and she will create. That we shall often talk of you both on our rambles be assured. We have both been ailing all the winter and spring, so that quiet and country air are on all accounts needed.

I am pleased to hear of Viller's pleasure in the Goethe and shall be glad

accompanied them to the photographers. Then took boat to Nine Elms [Battersea] to see about removing luggage to the cottage. Found Mrs. Burne Jones with Polly." (GHL Diary, 28 April 1871.)

7. "Master Brook" is the disguise as-

sumed by Ford to catch Falstaff in *The Merry Wives of Windsor*, e.g. III, v.

8. Anne Gilchrist (1828–85), widow of Alexander Gilchrist (1828–61), Brookbank, Shottermill, near Petersfield, Surrey.

to hear from him. Remember us to Liszt when you see him. We have had Tourguéneff here lately and seen much of him. He was an old fellow student of mine in Berlin in 1838 and we had not met since! He's a superb creature and a real genius. Do you know his Récits d'un chasseur?[9] if not, *do.*—Every Saturday I go to Mad. Viardot's—she has charming musical soirées, and as Polly declines to go out, Viardot kindly proposed to come to her some afternoon and sing as long as she liked. She did so, and a splendid exhibition it was![1] One of your appreciators and real well-wishers, Lady Castletown, pointed out to me what a group of genius and of what variety of genius there was standing in a small circle on that occasion—Tourguéneff, Viardot, Browning, Trollope, Burne-Jones, and Polly.

Your remembrance of Ben was touching; but alas! misplaced. He has gone where the good bulldogs go. I wonder whether life in the future regions will be 'diversified with cats'—as in this world?

Our love to your wife

Ever faithfully yours,

G. H. L.

V, 145:1 HERBERT ARTHUR LEWES TO GHL, WAKKERSTROOM, 6 MAY [1871]

MS: Nuneaton Public Library.

Falls of the | Assagai. 6th May.

Dear Pater

I have just received your last letter dated 7th February. I am very sorry indeed to hear of poor dear Grandma's death and M. Gillies.[2] I expect Charles and Gertrude miss her very much. If you should write or see Lizzie remember me to her. I am very sorry to hear of her husband's death.[3] Many thanks for the Box of Books, which I received in January. I have not been able to read many of them as yet, I've had too much to do. The only

9. See v, 143, n. 1. Turgenev's *Récits d' un Chasseur,* tr. E. Charrière, 2 vols., Paris, 1869.

1. GHL's Diary describes one of these parties, Saturday, 11 February 1871: "The entertainment consisted of an operetta composed by [Louis] Viardot, who played the accompaniments and sang tenor, a chorus of girls, and Tourguéneff read the Libretto. Home at 12.30." Other parties GHL mentions: 25 February, "a quartett of Beethoven, a Mdle Castillan played very finely on the violin and [Pauline] Viardot sang the sleep-walking scene in Verdi's Macbeth; her daughter some Spanish duets"; 18 March, 1 and 15 April. On Sunday 23 April Mme Viardot sang at the Priory.

2. Mary Gillies, with whom Charles and Gertrude Lewes lived in Church Row, Hampstead, died 19 June 1870.

3. Elizabeth Lee Huddy, whose husband John Huddy, a bricklayer, died 13 September 1870, aged 55.

time I read is of an evening before going to bed. There are two Books I should like to have had, that is Mutter's last two poems. My Father-in-law has answered your letter, I did not see it, but Eliza told me almost all he had said in it. I knew pretty well what his answer would be, he is too stingy to part with any thing. He could spare a span of oxen and some cows etc. and never miss them for he has plenty of cattle.

For some months past Mr. and Mrs. Harrison have been trying to make Eliza give me up. The poor girl has had a dreadful life of it. They want her to give me up because I am poor. In January Mr. H. in a fit of rage threatened to knock Eliza down and would have done so, if Mrs. H. had not been in the room and prevented him. (Lucky for him he did not strike Eliza, for I don't know what I would have done to the Brute.) That day Eliza packed up her things and left the house. It had been raining very hard for several days and the country was in a dreadful state, how the dear girl crossed all the swamps etc. on foot I don't know. She walked 5 miles to a friend's house, and stopped there for a few hours. While she was there an English farmer and his wife (name of Short) rode up to the house. They knew Eliza well, and when she told them what had happened they got a horse for her, and she rode home with them, and has been staying with them ever since. Mr. H. has tryed to get Eliza back, but she won't go. I think she is quite right not to go. Next month we shall be married. We ride to Newcastle and get quietly married by the Magistrate, and nobody will know anything about until it is over, except Mr. and Mrs. Short. They of course will ride with us.

In my last I think I told you I had sold Falls of the Assagai. When I went to take over the cattle, the Dutchman thought he had given too much, and backed out of the bargain. However, I have sold it again, for £130. in cattle—viz. A good span of oxen, 4 mares and 2 horses and £15. I was obliged to sell the place. I could not bring Eliza here to live, it would not have been safe, it is too close to the timber Bushes and there are always a lot of Bush workers passing, going in to Wakkerstroom and very often they are drunk. I could not have left Eliza alone for a day. I have hired a very good Farm for 5 years, close to Wakkerstroom, and close to plenty of English neighbors. This week I am going to shift and build a small brick house. Now I have got a good span of oxen again, I shall be able to earn a little, by riding timber, and transport. If I had now a little stock, 12 cows and a couple of hundred sheep, with care I should be well off in a few years. I often wish that I had learned some trade. A man in a colony ought to have some trade, if he has not got enough stock to live on a Farm with.

I have had hard times of it since I lost my cattle with the lung sickness. I have learnt some things I did not know before. If ever I have lungsickness again in my cattle I shall know what to do and shall not lose so many. There is a large store in Wakkerstroom now. Mr. Nisbet the manager a great friend of mine is talking of going to England in a few months he will very likely call upon you. The winter has just commenced we have plenty of frost now of a morning the grass is begin[ning] to get dried up. The next letter you get from me, I shall be on my new Farm and I hope married. The address will be the same as before only Kalbasfontein instead of Falls of the Assagai.

I think I have told you all the news. Love to Mutter, and Gertrude, Charles etc. I am

Your affectionate son
H. A. Lewes.

V, 148:1 GHL TO JOHN SIMON, SHOTTERMILL, 25 MAY 1871

Text: Copy made by Edwin Mallard Everett.

Brookbank Cottage | Shotter Mill | nr Petersfield | 25 May 71. My dear Simon

Dr. Payne[4] who is a candidate for a post at your Hospital wishes me to say a word in his favor, and although I cannot speak as one having authority I can't refuse to bear conscientious testimony to the real worth and ability concealed under his modest and unimpressive exterior. You will be the best judge of his qualifications—professionally—I can only say that I believe him to be a thoroughly good man with honest work in him. That is a kind of man rare as you know!

We are here amid lovely scenes and, what is more precious, intense solitude. Lord Houghton laughs at us for our St. Simeon Stylites kind of existence, and many other friends marvel that we can run away from London with all its season gaieties and our very [curious] wish to bury ourselves in the country. But *you* can understand it.

I am hard at work—digging at the foundations of things with but a distant prospect of reaching the artesian well. Meanwhile it gives life a purpose and the afternoon ramble a keener edge of enjoyment. Remember me to Helps whom I suppose you see often and whom I never see now.

Ever yours
G. H. Lewes.

4. Joseph Frank Payne. See v, 148, n. 7.

V, 152:14   HERBERT ARTHUR LEWES TO GHL, SANDFONTEIN, 14 JUNE 1871

MS: Nuneaton Public Library.

Sandfontein | June 14th 1871.

Dear Pater

Many thanks for the £200. which I received quite safe on the 22nd of last month. I hope I shall make better use of it than the money I have had before. It has just come in nice time. On the 25th of May I was married. We rode to Newcastle, in the morning, and were married quietly at 10 o'clock, had luncheon and returned the same day. 56 miles in one day is not bad. Is it? I shifted from Assagai about a month ago, and on Saturday I expect to take Eliza to Kalbasfontein to live. Jacob has been very hard at work, and built a small house with 2 rooms. In a couple of months I expect to have a 4 room house finished. I shall buy as many sheep as I can in September and if you send me the other £100. I shall lay it also out in sheep. I can't buy any sheep just now because I have no Kraals built and it is not safe to leave sheep out in the night. I have been staying at Sandfontein with my wife for the last Fortnight. The old folks are reconciled now, the quarrel has been made up. It is no use of us to be on unfriendly terms with them. I hope you will excuse this short letter. I have no news at all to tell. My wife and I are quite well. We both send our love to all at home.

I remain

Your affectionate son
H. A. Lewes.

Kalbasfontein Wakkerstroom

V, 152:14   GHL TO ROBERT LYTTON, SHOTTERMILL, 15 JUNE 1871

MS: Lady Hermione Cobbold.

Brookbank Cottage | Shotter Mill | nr Petersfield | 15 June 1871.

My dear Lytton

Cease all doubts and vexations at not having sooner heard from me about your Fable[5] which only reached me yesterday. My son went to the Priory for me and there found your letter which he forwarded. I have

5. "Fiat Justitia," in *Fables in Song*, 2 vols., 1874, II, 5–29, tells of Simplicius, who has a bird (Charm), a cat (Grace), a dog (Fidelity), and a bear (Humour).

read the Fable thrice and think it VERY GOOD—so good that it ought to be perfect and might perhaps be made so by a touch or two though I don't know how. Perhaps on remeditating and rewriting it you may discover the secret springs of imperfection. All that I can suggest is a certain lessening of the reader's prevision. For instance, slight as it is, I wouldn't have the Inn called the Sign of the *Bear*.[6] It is too *schematic* and seems to project a shadow over the coming catastrophe. Altogether I should urge your fixing your critical eye on the last part with a view of making it unfold itself as easily as the others.

Again, I doubt the felicity or propriety of calling it a Fable in cantos and *acts*—it is not a drama and the *acts* suggest misleading thoughts.[7] The writing is throughout admirable—good thought felicitously expressed. Let us have more such!

We are both distressed to think of your alarm respecting your sweet little wife (je maintiens le mot!) and beg you to write at once to relieve our distress by telling us she has not been laid up with anything worse than a cold. Thank her from Mrs. Lewes for her pretty welcome letter, which Mrs. Lewes would have answered at once had she not alas! been suffering continuously from biliousness, headache and neuralgia. I was at last forced to take her up to London to have medical advice.[8] She is better now but still feeble. Our country quarters, delicious as they are, have not benefited her yet.

For myself they have done wonders. I have got through more, and better work, during this six weeks, than during the whole year previously. I am still dipping at the "foundations of things" and you won't be surprised to hear I find them "rather infinite."

Although Petersfield is our post town Surrey is the county where we luxuriate in miles and miles of heath, park, lane, and picturesque undulating wooded hills. Our range of walks and drives is practically infinite. Had there not been so much cold wind we should have sat in the woods to read poetry and "talk of lovely things that conquer death" more than we have done—but it will doubtless come. Our cottage is an artist's cottage very picturesque but so far from the world that there are great difficulties in the commissariat. But if we don't live like "fighting cocks" we live like your philosophic Bruin, remote, unvisited, quite away from the dust, envy, turmoil, tittletattle and other uglinesses of London. Not a soul have we

Returning from a journey, he eats bear paws with tartar sauce at an inn, only to find that the bird let out of the cage by his servant, was eaten by the cat, which was killed by the dog, which was eaten by the bear, whose paws he himself had eaten.

6. Lytton retained "The Bear" as the name of the inn, II, 19.

7. The three cantos are entitled Theory, Practice, and Experience, without mention of acts.

8. See v, 151, n. 7.

seen except Blackwood who ran down one day[1] to have lunch with us on the scent of the new novel—a distant object—alas!

Love from both to both

Yours ever
G. H. Lewes.

We shall stay here till end of July. Gourmandise is permissible.

V, 157:16   GHL TO ROBERT LYTTON,
SHOTTERMILL, 24 JUNE [1871]

MS: Lady Hermione Cobbold.

Shotter Mill nr Petersfield | 24 June.

My dear Lytton

Yes indeed I got your last sad note (inclosing the charming letter from Villers) and its contents saddened both of us more than I can tell you.[2] We have been anxiously expecting to hear from you, scarcely daring to hope for good news, and your note just arrived is most welcome though it might have been more cheering. Let us hear soon how all goes on. That dear boy's image haunts us in these green solitudes. And the image of his poor mother too! We had such a terrible experience with our six months watching of Thornie that any *suggestion* of such a scene is exaggerated for us.

Enclosed is a scrawl for Villers in answer to his amusing fragment which I hope will be concluded some day.

We have had rather warmer weather of late and Mrs. Lewes seems to profit by it. When the severity of summer has passed I hope she will flourish.

Ever yours faithfully
G. H. Lewes.

V, 169:15   GHL TO MRS. WILLIAM CROSS,
SHOTTERMILL, [24 JULY 1871]

MS: Yale.

Brookbank Cottage | Shotter Mill | nr Petersfield | Monday.

My dear Mrs. Cross

I had addressed an envelope to you (by way of memorandum that I was to enclose a note when practicable) to tell you how Mrs. Lewes was going on and to tell Emily and Florence that if their German ardour is

---

1. John Blackwood and his nephew William came 31 May 1871.

2. Rowland Edward Lytton, born 19 September 1865, had whooping cough

sustained they can now not only get *Romeo und Julia auf dem Dorfe*,[3] which I once spoke about and which I believe Mr. Bullock made a note of, but can get two or three other tales in the 3rd volume of the *Deutscher Novellenschatz* edited by Heyse and Kurz. Each volume only costs 1/6, so they can begin with volume III and add to them, si le coeur leur en dit.

Mrs. Lewes is decidedly stronger and has got rid of her *tic*; but she is still not so flourishing as she could, should, might, ought to be. But then you women are so unreasoning and unreasonable! The Saturday Review says so[4]—and it must know. You, for instance, whom we had almost learned to regard as a judicious woman—could any thing be more irrational, misplaced, intempestive,—*a crosstic*—than your taking to yourself a Bronchitis—unless indeed a distant vision of the Champagne cure was the prompter! Now look at me—a male and rational animal—see how I brown here like a well fried sole—how I "put on flesh" like a prize pig (of the Breton sort, I regret to say, that is rather lanky, all ribs and ears)— how I digest (when I can get the food) and work at mathematics as if I were going in for honors. You don't see any injudiciousness in me. *I* don't coquette with Bronchitis or any other itis. I say unto them "get thee behind me; or visit some less rational party." Make me your model and it will be well with you!

We are glad you saw Tourgeneff—to see him is to like him. Tell Johnnie I quite agree in his estimate of Armgart—which makes me sure he *must* be a very profound critic! Seriously we were both pleased that you were all pleased with the poem; in spite of its misprints.[5] I suppose you noticed *s*araphrase for paraphrase and

Lay like frozen Rhine till a summer came

instead of

Lay like a frozen Rhine till summers came.

There are several small inaccuracies but printers are mortal.

Our united love to all

Ever yours truly
G. H. Lewes.

in May 1871, followed by an inflammation of the lungs of which he died 26 July 1871.

3. "Romeo und Julia auf dem Dorfe" by Gottfried Keller (1819–90), reprinted in *Deutscher Novellenschatz*, ed. P. Heyse and H. Kurz, Munich [1871–76], Vol. III. GE and GHL read it aloud 17–18 July 1871. (GHL Diary.)

4. The *Saturday Review* consistently ridiculed the feminist movement and education of women. One recent sarcastic article was a long review of Mrs. [Frances] Elliot's *Diary of an Idle Woman*, 17 June 1871, pp. 777–778.

5. "Armgart" appeared in *Macmillan's*, 24 (July 1871), 161–187. The misprints GHL notes on pp. 164 and 185 are corrected in *The Legend of Jubal and Other Poems*, 1874, pp. 85 and 142.

We shall be forced to leave this at the end of the month—although we don't go to Scotland[6]—probably to Harrowgate.

V, 171:20   GE TO [?],
SHOTTERMILL, 28 JULY 1871

MS: University of California Los Angeles.

Shottermill | Petersfield | July 28. 71.

My dear Madam

I am much obliged by your kind letter—by its expressions of sympathy and its indication of error.

It is long since I opened Adam Bede, and here in a country retreat, I have no copy by me. I am surprized to learn that there is the incongruous statement about the Leicester coach,[7] as my heart and thoughts were thoroughly in the imagination of the circumstances in 1858, when the book was written. Just at present there is no remedy as the current edition is stereotyped.

Believe me, dear Madam

Yours with sincere obligation
M. E. Lewes.

V, 182:8   GHL TO JOHN BLACKWOOD,
LONDON, 2 SEPTEMBER [1871]

MS: National Library of Scotland.

The Priory, | 21. North Bank, | Regents Park.
2 September.

My dear Blackwood

Home again and not sorry once for a while to enjoy the 'comforts of the saut market.'[8]

My arrangement with America is very simple and cannot in the least interfere with England.[9] The advance sheets are to be sent to Osgood & Co.

6. "Wrote to the Secretary of the Scott Festival saying that we could not attend." (GHL Diary, 26 June 1871.)

7. The Leicester coach is mentioned at the end of ch. 35 and the beginning of ch. 36. GE did not alter the text for the Cabinet ed. in 1878.

8. In Scott's *Rob Roy* Bailie Jarvie lives in the Salt Market in Glasgow.

9. See v, 179–180, for the agreement with J. R. Osgood of Boston, who offered GE £1200 for serializing *Middlemarch* in *Every Saturday.*

who will begin to print in their weekly paper at such a time as will allow their last instalment to be out before Part I reaches America. That is to say although we publish Part I in England a fortnight before they publish their last weekly instalment of the same, they will have the advantage of really being before the other Americans, though not before us. Only two copies of the paper come to England, one to me. These are posted. The slight advance in point of time given to them though of great importance to them will be of none to us. If they waited till we published in England before they began to publish they would of course be forced to print it as we do all at once. It is to give them their weekly advantage that the plan has been devised; and they pay for it.

As respects terms I think prudence rightly suggests that you should not take the risk when the adventure is so novel. But I also think that in that case the alternative I proposed is the only proper one. If the adventure is a failure your modified proposal would leave you at a disadvantage. If a success it would leave us at a disadvantage. Since the expences are *certain* to be more than covered, my plan leaves us both a risk only of diminished profit, with the chance of a good one.

Mrs. Lewes begs her kindest regards and says Mr. Simpson did *not* send *The Speech*[1]—or it did not come!

Ever yours truly
G. H. Lewes.

V, 184:24 GHL TO J. R. OSGOOD & CO., LONDON, 7 SEPTEMBER 1871

MS: Gordon N. Ray.

The Priory, | 21. North Bank | Regents Park.
7 September 1871.

Gentlemen

In reply to your letter of the 18 August apropos of Canada we shall be much obliged to you if you would make all the necessary arrangements, paying us 200£ additional as you propose.[2] This will save us trouble.

Mr. Blackwood is so very uneasy about our arrangement lest extracts should creep into our newspapers before we appear here that Mrs. Lewes has been for some time on the point of asking you to rescind it. But I think

---

1. John Blackwood's speech at the Scott Centenary banquet at St. Andrews.

2. For Canadian rights to *Middlemarch*.

on due consideration of the case both our interests may be served by your publishing larger weekly instalments[3] than you proposed—and indeed I think on a revision of the matter you will see that $\frac{1}{2}$ a volume ought only to occupy 5 *weeks* in publishing. This was your original estimate—viz. 30 weeks for 3 volumes. If you can manage this—while you will have the undisturbed priority—the book not appearing in America until your last weekly instalment also appears—we shall be tolerably secure against more than an extract or two since if you begin to print on the 4 November and we publish on the 1st December our part can't reach America till the 15th or later when you would have completed your publication; but on the other hand we could only have received in England the two numbers you had printed.

Can you therefore manage to publish each part in 5 or at the utmost 6 numbers? Please let me know about this.

Yours faithfully
G. H. Lewes.

Messrs. James R. Osgood & Co.

V, 189:1 EMILY SUSANNAH CLARKE TO GE, LICHFIELD, 16 SEPTEMBER 1871

MS: Yale.

Lombard House, Lichfield. | September 16. 1871.

My dear Aunt Polly

It grieved me to hear you were not well. It was very good of you to write to me but please do not do it again when you are not well. I know what it is to suffer from weakness and only wish I was somewhere near that I might be a comfort to you. I always feel proud when I hear you praised. Last week Canon Lonsdale[4] in his lecture to the children on church history said there was a very clever account of Savonarola in a novel called "Romola" written by one of the first writers of the day.

There were no painful reasons for the breaking off of Walter's engagement.[5] The young lady was rich, vulgar and a great flirt—it was one of those engagements that should never have taken place. Walter is very quiet and has very strict ideas of what a woman ought to be. Old Mr. Harpur[6] is

3. In *Every Saturday*. But see v, 216, n. 1.

4. John Gylby Lonsdale, B.A. Cambridge 1841, was Canon and Chaplain to the Bishop of Lichfield.

5. Walter Pearson Evans (1845–1920), son of Isaac Evans.

6. Henry Richard Harpur (1798–12 June 1870), the squire of Chilvers Coton.

dead there are very few people in Nuneaton that I know—the Buchanans still live there.

Some time I must tell you more about my life here. In ten days we have a week's rest, I shall go away but have not settled where until I know Miss Crockett's plans. A Mrs. Tibbits kindly has me at her house for any length of time I care to go—if Miss C. does not want me I shall go to Mrs. Tibbits. Rest is always welcome, more especially the week in the middle of the half year. I am much stronger, but it takes very little to "knock me up"—and then to work when one is ill is anything but pleasant. Both the Misses Crockett are very kind, being here so long makes me more like a relation than a teacher. I meant to have written only a line but somehow I have gone rambling on.

Please do not think I want an answer to this. It is kind of you to write and your letters do me good. With dear love

Your affectionate niece
Emily S. Clarke.

V, 190:1 GHL TO ROBERT LYTTON, LONDON, 18 SEPTEMBER 1871

MS: Lady Hermione Cobbold.

The Priory, | North Bank, | Regents Park.
18 September 1871.

My dear Lytton

For several days before we left our cottage I had made a knot in my mind to write to you to learn how you (especially Edith) were bearing up under your trials, and with what health you were awaiting the calm of resignation. The calm does come—but much depends on health.

In spite of my resolution and of Polly's reminders I never could exactly find the time when I had the energy or the energy when I had the time to write, and I now leave her sickbed (by her injunction) to do what should have been done before. When I say her sickbed you must not imagine anything serious, though yesterday I was alarmed about her for in spite of two doctors[7] she got worse and what seemed at first a slight illness threatened to be a serious dysentery. However she passed a good night, awoke free from fever, and today is decidedly convalescent, having begun with a cup of beef tea and half a cup of carrot soup.

I am raised to the post of Nurse in ordinary and while seated on her

7. See v, 191, n. 2.

bed quietly chatting as Nurses are wont (and are wanted) to do she again
recurred to that "sweet dear Mrs. Lytton whom you have never written to"
—so struck by the reproach I said: "I'll go and write now." "Do!" she
said: and I did it.

I know letter writing is no task to you and therefore I have no hesitation
in asking you to tell us all about yourselves; where you are, and how you
get through the days. We left Haslemere on the 1st having seen no one but
the Tennysons, who [*The rest of this letter is lacking.*]

V, 192:20 GHL TO WILLIAM BLACKWOOD,
[LONDON, 26 SEPTEMBER 1871]

MS: National Library of Scotland.

                                                                   Tuesday.
My dear Willie

Mrs. Lewes continues to improve in strength and is only too impatient
to get back to 'Middlemarch'—at which I protest, greatest haste being
worst speed in such cases.

We should be glad of two sets of proofs and I hope the printing is going
on *rapidly;* for the time is running very short, and if one of the mails were
to miss, the Americans might be unable to begin on November 4 as they
promise their subscribers. We agree with you that a new vignette would
be best.[8] It should be a town viewed from some country aspect—so as to
combine trees, stream, and meadows with distant spires and gables.

Our respectful bows to the great Captain! If he golfs with the severe
dignity and restrained fervor of Maga and J. B. it must be a sight to see.

                                                          Ever yours truly
                                                          G. H. Lewes.

8. George Simpson, commenting on GHL's remark [22 September] that GE was "charmed with the vignettes which are on the title-page of the cheap edition of her novels," wrote to Blackwood: "We cannot give in to Mr. Lewes' notion of using up some old cut on the cover of this '*bran*' new work of George Eliot's, but it would not cost more than £4.4 to have a little thing done on purpose and it would look nice. I believe our friend Adams here would work up a very nice thing from the hints in Mr. Lewes' letter. If you approve please send me back the letter. I am amazed to see an expression of satisfaction with the vignettes in our C. Ed. of G. Eliot's works. I understood they had proved most offensive in the eyes of the fair Author. I hope you will write at once to Mr. Lewes and get our page approved of, that we may start the setting up and arrange about Paper etc. I have retained a duplicate of the dummy volume which contains 214 pages." (NLS.)

V, 201:14   GHL TO CLEMENT MANSFIELD INGLEBY,[9]
LONDON, [12 OCTOBER 1871]

MS: Folger Library.

The Priory, | **21. North Bank,** | **Regents Park.**
Thursday.

My dear Sir

First let me say in justice to Jevons that you misunderstood me, or I expressed myself quite inaccurately. His machine[1] does *not* turn out the false conclusion from the true premises in such an example as No man is a stone etc. but simply that "A man is either an animal or not an animal." But his machine *does* justify Aristotle's example and thereby proves my case—which is the vanity of the mere syllogistic form.

My point is this: The syllogism is a mill which grinds fatally; all depends on what is put into it to be ground. You seem to consider Aristotle's example a true syllogism and my inversion of it a false one. I consider that both are true as forms, and that both conceal a paralogism and if this concealed paralogism be dragged into light, the whole is clear. Thus every man is a stone (man) every stone (man) is an animal ∴ every (stone) is an animal (stone). Although the proposition every man is an animal, when isolated, is true, this is not the conclusion *shut up* in the premises unless *stone* man and *stone* animal be understood. The judgment really is "Whatever man is animal is"; *if* man is stone man, and stone man is animal stone, then— Alter it into every man is a stone; every stone is a carrot ∴ Every man is a carrot. Here the conclusion is as obviously false as the premise. Yet it says: what man is stone is i.e. *carrot.*

I think therefore that if the Aristotelian form is correct, the inversion of it is equally so; and the conclusion is: No (stone) man is a (stone) animal: which is what the premises assert. If I say: No animal is-*immortal*: Dogs are-*animals*: no dog is-*immortal*—is not the form correct—and wherein (*as form*) does it differ from No man is-*a stone* etc.?

I am but superficially versed in Logical literature, but as far as I under-

---

9. Clement Mansfield Ingleby (1823–86) read metaphysics and mathematics at Trinity College, Cambridge, M.A. 1850; he published *Outlines of Theoretical Logic,* 1856.

1. William Stanley Jevons (1835–82), Professor of Logic at Owens College, Manchester, devised in 1866 a "reasoning machine or logical abacus,"

a rather simple set of slips marked ABC, AbC, ABc, aBC, etc., to demonstrate Boole's logic. It is described in his *The Substitution of Similars,* 1869. GHL had often pointed out the weakness of Aristotle's syllogistic form, e.g. in *The Biographical History of Philosophy,* 1857, pp. 211–218.

stand the syllogism it is that the conclusion is simply an *ex*plication of which is *im*plicated in the premises, whatever that may be; and therefore the truth or falsity of a conclusion never resides in the form but in the matter. You will correct me if I am wrong; and since logicians have as far as I know always maintained that a true conclusion could be deduced from false premises (*which I deny*) they ought to maintain that a false conclusion can equally be deduced from true premises. In either case it is necessary that the paralogism should occur, so that the conclusion expresses something not really given in the premises.

You will see that the gist of the matter is this: Can we *deduce* from premises what is not already shut up in them? And is not the false conclusion proof of a paralogism?

Yours in haste
G. H. Lewes.

V, 209:18   GHL TO MRS. WILLIAM CROSS, LONDON, [29 OCTOBER 1871]

MS: Bryn Mawr College.

The Priory, | 21. North Bank, | Regents Park.
Sunday.

Dear Friends

You will rejoice to hear that although Mrs. Lewes was rather knocked up by the journey she is this morning quite vigorous and feels the good effect of her visit. ("Letter of thanks" will come in due time—but I must "give my whole mind to it.") Indeed I have just been describing our visit[2] to one of her dear friends as a tonic compounded of high feeding, high adoration, high falutin', and a general sense that to be at Weybridge where "you may ring your bell at 3 in the morning and get beef tea or your corns cut," is eminently calculated to restore the vital vigor.

You cannot imagine what a sense we had of the presence of all of your ghosts at our solitary dinner table. Ghosts of jokes were saluted with ghostly laughter—unco' gash, perhaps yet as warming as toddy.

I have packed up Tourguéneff[3] and Séraphine,[4] and they will go by Rail.

2. On Sunday, 22 October 1871, John, Emily, and Eleanor Cross came to beg GE and GHL to come to Weybridge for a week's visit. They went on Tuesday, the 24th, and stayed till Saturday. (GHL Diary.)

3. GE and GHL had been reading Turgenev's *Dimitri Roudine* in July 1871. (GHL Diary.)

4. A play by Victorien Sardou, adapted by Dion Boucicault, 1869.

My minister of the Interior is quiet and rational again; whereas up to yesterday he was more like the interior of a minister. There was an intimation of another and a hotter world which was more theological than I could fairly appreciate.

Polly sends a handful of loves and kisses, which you will distribute for her. As for me the vision of the Salt Lake which I had, though but in a glimpse, beatifies Weybridge, and raises severe doubts respecting the selfishness of the American government in arresting Brigham Young.[5]

But I must get down Johnson's Dictionary and the Polite Letter Writer and compose the Letter of Thanks which you were promised. God bless you all

> Ever yours affectionately
> G. H. Lewes.

V, 212:8　GHL TO PHILIP GILBERT HAMERTON,
LONDON, 2 NOVEMBER 1871

Text: Philip Gilbert Hamerton, *An Autobiography and a Memoir*, London, 1897, pp. 408–9.

The Priory, | 21. North Bank, | Regents Park.
November 2. 1871.

My dear Hamerton,

We so often speak of you and your wife, and were so very anxious about you during the war, that we have asked right and left for news of you, and were delighted at last to get such good news of you both.

As to the books to be suggested for your work,[6] partly the fact that no one can really suggest food for another, partly the fact that I don't clearly understand the nature of your work—these perhaps make a good excuse if the following list is worthless. It is all I have been able to gather together.

Littré, *Vie d' Auguste Comte.*[7]
St. Hilaire, *Vie et travaux de Geoffroy St. Hilaire.*
Gassendi, *Vita Tychonis Brahei, Copernici.*
Bertrand, *Fondateurs de l' Astronomie Moderne.*

5. Brigham Young (1801–77) was arrested at Salt Lake City 2 October 1871 charged "under the Utah statute with lewdly and licentiously cohabiting with sixteen different women." (*N.Y. Times,* 18 and 27 October 1871, p. 8b.)

6. Hamerton had begun his book *The Intellectual Life,* 1873.

7. Maximilien Paul Émile Littré, *Auguste Comte et la philosophie positive,* Paris, 1863; Étienne Geoffroy St. Hilaire, *Vie, travaux, et doctrine scientifique,* Paris, 1847; Pierre Gassendi, *Tychonis Brahei, ... vita ... Nicolai Copernici,* Hague, 1654; Joseph Bertrand, *Les Fondateurs de l'astronomie moderne,* Paris, 1865; Henry Morley, *Bernard Palissy,*

Morley, *Life of Palissy* (passionate devotion to research).
Morley, *Life of Cardan.*
Berti, *Vita di Giordano Bruno.*
Bartholmess, *Vie de Jordano Bruno.*
Muir's *Life of Mahomet.*
Stanley's *Life of Arnold.*
Mazzuchelli, *Vita di Archimede.*
Biot's *Life of Newton.*
Drinkwater's *Kepler and Galileo.*

All these are first-rate, especially the two last, published by the Society for the Promotion of Useful Knowledge, together with some others under the title of *Lives of Eminent Persons.*

The *Biographie Universelle* will give you, no doubt, references as to the best works under each head.

We did not go abroad this year, but buried ourselves in absolute solitude in Surrey—near Haslemere, if you know the lovely region; and there I worked like a man going in for the Senior Wranglership, and Mrs. Lewes, who was ailing most of the time, went on with her new work. This work, by the way, is a panorama of provincial life, to be published in eight parts, on alternative months, making four very thick vols. when complete. It is a new experiment in publishing. While she was at her art, I was at the higher mathematics, seduced into those regions by some considerations affecting my personal work. The solitude and the work together were perfectly blissful. Except Tennyson, who came twice to read his poems to us, we saw no one.

No sooner did we return home than Mrs. Lewes, who had been incubating an attack, *hatched* it—and for five weeks she was laid up, getting horribly thin and weak. But now she is herself again (thinner self) and at work.

She begs me to remember her most kindly to you and to Mrs. Hamerton.

Ever yours truly,
G. H. Lewes.

the Potter, 2 vols., 1852, and *The Life of Geronimo Cardano of Milan, Physician,* 2 vols., 1854; D. Berti, *Vita di Giordano Bruno,* 1868; C. J. G. Bartholmess, *Vie de Jordano Bruno,* 2 vols., Paris, 1846–47; Sir William Muir, *Life of Mahomet and History of Islam,* 4 vols., 1858–61; Arthur Penrhyn Stanley, *Life and Correspondence of Thomas Arnold,* 2 vols., 1844; Giovanni Maria Mazzuchelli, *Notizie istoriche e critiche intorno alla vita, alle invenzione, ed agli scritti di Archimede,* Brescia, 1737; Jean Baptiste Biot, *Life of Sir Isaac Newton,* tr. [from *Biographie Universelle* by Sir H. C. Elphinstone]; John Elliott Drinkwater, *Life of Galileo* and *Life of Kepler,* 1833.

V, 214:1 GE TO NIKOLAUS TRÜBNER,
LONDON, 13 NOVEMBER 1871

MS: Yale. *Endorsed:* This is "George Eliot" and was given to me by Mrs. Trübner. I. Oppenheim.

The Priory, | 21 North Bank, | Regents Park.
November 13. 71.

My dear Mr. Trübner

I find that we possess the "Opuscules" of which you and I were speaking yesterday. Mr. Lewes tells me that he found them in a parcel on our return from the country, Mr. Van der Wegen having kindly sent them during our absence. Hence I shall have the pleasure of reading them without giving you the trouble of lending me a volume.

Always yours truly
M. E. Lewes.

V, 214:1 GHL TO JOHN H. BALFOUR-BROWNE,
LONDON, 16 NOVEMBER 1871

MS: Miss V.E.C. Balfour-Browne, who supplied text.

The Priory, | 21. North Bank, | Regents Park.
16 November 71.

Dear Sir

Mrs. Lewes is just now so absorbed and exhausted by work that I relieve her of all correspondence when practicable; she begs me, in her name, to thank you for your present of 'For Very Life'[8]—She wishes this done at once because some months must necessarily elapse before she will be free to profit by your kindness.

Yours truly
G. H. Lewes.

J. H. Balfour-Browne Esq.

8. *For Very Life* is not found in the British Museum or the National Library of Scotland.

V, 218:7 GE TO MME EUGÈNE BODICHON, LONDON, [24 NOVEMBER 1871]

MS: Berg Collection, New York Public Library.

The Priory, | 21. North Bank, | Regents Park.
Friday Morning.

Dear Barbara

Come to dinner at half past six—cold lamb and salad.

Yours ever affectionately
M. E. L.

We saw Mr. Bullock[9] yesterday but he knew nothing about Paris.

V, 223:1 GHL TO JOHN MORLEY, LONDON, [DECEMBER 1871]

Text: Copy by Edwin Mallard Everett.

The Priory, | 21. North Bank, | Regents Park.

Dear Morley

Thanks for your offer, which I may probably avail myself of in the early summer.

I am reading Voltaire[1] with intense interest. Last year I read Strauss's book[2] with such memories and impatience that I exclaimed, 'Is there no one to attempt this great task in a quite other style!' and lo! here is that other.

Yours ever
G. H. L.

I am plotting a little paper on Dickens for the Fortnightly—*not* a review of Forster,[3] so that you may hold yourself quite free on that score.

9. William Henry Bullock (later Hall) dined at the Priory 23 November 1871. (GHL Diary.)
1. Morley's *Voltaire*, 1872.
2. D. F. Strauss, *Voltaire*, 1870. GHL finished it 29 August 1870. (Diary.)
3. See v, 226, n. 6, and vi, 28, n. 6.

GHL's "Dickens in Relation to Criticism," *Fortnightly*, 17 (February 1872), 141–154. For an account of Forster's rage at this article see G. S. Haight, "Dickens and Lewes," *PMLA*, 71 (March 1956), 166–179.

V, 224:19   GE TO FREDERICK LOCKER,
LONDON, 4 DECEMBER 1871

MS: Knox College, Galesburg, Illinois. *Envelope:* Frederick Locker Esq. | 91 Victoria Street | S.W. *Postmark:* LONDON–N.W | 5 | DE 4 | 71.

The Priory, | 21. North Bank, | Regents Park.

December 4. 71.

My dear Mr. Locker

We shall be happy to dine with you on Wednesday next at 7.30.[4] And since you permit us, we will be with you soon after 7. in order that I may see the "Songs of Innocence."[5]

Yours ever sincerely

M. E. Lewes.

V, 225:7   MME EUGÈNE BODICHON TO GE,
HASTINGS, [10? DECEMBER 1871]

MS: Yale.

11 East Parade | Hastings.

My dearest Marian,

I have read your new book and I think it the most interesting subject you have ever given us and I think it is only too happy and beautiful a book for the horrid things coming after in her life. I feel intensely about it and I never felt so much interest in any story but 2 in my life.

I think it *is* your best work—no that I won't say but being the last I have read it does seem to me to day to be by far your best. I am sure it is the most interesting only I dread the unfolding and feel quite certain it is a horrible tragedy coming.

I hear people say it is so witty amusing and lively so it is but all is shadowed by the coming misery to me. I can't help feeling it desperately. I am very sorry for the poor thing[6] just as if she were alive and I want to

4. At dinner 6 December were Lady Charlotte Locker, their daughter Elinor Locker and her governess, Dean Stanley, and Lady Augusta Stanley. (GHL Diary.)

5. Among the poems copied into a notebook of GE's, now in the Berg Collection, NYPL, are "The Divine Image" and "London" from William Blake's *Songs of Innocence*. Two stanzas of the former poem form the epigraph of ch.76 in *Middlemarch*.

6. Toward the end of Book I of *Middlemarch* Dorothea Brooke leaves with Mr. Casaubon for her honeymoon in Rome.

stop her. She is like a child dancing into a quick sand on a sunny morning
and I feel a sort of horror at your story as if it were all real and going on at
this moment. I do not know if you meant to produce this sort of terrible
foreshadowing of inevitable misery and I see some of 'em have read it and
only see wit character and liveliness, and call it light reading now I find it
heavy reading to my heart though I think it a most noble book and thank
you for it.

I am going to read it again because I read it all through in one day as
hard as I could to take in the whole impression and I have given to you.
But then a great many do not feel it as I do.

I am enchanted with you for publishing it so that I can buy it at once
for myself and have it for my friends it is quite a progress and was the first
thing I blessed you for. Only I do not like the cover at all it is not artistic
enough—much better have nothing on the cover than that riggle and
landscape which are not worthy of your work at all. The green is not a
bad colour much better than the blue of the Spanish Gypsy which was a
very hard wicked blue and made me unhappy and a plain Roman letter on
that green would have been very nice, do not let them do what they like in
dressing your children it does make a difference and I like to see your
things in becoming clothes.

Ever yours
B.

I feel I have not expressed myself a bit.

V, 227:5 HERBERT ARTHUR LEWES TO GHL, NEWCASTLE, 15 DECEMBER 1871

MS: Nuneaton Public Library.

Coldstream, | 15 December 1871. | Newcastle.

Dearest Pater

I received your letter of the 13th September quite safely. I had been
expecting to hear from you for a long time. I am glad you got back from
your trip in good health. I suppose the house looks very nice since the alterations. It is a pity Grace and Emelia have left you, after having them for so
many years.

You will see by my address that I am not living any more at Kalbasfontein. After being there 5 months, and having built a nice house—I had
to leave. The man I hired the place from had no right to it. It being a disputed farm. I was advised by everybody to leave, before I got warning to

quit. So I took all the thatch off the house likewise window and doorframes, etc. I am staying in my Brother-in law's house close to Mr. Harrison, until I can get a farm. I bought 130 sheep in the winter but lost a good many of them from poverty, having to drive them a long way, where I bought them, and no grass. They are doing very well indeed now. I shall be glad when I have 500. I have been doing a little timber loading while I am stopping here. I must be doing something I can not remain idle. I am going to ride transport to Maritzburg soon. I want to get a larger wagon, then the one I have at the present. I can earn from £15 to £20 a Fortnight down to Maritzburg and the same up again, in the summer months. In the winter I shall work on the farm. Jacob has left me, after staying with me for nearly 5 years. When I go transport riding, I shall take Eliza with me. I could not leave her for a month alone on a farm. We are as happy as mortals can be.

I will write oftener, you know I am such a bad hand at letter writing. I think I have told you all the news for the present. With our best love to Mutter and yourself and anybody else at home I remain

Your affectionate son
H. A. Lewes.

V, 227:5 GHL TO MESSRS HARPER AND BROTHERS, LONDON, 16 DECEMBER 1871

MS: Wellesley College.

The Priory, | 21. North Bank, | Regents Park.
16 December 1871.

Gentlemen

In reply to your favor of the 6th I may say that two thirds of the new part of 'Middlemarch' will be ready in three or four days and will be sent to you through Mr. Sampson Low.[7] But although our copyright is not in danger, there is a danger of our being hurt by the newspapers here publishing 'extracts' in advance, if your Magazine—which finds its way over here —has much the same start of us. It was on this ground that in the arrangement with Messrs Osgood it was stipulated that they should so time the appearance of the weekly instalments that our complete part should be issued a fortnight before their final instalment, so that we reach America just in time to secure priority for the American reprint without running the risk of the American reprint reaching England before we appeared.

We publish with the February Magazines. If you divide the instalments

---

7. For the transfer of *Middlemarch* to Harpers see v, 216, n. 1.

so as to let your last instalment appear on the 10th or 12th February, all will be well.

Hoping this will meet your convenience I remain, Gentlemen,

Yours truly

G. H. Lewes.

Messrs Harper and Brothers

V, 229:1 GHL TO JOHN WALTER CROSS, [LONDON, 27 DECEMBER 1871]

MS: Yale.

Wednesday.

Dear Nephew

Certificate and Stock arrived safely.

Your uncle is just now laid up with a fiery sore throat and your Aunt doesn't flourish over a headache; but we shall be with you on Monday at 4.10—"or perish in the attempt"![8]

Ever yours

G. H. L.

8. "Started this morning for Weybridge on a visit to the Cross family. Delicious weather all the time we were there. Riotous fun and interesting talk. Bowen, Sandars, and Jowett the only guests besides ourselves. Played games and acted charades. Drove about the country each afternoon. Walked each morning. But Polly, who had been ailing (I also) for some days, got worse, so we shortened our visit. Returned home by the 11. train. On our way called on Sir H. Holland, who prescribed for Polly." (GHL Diary, 1–4 January 1872.)

Middlemarch

V, 231:1 GE TO WALTER W. SKEAT, LONDON, [1872?]

Text: English Dialect Society, *A Bibliographical List*, Part I, London, 1873, p. viii.[9]

It must be borne in mind that my inclination to be as close as I could to the rendering of dialect, both in words and spelling, was constantly checked by the artistic duty of being generally intelligible. But for that check, I should have given a stronger colour to the dialogue in "Adam Bede," which is modelled on the talk of N. Staffordshire and the neighbouring part of Derbyshire. The spelling, being determined by my own ear alone, was necessarily a matter of anxiety, for it would be as possible to quarrel about it as about the spelling of Oriental names.

The district imagined as the scene of "Silas Marner" is in N. Warwickshire. But here, and in all my other presentations of English life, except "Adam Bede," it has been my intention to give the general physiognomy rather than a close portraiture of the provincial speech as I have heard it in the Midland or Mercian region. It is a just demand that art should keep clear of such specialities as would make it a puzzle for the larger part of its public; still, one is not bound to respect the lazy obtuseness or snobbish ignorance of people who do not care to know more of their native tongue than the vocabulary of the drawing-room and the newspaper.

V, 233:6 GHL TO ALEXANDER MAIN, LONDON, [4 JANUARY 1872]

MS: Harvard.

The Priory, | 21. North Bank, | Regents Park.

My dear Main

We only returned half an hour ago from a stay with friends in the country[10]—it is my absence from home which has prevented my writing to you to say that the effect of your book[11] on my son and on myself is all that you could wish. As he says it is utterly free from the fragmentary scrapiness of extracts.

9. The MS of this letter, written in reply to Skeat's inquiry about GE's use of dialects, has not been found.
10. Visiting the Cross family at Wey-bridge, 1–4 January.
11. *Wise, Witty, and Tender Sayings ... of George Eliot*, Edinburgh, 1872.

Mrs. Lewes is far from well. I took her away in hopes the change would do good—but it hasn't.

Yours faithfully
G. H. L.

V, 238:7 GE TO MME EUGÈNE BODICHON, LONDON, 18 JANUARY 1872

MS: Berg Collection, New York Public Library.

The Priory, | 21. North Bank, | Regents Park.

January 18. 72.

Dearest B.

I am ashamed and grieved that I cannot help you with an address which you so kindly sought in my behalf long ago.

The fact is, we went to the said shop in Oxford Street, and bought some glycerine soap there; but I was disappointed in it, not finding it so nice as that which had won my affections at your Isle of Wight home. So I neglected the preservation of the address. I have since had some of the glycerine soap in prepared squares which comes nearer to my ideal.

Always thine uselessly,
M. E. Lewes.

V, 238:7 GHL TO ALEXANDER MAIN, LONDON, [19 JANUARY 1872]

MS: Harvard. *Address:* Alex. Main Esq | West Mary St | Arbroath | NB. *Postmark:* LONDON N.W | 4 | JA 19 | 72.

The Priory. Friday.

No news. Patience! Not likely to go off rapidly—nor to be much noticed by Press. From one reader to another will be its course.[1]

Mrs. L. better, but far from strong.

G. H. L.

1. See v, 239.

V, 246:22   GE TO [?],
LONDON, 7 FEBRUARY 1872

MS: Private Collection.

The Priory, | 21. North Bank, | Regents Park.
February 7. 72.

Dear Friend

The assurance that there is communion between us is very precious to me. I should be inclined to write much to you if I were not obliged to husband my nervous strength with a care which makes me appear very mean and unreciprocating. But—as I said the other day[2]—I trust to your comprehension.

Always yours lovingly
M. E. Lewes.

V, 250:14   GHL TO LORD HOUGHTON,
LONDON, [21 FEBRUARY 1872]

MS: Trinity College, Cambridge.

The Priory, | 21. North Bank, | Regents Park.
Wednesday.

Dear Lord Houghton

Will you kindly cast your eye over the annexed sketch of a Memorial to Gladstone in favor of poor Du Maurier[3]—*correcting* or *enlarging* it according to your wider knowledge of what is proper in such cases? and will you sign it when I have drawn up the amended draft?

That "Sunday Services for the People" (pleasant people!) are held at the Priory has not, we hope, been wholly forgotten by one whose "voice may have grown hoarse with singing of Anthems,"[4] but whose wit made very good incense!

Very truly yours,
G. H. Lewes.

2. Among the ladies listed in GHL's Diary for 4 February 1872 are Kate Field, Mrs. Burne-Jones, Mrs. Douie, Mrs. Rudolf Lehmann, Mrs. Pattison, Mme Bodichon, and Mrs. Wingfield.

3. George Du Maurier's eyesight failed 3 January 1872; and though the medical report two weeks later was favorable, he was panicky. He resumed work at the end of February 1872. (Leonée Ormond, *George Du Maurier*, 1969, pp. 236–237.) No record of the memorial is found among the Gladstone papers.

4. *II Henry IV*, i, ii, 213.

V, 252:7 ANTHONY TROLLOPE TO GE AND GHL,
MELBOURNE, 27 FEBRUARY 1872

MS: Yale. *Published: The Letters of Anthony Trollope,* ed. B.A. Booth, 1951, pp. 290–291.

Melbourne | 27 February 1872.

Dear Friends,

I was so glad to [get] a letter from the Priory! I ought to have written sooner myself;—but I am hurried from place to place, and have no rest for my foot, and do not do the things I ought to do. I am beginning to find myself too old to be 18 months away from home. Not that I am fatigued bodily;—but mentally I cannot be at ease with all the new people and new things. And I find myself asking myself that terrible question of cui bono every morning. I am struggling to make a good book, but I feel that it will not be good.[5] It will be desultory and inaccurate;—perhaps dull, and where shall I be then?

Forsters first volume is distasteful to me,—as I was sure it would be.[6] Dickens was no hero; he was a powerful, clever, humorous, and, in many respects, wise man;—very ignorant, and thick-skinned, who had taught himself to be his own God, and to believe himself to be a sufficient God for all who came near him;—not a hero at all. Forster tells of him things which should disgrace him,—as the picture he drew of his own father, and the hard words he intended to have published of his own mother; but Forster himself is too coarse-grained, (though also a very powerful man) to know what is and what is not disgraceful; what is or is not heroic.

Cigars! Yes, indeed, you in your comfort smoke cigars I dont doubt, and drink coffee, and look on the pleasant faces of books, and write with good ink at a comfortable table,—and are civilized. I am reduced to the vilest tobacco out of the vilest pipe, and drink the vilest brandy and water, —very often in very vile company. But perhaps I shall live to get home when,—not the noctes cænæque Deum—but the pleasant morning table may be spread for me again with just that sufficiency of the divinæ auræ which rescues an hour of sensual enjoyment from any touch of reproach.

My best and kindest love to both—

Yours always
A. T.

5. Trollope went to Australia in June 1871 to visit his son Frederick and to write his *Australia and New Zealand,* 2 vols., 1873.

6. John Forster's *Life of Charles Dickens.* See v, 226.

V, 252:7 GHL TO KATE FIELD,[7]
LONDON, 28 FEBRUARY 1872

MS: Boston Public Library. *Published: New York Tribune*, 14 February 1881, p. 5e.

The Priory, | 21. North Bank, | Regents Park.
28 February 72.

Dear Miss Field

Dining out is one of my costly pleasures—it means a headache next day and therefore I am very sparing in my indulgence. On this account and because I am going to dine out to-day—one excess being enough for one week—I am forced to decline your otherwise tempting invitation.

I shall invade you some afternoon with claims 'growing out' of this one.

Yours truly
G. H. Lewes.

V, 252:7 GHL TO JOSEPH MUNT LANGFORD,
LONDON, [FEBRUARY 1872]

MS: National Library of Scotland.

The Priory, | 21. North Bank, | Regents Park.

My dear Langford

Will you please in *future* send the parts of Middlemarch addressed to our son Herbert Lewes | Coldstream | Newcastle | Natal *instead* of to Kalbasfontein | Natal.

Ever yours
G. H. L.

7. See v, 272, n. 9.

V, 254:1   GHL TO LORD HOUGHTON, LONDON, 7 MARCH 1872

MS: Trinity College, Cambridge.

The Priory, | 21. North Bank, | Regents Park.
7 March 1872.

Dear Lord Houghton

About a fortnight ago I addressed a letter to you on the subject of Du Maurier and the Pension List. Did it reach you?

Yours faithfully,
G. H. Lewes.

V, 259:8   GE TO MR. AND MRS. ROBERT LYTTON, LONDON, 20 MARCH 1872

MS: Lady Hermione Cobbold.

The Priory, | 21. North Bank, | Regents Park.
March 20. 72.

Dear Friends both

It seems a restoration to my rights to know something about you once more. I am hungry for any details even to the smallest gossip, but I shall never earn them honestly by writing to you, so I shall trust to your generosity.

I had been fearing that illness was the cause of the long silence which somehow or other we fancy ourselves warranted in complaining of—I suppose simply because you have made precedents of kindness and affection which we turn into claims. The illness is a new tie and ground of understanding between us, for how can a wretch crawling between heaven and earth as I have been for a good part of the last year, have much community with robust flesh and blood? The words "nausea" and "depression" reveal more common experience between us than could be told in many letters. But Spring and Carlsbad will I trust do for you, dear Mrs. Lytton, what the clear days we are already having seem likely to do for me—turn the miserable consciousness of a stomach into healthy hunger and peaceful digestion.

I like to think of the Baby that is coming to make another sort of fresh Spring time. I don't promise to be delighted with endless babies, but this one I am really glad to expect for you. You will let me know, will you not, when it is safely arrived?

Mrs. Locke[8] promises to come and see me, and I am prepared to like her very much. At present she is a charming portrait to me and of course I prefer the original, objecting to every shade of difference.

I hope Mr. Lewes has told you how mathematics and psychological problems have been renewing his youth these last two years. He has still too much headache, but he is much stronger and looks, I think, younger than when you saw him. We are so unspeakably happy in all other respects that we ought not to grumble at paying a little tax in the form of bodily malaise.

We wish that you could be satisfactorily transplanted and brought nearer to England.[9] I wonder where you would best like to be—in Italy or in Germany? Meanwhile the Fables which are being copied on that enviable paper will come out in a pretty volume[1] and leave room for new studies—perhaps for science which will feed some new form of poetic production. I cannot help believing that there are fibres still to be stirred towards such a combination in you.

Mr. Ralston has just brought out a volume on Russian poetry and legends in which there is this little sketch of a story that Heine would have turned into a poem. "A poverty-stricken wretch tries to keep up appearances by singing, and hears another voice in unison with his own, for which he cannot account until he discovers that it belongs to misery, who is keeping him company."[2]

I usually scribble such letters as I write (Mr. Lewes in his angelic goodness undertaking to write all business notes for me) on my knee, the last thing before going bed, thus giving my friends the ragged edge of my day. This is a poor return for the delightful stories which have made us laugh, and all the other good things that we care for under your hand and —envelope.

Much affection and sympathy, dear Mrs. Lytton, specially in these weeks—much sincere tender friendship to you both at all times from

Yours ever faithfully

M. E. Lewes.

8. Mrs. Lytton's twin sister Elizabeth Villiers (1841–1938) married in 1862 Henry Brougham Loch, later Baron Loch. She spoke to GE after the concert 2 March 1872. (GHL Diary.)

9. Lytton was at Vienna.

1. John Blackwood wrote to Lytton, 28 March 1872: "I like the idea of your Fables very much indeed and shall be most happy to make arrangements for publishing them." (Blackwood Letter Book, NLS.)

2. W. R. Shedden-Ralston, *The Songs of the Russian People*, 1872, p. 29.

V, 260:8 ROBERT LYTTON TO GHL,
VIENNA, 23 MARCH 1872

MS: Yale.

Saturday 23 March 1872 | Vienna.

My dear Lewes

Edith charges me to inform the Prior and Prioress that yesterday at 2. 20 a.m. she gave birth to a little boy,[3] and that our young Astyanax as well as his dear Mother are going on famously. The February number of the Fortnightly only reached me yesterday, and I have read in it with the greatest interest your admirable paper on Dickens.[4] It is delightful reading and appears to me a very masterly piece of criticism. Fully recognizing the justice of your specification of the qualities which Dickens had and had not, I shall perhaps shock you however by the avowal that I rate higher the qualities he had, than those he had not. It appears to me that the reflective tendency, analytical faculty, æsthetic judgement and taste, culture, accurate drawing, accurate style, even in combination with other intellectual powers of a high order, do not of themselves constitute genius, though they are invaluable adjuncts to it,—as zeros are to units,—and greatly elevate the order of the genius to which they are joined. But a prolific imagination of unequalled intensity "furnished with the elements of universal power" able to create a whole world of fictitious images which it is impossible to contemplate without immediate involuntary and inevitable emotion is so undoubtedly genius that whatever the defects of art or intellect with which we find it combined, it stands for all time in a higher order than any combination of faultless talents standing alone.

That is why I can never, in my own view of them both, put Thackeray on a level with Dickens, though the critics seem to put him higher. I can see nothing in Thackeray but well trained talent of a very high order. Dickens is the Poet of the Bourgeoisie all the world over. He has poeticised the bourgeois virtues and vices. What is Thackeray the poet of? There is not a single touch in all his writings which affects me poetically, and he seems to me as immeasurably inferior to Dickens as talent is to genius, although he is as undoubtedly free from the defects of Dickens as Dickens is destitute of the merits of Thackeray. Those merits are certainly great. But have they

---

3. Henry Meredith Edward Lytton (22 March 1872–1 March 1874).
4. "Dickens in Relation to Criticism," *Fortnightly*, 17 (February 1872), 141–154. See G. S. Haight, "Dickens and Lewes," *PMLA*, 71 (March 1956), 166–179.

not been overrated by his Eulogists? You couple him incidentally with Fielding.[5] But I don't know whether you classify them together. My impressions put Fielding very high above him. Comparing the masterpieces of each, there is a cosmical fullness about Tom Jones, which I cannot find in Vanity Fair. One is the whole orbis veteribus notus in a focus, the other only May Fair under a magnifying glass. Thackeray's keen perception, and careful picturing of a certain section of society is put forward with a mighty flourish of trumpets by himself and his ἐπίγονοι as knowledge and portraiture of human nature. If one of Balzac's little fingers could have been cut off and planted in the social soil of London, it might have sprouted into a Thackeray. And even the vividness of vision with which he saw the society he describes I suspect to be largely owing to the fact that he was a parvenu in it. The commonest phenomena impressed him as vividly as common things impress children to whom they are new and unhacknied, and like children he was always inclined to see in such phenomena a volition which had no existence except in his own imagination. This struck me greatly in his conversation. He was incessantly referring the most trival actions to the most recondite motives. I think his influence on the literature of English Fiction has been unfortunate. His imitators are eternally painting in minute strokes, the characters and doings of a number of commonplace and vulgar persons, whom I, for one, would shun like the pest if I met them in real life, and then pausing at every chapter to say "See how sobre is our colouring, how accurate our drawing, how true to nature we are!"

Your illustration of the child's spotted horse on wheels is a master stroke.[6] It is one of those rare explanatory images which attain the perfect ideal of demonstration, giving concrete form to the result of a long train of the subtlest analytical thinking, and is worth folios of argument. It strikes me as eminently just and unanswerably cogent. But after all, how superlative is the merit of any imaginative writer who can reduce his readers involuntarily to the sensational condition of a child or a savage! And what matters it whether the subject we contemplate be a wooden horse, or a waxwork figure, if we contemplate it with such naïveté of sensation as to laugh or cry heartily at the sight of it? I suspect that with many, perhaps most of

5. "Dickens sees and feels, but the logic of feeling seems the only logic he can manage. Thought is strangely absent from his works. . . . Compared with that of Fielding or Thackeray his was merely an *animal* intelligence, *i.e.*, restricted to perceptions." (*Fortnightly*, p. 151.)

6. "Give a child a wooden horse, with hair for mane and tail, and wafer spots for colouring, he will never be disturbed by the fact that this horse does not move its legs, but runs on wheels— the general suggestion suffices for his belief." (p. 146.)

us, as regards works of imagination our appreciation of an author is greatly dependent on accident. Do we ever appreciate the poet we read for the first time in later life as heartily as we appreciated the Poet we read at eighteen when we were first in love? We may grow out of him in after life, but can we ever grow *into* any other poet as entirely? Imaginative writers appeal to our emotions. The response to their appeal depends more upon ourselves than upon them, and we ourselves depend so much on circumstance!

If you ever want to give me a great treat, you will write me a letter. My thoughts are more constantly with you and yours than I have any means of letting you know. The Baby is thin but healthy. He reminds me strangely of his poor brother—whom I think him very like—for I have now sufficient paternal experience to distinguish between the ugliness of one baby and that of another.

Edith and I are much excited by a letter, which I have just been reading to her, from Lizy[7] who says 'I am just going to call on Mrs Lewes': and much disappointed by finding at the end of the letter that Mrs Lewes was out when she called. Vale et seu memor mei. Nobody can admire and love you and your dear wife *more* than you are loved and admired by your affectionate

R. Lytton.

The Kladdersdatsch says—The Pope is ready to burn the Old Catholics for denying that $2 + 2 = 6$ and Dölinger[8] is ready to go to the stake for the assertion that $2 + 2$ *only* $= 5$!

V, 260:23   GHL TO ROBERT LYTTON, LONDON, 27 MARCH 1872

MS: Lady Hermione Cobbold.

The Priory | 27 March 72.

My dear Lytton

Our blessing on the Mottled and our love to his Mother! Tell her she has my entire approbation for having made arrangements to continue the male line of Lytton—not that I am disposed to share the Italian contempt of daughters, especially when there is a chance of their taking after such a

7. Mrs. Lytton's sister Mrs. H. B. Loch.

8. Johann Joseph Ignaz von Döllinger (1799–1890), leader of the Old Catholic Movement, was excommunicated by Pius IX in 1871 for opposing Papal infallibility.

sweet mother but still a boy's a boy and will have the best of it in this world of ours. I am writing this on my tablets because my head aches and won't allow me to bend over the desk. If I am particularly brilliant therefore you will attribute it to my genius, if particularly dull you will know where the dullness springs from!

Apropos of genius in your ingenious defence of Dickens you seem to imply that I did not sufficiently emphasize the fact of his unquestionable genius and that I meant to place Thackeray above him—which proves that my article was a very imperfect expression of my real opinion. I *meant* to bring out strongly the distinctive nature of his genius and to mark not only the defects of his works but also the reason why so many readers were impatient and intolerant. But I suppose as usual what was clear in my own mind was assumed to be clearly presented to the reader. With all you so admirably say of Thackeray I agree.

No Lizzy came to us—or rather came at proper time. But we saw her and her husband at the Concert though that was meagre and scrappy work and hadn't the pleasurable excitement of the former reconnaissance. However I dare say we shall get to know her some future time and she has a warm place prepared for her (I don't mean in the other world, but in the Priory) and if she doesn't find herself there it will be her fault.

Gobineau's[9] Medaillon will not be forgotten though unless I can biologize some rich man and persuade him that he passionately longs to possess what of course he doesn't, I don't see how my attention to the work will fatten Gobineau. Alfred Morrison[1] for example is frightfully rich and is always buying "the most perfect thing in the world, sir," but then whether he will take my view of the Medaillon or at any rate of the propriety of his buying it is another matter. I should say *not*.

Your capital stories—especially that one about the marriage certificate—demands repayment in kind. Grant Duff told us this: Gould, Fisk, and Tweed,[2] among other speculations ran steamboats. On panels of the cabin of the chief boat were portraits of Fisk and Gould; the panel for Tweed's not being filled up at the time, a Yankee quietly observed "Wal, they're certainly like but I miss Christ between them."

---

9. Lytton's *Orval, or the Fool of Time*, 1869, is dedicated to "Count Arthur de Gobineau, Minister of France at the Court of His Hellenic Majesty; Member of the *Société Asiatique* of Paris; Author of '*Esquisses sur l'Inégalité des Races*;' '*Traité des Écritures Cunéiformes*;' and '*Religions et Philosophies dans l'Asie Centrale*,' &c." See Edith Finch, *Wilfred Scawen Blunt*, [1938], p. 394. Lytton was Secretary of Legation at Athens in the spring of 1864.

1. Cf. GHL's account of his call on the Morrisons to see Houdon's bust of Voltaire, vi, 162, n. 7.

2. The notorious American speculators Jay Gould, James Fisk, and William Marcy Tweed.

Here's another: The Dukes of Argyll and Northumberland were in a railway carriage and a bagman who got in en route entered into talk with them and rattled away freely. The Duke of N. got out and left at a station midway; bagman getting out to stretch his legs at the same time was much struck with the deference paid his travelling companion and enquired who he might be; was told; and returned full of excitement to the Duke of A. "Do you know that was the Duke of Northumberland that just left. Only think of a great man like that talking so freely to snobs like you and me." These are not fit to paré off with yours but they are the last I have heard and I only hope they're not already familiar to you.

You want to know about my mathematical speculation. Could I only have you here over a cigarette, or have my own feet on your hearthrug I would discourse till the small hours and make you eternally repent your indiscretion in opening such a sluice. But I can't write about it. All I can say is that the higher calculus has opened a shaft in the metaphysical mine which if it doesn't lead me to the foundation of things will not be for want of digging or adventurous confidence. I sometimes think (so modest is Philosophy!) that as Descartes revolutionized science by his discovery of the application of Algebra to Geometry, expressing curves by equations, so a larger revolution may be heralded by an application of Algebra to the Cosmos, reducing all Science to Symbols and operations on Symbols.

Polly, who is suffering from a week's hemicrania, and would otherwise have written her love to Edith, bids me send all manner of tender messages, and especially to emphasize the fact of *it* (what else can *it* be?) being a Boy —a possible Casaubon![4] who however isn't likely to find a Dodo—that species being said to be extinct. And would you have that Zoological problem solved, why was the Dodo suffered to get 'improved' from the face of Gaea? The solution is extremely simple—Because such was the resultant of the component forces! I must not go on.

Ever yours affectionately
G. H. L.

3. George Douglas Campbell, 8th Duke of Argyll (1823–1900), and Sir Algernon Percy, 4th Duke of Northumberland (1792–1865).

4. *Middlemarch*, Book II, published February 1872, describes the Casaubons' honeymoon in Rome.

V, 263:1   GHL TO KATE FIELD, LONDON, 1 APRIL 1872

MS: Boston Public Library.

The Priory, | 21. North Bank, | Regents Park.
1 April 72.

My dear Miss Field

Ce que vous me demandez sort tout à fait de mes habitudes. Par conséquent, (telle est la logique humaine!) I will be there[5] "or perish in the attempt."

Yours ever
G. H. Lewes.

V, 268:21   GHL TO ALEXANDER MAIN, LONDON, [16 APRIL 1872]

MS: Harvard. *Address:* Alex. Main Esq. | 21 West Mary St | Arbroath | N.B. *Postmark:* LONDON N.W | 4 | AP 16 | 72.

The Priory, Tuesday.

Before closing my letter I forgot to say that I have sent 'Olrig Grange'[6] by this post. You can keep it as long as you please; we have both read it.

G. H. L.

V, 268:21   GHL TO WILLIAM ALLINGHAM, LONDON, [17 APRIL 1872]

MS: University of Illinois.

The Priory, | 21. North Bank, | Regents Park.
Wednesday.

My dear Sir

Can you lunch with us next Sunday at 1.30? Say yes!

Yours truly
G. H. Lewes.

W. Allingham Esq.

5. GHL attended Kate Field's private rehearsal of her lecture on Dickens, 4th April 1872. (GHL Diary.)
6. See v, 262, n. 7.

V, 268:21   GHL TO WILLIAM ALLINGHAM, LONDON, 20 APRIL 1872

MS: University of Illinois. *Address:* Wm. Allingham Esq. | 18 Neville Place | Onslow Gardens | S.W. *Postmark:* LONDON N.W | 12 | AP 20 | 72.

The Priory.

The Prioress has taken cold and will not be visible tomorrow. Can you postpone your visit till Sunday following, same hour?[7]

G. H. L.

V, 268:21   GE TO MRS. PETER ALFRED TAYLOR, LONDON, 24 APRIL 1872

MS: Yale. *Envelope:* Mrs. Taylor | 22 Marine Parade | Brighton. *Postmarks:* LONDON N.W | 5 | AP 25 | 72; BRIGHTON | A | AP 26 | 72 | A.

The Priory, | 21. North Bank, | Regents Park.
April 24. 72.

Dear Friend

Thanks for your letter about dear Mrs. Smith.[8] I have written to her.

How very generous Mr. Taylor has been in taking trouble about a house for us! We both of us felt that the place he had found was not only tempting in the description, but guaranteed by his judgment as well as it would have been by our own inspection. Unhappily, the distance from town is made all the graver obstacle by the state of my health, which makes me nervous about being away from all the succour to be found in my own home—without the sense that I could easily get back to it at any moment. I have been suffering from neuralgic pains and inflamed gums, and have been quite confined to the house for a week or more. The least draught, or exposure to an unfriendly wind brings some form of ailment in me, owing to my being in an unusually weak condition. However, what I wanted to tell was not the long chapter of my ailments, but my gratitude to Mr. Taylor for taking trouble on our behalf.

Mr. Lewes presents affectionate remembrances to Snowball and Buff with homage to their patroness. Our united thanks and regards to Mr. Taylor.

Yours ever lovingly
M. E. Lewes.

7. Allingham came to lunch 28 April   8. See v, 265, n. 8.
1872. (GHL Diary.)

V, 270:7 ROBERT LYTTON TO GHL, VIENNA, 29 APRIL 1872

MS: Yale.

Vienna 29 April 1872.

My dear Lewes

Procrastination is the Thief of Time, Time is the murderer of good intentions, and good intentions are the fraudulent bankers, the rascally psalmsinging Deane Pauls,[1] of honest innocent well disposed folks, like myself. I sat down to answer your last letter the day I received it,—was called away to receive visitors, meant to write to you the next day, on the same evening was laid up with an inflammation in the stomach from which I am only now escaped. It vexes me however to have left you so long under a false impression of my own impressions of your admirable paper on Dickens and his critics. I DIDN'T think you had underrated D's genius or set Thackeray above him on the score of genius. Your incidental mention of the two in connection with each other led me to talk of them both in reference to my own predilections when writing to you currente calamo. You never fail to express with fine accuracy what you mean: and the essay in question is crystal clear. It is I who must have expressed myself imperfectly if you thought I either mistook your meaning or dissented from it. All I meant was that in regard to authors, after criticism has said its last word pro and con about them, we readers, transcribing the verdict on the tablets of our own impressions, add, unconsciously for the most part, a saving or a damning clause dictated by personal predilections or prejudices which are stronger than all criticisms because they are not formed on critical grounds, or accountable to critical cannons, but the inevitable resultant of an infinite number of accidents which happen to have favoured or disfavoured the rapport between our own minds and that of the author under judgement. It is like the feather in the Egyptian Scale of the Dead, which, though of no weight in itself, just turns the scale after strict justice has adjusted the balance: or the talisman in the pretty German story about Charlemagne which to the astonishment and scandal of all his wise counsellors made him attach himself to whoever happened to have that talisman for the time being. I have often thought that from the rapport between two friends there results a third individuality common to both, but not completely residing in either. A calls it B and B calls it A. It is really A + B,

1. Sir John Dean Paul (1802–68), London banker, convicted of fraud in 1855 and sentenced to fourteen years' transportation, "was reputed to be a man of the highest religious principles." (*DNB.*)

and probably as regards works of imagination, their effect is quite as dependent on the imagination that receives as on the imagination that produces. Voilà tout ce que je voulais dire, in explanation of my own delight in D's genius—a delight undiminished by any critical consciousness of his defects in art, though those defects are patent and numerous.

How I wish I *could* have a chat with you au coin du feu, or rather under some tree in your garden, concerning the subject and scope of your present labours! Would I not just "bid you discourse" knowing that "you would enchant mine ear!"[2] The tiny and mysterious glimpse you give me of the road you are following—or making—bewilders my curiosity. I don't understand your dark saying—dark as seen from the depths of my ignorance, in which I welter whimsically amongst all sorts of fanciful conjectures, as for instance that I am now writing to a positivized Pythagoras, and how strange it would be if Physical Sciences should first reduce the explanation of all phenomena to a single force, and then Philosophy step in to reduce the logic of all explanations to a single formula. What a sword wherewith to open the world, our oyster![3] Perhaps the next generation will be able to travel through the universe like Mr. Cook's Tourists with tickets of admission to the sun and moon, and a portable guidebook explaining everything by the way. Perhaps knowledge will end where it begins at the Multiplication Table and perhaps the Fairy tale of the Belle au bois dormant was a prophecy of this. The Sleeping Beauty will wake up and say to her enterprizing fiancé Humanity, as she rubs her eye, "Well you have come at last, but what a time you have kept me waiting and how stupid of you not to have found out the secret sooner. You see now how simple it is!"

Your story of the Bagman is magnificent. I have been chuckling over it ever since I got your letter. And as the old women say of Mr. Spurgeon's[4] preaching "It is very comforting." For is not the Paladium of the British Constitution built on a granite foundation of Bagmans' heads? and how do those dear heads tingle with satisfaction when tenderly titilated by the toes of the temporal and spiritual Hierarchy that stands upon them! Baron Schwartz (not a descendant of the inventor of gunpowder, but the present director of the Great Vienna Exhibition, or Weltausstellung, for the year of our Lord 1873) has just officially proposed (by way of appropriately inaugurating that particular date of the Christian Era, and adding to the attractions of the great guinguette with which it is for ever after to be associated in the grateful memory of mankind)—to the Amergau Peasants

2. *Venus and Adonis*, line 145.

3. *The Merry Wives of Windsor*, ii, ii, 2.

4. Charles Haddon Spurgeon. See v, 121, n. 8.

to perform the Passion Play here on that occasion. Such is my sympathy with this sacred subject, that as you see, I have in speaking of it, fallen into the parenthetical style of St. Paul! Baron Schwartz is an Austrian-German, a Consul, and a Baron; I therefore presume that he is also a Jew—a fact which refines the spicy flavour of this invitation. But though the Vienna Jews (of whom there are no less than 30,000) would probably be willing to give more than thirty silver groschen (and could certainly afford to give *much* more) for such a second edition of the Crucifixion, I fancy that amongst the Amergau disciples Mr. Schwartz will not find any Judas willing to strike a bargain with these scribes and pharasees. The idea however was a great one.

We are going into the Country (thank Heaven!) in about 10 days to a little house with a garden and water mill and a troutstream which I have taken, at 2 hours distance from Vienna for the summer. Edith cannot [*The rest of the letter is lacking.*]

V, 270:7 MATILDA BETHAM EDWARDS TO GE, LONDON, 30 APRIL [1872]

MS: Berg Collection, New York Public Library.

18 Upper Baker St. N. April 30.

My dear Mrs. Lewes

I never can say what I want to say at the right moment or I should have told you on Sunday[5] how deeply I felt the truth and value of the few words you said to me about writing. "Speech," is as you have said, in that wonderful Shakespearian line, "but broken light, upon the depth of the unspoken,"[6] but a few such words as you said then stir those depths and are never forgotten. It is so much easier to be content with mediocrity in things spiritual and moral, as well as intellectual, than to be always striving for the best, that without coming in contact now and then with the highest thought, even an ardent nature is apt to yield to temptation, and live meanly without remorse. This more especially applies to literary work, which we were talking about; and I am sure you will easily believe what I said about wishing so much of my work unwritten. I am tempted to write and tell you all this that you may know how greatly I treasure the rare privilege of a little talk with you and how much good it does me.

5. Mme Bodichon and Miss Edwards were among the 20 callers 28 April 1872. (GHL Diary.)

6. *The Spanish Gypsy*, 1868, p. 98; Cabinet ed., p. 104.

Farewell till September and meantime may every summer breeze bring
health and enjoyment to you both.

I will venture to sign myself, yours affectionately and gratefully

M. B. Edwards.

I am sure you will take it for granted that I don't expect an answer.

V, 270:7   GHL TO KATE FIELD, LONDON, [APRIL? 1872]

MS: Boston Public Library.

The Priory, | 21. North Bank, | Regents Park.

My dear Miss Field

We may be obliged to go out on Sunday, but shall be at home again a
little after 4, if you think of again swelling the crowd, but I hope you will
be in London on our return.

Yours truly

G. H. Lewes.

V, 270:22   GHL TO CLEMENT MANSFIELD INGLEBY, LONDON 7 MAY 1872

MS: Folger Library.

The Priory, | 21. North Bank, | Regents Park.

May 7th 1872.

Sir

I am not aware of the existence of any such criticism on Shakspeare as
you inquire about. But since we have at last ventured to criticise the Bible
it is presumable that the heretical tendency may sooner or later extend to
Shakspeare.

I quite sympathize with you in your feeling of despair on this subject.

Yours truly

G. H. Lewes.

V, 276:21 ROBERT LYTTON TO GHL,
[KNEBWORTH, JUNE 1872]

MS: Newnham College, Cambridge.

Wednesday morning.

My dear Lewes

Your little line to Edith, received and warmly welcomed this morning, has been anticipated, as you will see, by little lines from both of us to your dear wife. I have nothing to add this morning except ("on behalf of self and Partner") this expression of the very great pleasure it has given both of us to hear from you. I am also, above all things, rejoiced, on the world's behalf, as well as my own, to learn that you are 'hard at work.' I wish I was. What with the reaction from a very laborious and anxious chargé d' affaireship and an extra supply of stupidity from shaken health, I pass my days just now in wishing much, and doing nothing. I can say of work however what the French lady said of Virtue—cela a toujours été pour moi un effort rarement couron[n]é de succés.

What is your son doing in Africa? I mean—besides being happy. Our two little girls are growing very fast, and growing very pretty.

I don't wonder at your being startled by the likeness between those two Dromias, Lizzie and Edith. I always tell my wife that she is half a charming woman. I don't [know] which has the best half of that charming woman, Henry Loch or myself. But I am well content with my own half.

Write again whenever you feel in a charitable disposition. Mr. Casaubon is excellent, but as he is quite good enough to die, and too good to change for the better in this world, I hope for Dorothea's sake that it will please her creator to remove him to another world before the end of the book.[7]

Here is a riddle for you, the character of which must be excused by your knowledge of my present domestic circumstances. What is the difference entre un conspirateur et une nour[r]ice? Le conspirateur a toujours un dessien caché. La nour[r]ice a toujours un des seins découverts.

Adieu! adieu! adieu! Your ever affectionate

R. Lytton.

7. Mr. Casaubon dies in ch. 43, published in Book v, August 18, 1872.

V, 276:21   GHL TO MONCURE DANIEL CONWAY, [REDHILL, JUNE? 1872]

MS: Historical Society of Pennsylvania.

Monday.

My dear Sir

Your letter has been forwarded to us in our retreat from the turmoil of London. Respecting your friend's proposal I can say little or nothing. Mrs. Lewes does not engage for unwritten or unprojected works, not keeping a manufactory of novels on which she could relie. But as it is quite possible that she may at some future time write another novel there would be no harm in your friend making his proposition, that you might have it before you in case of there being any work to sell.

All I would beg him to understand is that Mrs. Lewes neither undertakes to write again, nor affixes any time, nor that she would give any answer to any proposition now made for so contingent a transaction. It would be understood on both sides as merely a proposition en l'air serving as a memorandum for future guidance.

Yours truly

G. H. Lewes.

M. D. Conway, Esq.

V, 277:23   AN "AFFABLE" BARRISTER TO GE, LONDON, 4 JUNE 1872

MS: Yale.

12, King's Bench Walk, | Temple, E. C.

4th June 72.

Madam,

If a lawyer who reads your work with great interest and admiration may be allowed, without being thought intrusive, to tell you a bit of "shop" I will take the liberty of doing so.

Peter Featherstone makes two wills, one anterior to the other in date, and thinks by destroying the last to leave the other his legal "last will and testament."

In law this would not be the effect. He would die an intestate and his property would be divided among his heirs-at-law.

The destruction of the last would not revive the former, though if it passed undisputed it might be taken for his last will, but different solicitors having drawn them up it certainly would not pass without question.[8]

Hoping you will pardon this word on a purely technical point (which probably has been 50 times pointed out to you already),

I remain

Your faithful servant
An "affable" barrister.

V, 293:1   GHL TO ROBERT LYTTON, REDHILL, 27 JULY 1872

MS: Lady Hermione Cobbold.

Elversley, Red Hill | 27 July 72.

My dear Lytton

I conclude from not having seen nor heard from you that either you did not come to England or were too much occupied with others' business to find a day for our pleasure here. That you are at home now I also conclude and therefore send you this to say how very much Polly and I were pleased with the *mâle eloquence* and fine thought of the article on Beethoven[9]— an article such as one rarely sees. Not that we have not our differences of opinion! especially in respect to the sort of heaven-descended speciality assigned to Music. But this is a big subject—(you know the Yankees call the Mississippi a 'big drink'?) and not to be touched in a letter. Some day we may have a confabulation on it—may that day be near!

With regard to your Fable I am really at a loss what to say. It contains passages fine as any you ever wrote, but somehow es will mir nicht zusagen. I think its chief want is unity of feeling. It does not all seem moulded out of the same metal and in the same mould. But it is very easy to say this; easy to say one is not perfectly satisfied, and damnably difficult to put one's finger on a spot and say that that is not organic, normal, healthy, so I give it up. After all readers and critics must never forget how very probable it is that the darkness lies in their minds, rather than in the want of light in the poet!

---

8. In Book IV, ch. 35, GE wrote: "if he had done as he liked at the last, and burnt the will drawn up by another lawyer, he would not have secured that minor end" of surprising Mr. Standish. (1st ed., II, 201.) In Book V, ch. 52, published in August 1872, GE made Mr. Farebrother explain to Mary Garth: "I find that the first will would not have been legally good after the burning of the last: it would not have stood if it had been disputed, and you may be sure it would have been disputed." (III, 161–162.)

9. "Beethoven," *Fortnightly*, 18 (July 1872), 19–38.

You will be glad to hear that my son Charles—I forget whether you have seem him—is a father at last. Six years ago his wife was confined of a strangled daughter, and now at length she has produced a squalling daughter[10] —'pomegranate colored' according to maternal vision—'mottled' according to paternal. It is a great comfort to us that all has gone successfully at last.

And how is your sweet wife? and the chicks?—Not that I mean you to answer these questions until you have some reason for writing; only consider them as details of interest when you do write. Polly adds: And don't forget to tell us whether our wishes for your increase of fortune by Lord Dalling's death have been realized.[1]

We are getting on in our absolute solitude as well as two pregnant authors can be expected to get on. Polly's health has been very satisfactory but it doesn't make her less miserable over her work. My health has *not* been satisfactory, but it has not prevented my being jubilant over my work. There is the contrast! When I see her so diffident over work I know to be so fine, it makes me dread lest my confidence may not be altogether hallucination!

You ask about the Mole cricket? All I know is that I once took out his nervous system—nicht wichtig schien es mir—to quote Wagner (Faust's).[2] Of his habits I know nix. Love to Edith.

Ever yours truly
G. H. L.

V, 301:1 GE TO GEORGE CROOM ROBERTSON, REDHILL, 18 AUGUST 1872

MS: University College London.

Park Road | Redhill | August 18. 72.
Dear Mr. Robertson

On your own account simply, over and above the other ties which give me an interest in your engagement to Miss Crompton,[3] I am gratified to be told of it. For Mr. Lewes and I have long had a high value for your society,

10. Blanche Southwood Lewes (19 July 1872–1964).
1. Sir William Henry Earle Bulwer, Baron Dalling and Bulwer (1801–23 May 72), Robert Lytton's uncle, under whom he served when Bulwer was ambassador to Washington. By will he left all his estate to his widow except for his documents and manuscripts, which he left to his two brothers or their surviving sons to be kept or destroyed as they saw fit. (Somerset House.)
2. "Ich sah ihn lange schon, nicht wichtig schien er mir." (*Faust*, Part I, line 1148.)
3. George Croom Robertson (1842–92), married 14 December 1872 Caroline Anna Crompton, daughter of Sir

and have liked to think that we might number you among our friends. We congratulate you sincerely on a relation so full of promise. A good while ago Mr. Lewes had the pleasure of seeing Miss Crompton at a garden party and expressed to me when he came home his admiration for her sweet face.

Please give my love to my friends who are with you. I trust that Mrs. Harry Crompton's face has less of pearly delicacy than when I said goodbye to her, and that little Paul is flourishing.[4]

We have enjoyed our retreat in this pretty corner of the world, and Mr. Lewes has been on the whole prosperous in health as well as happily industrious in psychological studies. I am a little below my average condition, but we hope to start for the Continent by the middle of September, and a journey is often curative for me.

We shall be at home again at the end of October. Perhaps by that time you will be married. Do not forget us, and believe me always

Most sincerely yours

M. E. Lewes.

V, 325:10   GE TO COURTNEY STANHOPE KENNY, LONDON, 5 NOVEMBER 1872

MS: Ohio University, Athens, Ohio. *Envelope:* Courtney Kenny Esq. | Downing College | Cambridge. *Postmark:* LONDON-N.W | 2 | NO 5 | 72; N.W 20.

The Priory, | 21. North Bank, | Regent Park.

November 5. 72.

Mrs. G. H. Lewes (George Eliot) presents her compliments to Mr. Courtney Kenny[5] and thanks him for his kindness in wishing to help her by pointing out errata in "Middlemarch." Of the two cases which he has noted in Book III. the one on p. 8. 1. 15 will, she thinks, be seen by him not to be an error if he will take the trouble to reconsider it.[6] The real erratum of "nulli" for "nullo"[7] was corrected on a slip stitched into Book IV., and the page has since been cancelled and replaced by a new one in the stereotype.

Charles John Crompton, Justice of the Queen's Bench. She afterwards took a considerable share in the management of Girton College.

4. Henry Crompton (1836–1904), Caroline's brother, married Lucy Henrietta Romilly, daughter of Lord Romilly, 8 November 1870. Their elder son Paul with his wife and six children drowned in the *Lusitania* in 1915.

5. Courtney Stanhope Kenny (1847–1930), admitted a pensioner at Downing College 17 May 1871, had practised as a solicitor in Halifax since 1869.

6. In ch. 23 GE wrote: "though old manufacturers could not any more than dukes be connected with none but equals."

7. In ch. 29 Casaubon had addressed "a dedication to Carp in which he had numbered that member of the animal kingdom among the *viros nulli aevo perituros*, a mistake which would infallibly lay the dedicator open to ridicule in the next age." 1st ed., II, 103.)

V, 325:11   GHL TO [?],
LONDON, 8 NOVEMBER 1872

MS: Princeton.

The Priory, | 21. North Bank, | Regent Park.

8 November 72.

Dear Sir

Mrs. Lewes (George Eliot) is so much occupied just now that I relieve her, whenever practicable, of the labour of correspondence; and she is the more desirous that I should reply to your question, because she has a very slight experience on which to found a judgment, and I have had a tolerably large experience.

My advice is by all means not to throw yourself on Literature for a living. Very splendid talents and wide knowledge are often incompetent to secure bread and cheese and except in the department of journalism there is but a perilous outlook for any one who has not already proved that his talents are *commercially* valuable. Now it seems to me that this question you can decide for yourself. Assuming that your present employment is intolerable to you and that you have a strong bent towards Literature, I would urge you to ascertain decisively whether editors and publishers are willing and eager to *pay* you for your writing? If they are you can form some estimate of your probable success when you devote your whole energies to Literature. Meanwhile you can do what hundreds of others are doing, viz. cultivate Literature in your leisure hours, and try by your production to encrease your income and find a footing for yourself on the shifting sand of periodicals. To give up any honorable employment on the vague *chance* of success in Literature is what all rational men would advise against.[8] You must not confound your hopes and wishes with the condition of success. It is for you a question of pounds and shillings and pence not of literary activity—and that question you, like every one else, have the means of settling, by simply offering editors and publishers what you have written. Believe me both editors and publishers are for their own sakes eager to accept and pay for whatever promises to be commercially valuable; and no one will accept work that does not seem to promise such commercial advantage.

Yours truly

G. H. Lewes.

8. This advice parallels the opening section of GHL's "The Principles of Success in Literature," *Fortnightly*, 1 (15 May 1865), 85–95. Like Ran- thorpe, the hero of his first novel, GHL himself had given up unpalatable work and thrown himself on literature.

V, 325:10   HERBERT SPENCER TO GHL, LONDON, 11 NOVEMBER 1872

MS: London University. Only the signature is in Spencer's hand. *Brief extract published:* Haight, *George Eliot*, p. 446.

37 Queen's Gardens, | Bayswater, London, W. | 11 November 1872.
My dear Lewes,

Yesterday I forgot for the moment the proper course to be pursued. The proposal, according to the established arrangement, should be made through King, since the supposition is that the Committee is anonymous.[9]

Yesterday, after seeing you, I finished reading the last instalment of *Middlemarch*. It is altogether admirable. I cannot conceive anything more perfectly done. Hitherto, I have felt that the story, while it has been somewhat too uniformly full of fine things—too uniformly rich, has been a little wanting in breadth of light and shade; but this last portion seems to me to fulfil the requirements of the highest art in every respect.

Ever yours truly,
Herbert Spencer.

V, 333:13   GHL TO MRS. RICHARD STRACHEY, LONDON, [26 NOVEMBER 1872]

MS: British Museum. *Envelope:* Mrs. Strachey | 8 Rutland Gate | W. [*forwarded to*] Willenhall | Whetstone N. *Postmark:* LONDON-N.W | 12 | NO 26 | 72. *Published: TLS* 16 May 1968, p. 507.

The Priory, | 21. North Bank, | Regents Park.
Tuesday.

My dear Mrs. Strachey

I so much desire to have you as a neighbour[1] that if you will only send me word what style of house, how many rooms, and about what rent, you contemplate I will ransack St. John's Wood and Regents Park, get you

9. "Called on Spencer and spoke to him about publishing 1 vol. of Problems in the International Series." (GHL Diary, 10 November 1872.) The International Scientific Series was projected by Spencer's friend E. L. Youmans for the publication of "works of a certain class" by agreement among English, American, French, and German pub-lishers at specified rates of profit for the authors. See Spencer, *Autobiography*, 2 vols., 1904, II, 227. Henry Samuel King was the English representative of the publishers.

1. General and Mrs. Richard Strachey were among the guests at the Priory Sunday, 24 November 1872.

cards to view of any that seem promising and so take some of the bother off your hands.

Very truly yours
G. H. Lewes.

V, 333:13 GE TO MME EUGÈNE BODICHON, LONDON, [26 NOVEMBER 1872]

MS: Berg Collection, New York Public Library.

Monday Evening.[2]

Dear Barbara

If you can defer your visit tomorrow till $\frac{1}{2}$ past 4 I shall be at home by that time. But I am not wise enough to do Miss Cook[3] any good. You know, I have had no experience in teaching.

We have been to Weybridge today, so I could not write earlier. But I hope you will get this in time.

Yours always
Marian.

V, 334:1 GHL TO GEORGE SMITH, LONDON, [29 NOVEMBER 1872]

MS: Princeton. *Endorsed:* 408 pages = $12\frac{3}{4}$ sheets of 32 pp.

The Priory, | 21. North Bank, | Regents Park.
Thursday.

My dear Smith

The German publishers wish to know how many sheets the 'Story of G's Life'[4] will make. Would you ask the printers to send me about what quantity?

Ever yours truly
G. H. L.

2. Monday was 25 November. But GHL's Diary records their spending Tuesday, 26 November, at Weybridge and Barbara's call 27 November.

3. Rachel Cook, one of the Girton pioneers, became in 1874 the wife of Charles Prestwich Scott, editor and owner of the *Manchester Guardian*.

4. Heinrich Brockhaus (1804–74) of Leipzig paid GHL £50 for *The Story of Goethe's Life*, 1873. Smith proposed the abridgement 11 April 1872 and GHL finished it 6 November. (GHL Diary.)

V, 334:1 GHL TO [FRANZ DUNCKER], LONDON, 29 NOVEMBER 1872

MS: Yale.

The Priory, | 21. North Bank, | Regents Park.

29 November 1872.

My dear Sir

A brief absence from home[5] has prevented my sooner acknowledging your letter of the 11th inst. With respect to your question about the English reprint, it is, as you imagine, to be taken in hand by Messrs. Brockhaus, who published it originally.

I will send you the 'copy' from which our printers work, to save you all trouble in adapting your translation to the new.[6]

Yours truly

G. H. Lewes.

V, 334:1 GHL TO MRS. RICHARD STRACHEY, LONDON, [30 NOVEMBER 1872]

MS: British Museum. *Envelope:* Mrs. Strachey | Willenhall | Whetstone. *Postmarks:* LONDON-N.W | 2 | NO 30 | 72; LONDON | MD | NO 3 | 72. *Published: TLS,* 16 May 1968, p. 507.

The Priory, | 21. North Bank, | Regents Park.

Saturday.

My dear Mrs. Strachey

Of the houses on your list No. 1 Cunningham Place wants thoroughly cleaning and papering (the landlord will do whatever is wanted) and then might perhaps suit you. No. 19 Cavendish Rd.[7] is a house we so much longed for that although it was not to let I ventured to write to the tenant asking if there were any probability of his leaving it in 2 years. He said No, so we altered our house and remained there. Whether the accomdation would be all you desire I know not, but pray come and see it—the situation is worth a great deal.

I have also got the enclosed order to view four houses—the two first

5. With the Cross family at Weybridge 26 November 1872. (GHL Diary.)

6. Duncker accepted GHL's proposal to publish a German translation of *The Story of Goethe's Life* for £50. (GHL Diary, 14 November 1872.)

7. Now Cavendish Avenue, close to Lord's Cricket Ground. Both houses were near the Priory.

very likely to suit,—but I don't know whether you desire quiet or not. In that case the Finchley Rd would not do, but St. John's Park would.

Ever faithfully yours
G. H. Lewes.

V, 339:7 GE TO SIR JAMES PAGET, LONDON, 7 DECEMBER 1872

MS: Princeton. *Published: Memoirs and Letters of Sir James Paget,* ed. Stephen Paget, 1903, pp. 407–408.

The Priory, | 21. North Bank, | Regents Park.
December 7. 72.

My dear Sir James

Since I saw you a medical man at Ealing has written to me to express his regret that I have "blotted" the correctness of my representation on medical subjects by speaking of Lydgate's "bright dilated eyes" in such a connection as to imply that an opiate would have the effect of dilating the pupil.

It is a piece of contemptible forgetfulness in me that when I wrote those passages I had not present in my mind the fact which I had read again and again—that one of the effects of opium is to contract the pupil. What I had in my imagination was the appearance in the eyes which I have often noted in men who have been taking too much alcohol, and who are in the loquacious, boastful, or quarrelsome stage.

I am unhappy, as you may imagine, about this said "blot." And what I wish to ask of your goodness now is, to tell me whether you think the matter grave enough to urge my cancelling the two stereotype plates (certainly no great affair) before any more copies are struck off?

I am sure that your sympathy is large enough to take in this small trouble of mine.

Always most truly yours
M. E. Lewes.

Sir James Paget, Bart.

V, 340:16 FREDERIC W. H. MYERS TO GE, CHELTENHAM, 8 DECEMBER 1872

MS: Yale.

Brandon House | Cheltenham | December 8/72.

Dear Mrs. Lewes,

I have often wanted to write to you while Middlemarch was coming out, but have restrained myself hitherto, partly because you must be bored with many letters of the kind from slight acquaintances, like myself, or even from strangers, and partly because I felt hindered by the idea that you might think that I had expected an answer. But after reading the last volume my impulse to write is so strong that I shall yield to it. I do *not* expect an answer, and I write to give myself the pleasure and relief of thanking you for an enjoyment which has brightened the whole year.

Each reader of complex books like yours will care most for some particular strain which appeals most directly to his personal tastes and experience. Though I thoroughly enjoy the whole of Middlemarch I care far the most for the scenes between Ladislaw and Dorothea. Noble love making,—the surprised and pure contact of lofty souls,—is hardly ever described truly. When it is described truly, to read the description is better than to live through any scenes but such as those. Life has come to such a pass,—now that there is no longer any God or any hereafter or anything in particular to aim at,—that it is only by coming into contact with some other person that one can be oneself. There is no longer anything to keep an isolated fire burning within one,—all one can do is to feel the sparks fly from one for a moment when one strikes a kindred soul. Such contact in real life can make one feel for the moment immortal; but the necessary circumstances are so unusual! Mere love, delicate or passionate, will not do; to have its best savour love must be set among great possibilities and great sacrifices, and must demand the full strain of all the forces within one. Unless things can so happen the first moment of love is apt to be the best. And therefore it is that to read of Dorothea's night of struggle and visit to Rosamond is better, though it is only on paper and in a book, than an ordinary passion; for this is what one wants, though it be but a shadow; this is the best conception of life that in this stage of the world we can form. Scenes like these go straight into the only imperishable world, —the world which is peopled by the lovely conceptions which have disengaged themselves in successive generations from the brains of men. The interest of such conceptions is more than artistic; they are landmarks in the history of the race, showing the height to which, at successive periods, man's ideal of his own life has vision.

And you seem now to be the only person who can make life appear potentially noble and interesting without starting from any assumptions. De Stendhal, perhaps, while himself detached from all illusions has painted life in the same grand style. But he remains too much outside his characters, and though in his books nobleness seems possible it seems possible only as an aberration. And others who have shown more or less of the same power of rising into clear air, —Mme de Stael in Corinne, Mrs. Craven in Fleurange, George Sand in Consuelo, —have all needed some fixed point to lean against before they could spread wings to soar. But one feels that you know the worst, and one thanks you in that you have not despaired of the republic.

I remain, dear Mrs. Lewes,

> Yours very truly
> Frederic W. H. Myers.

V, 340:16   GE TO FREDERIC W. H. MYERS, LONDON, 9 DECEMBER 1872

MS: Trinity College, Cambridge. *Envelope:* F.W.H. Myers Esq. | Brandon House | Cheltenham. *Postmarks:* LONDON N.W | 5 | DE 9 | 72; CHELTENHAM | A2 | DE 10 | 72. *The letter has not been found.*

V, 340:16   GE TO MRS. WILLIAM CROSS, LONDON, 11 DECEMBER 1872

MS: Yale. *Envelope:* Mrs. Cross | Weybridge Heath | Weybridge | S.W. *Postmarks:* LONDON-N.W | 4 | DE 11 | 72; WEYBRIDGE STATION | A | DE 12 | 72.

The Priory, | 21. North Bank, | Regents Park.
December 11. 72.

My dear Mrs. Cross

We shall look forward to our Christmas holiday as if London were school and Weybridge home. A London Christmas is always dreary, to me, not being in the least after that country fashion to which I was bred. Please thank Mr. Hall on our behalf for his kind partnership in your hospitality, and feel yourself spiritually kissed by our gratitude.

If we have a fine morning on the 24th, George desires me to say, ⟨that⟩ we will be with you before lunch-time, but in case of rain he will console himself by doing his morning's work at home, and we will start by an afternoon train.

Yours always lovingly
M. E. Lewes.

V, 342:1 GHL TO GEORGE SMITH, LONDON, 11? DECEMBER 1872

MS: Princeton. *Endorsed:* Very near what was estimated—press in a few days.

Wednesday.

Dear Smith

I never saw the pamphlet on Oneida.[8] Ergo!—

Has the estimate of what my new version of Goethe will make been settled? and the type? and are they printing?

In haste

Ever yours
G. H. L.

V, 352:1 GHL TO JOHN BLACKWOOD, LONDON, [29 DECEMBER 1872]

MS: National Library of Scotland.

Sunday.

My dear Sir

The more I think over the suggestion I threw out respecting the guinea edition of Middlemarch on thinner paper the more I see its fairness and its chance of acceptance.[1] It should be advertised as ostensibly inferior to the other, and then no one need grumble at having paid more for the 'fine paper copy.'

Mrs. Lewes has just come back from a visit to country friends laid up with neuralgia and indigestion—not a good result of festivities! We hope you are enjoying Christmas without such consequences.

Yours truly
G. H. Lewes.

8. *Handbook of the Oneida Community,*   *Votaries,* New York, 1870.
1871, or John B. Ellis, *Free Love and Its*   1. See v, 350.

V, 352:24   GHL TO GEORGE SMITH,
LONDON, 29 DECEMBER [1872]

MS: Princeton.

The Priory, | 21. North Bank, | Regents Park.
Sunday 29 December.

My dear Smith

I should be glad if you would tell the printers to send proofs of the Goethe to Herrn F. A. Brockhaus[2] | Leipzig | as they are got ready.

We have just returned from a Christmas visit to country friends whose excessive hospitality has unhappily given Mrs. Lewes a fit of indigestion and the long drives a touch of face neuralgia. May your festivities have no such results!

Ever yours truly
G. H. Lewes.

V, 365:6   GHL TO GEORGE SMITH,
LONDON [JANUARY 1873]

MS: Princeton.

The Priory, | 21. North Bank, | Regents Park.

Dear Smith

I don't know which portrait you mean. Please send up specimens of both.[3] The *young* man is very unsatisfactory—on the other hand the *old* one gives no idea of him ever having been young and handsome like us!

Ever yours
G. H. L.

2. The firm was founded at Leipzig by Friedrich Arnold Brockhaus (1772–1823.)

3. An engraving by E. Radclyffe of the J. G. Stieler portrait of Goethe (1829) is used as the frontispiece in *The Story of Goethe's Life*, 1873.

V, 371:12 GHL TO JOHN WALTER CROSS, LONDON, [19 JANUARY 1873]

MS: Yale.

The Priory, | 21. North Bank, | Regents Park.
Sunday.

My dear Johnnie

Your misgivings are sadly misplaced!—I would rather concentrate the 2250 on *five* than on 10 railways—to be selected by you.[4]

We shall be at home on Tuesday. Is Hall coming on that day to dine here and meet Octavia Hill?[5] If so and you would like to join them (no one else coming) need I say how glad we shall be?

Yours truly
G. H. L.

V, 373:9 GHL TO ALBERT COHN, LONDON, 26 JANUARY 1873

MS: Princeton. *Endorsed:* To A. Cohn Esq.

The Priory, | 21. North Bank. | Regents Park.
26 January 73.

My dear Sir

It would be better to wait for the Easter returns before sending any payment on account—I hope those returns will prove more favorable than you anticipate—for 2000 copies seems to me but a small sale for such a work all over the continent.[6]

I shall be glad of the copies when they are ready, but of course as it is only to keep among others of the kind there has been no inconvenience from your clerk's forgetfulness.

Mrs. Lewes begs me to thank you for your kind wishes and to send hers in return.

Ever yours truly
G. H. Lewes.

4. Cross was investing in American railways the income from *Middlemarch*, of which an installment of £1433.10 was received in January 1873.

5. The dinner was postponed, GE having on Paget's advice gone to have a tooth pulled. W. H. Hall and Octavia Hill dined at the Priory on Saturday, 25 January. (GHL Diary.)

6. The cash account for June shows Cohn's payment of £138.19.6 for the English reprint of *Middlemarch*. (GHL Diary.)

Problems of Life and Mind

V, 373:9 GHL TO GEORGE JAMES HOWARD, LONDON, [3 FEBRUARY 1873]

MS: Mr. George Howard.

The Priory, | 21. North Bank, | Regents Park.
Monday.

My dear Mr. Howard

The Bowens are coming to lunch next Sunday at 1.30.[7] Is it probable that the fascinations of the *hateful* Stopford Brooke[8] will permit a certain person to accompany you, and make up a cozy party on that occasion? I assume that you are *disponible* and willing. If *Rosamund* writes to Sir Godfrey on the matter you have full permission (from me) to beat her![9]

Ever yours truly
G. H. L.

V, 373:9 GE TO GEORGE CROOM ROBERTSON, LONDON, 5 FEBRUARY 1873

MS: University College London.

The Priory, | 21. North Bank, | Regents Park.
February 5. 73.

Dear Mr. Robertson

We shall have much pleasure in welcoming Mrs. Robertson with you.

Can you come and lunch with us at half past one the Sunday after next? I mention that day, because I fear that next Sunday I might not be able to see so much of Mrs. Robertson as I should like, from preoccupation with other visitors.[1]

If you can come and lunch with us, we shall have some quiet space for chat.

Yours always truly
M. E. Lewes.

---

7. Bowens and Howards lunched at the Priory 9 February 1873. (GHL Diary.)

8. Stopford Brooke (1832–1916) became acquainted with the Howards in 1868, and spent part of his holidays with them at Naworth Castle for many years. He was Chaplain to Queen Victoria 1872–80, when he left the Church of England and became a Unitarian. GHL may have heard his opinion of *Middlemarch*, which he considered "inferior to any other of George Eliot's works." See *The Life and Letters of Stopford Brooke*, 2 vols., 1917, I, 259.

9. In *Middlemarch* Rosamond writes secretly to her husband's uncle Sir Godwin Lydgate asking for money. GHL is careless about both names.

1. "Professor Robertson and his

V, 381:12   GHL TO SIR ARTHUR HELPS,
LONDON, [28 FEBRUARY 1873]

MS: Nuneaton Public Library. *Published: Correspondence of Sir Arthur Helps*, ed. E.A. Helps, 1917, pp. 343–344.

The Priory, | 21. North Bank, | Regents Park.

Friday.

My dear Helps

So excellent a *right* had I to your book[2]—a right grounded on my being one of those who would most sympathize with it—that I had read nearly half of it before the second copy—your's—came to hand. I had been gurgling with suppressed laughter and emphasizing with pencil approbations—at almost every page; and, having friends[3] to dinner yesterday, had nothing more pressing than to impart several of the 'good things' as the conversation suggested them and after they had all departed to their virtuous, let us hope, beds, I found your letter had arrived. This morning the book itself arrived.

Of course you knew that I should like it, and of course also you knew that I should *not* have written certain parts better—(at least of all the pages I have yet read) though confounded modesty makes you say so.

That scientific hypothesis of the genesis of Boys[4] is, to use the reviewer's phraseology, "worth the whole price of the volume." But it is the undercurrent of really serious thought which will give the book its lasting value, however much the lambent play of humour may brighten it. In the name of all the animals this animal lover thanks you!

Ever yours

G. H. L.

Have you seen 'Nature' with the letters from Darwin, Wallace and others respecting hereditary hatred of butchers in a family of mastiffs?—These letters were in the numbers 172 and 3—perhaps this week's 174 will contain more.[5]

bride, Du Maurier, and Barbara to lunch. Trübner, Mrs. Orr, Burne Jones, Hall, Roundell, Dr. Andrew Clark, Johnnie Cross, Charles and Gertrude, Sir H. Holland." (GHL Diary, 16 February 1873.) There were 20 guests on 9 February.

2. *Some Talk about Animals and Their Masters*, 1873.

3. Mr. and Mrs. Frederic Harrison, Sir Henry Maine, Spencer, Burton, and W. H. Hall. (GHL Diary, 27 February

1873.)

4. "It is my firm belief that misfortune breeds boys without any superfluous assistance from parents " (p. 4.)

5. Charles Darwin's letter "Inherited Instinct" was published in *Nature*, 7 (13 February 1873), p. 281, with a letter from William Huggins, who first brought up the subject of dogs and butchers. Alfred R. Wallace, "Inherited Feeling," 7 (20 February), 303, was followed by G. Croom Robertson's

V, 381:12   GE TO MRS. JOHN CASH,
LONDON, 1 MARCH 1873

MS: Nuneaton Public Library. *Envelope:* Mrs. Cash | Grosvenor Hotel | W. *Post-marks:* LONDON–N.W | X | MR 1 | 73; LONDON N.W | A | MR 1 | 73.

The Priory, | 21. North Bank, | Regents Park.

March 1. 73.

Very happy to see you, my dear Mrs. Cash[6]—with or without your daughter—at any time tomorrow between 3 and 5.

[*Signature cut away.*]

V, 382:9   GHL TO SIR ARTHUR HELPS,
LONDON, [2 MARCH 1873]

MS: Nuneaton Public Library.

The Priory | 21. North Bank, | Regents Park.

Sunday.

My dear Helps

I have now finished the book, and have only one regret—that it was not longer! A good fault. Àpropos of faults, I noticed two trifles, and one serious—1st. Telliamed was not an Arabian author, but the anagram of *De Maillet*[7] one of Darwin's absurd predecessors. 2d. It was *Dr. Johnson* who supposed some men's nonsense suited their nonsense.[8]

"External Perception in Dogs," 7 (27 February), 322–323, accepting Wallace's view.

6. Mrs. Cash wrote in 1884: "More than twenty years elapsed before I had again the privilege of seeing George Eliot, and that on one occasion only, after her final settlement in London. It touched me deeply to find how much she had retained of her kind interest in all that concerned me and mine, and I remarked on this to Mr. Lewes, who came to the door with my daughter and myself at parting. 'Wonderful sympathy,' I said. 'Is it not?' said he; and when I added, inquiringly, 'The power lies there?' 'Unquestionably it does,' was his answer; 'she forgets nothing that has ever come within the curl of her eyelash; above all, she forgets no one who has ever spoken to her one kind word,'" (Cross, New Edition,

pp. 59–60.)

7. The 1st ed., 1873, p. 121, reads: "an Arabian author named Telliamed." In the 2d ed., 1873, 3 lines have been reset to read: "Telliamed, whose real name was De Maillet." Benoît de Maillet wrote *Telliamed: ou entretiens d'un philosophe indien avec un missionaire françois, sur la diminution de la mer, la formation de la terre, l'origène de l'homme,* etc. 2 vols., Amsterdam, 1748.

8. On p. 150 Helps tells of a dull candidate who was returned in the general election because "his nonsense suited their nonsense." GHL may have been thinking of Johnson's saying to Mrs. Thrale, "Nonsense can be defended but by nonsense." (Boswell, *Life of Johnson,* ed. G. B. Hill and L. F. Powell, 6 vols., Oxford, 1934, II, 78.) Helps did not insert any reference to Johnson.

3d. What you say on Vivisection[9] though excellent in spirit proceeds on two misconceptions. First that it has not led to discovery. Secondly that it is necessarily accompanied with pain. *All* physiological discovery was made through experiment, and of experiment the greater part is Vivisection. Since the discovery of anæsthetics almost all experimenters render the animals unconscious, not only for the sake of sparing pain, but for the precision of the operation. I have performed hundreds, and never once, except in very trifling cases, operated without anæsthesia. Nor indeed could I *see* another operate without it. There are some experiments which do not admit of the application of anæsthesia but these are few and one of the very greatest living experimenters, Schiff,[1] *always* narcotizes. In France they are culpably reckless on this point—a tradition with them. Now it would make your indignation all the more effective if it were to be thrown solely on the gravamen of the case—the *needless* vivisection and the *carelessness* as to pain. In the way you state the case only those who know vivisection from indignation pamphlets can agree with you. Pray see to this in a second editon, as you, one of the justest of men, would certainly not be cruel to animals nor to vivisection.

Ever faithfully yours
G. H. L.

If you had ever stood by and seen a rabbit wake up after an operation (the mere *pain* of which would have killed him had he not taken chloral or chloroform) and begin to munch his cabbage just as if nothing had occurred, you would have no doubt about the comparative indifference to him of having been experimented on.

V, 384:18   GHL TO SIR ARTHUR HELPS, LONDON, [6 MARCH 1873]

MS: Nuneaton Public Library. *Published: Correspondence of Sir Arthur Helps*, 1917, pp. 345–346.

The Priory, | 21. North Bank | Regents Park.

Thursday.

My dear Helps

As the book undoubtedly will go to a second edition I will tell you what modifications I should like to see in it. Preserving the spirit of your remarks you might say that while recognizing experiment as indispensable to the

9. "There have been horrors in the way of vivisection—especially those perpetrated in France and Germany—against which I think direct legislation might be claimed." (p. 43.)

1. Moritz Schiff (1823–96), Professor of Physiology at Berne.

physiological *inquirer* (vivisection being only one large branch of experiment) the humane and considerate man would never keep out of sight the fact that he was *injuring* or *paining* animals, and therefore would altogether refrain from vivisection when *teaching* physiology to students unless his teaching were of some contested point and he wanted to *prove* his position. All established or uncontested results of vivisection should be simply stated, not reperformed in presence of students.

Then too the inquirer himself should consider carefully *what* it is his experiment is going to prove and whether if successful it will do so. This would save a great mass of reckless inconsiderate experiment.

Finally since there are but few experiments which cannot better be performed on an animal rendered insensible by chloroform ether or chloral the inquirer should never dispense with that mode whenever it is practicable.

The object of your remarks should be to lessen the injury to animals, by instilling more serious views into the operators. I remember at one of the meetings of the Medical Association the Rev. S. Haughton[2] produced a striking oratorical effect—touching on vivisection—(all present were alert) he said "I consider that I have a perfect right to subject my dog to any experiment however painful—which I am willing for science to *undergo myself.*"[3]

> In great haste ever yours
> G. H. L.

If you send me a proof of your modification when made I will annotate it.

V, 384:18 GHL TO SIR ARTHUR HELPS, LONDON, [7 MARCH 1873]

MS: Nuneaton Public Library. *Published: Correspondence of Sir Arthur Helps,* 1917, p. 346.

The Priory, | 21. North Bank, | Regents Park.
Friday.

My dear Helps

In my hurry yesterday I forgot to add a note about Descartes confirming your impression that he did not maintain animals to have no feeling. With

2. Samuel Haughton (1821–97), an ordained priest, was Professor of Geology and Chairman of the Medical Committee at Dublin University.

3. There was no alteration of these passages in the 2d ed. GHL wrote a letter to *Nature,* 9 (25 December 1873), 144–145, elaborating these remarks on vivisection and adding that his "sympathies are unusually active in the direction of animals; and it was my inability to witness pain which prevented my pursuing the profession of a surgeon."

regard to your difficulty in finding any passage in which his opinion was distinctly expressed the only one I know is that in his Letters (Œuvres,[4] vol. 7, p. 393) in which however you may observe that he qualifies the denial of feeling by saying *comme en nous et aucun vrai sentiment*. Now if you compare this with the passage vol. X, p. 208 you will see that he speaks of *thought*, non de la vie ou du *sentiment*. He adds je ne leur refuse pas même le sentiment autant qu'il dépend des organes du corps. Ainsi mon opinion n'est pas si cruelle aux animaux.

Ever yours faithfully
G. H. Lewes.

V, 385:1   GHL TO JOHN BLACKWOOD, LONDON, [11 MARCH 1873]

MS: National Library of Scotland.

The Priory, | 21. North Bank, | Regents Park.
Tuesday.

My dear Blackwood

The great Work bears the title *Problems of Life and Mind*; and the first batch thereof goes by this post *registered*.[5]

I think it should be a volume resembling Hamilton's Lectures[6]—but as there will be no marginal headings we may have a broader line. It will be desirable to make it as cheap as one can, by using a thin paper; but it ought also to look *libraryish* and handsome—as all your books do.

I am quite ready to keep the press going but don't send more m.s. at a time than is needful because I have often revisions to make—Casaubon-like.

Your news about the sale of the guinea edition is cheering, and un-expected. The *Times* review[7] is very well written but not specially re-markable I think. Others—because it is in the Times?—seem to think it a grand affair; and one or two friends cannot understand that Mrs. Lewes should not read *that*.

4. René Descartes, *Œuvres*, ed. Victor Cousin, 11 vols., Paris, 1824–26.

5. "Sent *Problems* to Blackwood—first batch of m.s." (GHL Diary, 11 March 1873.)

6. Sir William Hamilton, *Lectures on Metaphysics and Logic*, 4 vols., published by Blackwood, 1858–60.

7. The review of *Middlemarch* in *The Times*, 7 March 1873, pp. 3d–f and 4a, an extraordinarily long and favorable article, begins: "There are few novels in the language which will repay reading over again so well as *Middlemarch*." It was written by Frederick Napier Broome. (*History of The Times*, II, 489.)

Port Royal Logic[8] arrived and was welcomed. We have just returned from Tunbridge looking after a country house—found what we wanted and found it already let![9]

Mrs. Lewes begs to be kindly regarded by both of you.

Ever yours truly

G. H. L.

V, 388:1 GE TO MME EUGÈNE BODICHON, LONDON, [MARCH 1873]

MS: Berg Collection, New York Public Library. *Endorsed:* March 1873.

The Priory, | 21. North Bank, | Regents Park.

Sunday.

Dearest Barbara

Mr. Lewes read your note this morning without sending it up to me— else I should immediately have written a line to say, first how vexed I was to have missed you the other day. Next, I will remember your message to Mrs. B. Jones.

The word you send me of a life so bound up with your early years being suddenly brought to a premature close,[10] makes me imagine how your thoughts are saddened and solemnized in these first succeeding days. For her sake—even for the children's—the passing away seems a good. But every death that comes at all near to one makes one in some sense a mourner.

The precious flowers are duly cherished.

Your ever grateful

M. E. L.

8. See v, 380, n. 3.

9. It was Val Prinsep's house. (GHL Diary, 10 March 1873.)

10. Her sister Bella, the wife of Major General John Ludlow, died at Mereworth, Kent, 6 March 1873. She left two sons, the elder eleven years old.

V, 388:1   GE TO OSCAR BROWNING, LONDON, 16 MARCH 1873

MS: Yale.

The Priory, | 21. North Bank, | Regents Park.
March 16. 73.

My dear Mr. Browning

Thanks for the Curtius[11] which came to me the other day. I have already found some nutritive bits in it, and am very glad of the opportunity which your kindness has given me.

Also your generous pains to let me see the photographs were more highly appreciated than I was able to tell you.

Madame Novikoff[1] presented herself today, so that the task which your friend's letter laid on you has been successfully fulfilled.

Yours always truly

M. E. Lewes.

V, 389:13   GHL TO ALEXANDER MAIN, LONDON, 19 MARCH 1873

MS: Harvard. *Address:* Alex. Main Esq | West Mary St | Arbroath. *Postmark:* LONDON-N.W | 2 | MR 19 | 73.

Dear M.

Correspondence so enormous only the *indispensable* can be accomplished. Your guess about rehearsals right. I will do my best as to book.[2]

G. H. Lewes.

11. Ernst Curtius, *Griechische Geschichte*, 1857–67; English translation by A. W. Ward, 3 vols., 1868–73.

1. Olga Novikoff called 16, 23, and 30 March 1873. (GHL Diary.)

2. "Called on Chapman and proposed that Main should execute my plan of a 'Life of Johnson founded on Boswell's.'" (GHL Diary, 20 March 1873.)

V, 389:13 GE TO MRS. ERNST LEOPOLD BENZON,
LONDON, 20 MARCH [1873]

MS: Birmingham Reference Library.

The Priory, | 21. North Bank, | Regents Park.
March 20.

Many thanks, dear Mrs. Benzon. We *should* like to go.[3]

Yours affectionately
M. E. Lewes.

V, 394:26 LORD LYTTON[4] TO GHL,
LONDON, [21 MARCH 1873]

MS: Yale.

12 George Sq. Friday.
My dear Lewes,

I *do* know Madame Olga.[5] She *is* sister in law to the Russian Minister at Vienna, and the whole Novikoff Family were the bêtes noires of Vienna when I was there.

I believe that Novikoff's previous career had been chiefly Consular and in the East. I doubt if he was ever before dans la haute. Both he and his wife are very underbred ridiculous people. She (a country vulgar precieuse) got into some silly scrape at Vienna—nothing whatever "improper": but she wanted to get P[rince]ss Metternich[6] to come to her receptions, applied with that object to the good offices of a petit crevé

---

3. "We went with Mrs. Benzon to an entertainment given by Lady Smith for the Normal School of Music for the Blind. The blind children sang, played, recited, answered questions in mental arithmetic and geography. Altogether an interesting and affecting experience. Home at 11.30." (GHL Diary, 20 March 1873.)

4. Robert Lytton succeeded to the title of Baron Lytton on the death of his father, 13 January 1873.

5. Olga Alexéevna Novikova, *née* Kiréeva (1840–1925), wife of General I. P. Novikov, writer and journalist. Turgenev wrote to Pauline Viardot

7 June 1868 about an encounter with her in St. Petersburg: "Malheuresement au moment d'entrer au Musée Campana je suis tombé sur la grosse patapouffe Mme Novikoff—et il n'y a eu plus moyen de regarder tranquillement; j'ai dû m'enfuir. Elle m'a naturellement beaucoup questioné sur vous, sur les opérettes; elle menace Bade de sa visite.... Quelle glu!". (*Lettres inédites,* 1972, pp. 147–148.)

6. Princess Pauline Metternich (1836 –1921), wife of Prince Richard Klemens Lothar Hermann von Metternich, Austrian Ambassador at Paris 1859–71.

patronised by Mad[am]e Metternich; he said something impertinent to
her in her own house. She complained to her husband who made a "scene."
There was a talk of half a dozen duels, none of which came off, and a nine
days gossip. After which the fat sister-in-law to whom your enquiry refers,
arrived, giving out privately that she had been sent by the court "pour
former sa soeur." She is the vulgarest of the three. A pushing, gushing,
toadying, fulsome fat woman with the manners of a second rate adventuress.
She introduced herself to my wife with the assertion that she was the bosom
friend of my mother in law.[7] But in spite of the warmth as well as the magnitude of both her bosom and her friendship, Edith, who can be, when she
pleases, a perfect refrigerator, iced the volcano at the first eruption. The
truth was that she had only once met my mother in law in the streets at
Ryde. She then went back to England and hurled herself at Mrs. Villiers
as the bosom friend of my wife. She told me she was in close correspondence
with my Uncle Henry[8] and Charles Villiers.[9] I believe the correspondence
was chiefly unilateral. *They* told me they were much bored by her (they
had met her at Ems) and asked me who she was.

After her return to Vienna, there was an odd story about some Diamonds, missed by her sister-in-law one evening when there had been a
reception at the Russian Legation. Novikoff went to the Police about them.
The police after some days' investigation declared that the diamonds were
not stolen and that Madame Novikoff and her sister knew all about them.
The matter was then hushed up. The Buchanans[10] told me that Madame
Olga was in no sort of society at St. Petersburgh and they have always
refused to know her. I believe however that she *is* in correspondence with
Gortchakoff,[1] whose "bosom" friend she is said to be. Her wish is to pass
for a femme politique, but she is not a Madame de Lieven.[2] In England I
am told that she really has obtained a very good footing. We are not a
very refined people: and I suspect that pushing gushing and flattering are
not unserviceable instruments of success with us. However the long and
the short of it is—I don't like Madame Olga, but I know of no reason
whatever why you should refuse to have the pleasure of adding G. Elliot

7. Mrs. Edward Ernest Villiers,
Lytton's mother-in-law.
8. Sir Henry William Earle Bulwer,
Baron Dalling and Bulwer.
9. Charles Pelham Villiers (1802–
98).
10. Sir Andrew Buchanan (1807–
82), Ambassador to Austria 1871–78,
where Lytton served under him, had
been Ambassador-extraordinary to
Russia in 1864.
1. Prince Aleksandr Mikhailovich
Gortchakov (1798–1883), Ambassador
at Vienna in 1854, became Chancellor
of Germany in 1863.
2. Dorothea Christophorvna de
Benkendorf, Princess Lieven (1785–
1857), Russian noblewoman, whose
salon in Paris attracted Wellington,
Metternich, and Guizot.

and yourself to the list of her "distinguished acquaintances"—(especially if by granting her that pleasure you would please any one you like) beyond the anticipation that you will not greatly care for her.

I do indeed rejoice to hear that Mr Casaubon has given birth to his first vol.[3] I am longing to see you both my dear friends. But oh, I am almost overwhelmed by troublesome business of all kinds. I have concentrated as much of it as I could, at Knebworth; where, as I daresay you may remember[4] there is a woeful dearth of bedrooms. The only double bedrooms in the house are now occupied by our nurseries and my mother in law who is staying with us, so that we cannot put up another couple. But can I induce you "one of these fine days"—which are I hope at hand—to come to us for a couple of days en garçon—and have a chat? If so rejoice my heart by letting me know—and I'll send you lists of trains and all needful instructions how to get to us. So very much that I should like to talk over with you if I could!

Our dearest love to your most dear wife. I write this from town, but am only here for a few hours on business. Adieu.

Your affectionate
Lytton.

V, 394:26 EDWARD BURNE-JONES TO GE, LONDON, [21? MARCH 1873]

MS: Yale.

The Grange, Northend.
dear Mrs. Lewes

It ought to be the easiest thing in the world for me to say how grateful I am for your letter, but I feel as if I couldn't say it strongly enough or make you quite believe how important your praise is to me.—Indeed you have written so sweetly and comfortingly to me that you have made me seriously happy, and given me more courage than I have felt for many a day. You know I am not so silly as to take all this praise and hug myself contentedly (which I feel inclined to—nay even to strut a while) but this understanding sympathy of yours does go to my heart and encourage it mightily.

please believe me I hold this a very precious letter that will help me to feel less dismayed at my own fogginess and bewilderment (which is plenti-

---

3. Of *Problems of Life and Mind.*
4. GHL spent a night at Knebworth with Sir Edward Bulwer Lytton 19 September 1863.

ful always) since you can see any light at all in me. It was a kind thought
to send me such a letter.

Ever yours sincerely

Edward Burne Jones.

poor Georgie is a most suffering mortal by reason of toothache—disclaims
what you impute to her also and sends much love.

V, 397:20   GHL TO JOHN BLACKWOOD, LONDON, [28 MARCH 1873]

MS: National Library of Scotland.

Dear Blackwood

I send you such a letter as you may send to Tait and will put him in
possession of what is asked of him.[5] The type and aspect are all that could
be desired. Please ask Mr. Simpson to order the m. s. to be sent along with
the proofs.

'Kenelm Chillingly'[6] arrived this morning. May it prosper! The *Times*
notice was not a good one for those who read carefully; but the mass don't
read, they glance.

Every American mail continues to bring gushing testimonies about
Middlemarch. Mrs. Lewes is not the thing and longs for quiet and the
country. On Sunday we had 23 at our gathering from 1.30 to 6.30.—
Darwin, Kinglake, Grant Duff, Clifford, Joachim, Roundell, Browning,
and some 'swells.'[7] We went to bed at 9!

We hope the new edition[8] continues in demand. Does not this delicious
weather rejoice your heart? Kind regards to Willie.

Ever yours truly

G. H. L.

Here comes more m. s.

5. Peter Guthrie Tait (1831–1901),
mathematician and physicist, Professor
of Natural Philosophy at Edinburgh,
was at GHL's suggestion to be asked to
read the proof of *Problems of Life and
Mind.*
6. Bulwer Lytton's last completed
novel, published by Blackwood, 3 vols.,
1873.
7. The people named are listed in
GHL's Diary 23 March 1873. Lady
Castletown, her daughter Mrs. Wingfield, and the George Howards are
probably the "swells." Commenting on
GHL's social life, John Forster in a
letter to Lord Lytton, 12 April 1873,
wrote: "Your friend Lewes points to
Browning as dining out everywhere to
all invitations and being invariably
pointed at as 'the husband of Mrs.
Browning the poetess.' 'Now,' continues Lewes, 'that is just the reason
why I *don't* go out—why I refuse all
invitations. Because I am not going to
be pointed at as "the husband of George
Eliot the novelist." ' " (Lady Hermione
Cobbold.)
8. *Middlemarch,* Guinea edition, 1873.
See v, 386.

V, 398:1   GE TO MME EUGÈNE BODICHON, LONDON, [30 MARCH 1873]

MS: Berg Collection, New York Public Library.

I was under a delusion this afternoon in talking to Mrs. Sitwell.[9] I imagined that she was speaking of some definite plan for helping forward the higher education of girls, and it was in reference to such a plan that I thought it desirable to exclude lady-associates of the kind you wot of. When I found that it was only the Conversazione scheme, I was quite sorry that I had made my unnecessary remarks. For that sort of project
[*top half of page torn off*]
If you want histories, there are Mommsen's history of Rome, and Curtius's history of Greece. But they are both translated. Still they are admirably well written and therefore good to read in German. Grimm's Kinder und Hausmärchen, and Grimm's Deutsche Mythologie might be thought of.

Gervinus's book on German poetical literature is too heavy, and presupposes all knowledge in the reader. There is a voluminous History of German Literature by Julian Schmidt, for one.[1] But [*half of page torn away*] less useful writing, because it [*half of page torn away*]

V, 398:1   GE TO CHARLES DARWIN, LONDON, 31 MARCH 1873

MS: Yale.

The Priory, | 21. North Bank, | Regents Park.
March 31. 73.

My dear Mr. Darwin
    We shall be very happy to see Mr. and Mrs. Litchfield[2] on any Sunday when it is convenient to them to come to us. Our hours of reception are

9. Mrs. Sitwell and Barbara were among the visitors 30 March 1873. (GHL Diary.)
1. The books mentioned in this letter were possibly suggestions for Girton, where the girls were discussing preparation for the Little-go and the Tripos. See Barbara Stephen, *Emily Davies and Girton College*, 1927, pp. 277–280.
2. Charles Darwin, who had called

at the Priory 23 March 1873, wrote to GE 30 March asking "whether his daughter and son-in-law, Mr. Litchfield, may call on her, and concluding: 'My wife complains that she has been very badly treated and that I ought to have asked permission for her to call on you with me when we next come to London; but I tell her that I still have some shreds of modesty." (Sotheby's, from $\frac{1}{2}$ past two till six, and the earlier our friends can come to us, the more fully we are able to enjoy conversation with them.

Please do not disappoint us in the hope that you will come to us again, and bring Mrs. Darwin with you, the next time you are in town.

Yours most sincerely

M. E. Lewes.

V, 401:9   GHL TO JOHN BLACKWOOD, LONDON, [15 APRIL 1873]

MS: National Library of Scotland.

The Priory, | 21. North Bank, | Regents Park.

Tuesday.

My dear Blackwood

If you have kept my last you will find with it a letter specially intended to be sent to Prof. Tait, carefully indicating all I wished him to do. If you have destroyed it drop me word on a post card and I will 'give my mind' to the composition of another. Here is more m.s.

We rejoice that your watery ordeal[3] has proved successful, and hope for no recurrence. Fancy you one of the Alliance—cheek by jowl with Sir W. Lawson![4]

Mrs. Lewes is deep in the Greek poets,[5] but without being positively unwell cannot get up her strength and energy to set to work. We are looking out for a country retreat, and hope that quiet and sunshine (if to be had) will bring the bloom on her cheek and her pen to the paper.

The news about 'Middlemarch' very acceptable. She begs to be most kindly remembered to you and Willie.

Ever yours truly

G. H. L.

6 March 1934, item 434.) Henrietta Darwin and her husband Richard Litchfield called 6 April 1873. (GHL Diary.)

3. See v, 401.

4. Sir Wilfred Lawson, 2d Baronet (1829–1906) introduced a permissive bill in the House of Commons in 1864 giving districts a veto on the granting of liquor licenses. He was president of the United Kingdom Alliance.

5. A Notebook of GE in the Folger Library (Ma. 14) contains extracts from many Greek poets.

V, 402:19   GHL TO GEORGE SIMPSON, LONDON, [18 APRIL 1873]

MS: National Library of Scotland.

The Priory, | 21. North Bank, | Regents Park.
Friday.

My dear Sir

By this post, registered, I send more m.s. and should be much pleased if you could put on the steam so as to have the sheets ready by the end of this month because I want the proofs to be read by a friend before he leaves town. Unless we hurry a little the book will not be out this year. You need not send Prof. Tait the proofs—unless I specially name it—because they have nothing mathematical and it is needless to trouble him with them.

Ever yours truly
G. H. Lewes.

V, 404:1   GHL TO JOHN BLACKWOOD, LONDON, [21 APRIL 1873]

MS: National Library of Scotland.

The Priory, | 21. North Bank, | Regents Park.
Monday.

My dear Blackwood

Tait's suggestions will be immensely useful—I have written to thank him for the trouble he has taken in reading the proofs[6] so carefully and

6. Peter Guthrie Tait wrote to John Blackwood, 17 April 1873, that he had just managed to go through GHL's proofs. "I cannot understand what he means by the debt he owes me. Beyond pitching into *so-called* Metaphysicians whenever I had a chance, I am not aware of having done anything in his direction. I enclose a translation of a lecture of mine bearing on those matters. Lend it to him with the mangled proofs enclosed; and refer him to my short correspondence with Mr. Ingleby in 'Nature' about a couple of years ago. I took him at his word as you will see, and deliberately marked every point I did not agree with—or on which I differed (ever so little) from him. I fear I shall get scant thanks for my impertinence; but if a man *will* go into a shower-bath and pull the string, he has no right to swear at the consequences. I found it pretty stiff reading, far worse than double its amount of analytical formulae: but it is very interesting indeed, and will thoroughly rile the so-called Metaphysicians." (NLS.) In *Problems of Life and Mind*, I (1874), 28, GHL quotes Tait's comment on quaternions from his *Address before the Mathematical Section of the British Association*, 1871.

expressing himself so unreservedly. Even when I do not adopt his corrections they are useful. I happened to have had a great mathematician and a great scholar[7] with me yesterday and they both endorse my 'insoluble' and reject 'insolvible.' The book will gain greatly by such a revision!

There seems to have been a good deal of curiosity excited by the announcement of the work being in the press—how much will be due to interest in Dorothea? Good public to be still hungry for her! The Quarterly article[8] will no doubt be savage, as their previous article was, but it will be a good advertisement and she is beyond the reach of criticism.

The Country House is not forthcoming alas!

Ever yours truly
G. H. L.

V, 408:1   GE TO FREDERIC W. H. MYERS, LONDON, 29 APRIL 1873

MS: Trinity College, Cambridge.

The Priory, | 21. North Bank, | Regents Park,

April 29. 73.

Dear Mr. Myers

We should like, please, to have you to lunch with us on Sunday the 11th at half past one, and may we beg that you will keep a broad space of time free for us afterwards?[9] In this way we count on the most undisturbed enjoyment of your conversation.

The temptation you offer us is too strong to be resisted, and we gratefully accept your hospitality for Monday and Tuesday, the 19th and 20th, according to the programme which you have kindly made out for us.[1]

Mr. Lewes unites with me in thanks and kind regards.

Yours always truly
M. E. Lewes.

7. William Kingdon Clifford and F. W. H. Myers. (GHL Diary, 20 April 1873.)

8. Robert Laing wrote the review of *Middlemarch* in the *Quarterly Review*, 134 (April 1873), 336–369.

9. The other guests were Mr. and Mrs. Charles Bowen and W. K. Clifford. After lunch F. W. Burton, Charles Lewes, Prof. and Mrs. Allmann, Edith Simcox, Mrs. Orr, Frederic Leighton, William Allingham, George Howard, and Sir Henry Holland called.

1. Myers wrote to GE, 27 April 1873: "On Saturday May 17 I go to Cambridge: the boat races begin Monday May 19, and I do hope that you and Mr. Lewes will be able to give me the great pleasure of staying with me at Cambridge for a few days during that week." He suggests that they reach Cambridge on Tuesday, May 20 in time

V, 408:1 GE TO MRS. MARK PATTISON,
LONDON, 2 MAY 1873

MS: British Museum.

The Priory, | 21. North Bank, | Regents Park.
May 2. 73.

[The rest of the first leaf has been cut away.][2]
is sad to hear that the Rector's

private view at Burlington House, and are wishing that we knew beforehand which pictures we should do well to look at.

Yours affectionately
M. E. Lewes.

V, 408:23 GE TO [EDWARD BURNE-JONES],
LONDON, 12 MAY 1873

MS: University of California Los Angeles.

The Priory, | 21. North Bank, | Regents Park.
May 12. 73.

Dear Friend

I am sure you will be glad to help Mr. Pigott in any way possible to
you.[3]

The secretaryship of the Royal Academy is vacant, and an acquaintance
of Mr. Pigott's has suggested to him to try for the post. It is resolved that
no artist shall be appointed, and I should think that our old friend has just
the requisite accomplishments for such an office. His command of French
is rare, and he has a peculiar felicity in letter-writing. Then, his gentlemanly

for luncheon, see the boat races on that evening and Wednesday evening, returning to town on Thursday morning. (University of Virginia.)

2. An example of Sir Charles Dilke's treatment of GE's letters to Mrs. Pattison.

3. "Pigott called to speak about his candidateship for the Royal Academy. Arranged with him what we would do." (GHL Diary, 12 May 1873.) "Occupied writing letters about Pigott. Called on Millais on the same subject. After lunch we had the brougham and went to see Watts and Leighton; both promised their votes, and Leighton gave me a letter to Calderon, whom I called on, got his vote, and had a long pleasant chat with him. After dinner Pigott came in to hear and report." (13 May 1873.) He came again 18, 22 May, and 2 June.

feeling and agreeable manners would make personal relations with him comparatively easy even to artists with grievances.

The prospect of such a post with £600 a year is the prospect of as much affluence, won by useful work, as he would need to give him thorough contentment and he longs very much to get a release from the sort of labour which he has been chained to for the last 13 or 14 years.

It seems to me that any effort to get him into this office would be justly bestowed. If you think so too, will you speak on his behalf to artists or other influential persons whom you may judge to lie within your reach, mentally and physically.

I write in great haste in order to post the letter forthwith, as I go out.

Yours always sincerely

M. E. Lewes.

V, 409:11   GE TO LORD HOUGHTON, LONDON, 13 MAY 1873

MS: Yale.

The Priory, | 21. North Bank, | Regents Park.

May 13. 73.

My dear Lord Houghton

I think you know our friend Mr. Edward Pigott, for whom we have a respect founded on an acquaintance of twenty years.

It has been suggested that he might possibly obtain the Secretaryship of the Royal Academy which is about to be declared vacant and which is *not* to be given to any artist or art critic.

So far as I can imagine the Duties of the office, Mr. Pigott seems to me to have just the requisite qualifications. He has a perfect command of French both for conversation and correspondence—not an ordinary accomplishment in an Englishman, as you have had reason to complain in a certain essay of yours—and I suppose that this must be a chief demand on a Secretary to the Academy with its present cosmopolitan admissions. Then, he has the sympathetic manners which would make difficult business relations easier, and his letter-writing is peculiarly felicitous. He has a fine literary sense, and in spite of fourteen years' hard work at journalism, he retains his finesse of expressions and has not lost the discrimination of epithets.

If anybody asks whom he "boasts himself to be"[4]—he is a younger son

4. *The Winter's Tale*, iv, iv, 168.

of a Somersetshire gentleman, made a good figure at Eton and Baliol (the present master of Baliol is one of his best friends), spent some time in France, and finally coming to London bought the Leader newspaper in which he sank all the portion that fell to him as a younger son.[5] He took this check of fortune very gracefully, put himself into heavy harness without grumbling, and has ever since been deepening the respect of his friends.

Those who know his value—and among them are some of the best people both French and English—must be heartily rejoiced at his getting a post which would give him both a comfortable maintenance and a suitable change of work. But his success of course depends on his recommendations being straightway made known to those who have the power in their hands. Every day is of importance.

If, from what you know, you believe that his appointment would be a good service to the Academy as well as to himself, will you be so kind as to write a letter to me expressing your favourable wishes on Mr. Pigott's behalf—a letter which might be put in as an informal sort of testimonial? You may possibly have knowledge which would correct my uninstructed suppositions. In that case you will consider my request to be retracted. But I make no apology for trusting in your readiness to give help wherever you can.

I remain, my dear Lord Houghton

Yours very sincerely
M. E. Lewes.

V, 409:11   GHL TO [THE ROYAL ACADEMY], LONDON, 13 MAY 1873

MS: Mr. Gordon N. Ray. *Endorsed:* From Mr. George Henry Lewes.

The Priory, | 21. North Bank, | Regents Park.
13 May 1873.

I have known Mr. Edward Pigott very intimately for more than 20 years, and known him as a man of high honor, fine taste, and universally agreeable manners. His unusual accomplishments and his unusually amiable disposition, seem to me to constitute rare qualifications for the position of Secretary to such an Institution as the Royal Academy.

G. H. Lewes.

---

5. For Pigott's purchase of the *Leader* and his efforts to keep it afloat see Allan   R. Brick, *The Leader,* Yale dissertation 1958 (unpublished), pp. 205–245.

V, 409:11   GE TO JOSEPH MUNT LANGFORD,
LONDON, 17 MAY 1873

MS: Mrs. Dorothy Hicks.

The Priory, | 21. North Bank, | Regents Park.
May 17. 73.

Dear Mr. Langford,

Will you kindly send me a copy of the Spanish Gypsy?[6]

Yours sincerely
M. E. Lewes.

V, 409:11   GE TO [THE ROYAL ACADEMY],
LONDON, 19 MAY 1873

MS: Mr. Gordon N. Ray. *Endorsed:* George Eliot.

The Priory, | 21. North Bank, | Regents Park.
May 19. 73.

So far as I am able to imagine what are the duties attached to the Secretaryship of the Royal Academy, it seems to me that few men can be better fitted for the post than Mr. Pigott; and I say this on the warrant of an observation which has extended through twenty years.

Such an office should surely be filled by one who adds to a power of writing with distinction and taste, a large experience of the world and of work demanding regular application, delicate generosity of feeling, and a fine sense of what belongs specifically to the intercourse of gentlemen.

These are qualifications which I have had continual opportunities of noting in Mr. Pigott.[7]

George Eliot

6. To take to Myers at Cambridge?
7. After John Prescott Knight resigned 12 April 1873, it was decided that (for the first time in its history) "the Secretary shall not be a Member of the Royal Academy." The post was advertised. Of the 107 applicants, eight were selected by the Council, including Pigott. At the General Assembly, 10 July, Frederick A. Eaton was elected.

V, 410:5 GHL TO WILLIAM R. SHEDDEN-RALSTON,
LONDON, [20? MAY 1873]

MS: Pennsylvania State University.

The Priory, | 21. North Bank, | Regents Park.
Tuesday.

Dear Mr. Ralston

Mrs. Lewes is naturally much gratified by Mr. Ruskin's opinion, which however is too flattering to her, she having little experience of practical organization. But it will give us both much pleasure to see Mr. Ruskin any Sunday he may be disposed to call to talk the matter over.[8]

I'm both glad and sorry about Deutsch.[9]

Ever yours truly
G. H. Lewes.

V, 410:5 GE TO FREDERIC W. H. MYERS,
LONDON, 22 MAY 1873

MS: Trinity College, Cambridge. *Envelope:* Frederic M. Myers Esq. | Trinity College, | Cambridge. *Postmarks:* LONDON N.W | 5 | MY 22 | 73; CAMBRIDGE | A | MY 23 | 73.

The Priory, | 21. North Bank, | Regents Park.
May 22. 73.

My dear Mr. Myers

Nothing perturbs my memory of our delightful visit to Cambridge but (as usual) the sense of my own misdoing. That brooch about which I troubled my friends was all the while safely nestled in my drawer at home, and had not travelled to Cambridge otherwise than in my false imagination, which you perceive has a fatal facility in representing things as they are not. I am ashamed and sorry; yet I confess that I prefer the mistake to the loss of the familiar brooch, and so I think, will your benevolence.

Mr. Lewes and I have said several times to each other that we have had two days full of enjoyment—and we owe them to you. You will your-

8. John Ruskin met GE and GHL at the Water Colour Exhibition, 11 December 1869, and sat beside GHL at the Circus, 14 January 1874, when the invitation to call was probably repeated. His only recorded call at the Priory was on Sunday, 8 February 1874. (GHL Diary.) I cannot explain Ruskin's plan for GE.

9. Emanuel Deutsch died at Alexandria, Egypt, 12 May 1873 after long suffering from cancer.

self some time know by experience, I trust, that happy husbands and wives can hear each other say the same thing over and over again without being tired.

I wish that all the pleasant acquaintances I have made since Monday may bear me in mind kindly. I have a little bit of confidence that you yourself will do so, and will like to believe in the truth that I am with high regard

Most sincerely yours
M. E. Lewes.

V, 416:21   GHL TO JOHN BLACKWOOD, LONDON, [27 MAY 1873]

MS: National Library of Scotland.

The Priory, | 21. North Bank, | Regents Park.
Dear Blackwood

Friday we shall not be at home till 5 o'clock having to go in the middle of the day to see the gentleman and the House we propose to take.[1] But if you are free from engagements or bores in the afternoon we shall be glad to see you.

Ever yours truly
G. H. L.

V, 417:9   CHARLES VILLIERS STANFORD[2] TO GE, CAMBRIDGE, 28 MAY 1873

MS: London University.

Trinity College | Cambridge | May 28th /73.
Mr. C. V. Stanford presents his compliments to "George Eliot," and hopes he may be excused for troubling him with the following request. He has lately finished writing music to three songs from "The Spanish Gypsy," namely "Bright Fedalma," "Spring comes hither," and "Came a pretty maid," and hopes eventually to complete the music to the whole subject. He trusts that it may not be thought too much if he asks for permission

---

1. "Went to Chislehurst to see a house Lady Lubbock had found for us. Delighted with it." (GHL Diary, 23 May 1873.)

2. Charles Villiers Stanford (1852–1924) was appointed organist of Trinity College, Cambridge in 1873.

to publish the songs he has already written; and if the author would add permission to publish the remainder when completed, he would feel doubly grateful. The songs have received the approval of several good judges, and so he hopes that they may prove adequate to their subject.

V, 417:9 GE TO CHARLES VILLIERS STANFORD, LONDON, 29 MAY 1873

MS: Royal College of Music.

The Priory, | 21. North Bank, | Regents Park.
May 29. 73.

Mrs. G. H. Lewes (George Eliot) presents her compliments to Mr. C. V. Stanford and begs to say that she has no objection to the publication of the music which [he] has written or may write to the songs in "The Spanish Gypsy."

V, 417:9 GHL TO HENRY CROMPTON, LONDON, 29 MAY 1873

MS: Mrs. Rosamond Crompton Tinayre. *Address:* Henry Crompton Esq. | Phillimore Gardens | Kensington W. *Postmark:* LONDON N.W | 29 MAY | 1873.

The Priory, Thursday.

Can you lunch with us on Sunday at 1.30. There is a Medicus[3] coming whom I think you would like to meet.

G. H. Lewes.

V, 417:9 FREDERIC W. H. MYERS TO GE, LONDON, 31 MAY 1873

MS: University of Virginia.

Education Department | Whitehall S. W.
May 31/73.

My dear Mrs. Lewes

I was very glad to know that you had found your brooch, and to get your note telling me so. I feel a sort of instinctive conviction that when

---

3. John Hughlings Jackson (1835–1911) and Crompton came to lunch 1 June 1873. (GHL Diary.)

people tell you how much good you have done them you feel, not complacency but rather compassion for mankind, dwelling as they do in such
forlorn darkness that what no doubt seems to you the feeble and smoky
glow of your own presence and character should nevertheless be to so many
of them the masterlight of all their day.

I shall not therefore enlarge on the effect of your visit to Cambridge on
more than one man whom you met there: you seem to bring to everyone
what he needs, to me your presence, like your writings, gives most of all
the sense of example and companionship in the higher and unknown
struggles of the soul, and will cause them to be something less lonely and
bitter in the victories of Honour.

As for Mr. Lewes, he has friends, I don't doubt, in every University
in Europe, but nowhere, I venture to say, more sincere and more anxious
to see him again than in the ancient but only-partially-effete foundation of
King Edward III.[4]

> Very sincerely yours
> Frederic W. H. Myers.

V, 417:9   GHL TO JOHN BLACKWOOD, LONDON, [31 MAY 1873]

MS: National Library of Scotland.

The Priory, | 21. North Bank, | Regents Park.
Saturday.

My dear Blackwood

I am glad to think that arrangements have been made as to printing
which prevent any loss having occurred,[5] and hope that the loss of time
may be in some degree lessened by encreased energy in future. I sent back
the six sheets yesterday.

When the guinea edition of Middlemarch was first contemplated we
both thought it a risk and neither you nor I imagined that we should sell
more than 500 copies at that price. On such a supposition your proposed
royalty was quite acceptable; but now the event has turned out so very
differently, and the rapid sale of 1500 has so pleasantly disproved our
calculations ought not the royalty to be encreased?

4. King's Hall, founded by Edward
III in 1336, was absorbed in the new
Trinity College in 1546.

5. For Blackwood's decision against
publishing *Problems of Life and Mind* see
v, 410 and 416.

We were sorry to miss seeing you yesterday—all the more so because after all we did not have to run down to Chislehurst, the gentleman having written to postpone our visit till Monday.[6]

Ever yours truly

G. H. Lewes.

John Blackwood Esq.

V, 420:1   GHL TO GEORGE JAMES HOWARD, LONDON, [3 JUNE 1873]

MS: Mr. George Howard.

The Priory, | 21. North Bank, | Regents Park.

Tuesday.

My dear Howard

Thanks for the good news. Give the dear Lady our congratulations and from *me* this advice—another time let her bear the words of 'the Swan' in memory—

> If 'twere done when tis done then 'twere well
> If 'twere done *quickly*[7]

and not keep husband in unexplained suspence, or friends fidgetting at not hearing reports! Further let this be a lesson to her on the 'relativity of knowledge' and the delusiveness of 'feminine intuition.' She was so certain and so wrong!

More advice: Since she will of course desire that 'this fifth transmitter of a lovely face'[8] should be reared on strictly philosophical principles, she can't begin her experiments too early. Here is one: let her order a huge block of Wenham Lake ice, have a hole cut in it sufficient to form a mould for the mottled stranger, and gently *pour him* into it. If he screams, it will be a proof—that he doesn't like his quarters—or that *his* quarters don't like the ice. Much may be done in this way in ascertaining his views of things. But for this I should need a volume instead of a note: verbum sap.

Ever yours faithfully

G. H. L.

6. "We went to Blackbrook. Mr. Hamilton showed us over the house, with which Polly was delighted." (GHL Diary, 2 June 1873.)

7. Cf. *Macbeth*, i, vii, 1.

8. Cf. Richard Savage, *The Bastard*, 1. 8: "No tenth transmitter of a foolish face." George Howard's fifth child Christopher Edward Howard (2 June 1873–1 September 1896).

V, 421:29 GHL TO JOHN BLACKWOOD, LONDON, [10 JUNE 1873]

MS: National Library of Scotland. *Endorsed:* June 11/73.

The Priory, | 21. North Bank. | Regents Park.
Wednesday.

My dear Blackwood

We returned last night from a visit to Jowett at Oxford where from Saturday we have been in one continuous excitement of talk, and are proportionately knocked up.[9] Among a heap of letters was yours with a perfectly satisfactory explanation and a delicious burst about golfing which amused us much. In a few days now I hope we shall get away for a quiet saunter through France and Switzerland.

We have got our country house[10] at last—but can't take possession till September. It is quite an ideal place got for us by Lady Lubbock near her and the Darwins. We have for it a year on trial with the option of a long lease if approved of! It is near Chiselhurst only $\frac{1}{4}$ of an hour from London Bridge.

Ever yours faithfully
G. H. L.

V, 423:11 GHL TO WILLIAM BLACKWOOD, LONDON [23 JUNE 1873]

MS: National Library of Scotland.

The Priory, | 21. North Bank, | Regents Park.

My dear Willie

I am awaiting the proofs from Tait who being much occupied takes his time, and now I must start without them. He is to send them to Ballantynes[11] who are to send them to me. Will you please let them know that they can send me whatever they have ready to *Fontainebleau* poste restante

---

9. W. L. Courtney, one of the under-graduates who saw GE in the Common Room at Balliol, wrote: "The face was that of a tired woman, the large features being remarkable for only occasional flashes of inspiration. But her eyes were a different matter. They were wonderful eyes—eyes that now and again seemed to flash a message or analyse a person-

ality." (*The Passing Hour*, 1925, pp. 119–120.)

10. At Blackbrook, near Bickley and Chislehurst, Kent. The Darwins lived at Downe, about three miles away.

11. *Problems of Life and Mind* was printed by Ballantyne & Co. and published by Trübner.

⟨provided⟩. But I shall probably not be there till the 28th and not stay over the 29th. When I have got Tait's proofs I can soon liberate some type.

We were both very sorry to hear of the aristocratic gout making his appearance in your honorable tissues. May German baths wash it out!

We start tomorrow at 7.30.

Yours truly
G. H. L.

V, 423:11   MRS. EDWARD BURNE-JONES TO GE, LONDON, 23 JUNE 1873

MS: Yale.

The Grange | Monday, June 23rd/73.

Dearest Mrs. Lewes

This is instead of another touch of the hand and spoken farewell between us all—we felt leaving you in that way, but were sure you would prefer it to the public defection of two out of M—?'s limited circle of hearers and admirers. We reached home by 7 and ½ and found Mr. Allingham and Mr. Sanderson[1] both here and hastened to feed them and our other friends. I do hope this heavenly weather will go with you across the channel—and yet remain to bless us here. If it is in your kind heart and power to send me a word from any point of your journey, I shall be grateful—but do not do it unless it comes of itself to you to do it.

We both send real love to you both—and fresh thanks come into my mind for all your tender kindness to me. I don't feel, even now, that I have neglected my chances of coming to you—I have done so when I could.

Good bye, dear, kind friend—I am ever your loving and faithful

Georgie.

V, 428:24   HERBERT ARTHUR LEWES TO GHL, NEWCASTLE, 10 AUGUST 1873

MS: Nuneaton Public Library.

Belfast Newcastle | 10th August 1873.

My dear Pater

I had thought you had quite forgotten me, it is so long since I last heard from you. I have written to you and the little Mutter twice, and once to

1. David Masson and T. J. Cobden Sanderson were both at the Priory 22 June 1873. (GHL Diary.)

Charles and have not yet received any answer. I have been very busy riding timber, I have had to work the whole winter to make up for not doing any thing in the summer as I had to stop at home to nurse Eliza. I got a span of young oxen to brake in from my Landlord J. O'Neil. I have the use of them for one year. Ten of them I have broken in, I have two more and then my span is complete. If I can manage it I intend to ride with two wagons this summer, as I have two spans of oxen. This month and next I have to stop at home and attend to the sheep. They have commenced lambing, we have 8, at present. I don't know how many we shall have this year. I will let you know in my next.

When the Cows left off giving milk, at the commencement of the winter we bought two Goats, to milk for Marian. She has thriven very well on Goats milk. She is a lively little darling and so good. She is now 9 months old, and has two teeth and can say Mamma and papa. We shall be very glad indeed to receive a Box of Books, as we have read all the last, that you sent. If you address the Box to Mr. J. Brickhill Natal Bank Durban that will do, he will then forward it on to me. I have been troubled for the two last months with chronic rheumatism which gives me a great deal of pain. We hope the trip to France will quite recruit the little Mutter and yourself.

Our united Love to the little Mutter and yourself,

Your affectionate son,
H. A. Lewes.

V, 439:4 GE TO ALEXANDER MACMILLAN, BLACKBROOK, 18 SEPTEMBER 1873

MS: University of California Los Angeles. *Partly published:* v, 434.

Blackbrook | Bickley | Kent.
September 18. 73.

My dear Sir

I venture to send you as the publisher of our most successful books for boys, a M.S. story written by my friend Mrs. Charles Bray.

The want of some book placing duty to animals on the true basis of sympathy and written so as to rouse the interest of poorly-taught children, had been mentioned to me by several persons who are good judges on such a subject—among the rest, by Mrs. Schwabe, who would be glad to get such a book translated into Italian for the benefit of the small Neapolitans who are great tormentors of smaller animals than themselves.

I therefore suggested to Mrs. C. Bray—who has had abundant opportunity of observing what sort of narrative can win its way into rather stupid and ignorant young heads—that she should try her hand at a longer story of the same kind as a certain short one which she had already written, and as a result she has just sent me the said M.S., which I have read through and have found interesting, as well as thoroughly sound in feeling.

Will you also, for the sake of that precious element in education which the story is meant to enforce, read it through and let me know whether you judge it to be of a kind suitable to appear in your list?

Possibly you may conclude that it would be more properly classed in a catalogue devoted to books for children and schools of the humbler sort. In this case you would perhaps be kind enough to advise me as to the most suitable publisher.

I remain, my dear Sir,

Yours sincerely

M. E. Lewes.

V, 442:9 GE TO FREDERIC W. H. MYERS, BLACKBROOK, 1 OCTOBER 1873

MS: Trinity College, Cambridge.

Blackbrook | Bickley | Kent.
October 1. 73.

My dear Mr. Myers

We shall be delighted to see Mr. Gurney[2] in town (we shall be up again some time early in November). But just now we prefer having you and Mr. Sidgwick only.[3] Mr. Lewes has not been very well of late and is easily tired, so that we wish all our friends—except the exceptions—to consider us *en retraite*. You and Mr. Sidgwick are just the sort of exceptions that we choose, but please don't tell.

I should be very sorry to think that I should *not* see more of Mr. Gurney, who greatly charmed me. I trust that I am only deferring a pleasure. In haste,

Yours always sincerely

M. E. Lewes.

2. Edmund Gurney (1847–88), a Fellow of Trinity College, whom GE met at Cambridge.

3. Myers and Henry Sidgwick came to lunch 4 October 1873. (GHL Diary.)

V, 443:1   GHL TO MR. AND MRS. GEORGE HOWARD,
          BLACKBROOK, [9? OCTOBER 1873]

MS: Mr. George Howard.

                                    Blackbrook, Bickley, Kent | Thursday.
Dear Friends
    A hamper of game which anonymously arrived at the Priory and was
sent on here, we conclude to have come from you.[4] You might have sent
some *jelly* with the hare—in the shape of a letter telling us all about yourselves and your wanderings since we last saw you. Had you done so I would
have told you, what I won't now, how we sauntered through France in
search of unfindable health—reached Plombières where we stayed three
weeks and were perfectly delighted with it. I would have told you how we
went from Plombières to Luxe[u]il and Nancy—I being goaded by malaise
to change from place to place till we reached Homburg and stayed there
a fortnight to get thoroughly sick of it. I would have told you of our tour
through the war district, and of our settlemant at last in this lovely solitude
but most uncomfortable house. I would have told you that we often talked
of you and wondered whether you were in the mountains of Cadore[5] or
in the North (not with the Buggs!) and how we propose being once more
at the Priory at the end of this month—with hopes that even Stopford
Brooke would not always seduce some one from her allegiance, and that
she would remember the religious house! All this I would have told you—
and you see what you have lost for the want of a little jelly!
    Dorothea, who is not yet strong, though without positive ailment, sends
her love to both.

                                    Ever yours affectionately
                                    G. H. Lewes.
We have heard nothing of Mignon. How is she? And B. J.?

4. Mrs. Howard replied, 13 October 1873: "I fear I must undeceive you about the game. We sent none, for the best of reasons which is that we had none to send, all the game having died off on the moors this year, so that for one year at least George has been deprived of his barbarous sport." (Yale.)

5. The Dolomites.

V, 447:4 GE TO MRS. ROBERT HAMILTON,
[BLACKBROOK, 13 OCTOBER 1873]

MS: Girton College, Cambridge.

My dear Mrs. Hamilton

We should have liked, of all things, to have had the delicious drive you kindly offer us, but I am vexed to be obliged to give it up on the ground of an engagement which is likely to be good for nothing.[6]

Mr. Lewes has made an engagement with Mr. Layton that we should go to see his house about 3 o'clock, and after giving this trouble to our neighbour we must not venture to change our hour. I have not the least belief that Mr. Layton's[7] house would do for us—indeed I am disgusted with all places when I compare their ugliness with the charms of our lawn, which looks lovelier to me every day. Alas!

Yours very truly
M. E. Lewes.

I have not thanked you yet in word, though I have in feeling, for planning this pleasure for us.

V, 447:19 GE TO CHARLES WARREN STODDARD,[8]
BLACKBROOK, [OCTOBER 1873]

Text: C.W. Stoddard, *Exits and Entrances*, Boston, [1903], pp. 139–140.

Blackbrook.

My dear Sir

Your note has been forwarded to me in the country. We shall not be in town again for a fortnight; but if you are still there on Sunday, the 16th,

6. The drive was postponed till 25 October, when Mrs. Hamilton "drove us to Hayes and Shirley Commons and home by West Wickham. We called with her to see Hayes Place (Pitt's home) and Mr. Wilson the proprietor showed us his grounds, animals, etc. Not home till 6." (GHL Diary.)

7. Edward John Layton, Parkhurst, Bickley, Kent.

8. Charles Warren Stoddard (1843–1909) sent GE from San Francisco his *Poems*, 1867, and received a thoughtful letter of acknowledgment: "The writer of this letter said that she imagined me an almost solitary singer in a remote corner of the earth; that she loved to think of my diligently cultivating a little garden in a vast desert; that I seemed to have had no inspiration but that of nature, which was the best of all inspirations; that she hoped I would keep my heart pure and my voice clear; and she begged that I would ever remember what that marvellous philosopher Marcus Aurelius had written (she had just laid aside the volume of his thoughts), namely, an instrument that is left un-

and will call at the address which you know, I shall be happy to see you at any time between half-past two and five.

I remain, sincerely yours

M. E. Lewes.

V, 450:1   HERBERT ARTHUR LEWES TO GHL, NEWCASTLE, 29 OCTOBER 1873

MS: Nuneaton Public Library.

Belfast Newcastle | 29th October 1873.

Dearest Pater

I am sorry you have so often to complain of my not answering your letters sooner, I have not always an opportunity of sending to the post, and letters sometimes lay for weeks before they are posted. I will endeavour for the future to write oftener. On the 25th October I received your two letters with the Bill for £50.

We both thank you and the little Mutter very much for your kindness in sending the money. I have written to Durban to Mr. Leo Hirst to send me a piano. I am not able to go to Durban myself on account of the epidemic amongst the cattle. We are very pleased at the prospect of having a piano, it will afford us amusement for many a long evening. I shall send you all particulars when I receive the instrument. Many thanks for the seeds.

We are glad to hear your trip did the little Mutter good, but sorry it did not benefit you. We hope your country residence will prove beneficial.

Little Marian thrives well, she can stand alone now. She has not had a days illness since she was born. We are obliged to keep a Kaffir Boy to nurse her now she crawls about so much. I am still suffering from Neuralgia in my back and hips, and have got quite a skeleton. I am happy to say dear Eliza is getting a little stronger. We have had a very long dry winter, and our oxen have been very poor, we lost three from poverty. I have not commenced to ride timber as yet, but hope to do so in a weeks time. Our Cows have just now begun to calve. Our sheep have done well this winter. I have looked after them well, and not lost any. We have now 52 lambs and I think we shall have a few more. Tomorrow I commence shearing. Next year we hope to have 160 lambs, if we have any luck at all. The 100 Ewes I bought last January will then lamb. You did not tell me

strung for a season can never again be kept in tune; and that she was my friend and well wisher—George Eliot." (*Exits* *and Entrances*, pp. 137–138.) He called at the Priory 16 November 1873. (GHL Diary.)

the name of your last Work. I have read a great deal lately of a night, not being able to sleep through pain.

Love from Eliza, Marian and myself, to you and little Mutter.

Your affectionate son
H. A. Lewes.

V, 453:1 GHL TO JOHN WALTER CROSS, LONDON, [4 NOVEMBER 1873]

MS: Yale.

The Priory, | 21. North Bank, | Regents Park.

Friday.

My dear Nephew

Your aunt desires to make trial of *Draper's Dichroic Ink*[9] which is not to be had in these regions, but may be had at *W. Edwards, 38 Old Change.* Will you get a 6d bottle and put it in your pocket the first time you bring your welcome face into these regions?

Did you see your Cigar friend?

Ever yours truly
G. H. L.

9. The black ink GE used gave way to a violet ink in February 1872. A darker purple ink begins in GHL's Diary 7 November 1873. Since this letter is on paper watermarked 1873, GHL must be referring to the darker ink.

The Writing of Daniel Deronda

V, 460:24 GHL TO HENRY AUSTIN DOBSON, LONDON, [13 NOVEMBER 1873]

MS: University of London.

The Priory, | 21. North Bank, | Regents Park.
Thursday.

Dear Sir

Although I have read—or rather it would be truer to say *because* I have read several of the poems as they appeared I am delighted to have them in a more permanent and accessible form. Accept my thanks for the volume.[1]

Every yours truly
G. H. Lewes.

Austin Dobson Esq.

V, 460:24 GHL TO CHARLES WARREN STODDARD, LONDON, [14 NOVEMBER 1873]

Text: C.W. Stoddard, *Exits and Entrances*, Boston, [1903], p. 140.

The Priory | Friday.

We shall be glad to see you on Sunday—at least I shall be visible, though probably Mrs. Lewes may not, she being ill this week. If you are able to be in town Sunday week,[2] that would be the better time to see Mrs. L.

George H. Lewes.

1. Henry Austin Dobson (1840–1921), *Vignettes in Rhyme*, 1873, dedicated to Anthony Trollope, under whose editorship some of the poems appeared in *St. Paul's Magazine*. GHL's copy inscribed "To G. H. Lewes Esqre with the author's compliments Nov. 11. 1873" is at Yale.

2. Burne-Jones lunched at the Priory 16 November. "Mr. Stoddard (from California)," the first arrival afterwards, describes GHL as "a slender, nervous, scholarly-looking gentleman," who greeted him cordially, led him into the drawing room, and said "My dear, here is Mr. Stoddard!" Burne-Jones rather shocked the Californian by wearing a blue merino shirt and artist jacket. When it was time to go, GHL went to the door with Stoddard and offered him a "cigar of the very best brand." As they were shaking hands, a young woman without escort "stalked solemnly up the gravel path, gurgled at the threshold, and passed into the presence of the high-priestess." GHL whispered, "That is Miss———" but Stoddard failed to catch the name. It was Edith Simcox. Among others whose names he missed were the Beeslys, the Lyulph Stanleys, the Du Mauriers, and John and Emily Cross. (GHL Diary, 16 November 1873, and C. W. Stoddard, *Exits and Entrances*, Boston, 1903, pp. 143–147.)

V, 462:16   GE TO JOHN BLACKWOOD, LONDON, 21 NOVEMBER 1873

MS: Lady Hermione Cobbold.

The Priory, | 21. North Bank, | Regents Park.
November 21. 73.

My dear Mr. Blackwood

Thanks: you judged as I expected. I wrote strongly to you, feeling sure that you would not unnecessarily communicate anything likely to give pain. After my letter[3] was gone I had some fear that I had fallen into exaggeration of the misunderstanding to which the sentences in the little Preface were liable. But in any case, the decision now arrived at is, I think, the wisest that could be suggested in the matter.

I return today the corrected proofs to p. 64.[4] Of course one cannot like the 7/6 type so well as the original spaciousness, but I see no other fault to be found with it. The page seems rather long, but the size of the proof paper causes some illusion.

It is printed with admirable correctness, but I find one or two errors of print which I had allowed to pass in the first Edition, and also an important error of my pen which I am indebted to Mr. Main for pointing out. I had put (p. 50) 'any more than vanity *will help us to be* witty'[5] instead of 'makes us witty.'

I can imagine that you get interesting letters about Parisian affairs— from Lord Lytton[6] for example, and from Mr. Oliphant. Lord L. is one of the most delightful letter-writers I know of in these hurried penny-post days. But we have heard nothing from him for these seven months. He must be quite enough occupied with immediate claims, in a position so much more responsible than that he held at Vienna.

We are having some fine days, which I hope you are sharing. With best wishes to the suffering prisoner,

Yours always truly
M. E. Lewes.

3. See v, 458–459, 461, for GE's objection to Main's Preface to the 2nd ed. of the *Sayings*.

4. Sheets A–D of *Middlemarch*, New ed., 1874.

5. *Middlemarch*, 1st ed., i, 121. Main discussed the sentence in a letter to GE, 8 January 1873. See v, 366.

6. Lytton was Chargé-d'affaires and Secretary of Embassy at Paris, 1873–74.

V, 462:16 RALPH WALDO EMERSON TO GE, CONCORD, 21 NOVEMBER 1873

MS: Newnham College, Cambridge.

Concord, Masstts | 21 November 1873.

Will Mrs. Lewes allow me to introduce to her Mrs. S. M. Downes,[7] a young friend of mine, who grew up in this town, but lives now in Andover, where she makes herself useful and beloved by all the readers of good books from Chaucer down to George Eliot. At least that was my fortune in a visit I made to that theological town to find my young friend a centre of of the lay scholars. You will not wonder that in coming to England she earnestly wishes to see your face.

With very kind regards and recollections,[1]

R. W. Emerson.

Mrs. G. H. Lewes.

V, 469:15 GHL TO SIDNEY COLVIN, LONDON, [8 DECEMBER 1873]

MS: Nuneaton Public Library.

The Priory, | 21. North Bank, | Regents Park.
Monday.

My dear Sir

Henry Sidgwick is coming to town and will dine with us on Friday the 19th. I have asked Bowen, Beesly, Clifford and Otter to meet him,[2]

7. Annie Sawyer Downes (1839–1901), wife of Samuel Downes, teacher of music at Abbot Academy, Andover, Massachusetts, having called at the Priory 4 January 1874, rewarded GE's hospitality with a detailed account of the visit in the *New York Tribune*, 25 March 1876, p. 7d, under the headline: "George Eliot. One of Her Receptions. Face — Figure — Manner — Voice — Dress." See Haight, *George Eliot*, p. 461. An obituary describes her as "a well-known poetess" and "a personal friend of Emerson, Hawthorne, George Eliot, and other famous authors." Her call was never repeated.

1. On 30 October 1867 Emerson confided to Lady Amberley that "he does not care a bit for Mrs. Lewes's

novels and cannot read them" (*The Amberley Papers*, 2 vols., 1937, II, 68.) GHL dined with Emerson at C. E. Norton's, 17 April 1873. After dinner, when Goethe was being discussed, Emerson said energetically, "I hate *Faust*. It is a bad book," and according to Norton GHL was annoyed. (*Letters of C. E. Norton*, 2 vols., Boston and N.Y., [1913], I, 488.) But in his Diary GHL merely notes: "Emerson was there (very sweet, simple; young, healthy-looking for his age—over 70)." On 21 April GE and GHL lunched with the George Howards to meet Emerson.

2. Colvin and Beesly did not accept. E. F. S. Pigott and Dr. Richard Liebreich filled their places. After dinner the Charles Leweses, the George Du

and should be glad if you are likely to be in town on that day and will join us
at ¼ to 7.

Yours truly

G. H. Lewes.

Sidney Colvin Esq.

V, 470:17   GHL TO HENRY AUSTIN DOBSON, LONDON, 19 DECEMBER 1873

MS: University of London.

The Priory, | 21. North Bank, | Regents Park.

⟨20⟩ 19 December 73.

My dear Sir

I have been slowly sipping and resipping the small flask of Falernian you
were good enough to send me, and cannot resist telling you how charmed
I have been with the delicacy, ease, and real poetic feeling of this vintage.
To drop the clumsy metaphor and to keep within the region of sincerity
I will add that many times in the course of the volume I have regretted a
too artificially colloquial expression—and the scraps of French which give
a patchy and ostentatiously frivolous aspect to a Muse which in her better
moods is wholly charming. If I did not admire many of the poems very much
you will believe me when I say that I should never have thought of speci-
fying what seems not admirable.

Yours very truly

G. H. Lewes.

Austin Dobson Esq.

V, 475:13   GHL TO GEORGE SMITH, LONDON, [1873?]

MS: Princeton.

The Priory, | 21. North Bank, | Regents Park.

My dear Smith

The bearer of this letter, Mr. Tracey,[3] I have known and thought highly
of for some years. I cannot of course say how far his talents will suit him

Mauriers, Oscar Browning, and Mrs.
Liebreich came, and there was singing
till midnight. (GHL Diary, 19 December 1873.)

3. George Henry Tracey is listed in

the *Post Office London Directory* for 1873
at 1 Manor Road, Walworth S. E. There
is no other mention of him in GHL's
correspondence.

for the post to which he aspires, but he has better referees than me to lend him their good word. I only wish to say that if in other respects you think him qualified, I believe you will find him a pleasant coadjutor.

Ever yours truly
G. H. Lewes.

George Smith
Written in great haste but not inconsiderately.

VI, 13:12   GHL TO ALEXANDER MAIN, LONDON, [28 JANUARY 1874]

MS: Harvard. *Address:* Alex. Main Esq. | West Mary St. | Abroath | Scotland. *Postmark:* LONDON N.W | B 7 | JA 29 | 74.

Wednesday Evening.

C. promised me to send at once.[4] If you do not hear by Saturday let me know.

G. H. L.

VI, 13:12   GHL TO JOHN BLACKWOOD, LONDON, [31 JANUARY 1874]

MS: National Library of Scotland.

The Priory, | 21. North Bank, | Regents Park.
Saturday.

Dear Blackwood

In a letter from Main just received he says his bookseller answered an inquiry respecting the Spanish Gypsy by saying it was "now being re-printed."[5] Is this true? Because Mrs. Lewes wishes her corrected copy to be printed from.

She would also be glad of a copy of Page's Advanced Text Book of Geology[6] if you will kindly send her one, and I should be glad of Volume II of the "Physiology of Common Life"—in *parts*, if you have the parts. I want to make use of several passages, and don't care about sending my bound copy to the printers.

4. GHL called on Frederic Chapman, 28 January 1874, to discuss payment for Main's *Life and Conversations of Dr. Samuel Johnson*, 1874. (GHL Diary.)
5. Main's letter has not been found. The 5th edition of 525 copies in 1874 was the first reprinting since 1868. GE's copy of the 4th edition with her corrections is at Yale.
6. Blackwood printed the 5th ed. in 1873.

Don't believe a word Mrs. Lewes may say in depreciation of her new book—it's famous![7]

Ever yours truly
G. H. L.

VI, 13:12   GHL TO ALEXANDER MAIN,
LONDON, 31 JANUARY [1874]

MS: Harvard. *Address:* Alex. Main Esq. | West Mary St. | Arbroath | NB. *Postmarks:* ST. JOHNS WOOD N.W | D 2 | FE 2 74; ARBROATH | B | FE 3 | 74.

The Priory, 31 January.
My dear Main
Your letter with enclosure arrived safely this morning. Will write shortly.

G. H. Lewes.

VI, 13:12   GHL TO LADY [?],
LONDON, [5 FEBRUARY 1874]

MS: Historical Society of Pennsylvania.

The Priory, | 21. North Bank, | Regents Park.
Thursday.
Madam
Mrs. Lewes has been in bed with an attack (we fear of gravel) and has been unable to write, but in the intervals of pain she has read your ladyship's pamphlet and wishes me to say how excellent she thinks it, and her hopes that it will effect something at least in the direction aimed at.
I remain, Madam

Your ladyship's truly
G. H. Lewes.

7. *Daniel Deronda.*

VI, 19:20 GE TO MRS. WILLIAM HENRY SMITH, LONDON, 18 FEBRUARY 1874

MS: Drew University Library.

The Priory, | 21. North Bank, | Regents Park.
February 18. 74.

Dear Friend

Mr. Browning writes me word that M. Milsand's[8] address is 31 rue Perronet, Neuilly, Paris. And he adds "I am glad indeed that he will get so pleasant an evidence that his work has had the effect he would most wish."

I hope I am not doing wrong in sending you the enclosed letter. In all fellowship there is strength—even in that of irremediable sorrow.

Yours ever affectionately
M. E. Lewes.

Burn the letter—you need not return it. Of course it is for no eyes but yours.

VI, 24:1 GHL TO JOHN WALTER CROSS, LONDON, 21 FEBRUARY 1874

MS: Yale. *Address:* J.W. Cross Esq. | Weybridge Heath | Weybridge. *Postmark:* LONDON N.W | 4 | FE 21 | 74.

Saturday.

If we don't see you at the Concert today, we shall expect you and two of the Doves to lunch tomorrow.[9] No excuse valid!

G. H. L.

VI, 25:1 IVAN TURGENEV TO GE, PARIS, 25 FEBRUARY 1874

MS: Berg Collection, New York Public Library.

Paris | 48, rue de Douai
Wednesday, 25th February 74.

Dear Mrs. Lewes

I have to thank you for your very kind and most flattering letter.

You may well fancy, dear Madam, both the pleasure and pride I felt

8. See VI, 18, n. 3.
9. Mary and Florence Cross came to

lunch with Albert Druce. (GHL Diary, 22 February 1874.)

in reading it. To have written something approved of by George Eliot, that is to say by one of the greatest and most sympathetic authors of our time, is gratifying indeed and again I thank you for what you have said.

I have a great wish to return to England and by so doing, have some hope of seeing you. I regret much having been unable to go last year to Mr. Hall's, the more so when you tell me I would have been fortunate enough to have met you there; but perhaps that pleasure may be given me next autumn.

I transmitted to Madame Viardot the kind passage of your letter concerning her—and she wishes me to say you that she too keeps a vivid remembrance of the day[1] when, through her singing, she was able to please one whose noble and sure talent she most admires.

Pray, dear Mrs. Lewes, be so kind as remember me to your husband very cordially, and accept for yourself the affectionate expression of the admiration with which I remain

Yours very truly

Ivan Tourguéneff.

VI, 25:25   GE TO MME EUGÈNE BODICHON, LONDON, 5 MARCH [1874]

MS: Berg Collection, New York Public Library.

The Priory, | 21. North Bank, | Regents Park.

March 5.

Welcome, dear Barbara. Come to lunch with us on Sunday.[2] We shall be alone then, and as nobody is likely to come before 3 or $\frac{1}{2}$ past, we shall have time for a good chat.

Yours always

Marian.

1. See v, 143, n. 8.
2. "Barbara to lunch." Among the callers listed in GHL's Diary, 8 March 1874, are Trollope, Sir James and Lady Colvile, William Allingham, Mr. and Mrs. F. Harrison, Gurney, Woolner, G. A. Simcox, John Ferguson McLennan and his brother, and Charles Lewes.

VI, 30:5 GHL TO [GEORGE SIMPSON], LONDON, 11 MARCH [1874]

MS: National Library of Scotland.

The Priory. 11th March.

The proposed page for Jubal is quite satisfactory. I shall write to Mr. Blackwood in a few days.

G. H. Lewes.

VI, 32:15 GE TO LADY LYTTON, LONDON, 21 MARCH 1874

MS: Lady Hermione Cobbold. *Envelope:* The Rt. Honble | Lady Lytton | English Embassy | Paris. *Postmarks:* LONDON N.W | 5 | MR 21 | 74; ANGL. CALAIS | 22 MARS | 74.

The Priory, | 21. North Bank, | Regents Park.

March 21. 74.

Dear Lady Lytton

I am perhaps the very last in writing to you, though since I knew of your trial[3] there has not been a day in which I have not called it to mind. It is so long since we saw each other that my usual spirit of distrust has taken possession of me, and thinking of you as surrounded by a world of nearer friends, I have hardly been able to persuade myself that there would not be some obtrusiveness in sending you my helpless words. Very helpless —carrying only affectionate sorrow in your sorrow, and grateful sweet remembrance of you.

Those who have known you, though but briefly and interruptedly, cannot help counting you among their possessions—caring much lest any harm should befal you—wishing that you should not be quite loosed from them. And I cannot see my writing now in any other light than that of a self-indulgence which needs forgiveness. You will not deny me this.

I trust that your health has borne the pressure of grief, and that your life in Paris is not too arduous for you socially. I find the most effective source of resignation—and resignation makes half our spiritual life—in thinking of sorrow and pain as part of a sum which is shared among poor mankind. In that way one gets calmer about oneself, remembering others.

Please let me tell you of a pleasure I have had lately, namely, reading

3. Lady Lytton's second son Henry Meredith Edward Lytton died 1 March 1874.

that page of your husband's which contains the stanzas to E.L. They are perfect, and give me a delight which includes you both.

Mr. Lewes unites with me in offering to yourself and Lord Lytton a deeply felt regard and sympathy. In this busy world we are obliged to live in all senses by faith in each other, which nullifies silence and separation.

Always, dear Lady Lytton,

Yours faithfully and affectionately

M. E. Lewes.

VI, 36:21   GHL TO LORD LYTTON, LONDON, 30 MARCH [1874]

MS: Lady Hermione Cobbold.

The Priory, | 21. North Bank, | Regents Park.

30 March.

My dear Lytton

It is sad to have your long silence broken by such a calamity.[4] For months we have been "wondering" at not hearing from you or Lady Lytton; and then checking the "wondering" by the reflection that in the whirl of the Parisian life, and with your important functions added thereto, friends have no right to expect letters unless on some definite impluse; and therefore we would not write to you to ask why you were remiss.

By this post I send you the Academy which you may probably not see. It contains an article on the Fables[5] which we both think very gratifying, not because it is an adequate account of them, but because it is a very honest expression of enthusiasm in a man who, writing poetry himself, might not be thought easy to please. In private he expresses himself even more strongly on the Fables and his admiration for them; and because I know he is a genuine, though queer fellow, I think you ought to be glad of his sympathy. I like the Fables more than anything I have read for a very long while—and if you were only dead I think the critics would be loud in their discrimination. Mais que voulez vous? They must "labour in their vocation."[6]

The volume of poems which Polly has in the press is a small affair. Reprints of Jubal, Armgart, etc. with some new pieces added.

The first of my opus magnum about which you inquire is "Problems

4. See VI, 26, n. 2.   333–334.
5. George Augustus Simcox, "Fables   6. *I Henry IV*, I, ii, 117.
in Song," *Academy*, 4 (28 March 1873),

of Life and Mind"—published by Trübner. Blackwood began to print it and then let it drop like a hot potatoe—his Scotch caution being alarmed at its speculative audacity. He was wrong, however, for the book has sold surprizingly (1000 copies gone) and no one has attacked it on the score of its heresy.

We shall be here probably till the end of May. If you don't come to England before we leave for the country you must bring Lady Lytton down to see us, wherever we are, that we may have an undisturbed "talk over lovely things that conquer death." Give her our love—our sympathy she knows she has—and believe me

Ever faithfully yours
G. H. Lewes.

VI, 36:21   GE TO ALICE HELPS,
LONDON, 31 MARCH 1874

MS: Dr. Peter Helps.

The Priory, | 21. North Bank, | Regents Park.
March 31. 74.

Dear Ministering Spirit

I want to write to you this morning because I have no other way of trying to let you know that your kindness still keeps me company and makes me the happier. The sweet services and signs of care for me which you call little are to me very great, and create a warm soothing climate for my rather shivering personality—and it is the result of making other lives than your own easier which I perceive is a chief end of yours.

Thinking how I came by them I shall find a spirtual as well [as] bodily comfort in my warm capote and cloak. But you must not, please, take any tiring trouble for my sake—only let me come into your work as an easy parenthesis.

I trust to your quick kind instinct not to mention the name of my dear friend in connection with the difficulties of my toilette. Her taste is exquisite, but all experimental beginnings are hazardous with my unlovely form, and you saw only a rough tentative representation of her design. Those sleeves which you did not like, are charming on her—or on pretty Mrs. G. Howard. She has a fairy deftness and tact—a bright-glancing wit like your own.

I must tell you a bit of humour that has just come to me in a letter. Having called "Society" a huge boa-constrictor in its demands, our friend goes on—I wonder whether the rabbits of Java, as they walk down the throats of the anacondas, say to each other, "You know I hate these crushes, but one mustn't shirk one's social duties."

Yours always sincerely

M. E. Lewes.

VI, 36:21   GE TO ALICE HELPS, LONDON, [APRIL? 1874]

Text: Maggs Brothers Catalogue 451 (Summer 1924), item 811.

North Bank, | Regents Park.

Since the man once cast the blame on the woman, I will for once again cast it on the man and tell you that the verdant folly of writing to you at Burlington House was committed by a Mr. Lewes's advice. He had a romantic idea that somebody lived there, very high and mighty, whom you were visiting. Else, I should have acted on what was my interpretation of your request and have gone to meet you there. . . .

Among the dresses which Mrs. Martin[7] has kindly spared me, there is nothing with the full front like yours and the agreeable bishop sleeve.

I cannot bear to have seemed for a moment sluggish and neglectful about answering a letter. That is not one of my vices.

VI, 39:6   LORD LYTTON TO GHL, PARIS, 3 APRIL 1874

MS: Yale.

Paris, 3 April 1874.

My dear Lewes

Your kind letter was terque quaterque welcome. Now that the navette is retablie I hope it will go on spinning. Your good opinion of the Fables gives me very great pleasure. It is extraordinary what immense pleasure can be given by a word or two of approbation or sympathy at certain moments to certain temperaments. Had I been an "ancient Greek"—and a eupatrid, I would have built a temple to the God Apropos, and invited you to become his high Priest—a function not at all inappropriate to the

7. Mrs. Theodore Martin was the actress Helen Faucit. GHL wrote in his Diary, 30 March 1874: "Alice Helps brought cloak and hood, and talked over costumes with Polly. She stayed to dinner."

investigation of "Problems of life and mind." He is the Prompter of the Muses, who do not always know the right word to say, and the younger brother of the Graces, who do not always know the right thing to do. He is nimbler than Hermes and more multiform than Proteus, and what other Divinity can always arrive just when he is wanted, in just the shape which happens to be most helpful, a bed for the weary, or a mutton chop for the hungry?

But indeed the Fables have a certain claim upon your good will since you are partly responsible for their introduction into the world. What would be said by the Timé who has not yet succeeded in doing so, if he knew they had already entered the Academy? I am most obliged to you for sending me Mr. Simcox's valuable notice of them, and very grateful for the notice itself. It is not much to say that it is the best I have seen, for in fact it is the only good one. But it is very good—good not only as regards its appreciative generosity—(although to appreciate generously the aim of any honest work is in my opinion the sign and mark of superiority in criticism). But good also in every way—good thinking and good writing. I feel honoured by such candid attention on the part of so able a writer to whom I am personally unknown, and very much pleased and encouraged by his favourable verdict. As I don't know Mr. Simcox I don't like to write to him about his Paper in the Academy, since he might attribute my so doing to some interested motive. But what I say to you is no more—indeed it is less than I feel. By the way, as for the Fables themselves, their tribe has increased beyond all bounds, and still they multiply as fast as if they were jews. Oddly enough I am able to pay you at once my debt for 'the Academy' by a Promissary Note from Villers (our Vienna friend). If you have not already seen the review of G. Eliot which he mentions and if you care to see it, let me know and I will immediately get it from him and forward it to you.

My wife is only so so, our little girl much better. Ever my dear Lewes
Your affectionate
Lytton.

I hope to be in England about the beginning of June. But it depends on my being able to get finished before then some new bedrooms much wanted, which I am building at Knebworth.
L.

VI, 39:27   GE TO MRS. WILLIAM CROSS, LONDON, 20 APRIL 1874

MS: Bryn Mawr College.

The Priory, | 21. North Bank, | Regents Park.

April 20. 74.

My dear Mrs. Cross

My little master and great philosopher decides that we must not leave home for more than part of a day, because he is anxious to finish a certain portion of his work before we leave town and the easy access to books only to be had in town.

Therefore your pretty plan[8] for our health and pleasure must be renounced, but we could start from this house after 12 o'clock some day, and thus satisfy our souls by seeing a little more of you than you and destiny gave us yesterday. If you or Johnnie could gather for us that the promising house you spoke of is to be let, we could occupy an hour in the afternoon by looking at said house without, I hope, losing the advantage of your company.

The poor sufferer's head is not well yet—such is the price of London "pleasures." In haste

Always yours lovingly

M. E. Lewes.

VI, 40:1   GE TO ALICE HELPS, LONDON, 23 APRIL 1874

MS: Dr. Peter Helps.

The Priory, | 21. North Bank, | Regents Park.

April 23. 74.

Dear Alice

Your lovely flowers are blooming still and remind me every day of your kindness. Hence they have reminded me that on Sunday I was too absent-minded to ask you à propos of the workwoman about whom you have taken trouble for your friends' sake—whether she is one who would take her work home or one who expects always to work at the houses of her

---

8. Mrs. Cross and her daughter Eleanor were among the visitors at the Priory Sunday, 19 April 1874. On Friday the 24th, GE and GHL spent the day with the Crosses at Weybridge and looked over two houses there. (GHL Diary.)

employers. If the latter, I must renounce her, because I have an objection to supernumeraries. They make buzzing noises in the rooms above and below us and distract our poor nerves.

I hope that this note will be in time to make the matter entirely unimportant—I mean, to prevent your having said a word to the workwoman which will have to be retracted.

We have decided on a house for the summer. It is on Earlswood Common near Redhill, and we are likely to flit even before May is well out—at the latest on the 1st of June. [*The rest of the letter is lacking.*]

VI, 43:18 GE TO MRS. THEODORE MARTIN, LONDON, 29 APRIL 1874

MS: University of California Los Angeles.

The Priory, | 21. North Bank, | Regents Park.
April 29. 74.

My dear Mrs. Martin

How very kind of you! Since you let me choose my time for being with you, we will drive to your house on Saturday about 3 o'clock. I shall be very glad to secure the pleasure of seeing you again before we take flight.

With best regards

Sincerely yours
M. E. Lewes.

VI, 44:21 ANTHONY TROLLOPE TO GHL, LONDON, 3 MAY 1874

MS: Yale. *Published: The Letters of Anthony Trollope,* ed. B.A. Booth, 1951, p. 318.

39, Montagu Square.
3 May 1874.

My dear Lewes.

This is a begging letter, and I hate begging. It is intended for you and your wife alike. Shirley Brooks, who had been engaged for 35 years in literature, has died leaving a life insurance for £4000 with a wife and two sons, and not a penny else. His friends want to save the assurance for permanent income and if possible to add something,—also to raise a sum for immediate wants. I am acting as Treasurer. Dont be angry, and if you disapprove merely say so[9].

God bless you

Yours

A. T.

VI, 53:24 GHL TO ALEXANDER MAIN, LONDON, 1 JUNE [1874]

MS: Harvard. *Address:* Alexr Main Esq. | West Mary St | Arbroath | NB. *Postmark:* ST. JOHNS-WOOD N.W | B 2 | JU 1 | 74.

The Priory 1 June.

Our address henceforth will be

The Cottage | Earlswood Common | Red Hill | Surrey.

Drop a line two days before you come as we may be away.

G. H. L.

VI, 55:1 LORD LYTTON TO GHL, KNEBWORTH, 8 JUNE [1874]

MS: Yale.

Knebworth, | Stevenage, Herts | 8 June.

My dear Lewes,

I have long been wishing to write you a line, but there have been intervening if not extenuating circumstances.

I know not whether it is to "George Eliot" or to Blackwood that I owe the welcome receipt of a copy of the new volume of Poems[1], (which reached me just before we left Paris), but "without being *personal*" I wish to express my most grateful thanks for it. There are some notes sounded by this little book (which is worth all the *big* books of modern verse put together) in a key which I had not associated with the writer's masters' touch. In such a key is the whole stream of that most exquisite poem 'Brother and Sister.' To me this poem presents in one harmonious effect all the aspects of poetic beauty—genuine and sincere human sentiment of a high order, wrought

9. The detailed accounts in GHL's   1. *The Legend of Jubal and Other Poems,*
Diary for 1874 list no contribution for   1874.
Mrs. Brooks.

to a high lyric utterance, and yet in sympathy with what is common to universal experience, sustained melody in union with a sustained strain of emotion, both the sense and the purest delicacy of thought and word. The Minor Prophet is a masterpiece like one of those antique cameos which, within the narrow compass of a finger ring, is so wrought as, by the sharpness of its cutting and the largeness of the sentiment, to affect one with a sense of colossal size.

I think that G. Elliot's greatest effects are generally most appreciable when presented on a large canvass, on which she has had plenty of room to develop the spaciousness of her genius, and the poems in this volume which I like least are the purely lyrical ones. But from these Arion stands out on a promontory of his own with all the essentials of grandeur. All my old favourites I like more and more; of the more elaborate pieces the one I appreciate most coldly, recognizing its great merits but without enthusiasm, is Agatha. 'Stradivarius' is delightful in every detail, and a grand poem altogether.

What I have seen of the reviews, laudatory and respectful though they be, exasperates me to the highest degree of disgust. The British Public, as represented and educated by the critical press, is always burying alive in their own reputations its greatest literary benefactors, by walling them round forever with materials taken from their own books. The development of every original genius is ever, as it seems to me, in our Country, impeded and obstructed by the Public's hasty classification of it, for the public having an uncomfortable consciousness that such classifications are premature and imperfect, is always disinclined to acknowledge the necessity of abandoning them. Tennyson has been stunted and atrophied like a Chinese oak by the fear of ever outgrowing the small flower-pot of an established success. I hope that the author of Jubal and the Spanish Gypsy will not listen, and that you will not allow her to listen to those oafs who exhort her not to write Poetry because she can write such great prose. Her Poetry is, in its own sphere, quite as great as her prose, and just as much a genuine part of her. Her genius will miss its own completion if she neglects this side of it. If I may venture to say it without appearing to you presumptuous, what has particularly struck me in this last volume is the encreased spontaneity of the purely lyric note, the bird note which chirps in the soul of every poet, but which *intellectual* poets sometimes deaden by building too elaborate a nest for the bird, and choosing too high a tree for the nest.

I got your book[2] just as I was leaving Paris, but have not yet been able

2. GHL, *Problems of Life and Mind. The Foundations of a Creed*, 1874.

to begin it. My mind is at sixes and sevens just now, and incapable of grappling with any problem of life of more general importance than the personal one which is now pressing on it, whether or not to resign my post abroad and settle in England. To be or not to be.[3] The pros and cons of this personal problem are so nicely adjusted that I cannot yet succeed in making one scale outweigh the other, though I lie awake all night turning the balance and shifting the weights. Chapters on Free Will and Necessity might be illustrated from my present mental condition if a philosopher could analyse it.

I returned only a week ago from Yorkshire, where I have been speechifying to Mechanics[4] (an experimentum in corpore vile) and am now settled for two months at Knebworth; the place itself being altogether unsettled. The new bedrooms I have been building here for nearly twelve months are still unfinished and we live en bivouac, surrounded by bricklayers dust and through draughts. My poor wife is still *very* seedy, and indeed has never rallied at all from the effects of that last great blow. We hope to be in England till the 1st of August. Between this and then how are you and I to meet? I earnestly desire your practical assistance in the solution of this problem, which is one of life and mind in which I am directly interested.

What an amazing and unpleasant story this of Browning's matrimonial engagement to the widow Benzon![5]

Adieu my dear old friend,

Your ever affect[ionate]
Lytton.

VI, 55:1   LORD LYTTON TO GHL, KNEBWORTH, 13 JUNE 1874

MS: Mr. James L. Harlan.

Knebworth 13 June | 1874.

My dear Lewes

Your kind and charming letter[6] was thrice welcome. I hope that, before we leave England, we may both of us be able to pay you a visit, but my poor wife will not yet a while be able to creep out of her shell here. I wish I could give you a better report of her health.

If however you will tell me how to get to you from town, I thmk I shall

---

3. *Hamlet*, III, i, 50.
4. To the Mechanics Institute at Leeds.
5. To the widow of Ernst Leopold

Benzon. See G. S. Haight, "Robert Browning's Widows," *TLS*, 2 July 1971, pp. 783–784.
6. Not found.

very probably before long ask you to give me a day's hospitality at Redhill and there 'delight my soul with talk'[7]—neither of knightly nor of nightly deeds—but of all those things in heaven and earth which are dreamed of in your philosophy.[8]

Your disbelief in the rumoured Browning marriage I rejoice to know— and indeed I feel that I ought not, by alluding to it, to have given currency to a story which I myself have refused to credit—But . . . but—well, it distresses me that his numerous new acquaintances should regard as probable or actual, many doings and sayings of his, which I should have once believed—more firmly than I do now—to be impossible.

How well I appreciate the impatience with which you must listen to the folks who wish that Geo. Elliot 'would only write novels'! If genius listened to such folks (whose advice must be one of the drawbacks of a great popularity) its work would be like that of the village painter in Canning's[9] capital story of the Red Lion. His only idea of decorative variety was to paint little red lions for the small pannels because a big red lion was so effective in the large ones.

Your liking for the fables gives me more pleasure than anything else in connection with them. I see you mention the possibility of *riding* from Knebworth to Redhill—I should like that very much if it be possible. Can it really be done? I would prefer a long and a hard day's ride to an hour's rail, if there be any inn at Redhill where I could put up my horse—and if the distance be within a day's ride.

Ever dear friends

Your most affectionate
Lytton.

VI, 67:1 GHL TO PORTER & COATES,[1] EARLSWOOD COMMON, 11 JULY 1874

MS: Haverford College.

The Cottage | Earlswood Common | Red Hill, Surrey | 11 July 74.
Gentlemen

In reply to your letter to Mrs. Lewes of the 25th June I have to say that she never makes any arrangement respecting her books until they are

---

7. Tennyson, "Morte d'Arthur," line 19.

8. *Hamlet,* I, v, 166.

9. Charles John Canning, Earl Can-

ning (1812–62), Governor General of India 1856 and first Viceroy 1858.

1. Publishers of Philadelphia, offered £1500 for advance sheets of *Daniel De-*

finished, or very nearly finished; and the novel on which she is now engaged will not be finished for many months. As soon as she is sufficiently advanced to entertain a proposal I shall inform you thereof; meanwhile be pleased not to mention the fact or I shall have half a dozen more letters to write to others.

Yours truly
G. H. Lewes.

Messrs Porter & Coates

VI, 71:23   GHL TO MRS. GEORGE JAMES HOWARD, EARLSWOOD COMMON, 27 JULY 1874

MS: Mr. George Howard.

The Cottage, Earlswood Common
Red Hill, 27 July 74.

Sweet Person!

Reprehensible Person!

With the faithlessness of our sex you have fulfilled your promise. What promise, saith you? That Sunday afternoon[2] when good-bye was said, did I not ask you to write and let us know how it went with you on your journey; and when with misplaced modesty you exclaimed "As if you would care for a letter from me!" did I not quash that remark with a strong expression, and did you not then and there promise that letters should be written?

Since then what reams of cold pressed have you not despatched! The Post Office has been forced to place on an extra carrier for this beat, and the two have struck for higher wages, the mass of your letters being more than they can be expected to deliver at the price! Reprehensible Person!

And out of all these letters I gather not a syllable as to your journey and what befel you—(Palgrave[3] alluded to your 'little accident' as if I knew all about it.) what sketches Howard made, and how dull you found it being together. Did you find it dull? *We* are constantly threatened by some of our friends when we speak of retiring to our perfect solitude that we shall "find it terribly dull." But we are too dull to find it out. Isn't that your case too? Doesn't Love create its own world—and that world perhaps

---

ronda. (GHL Diary, 10 July 1874.) He wrote to them again, 16 September 1875, but his letter has not been found.

2. 29 March 1874. (GHL Diary.)

3. Francis Turner Palgrave (1824–

97), poet and critic, compiled *The Golden Treasury of Songs and Lyrics,* 1864. He called at the Priory 31 May 1874. (GHL Diary.)

on the whole not inferior to "the best society"? Isn't the sweet monotony your idea of Paradise?—Whether it is or isn't, Polly and I would both like to hear how your honeymoon slipped by.

It wouldn't *more* than break the postman's back if you were to add some news about yourselves and Burne Jones and Mignon. We have seen no one; and scarcely heard from any one. Our solitude will be unbroken till the end of September when I don't know what we shall do for the fortnight or three weeks of October when the Priory is cleaned and restored and recarpeted; but somewhere we shall be, and at home again in November. This lovely country is greatly enjoyed by us, but my health is no better than in town and Polly's not much. But her mind is more in repose, and that must tell.

We were much pained at the sudden death of Lady Amberley[4] which came upon us all the more startlingly because she looked so very robust when we saw her a few weeks before. It must be unspeakably sad for him.

Polly doesn't know I'm writing or she would send her love to you both —but I suppose my authority will suffice?

Ever faithfully yours
G. H. Lewes.

VI, 77:7 GHL TO JOHN WALTER CROSS, EARLSWOOD COMMON, [8? AUGUST 1874]

MS: Yale.

The Cottage.

Dear Nephew

Statement and checque received—thanks—glad to hear of Eleanor's improvement and Florence's fat. Can't say much for the avuncular health! Headaches as frequent as in London. Nor is the Aunt what could be wished. She has gone back again after having shown decided improvement. Love to all

Ever yours truly
G. H. L.

4. Katherine Louisa Stanley, Viscountess Amberley, died of diphtheria 28 June 1874.

VI, 77:7   GHL TO ALBERT COHN,
EARLSWOOD COMMON, 11 AUGUST 1874

Text: Maggs Bros. Catalogue 309 (May–June 1913), item 1882.

Red Hill, August 11. 74.

The bank bill for Jubal[5] arrived last evening. . . . I hope the cheap edition of the Middlemarch will have some of the success our 7s. 6d. one is having; it goes like batches of loaves, over 6,000 in the last two months and the demand not slacking.

VI, 79:9   GE TO MRS. COLERIDGE KENNARD,[6]
EARLSWOOD COMMON, 31 AUGUST [1874]

MS: Bancroft Library, University of California Berkeley.

The Cottage | Earlswood Common | August 31.

Dear Mrs. Kennard

A thousand thanks for the trouble you have so kindly taken. Mr. Lewes had just written you a note to say that the prospect of the cloak kept my imagination in too restless a state, when the post brought your letter.

In the choice of a cloth I should have trusted to your judgment more willingly than my own. I hope you will approve my preference for the bronze which I return.

We have been all the happier for the warmth, rejoicing in the prosperity of the harvest as well as in our own bien-être.

The cloak will be very welcome and in wearing it I shall often be reminded of you on your lovely background of the Riviera. I trust that the wintering in that kindly region will be propitious to the health both of yourself and your dear little girl.

Mr. Lewes has been rather ailing this last day or two, but is in better force this morning. He unites with me in best regards to you and Mr. Kennard, who, I hope, knows that we feel much obliged for the pains he took to get us acquainted with Oakfield—a bit of knowledge which we value.

Sincerely yours

M. E. Lewes.

5. GHL's account lists £50 for *The Legend of Jubal* in Asher's Collection of English Authors, vol. 99.

6. Coleridge John Kennard drove GE and GHL from the station to his house, the Grove, Penshurst, where they

VI, 80:7   HERBERT ARTHUR LEWES TO GHL, BELFAST, 13 SEPTEMBER 1874

MS: Nuneaton Public Library.

Belfast | 13 September 1874.

Dearest Pater

My Neuralgia pains have left me at last. I have been very weak from the effects, I am now still not well or strong. Eliza has not been well lately. We shall both be glad to start again for Leydenburg with a Transport load. The rest does Eliza a great deal of good.

I forgot to thank you and the little Mutter for sending the Book of poems, which we both enjoyed reading very much. Our sheep commenced lambing last month, we have over 100 lambs and expect about 50 more. We have lost 30 lambs or more my being unwell and not able to look after them. We have also lost 20 Ewes from poverty.

We have not heard from you lately. How do you like your House in Surrey. Shall you return to the Priory for the winter. The Box of Books and piano are still in Durban no wagon to be had to bring them to Newcastle. I hope we shall soon receive them. The grass is now growing and people will begin to ride transport. Little Marian grows splendidly, and gets in to every sort of mischief, she is very fond of animals. She like[s] to take my horse by the bridle and lead him round the house. She some times stands on the sofa and pats your portrait and says "Dada"

Writing every month I find nothing new to tell you.

Love from us all to you and little Mutter

Your affectionate son
H. A. Lewes.

Excuse bad pen.

lunched; then walked with them across the Park to Oakfield, a house belonging to the Hon. Charles Lane-Fox, which he wished them to rent. (GHL Diary, 31 July 1874.) Going again 12 August, they went over the house and rambled in South Park.

VI, 84:4 GE TO ROBERT EVANS, LONDON, 26 SEPTEMBER 1874

Text: Copy supplied by Mr. Percival R. Allen. *Envelope:* Robert Evans, Esq. | The Park | Nottingham. *Postmarks:* st johns wood n.w | c 3 | sp 26 | 74; nottingham | a 3 | sp 27 | 74.

The Priory, | 21. North Bank, | Regents Park.
September 26. 74.

My dear Nephew

I enter fully into the duteous and affectionate anxiety which prompted the letter I received from you last night, precisely on my arrival for a few days stay in town. The correspondence between me and your Aunt Fanny ceased simply by her ceasing to write to me, the last letter between us having been written by me;[7] at least, I have never since received from her the slightest sign of remembrance. Your good mother has written to me more than once,[8] but there was no word in her letters implying that your Aunt Fanny retained any affectionate regard for me. All that I have heard concerning her is this—that some (perhaps eight or ten) years ago, she spoke of me with dislike and unkindness, on an occasion in which I think my informant could have made no mistake. But I bear my Father's memory in too deep reverence willingly to dwell on anything painful in the conduct of those who were near to him; also I feel grateful for all goodness shown to me in my childhood and youth, and I have entertained only kind and admiring recollections of my sister.

But from the delicacy manifested in your letter I feel sure you will understand me when I tell you that during the seventeen years in which I have heard nothing from your Aunt Fanny, my connexions and duties, with consequent claims on my time and effort, have been continually multiplying. My strength, never quite equal to the demands upon it, naturally diminishes rather than increases with the increase of those demands, and I am constantly obliged not only to decline invitations but to escape from the pressure of visits and correspondence by retreating into the country out of the reach of all but the most intimate friends. I fear it is too late, my dear Nephew, for your Aunt Fanny and me to meet again. I cannot sustain agitating renewals of past relations in addition to the many social and family duties which have accumulated on me in the intervening years

7. For GE's last letter 2 June 1857 see II, 336–337.

8. One letter from Jane Attenbo-rough Evans, 15 March [1864], telling of her husband's death, is at Yale.

Life goes on urgently, and those who willingly renounce a friendship cannot after a long lapse of years recover it at a given moment.

I have a keen recollection of all the pleasant affectionate intercourse I had with my sister in my childhood and youth, and especially I bear in mind the tenderness we felt in common for our dear Father. But I have no store of nervous energy, no superfluous time, to make it right for me to encounter the excitement of reviving those memories actively in personal meetings. I am not conscious of having ever, either by word or deed, done anything injurious to my sister, and I have a lively satisfaction in hearing from you of her comfort and welfare. But I cannot respond to your suggestion (made, I am sure, with the best sympathetic motives) that I should reopen communication with your Aunt by writing. My correspondence is very onerous to me, and I must not enlarge it in any way that does not wear the aspect of a duty.

I gather from your very kind and delicate letter that you have not spoken to your Aunt of your intention to write to me, and that your view of her desires is a matter of interpretation. I trust to your evidently good judgment to comprehend my feeling and position without a more lengthy explanation, and also to withhold everything from your Aunt Fanny which might cause her unnecessary sadness. You can assure her with truth that I bear her in sisterly remembrance.

I rejoice to hear of your happy family circumstances. The youngest who bears the dear name "Robert Evans"[9] will I trust, grow up to be a comfort and delight to you. Pray offer my best regards to your Mother when you have an opportunity of doing so. I was deeply touched by that last (I think it was the last) letter of hers to me in which she gave me an account of your Father's death, and I always bear in tender remembrance his uniform brotherly goodness to me.

Believe me, my dear Nephew,

Your sincerely well-wishing Aunt
M. E. Lewes.

9. Robert Evans IV (1863–1927).

VI, 84:4 GHL TO JOHN WALTER CROSS, LONDON, [29 SEPTEMBER 1874]

MS: Yale.

The Priory | Tuesday

Dear Nephew

I seem to have stowed away some of your notes of purchase and can't think where they are. Will you kindly have made a list of all your purchases for me with the prices, and send the same to your uncle?

We came back on Friday and since Saturday I have been struggling against one of my inevitable return headaches. We decidedly gained strength however in the last days of our country quiet and I hope shall be able to face the 'London season.'

Ever yours
G. H. L.

VI, 88:1 GHL TO MRS. GEORGE JAMES HOWARD, LONDON, [2 NOVEMBER 1874]

MS: Mr. George Howard.

The Priory | Monday.

Dear Mrs. Howard

You were right to count upon our sympathy and real distress at the sad tidings of your letter. What you must have gone through makes us both tremble to think of. There is a streak of sunshine however in the closing sentences; and we hope it may not be inconvenient to you and improper for him to receive us one day on your passage through town. You mustn't think of coming to us—just drop a card to name day and hour and we will come to you.

As for your silence and your hope of forgiveness—"forgiveness"? *What* was there to forgive? Is not my paternal affection robust enough to see or *invent* excuses for any silence? We did at first 'wonder' whether you had received my letter—it might not have been forwarded and the thought that you might perhaps be ill or have your house full of guests who claimed attention was quite enough ground for silence. I could not be so poor spirited as to suppose there was either indifference or forgetfulness in the case.

The only scrap we heard of you was from Mignon[1] telling us of her

1. Mrs. Burne-Jones's letter has not been found. For her husband's troubles in these years see Penelope Fitzgerald, *Edward Burne-Jones*, 1976.

husband's illness, of George's offer to go with him to Egypt and your generous readiness to part with him on such an occasion; and as we only returned home on Saturday, we could hear nothing more.

I have a heap of letters to write so won't say a word more of ourselves than that we have come home prepared for the season's fatigues. Mrs. Lewes sends her love to you and the dear sufferer, and counts on hearing of a continued improvement.

Ever yours faithfully
G. H. Lewes.

VI, 88:19 HERBERT ARTHUR LEWES TO GHL, BELFAST AND NEWCASTLE, 9–14 NOVEMBER 1874

MS: Nuneaton Public Library.

Belfast | 9th November 1874.

Dearest Pater

I have just received your letter with the cheque for £25, for which we are very much obliged. We are expecting the piano every day, it has been a long time coming from Durban owing to the difficulty in getting transport. I also expect the Box of Books to arrive at the same time.

Newcastle 14th 1874.

I find on my arrival in Newcastle the piano has arrived. But not the Books. Since I last wrote I have been well for a few weeks. But foolish like I drove my wagon to get some timber from the Bush when I returned I was layed up again as bad as ever. However I got some more Strychnica and Iron and am now getting better again of the Neuralgia but feel ill from the effects of the Strychnica. Eliza is better then when I last wrote. Marian was 2 years old on the 2nd November her height is 32½ inches, and broad in proportion. Our sheep are doing well we have just done shearing we got 591 lbs. of wool this time. We have 3 calves, the rest of our cows have not yet calved they are very late this year. If they all calf we shall have 11 calves this year.

I think that is all the news I have to tell. Love to all

Your affectionate son
H. A. Lewes.

VI, 88:19 GE TO JOHN BLACKWOOD, LONDON, 11 NOVEMBER 1874

MS: National Library of Scotland. *Published: Journal of English and Germanic Philology,* 47 (October 1958), 705–706.

The Priory, | 21. North Bank, | Regents Park.

November 11. 74.

My dear Mr. Blackwood

Don't despair of me. I am settled down now, and the thick slice of manuscript which had passed into the irrevocable before we left Earlswood, had been read aloud to my private critic and was immensely approved by him. I did not think it up to the mark myself, but he vows it is.

Charles showed me your letter when he was here on Sunday. I have not read his article,[2] so that I have no judgment to give, but I should have been glad to have it appear for Mrs. Senior's sake, who had read and approved it. However, it may do for some other niche.

Charles is a monumental reminder to us of our venerable years. He is the father of two children, wears spectacles, and has just been appointed head of a department in the P.O. with twenty men under his direction. And it seems to us but the other day when we brought him from Hofwyl looking like a crude German lad of seventeen. He is not, thank Heaven, a literary dabbler, but he sometimes writes on practical questions that interest him.

You are rather hard on the Master of Baliol,[3] who is a favourite of mine. But he certainly is not a specimen of muscular Christianity. And he is wonderfully old-seeming for his years. I get on with him delightfully.

If you feel it a grievance to migrate from the country to Edinburgh, think what it is for your wretched fellow Britons who are doomed to London—a much vaster wilderness of brick and mortar without the grand breaks and outlines of Edinburgh. But I suppose that Miss Blackwood thinks the Londoners the more enviable among the doomed, and indeed

2. See VI, 87, for GE's request for return of Charles Lewes's article, which appeared ultimately in the *Edinburgh Review,* 142 (July 1875), 89–110. It dealt with Mrs. Nassau Senior's *Report as to the Effect on Girls of the System of Education at Pauper Schools,* 1874, and the controversy it stirred. By personal investigation of many of the girls Mrs. Senior showed the system a failure; she recommended the boarding out of orphans, smaller schools, and industrial training. (p. 102.)

3. "Modern Scientific Materialism," a long article in *Blackwood's,* 116 (November 1874), 519–539, attacks John Tyndall's address as President of the British Association; the same number has a verse satire on it, pp. 582–583. Neither refers to the Master of Balliol, who may have been mentioned in Blackwood's letter.

I am not sure that I should like the Edinburgh life as a whole better than what we get here. As an equivalent for golf, I am going to see some tennis playing which, they tell me, is very fine, and possible as a private institution for ladies.

Always yours truly
M. E. Lewes.

VI, 95:1   GE TO ALICE HELPS, LONDON, 23 NOVEMBER 1874

MS: Yale.

The Priory, | 21. North Bank, | Regents Park.
November 23. 74.

My dear Alice

I was continually reminded of you in our country life by the sight of the book chest which your clever kindness devised for us. And being as unreasonable as most persons who do nothing for their friends, I was disposed to grumble at you for not writing to me (without the slightest expectation of an answer). I am base enough to be glad that you wrote, though you took that trouble in vain, because I like the assurance that you bore us in mind.

Thanks for your kind thought about getting us tickets for the Beatrice.[4] We can't go because of our Concert. No, you can do nothing for us, but come to see us, which we count a pretty service and shall be glad of whenever you can do it without unpleasant effort.

I rejoice to hear of your having had a healthy inspiriting bit of travelling. Better by half go to by-places in our own lovely country, and drive in carts over breezy lovely hills than go moiling on railways to see places not comparable for beauty with what one leaves behind.

I will tell you what we did when you come to see us. We are tolerably robust for rickety personages and are comfortably settled down for the winter.

Mr. Lewes will soon have done correcting the proofs for his second volume, and will then start off on a new one. He sends his love to you and I am

Always yours affectionately
M. E. Lewes.

---

4. Helen Faucit at the Haymarket, 12 December 1874, played Beatrice in *Much Ado about Nothing*, a benefit performance for the Royal General Theatrical Fund.

VI, 95:13   GHL TO HERBERT SPENCER,
LONDON, [28 NOVEMBER 1874]

MS: University of London.

The Priory, | 21. North Bank, | Regents Park.
Saturday.
Dear Philosopher
Polly wants to read Mill's Essays on Religion—can you lend her the
book?[5] It would be amicable of you to bring it and diagnose a lunch.

Ever yours truly
The Problematical Thinker.

VI, 102:12   GHL TO SIR ARTHUR HELPS,
LONDON, [DECEMBER 1874]

Text: Correspondence of Sir Arthur Helps, K.C.B., ed. E. A. Helps, 1917, pp. 387–388.

The Priory, | 21. North Bank, | Regents Park.
Wednesday.
My dear Helps
    I have been solacing myself the last four nights with the conversations
of your Friends in Council[6] which remind me so vividly of the many delightful conversations at Vernon Hill—only more delightful than those of
the Milverton group because I sometimes had the satisfaction of hearing
the sound of my own voice! What a characteristic—and delicious—touch,
for instance, is that at p. 148, where Ellesmere remarks that "Milverton
says very good when I answer his secretary's objection. He did not say so
when I answered his own." But the book is full of good things.
    Query: wasn't the unknown sayer of that saying at p. 84 Goethe?[7] I
have a dim sense that he was. But I am quite certain that Carlyle is not the

5. John Stuart Mill, *Three Essays on
Religion*, 1874. GHL notes his reading of
it 7–8 December 1874. (GHL Journal.)
    6. *The Social Pressure*, 1875 (BM copy
received 28 November 1874) consists of
conversations by the Friends in Council
of Helps's earlier volumes.
    7. "Essay on Intrusiveness": "When
a man has once done anything well, the
world will take care that he shall not do

anything more of the same kind." (p.
84.) In discussing *Werther* Goethe said:
"Wenn man der Welt etwas zu Liebe
gethan habe, so wisse sie dafür zu sorgen
dass man es nicht zum zweitenmal
thue." (J.P. Eckermann, *Gespräche mit
Goethe*, ed. W. von Biedermann, 27
January 1827. 10 vols., Leipzig, v
(1890), p. 19.)

author of the Valet de Chambre appreciation of the hero.[8] He got it from Goethe who got it from Hegel (it occurs in the *Philos. der Geschichte*); correct this in your next edition and also modify that passage at p. 392 about the rapidity of nerve transmission.[9] You must have read a very inaccurate account of the experiments, for the impressions do not travel much quicker in one man than in another—there are individual variations, but these all lie within very narrow limits, 29 to 33 metres in a second. (You see I can't move from my last, like a virtuous cobbler!)

I could go on scribbling for some pages, but the cloth is being laid for lunch, and you are spared further remarks.

> Ever yours affectionately,
> G. H. Lewes.

VI, 110:13 GHL TO WILLIAM ALLINGHAM, LONDON, [5 JANUARY 1875]

MS: University of Illinois.

The Priory, | 21. North Bank, | Regents Park.
Tuesday.

Dear Mr. Allingham

As you were kind enough to say you would send us 'Frazers'[10] regularly I should be glad of the January number so as to make the year complete.

Say sweet things from us to the sweet wife and let us see you both soon.

> Yours ever
> G. H. Lewes.

8. "Carlyle's shrewd observation that 'the hero is not a hero to his valet, because the valet is a valet, and not because the hero is not a hero,' does not exhaust that question." [p. 183.] Cf. Goethe, *Maximen und Reflexionen*, 47: "Es gibt, sagt man, für den Kammerdiener keinen Helden. Das kommt aber bloss daher, weil der Held nur vom Helden anerkennt werden kenn. Der Kammerdiener wird aber wahrsche- inlich seines Gleichen zu schätzen wissen." (Weimar, 1907, p. 8.)

9. Helps wrote: "it seemed to be proved that sensations and impressions of all kinds were conveyed to the brain of one man much quicker than to that of another."

10. Allingham became editor of *Fraser's Magazine* in 1874. He and his wife called at the Priory 3 January 1875. (GHL Diary.)

VI, 114:1 GHL TO FREDERIC W. H. MYERS, LONDON, [11 JANUARY 1875]

MS: Trinity College, Cambridge. *Envelope:* F. W. Myers, Esq. | Education Office | Downing St. *Postmark:* LONDON N.W | D 2 | JA 11 | 75.

The Priory, | 21. North Bank, | Regents Park.

Monday.

My dear Myers

I wanted to ask you yesterday if you are disengaged next Sunday and would come to lunch at 1.30? The discussion of Spiritualism drove it out of my head; probably by mediums of unknown powers?

Shall I ask the Harrisons? Or is there any one else you would wish to meet?[11]

Yours ever

G. H. Lewes.

VI, 116:20 GHL TO WILLIAM ALLINGHAM, LONDON, [13 JANUARY 1875]

MS: University of Illinois.

The Priory, | 21. North Bank, | Regents Park.

Wednesday.

Dear Mr. Allingham

Your distrust and dismay might be justifiable were I one of those lofty people who think everything easy because they have never tried to do any one thing, and who supposes that to get "brilliant papers" depends on the editor, not alas! on his contributors. But I have had so many years editorial experience that you might trust me not to confound editor with contributor!

Further your dismay might be justifiable if your sending the Magazine was a peremptory claim on my reading it—dull or not. Whereas the dull papers would be left untouched, without misgiving and only what interested me taken notice of.

Ainsi! Concluez!

Yours ever

G. H. Lewes.

11. Myers was among the callers at the Priory 10 January 1875 but not at lunch 17 January, when the Frederic Harrisons came. (GHL Diary.)

VI, 120:1   GHL TO GEORGE CROOM ROBERTSON,[1]
LONDON, [22 JANUARY 1875]

MS: University College, London.

The Priory, | 21. North Bank, | Regents Park.

Friday.

My dear Robertson

After battering my brain till it is sore I have only been able to knock out this title as an acceptable one: *The Annals of Psychology* (*or* the *Archives of Psychology*)—a quarterly journal of progress (*or* of research) in questions relative to the Science of Mind (*or* in questions subsidiary to and arising out of the Science of Mind).[2]

I think this embraces all you require in a title.

Yours ever

G. H. Lewes.

VI, 126:1   GHL TO JAMES SULLY,
LONDON, [18 FEBRUARY 1875]

MS: University College, London. *Envelope:* James Sully Esq. | 17 Nicoll Road | Willesden | N.W. *Postmark:* ST JOHNS-WOOD N.W | B 12 | FE 18 | 75. *Endorsed:* G. H. Lewes Feb. 18/75. On Senn and Intuition. | Glad to see *me*.

The Priory, | 21. North Bank, | Regents Park.

Thursday.

My dear Sir

I read your "Sensation and Intuition"[3] with so very much interest that it will be a real pleasure to see you tomorrow about 4.30 if that will be convenient (if not, Monday at the same hour) though I fear I cannot be of the slightest aid to you.

Yours truly

G. H. Lewes.

James Sully, Esq.

1. Robertson came to lunch Sunday, 17 January 1875, and consulted GHL "about the new review of Psychology." (GHL Diary.)

2. "In January 1876 appeared the first number of 'Mind,' a title suggested by himself for the only English journal devoted to philosophy." (*DNB*, XVI (1909), 1294.)

3. James Sully (1842–1923), *Sensation and Intuition. Studies in Psychology and Aesthetics*, 1874. GHL's copy is in Dr. Williams's Library. He called Monday, 22 February, "to talk over his projected work on the Psychology of Art." (GHL Diary.)

VI, 126:24 LORD LYTTON TO GHL, PARIS, 19 FEBRUARY 1875

MS: Yale.

B[ritish] Embassy Paris | 19 February 1875.

My dear friend,

I begin this letter feeling like Virgil's ghost 'whose voice long silence had made faint.'[3a] But ever since my return to Paris, whither I was summoned by telegraph the very evening after my pleasant day in the country with you and your dear wife, my life has been one incessant fatiguing *hurry*—suspended only by intervals of ill health—my nearest approach to rest.

I write now with a special purpose. When I last saw you I had with me a printed copy of a poem which has been long between hammer and anvil, and about which I then spoke to you. You wished to see it, and I greatly wished to shew it you, but kept it by me to correct some misprints. My sudden change of place and occupation however put this and many other things for a while out of my head—and then I began to retouch and little by little to recast the poem—always seeing before me some further improvement to be made in it. I did not like to send it you in its transition state—but I have now had a fresh copy printed for my own convenience—and this copy I should greatly like to submit to you before it passes the rubicon of publication.

I remember however that when we were last together you were thinking of a flight into Egypt—and I know not whether this letter will find you in England. If it does pray spare me a line to say whether I can forward the poem to you.

I have accepted the post to Lisbon chiefly for the sake of rest and economy which fail me here. I expect to be, with my ménage, in England shortly—probably in the course of next month—and I think we shall not start for our new post before May, so that we count on seeing you twixt this and then. Edith joins me in numberless affectionate loves to George Elliot and yourself. How are you, dear friends?

Our friend Villers who has come from his Austrian Farm to share with us our last days at Paris, and is now staying with us greets you cordially. Pray believe me

Your ever affectionate
Lytton.

3a. Dante, *Inferno*, I, 63.

VI, 126:24   GHL TO LORD LYTTON, LONDON, [21–22 FEBRUARY 1875]

MS: Lady Hermione Cobbold.

The Priory, | 21. North Bank, | Regents Park.
Sunday.

My dear Lytton

Last night the "Fables" came back having been lent to a sympathetic reader; and this morning I have been rereading some of my special favorites. This naturally carries my thoughts to Paris and from Paris to Earlswood Common with memories of the too brief visit you paid us there[4] and the promise you then made to send me a proof of your new poem.[5] I don't reproach you for not having done so because of course hurried and harried as you must have been since then you could not think of such matters, and as I see no advertisement of the poem as forthcoming I suppose you haven't even been able to read the proof yourself.

The news of your being appointed to Constantinople was contradicted but that of your appointment to Lisbon[6] has not been contradicted, so we conclude it is true. You will come to England of course before going to Cintra and if you have any shred of decent friendship left, you won't be so niggardly of yourself and donna as you were last year, but let us have a good spell of you if you can.

My second volume is out at last,[7] and I shall be curious to know what impression the final problem makes on you with its complete turning the tables on the materialist hypothesis of Feeling as a mode of Motion.[8] I am now hard at work and at *the* subject nearest my heart—indeed I compare myself now to a duck which after painfully and ungracefully picking its way over the stony bank glides on to the water and expresses its complacency at once more finding itself in the proper element by a conceited wagging of the tail. I wag continuously!

Madonna is also at work but, unlike her duck is not to be induced to wag her tail or feel anything but the misery of misgiving and a profound

---

4. Lytton came 21 August 1874 to spend the day and night. See GHL Diary, 21–22 August 1874.

5. *King Poppy*, proof of which GHL read 24 February–2 March 1875, was privately printed 1875, but not published until 1892.

6. Lytton was appointed Envoy-extraordinary and Minister-plenipotentiary to Portugal 26 November 1874.

7. *Problems of Life and Mind. First Series. The Foundations of a Creed*, vol. II, was published 23 February 1875.

8. Problem VI. "The Absolute in the Correlations of Feeling and Motion," pp. 425–506.

sense of her own impotence. She bids me send her love to your donna, whose sweet hands I also kiss.

You generally send me a good story. Here is one I send as a *bait*. The frightful poisonings of the Borgias were being talked of in presence of a papal nuncio, and on his being asked how it was that such horrors could be committed, he rubbed his unctuous hands and blandly said, Monsieur, ça peut simplifier bien des choses.

Ever yours
G. H. L.

I open this (Monday morning) to say your note, just come in, has answered it.

VI, 127:11   GHL TO LORD LYTTON, LONDON, 3 MARCH 1875

MS: Lady Hermione Cobbold.

The Priory, | 21. North Bank, | Regents Park.

3 March 75.

My dear Lytton

I have gone slowly and scrutinizingly through your proof—and, as you will see from the smallness of some of the details objected to, not passed over anything that fastidious anxiety for perfection could pass over. Since I have restricted the remarks to fault-finding and queries, let me say with as distinct an emphasis as I can that my admiration and delight were so great that if the poem does not achieve a great and lasting success it will be your fault—that is it will, I firmly believe, be placed among the few poems that deserve to live provided you are stoic enough to inflict severe gashes on your child and cut its fair proportions into one volume. Hazlitt used to say fortitude of mind was *the* great quality of a dramatist since he was enabled to suppress the fine things suggested to him at every step in favor of those only which were dramatically in keeping. Now it is this fortitude which you have not displayed—but you may yet display it when you come to realize the old Greek adage "the half is better than the whole,"[9] for on this point and the reasons for the excisions—I must have a long quiet talk with you. I couldn't say what I want in a letter however lengthy; for I must know your feeling about certain points.

Remember that as a fantastic poem—(by the way would it not be well to christen it a Phantasy?) it must justify itself by unusual perfection of

9. "The half is greater than the whole." Hesiod, *Works and Days*, 40.

treatment.[10] Now that perfection it has—in parts—and *may* have through-out. My criticisms have been almost exclusively verbal; and the sort of things I should say unter vier augen only.

Not knowing when you leave Paris I send this to Knebworth with the copy.

Ever yours faithfully
G. H. L.

VI, 128:21   GHL TO LORD LYTTON, LONDON, [7 MARCH 1875]

MS: Lady Hermione Cobbold.

The Priory, | 21. North Bank, | Regents Park.
Sunday.

My dear Lytton

Your niece[11] told me yesterday, at the Concert that you were coming to Cavendish Square[1] and not to Knebworth. Now I presupposing that you would go there dispatched my criticisms and the copy to that address. Send for them, and read them as the remarks of one truly interested in your success, and therefore *not* willing to slur over objectionable points. I firmly believe you have only to hold out your hand to grasp a great and lasting success. No such fantastic poem has come in my way for many years—and by it I think you may realize the promise of your youth. But severe surgery will be necessary and the two volumes must be reduced to one.

In great haste

Ever yours
G. H. L.

10. Phantasos is one of the characters in *King Poppy*.

11. The Lyttons' nieces were still infants. GHL probably saw Lady Lytton's sister Mrs. Charles William Earle. See v, 88, note 7.

1. To Marshall and Thompson's Hotel.

VI, 129:15 LORD LYTTON TO GHL,
[LONDON, 16 MARCH 1875]

MS: Yale.

Tuesday.

Dearest Lewes

We propose a pilgrimage to the Priory next Thursday.[2] Will the Prior and Prioress receive us at 3.30 p.m.? I find that 4.30 will be too late for Edith.

You have my dear friend been so singularly kind and helpful about my Poppy[3] that I am encouraged to bespeak for myself the advantage of ten minutes' talk with you about it when we meet. I think I need not then detain you a moment longer—on that subject—if in the meanwhile you can oblige me by glancing over the accompanying copy—on which I have marked proposed omissions some of them contemplated before I received your letter, others suggested by your letter. The marks are slovenly—but as regards the particular point (my abridgment) which it is desirable to settle before considering other alterations (of meter or expression) I think you will find them sufficiently intelligible.

If you will give me on Thursday your opinion upon these proposed omissions with any further suggestions that may have occurred to you— I will then take back with me the copy now sent. I have not yet attended to all your suggestions for verbal alteration but every one of them shall be carried out.

I was so glad to make your son's acquaintance the other day.[4] What a bright *sympathetic* frank face and manner he has!

Not a word have I yet had with Mrs. Lewes. Sunday is a very interesting day, but as it is her Court day when one can only pass and kiss hands I shall hope for a private audience now and then.[5]

There are two things I much want to speak to you about. Pray remind me to do so next Thursday. One is a matter about vivisection, and the other is about some unpublished plays of my father.

Your affect.

Lytton.

2. Lord Lytton and Lady Lytton called and chatted for an hour, Thursday, 18 March 1875. (GHL Diary.)
3. GHL had been reading proofs of Lytton's *King Poppy* since 24 February.
4. Charles Lewes was at the Priory Sunday, 14 March, when Lytton called.
5. Lord Lytton and Lady Lytton called Friday, 26 March, and went with GE and GHL to see Burne-Jones's studio. (GHL Diary.)

VI, 134:18 HERBERT ARTHUR LEWES TO GHL, BELFAST, 29 MARCH 1875

MS: Nuneaton Public Library.

Belfast | March 29th 1875.

Dearest Pater

I have been so ill I have not been able to write or I should have done so long ago. I think I am getting a little better, but am far from strong or well. My weight now is 118 *lbs.* The Neuralgia "thank goodness" has left me, and I hope will never return.

Many many thanks for the 100£.⁶ I at once took your advice and bought myself a case of Porter and got other medical advice. Eliza is not well, she expects to be confined in May. Marian grows very well and interesting. I have no more news at present.

Love to you and Little Mutter from us all.

Your affectionate son
H. A. Lewes.

VI, 136:31 JOHN BLACKWOOD TO WM. BLACKWOOD, EDINBURGH, 22 APRIL 1875

Text: John Blackwood, p. 386.

I had great pleasure in receiving your letter to-day. The interview with the Leweses must have been deeply interesting, and I only wish you could have reported her looking better. I have seen her several times in those depressed states about her work, but always when she fairly began to speak one felt that there was occasion not for depression but for rejoicing. Certainly she does seem to feel that in producing her books she is producing a living thing, and no doubt her books will live longer than is given to children of the flesh.

6. GHL received a letter 2 December 1874 from Bertie's father-in-law Mr. Harrison about his health and poverty. He sent Bertie £100 on 4 December, and his list of charities for 1875 is headed with another "Bertie £100." (GHL Diary.)

VI, 138:1 GHL TO LORD LYTTON,
LONDON, 28 APRIL [1875]

Text: Copy in the collection of Lady Hermione Cobbold.

The Priory, | 21. North Bank, | Regents Park.

28 April.

My dear Lytton

I began the poems[7] with the intention of trying half a dozen, and read every one of them—some twice. From this alone you will gather that I am decidedly of your opinion as to the vintage being truly that of the grape, and not the gooseberry. But some of the bottles taste 'corked,' and some have allowed the alcoholic fermentation to pass into the acetic. They are in truth of very unequal quality. They all however have a real *poetic quality*, and I was particularly struck with the fact that although the work of a young writer they have neither the ordinary reflex of any one of the poets of the day—are neither Tennysonian, Browningian, Swinburnian, nor Morrisian—nor have they the other defects of young writers namely the tinsel and trick of 'poetic diction,' and the extravagance mistaken for effect. All *coule de source*; and with a quiet reserve of power which is very unusual. There are real notes of feeling, and genuine expression of thought, which promise in the writer a remarkable poet—but if you want the counsel of *un vieux renard*, it is to the effect that the author would be wise not to publish at present. Let him put these poems by, and not look at them for two or three years; if at the end of that time he, coming upon them with a fresh eye, still finds them the expression of what he feels and means, then by all means let him trust them to the public; but my belief is that he will *then* be very glad he did not prematurely come before the public; and will reject several, altering others.

The very selectness of the quality implies only appreciation from a select audience, and for that audience nothing but what is exquisite should be preserved. There is a great difference between poems it is worth writing and preserving for oneself, and poems to be given to the public. A flaw which is not remarked in delf, becomes serious in china. Were the author less unmistakably a poet I should not urge the delay; but in his case, I think the delay of primary importance. At any rate should he decide on publica-

7. "Lord Lytton sent me some M.S. poems of a friend of his to advise upon. Read them." (GHL Diary, 27 April 1875.) The friend was probably Wilfrid Scawen Blunt (1840–1922), who came himself to the Priory and "brought his M.S. poems for me to decide on." (GHL Diary, 7 May 1875.) His *Sonnets and Songs by Proteus* were published in 1875.

tion let him be firm in keeping to the anonymous—for this reason: the public always *classes* a writer, and having classed him according to one standard, is very unwilling to view him in any other light. I write in haste, but not hastily.

Ever yours truly
G. H. Lewes.

Since I have no hesitation in my opinion, and would say publicly what I have said here as to the power of the poems, you may, if you think fit, tell the author my name. I mean if you think that it will add to the *sincerity* of the advice.

VI, 140:1 C. L. LEWES TO MRS. NASSAU SENIOR, LONDON, 3 MAY 1875

MS: Birmingham Reference Library.

3 May 1875.

My dear Mrs. Senior,

At last the great work is finished![8] I propose if you think you will be well enough to see me to bring it down to you tomorrow afternoon after office, reaching you about five.[9] I will read it to you and if necessary leave it with you to go through afterwards by yourself. I will bring back at the same time the books you have so kindly lent me. I am looking forward to seeing you again, and hope you will be well enough to see me. But don't let me fatigue you. If it will fatigue you, I can send the article to you by post, or rather as there is so much to return I will come down, but won't see you, if you are not fit. Please send me a line, because if you will not be well enough, I have some friends near with whom I will go and spend the evening, as I shall be in their neighbourhood and I must let them know I'm coming.

Yours ever
C. L. Lewes.

8. See GE to John Blackwood, 2 and 11 November 1874. Lewes's article entitled "The Education of the Children of the State," *Edinburgh Review*, 142 (July 1875), 89–110, defends Mrs. Senior's *Report as to the Effect on Girls of the System of Education at Pauper Schools*, the 3d annual report of the Local Government Board, 1874, which had been attacked by Edward Carleton Tufnell, a former Inspector of Poor Law Schools in London, 8 February 1875; Mrs. Senior's *Reply* listed the names of ladies who had helped her investigate some 670 girls.

9. Mrs. Senior lived at Brighton.

VI, 140:1   GHL TO LORD HOUGHTON, LONDON, 4 MAY [1875]

MS: Trinity College, Cambridge.

The Priory, | 21. North Bank, | Regents Park.
4 May.

My dear Lord Houghton

Mrs. Lewes is at present unable to write, being confined to her bed; and although I have no reason to suppose she would not be well enough on Saturday to accept your kind invitation yet as she *may* be still disabled, and it would not do to leave two gaps in your party which might so well be filled up, I had perhaps better take the safe side and ask you to excuse us.

Hoping to see you soon, Believe me

Yours truly,
G. H. Lewes.

VI, 140:1   GHL TO LORD LYTTON, LONDON, 4 MAY 1875

MS: Lady Hermione Cobbold.

The Priory, | 21. North Bank, | Regents Park.
4 May 75.

My dear Lytton

We were both greatly delighted at the *recognition* which the splendid offer[1] implied, but were quite of opinion that you are right in declining it. Money and dignities are good things, but they are very small things in comparison with Health and the Affections. Moreover there is this reflection: since the government recognize your fitness for so high a post they will recognize it for some less considerable and more acceptable post. You won't be long at Cintra!

We had a delightful visit to Jowett.[2] The only guests in the house were Charles Bowen[3] and the Lansdownes[4]—the latter we had not seen. He is

1. In January 1875 Lytton was offered the governorship of Madras, which he declined. He returned to Lisbon 13 May.
2. See vi, 138–139.
3. See v, 234, n. 7.
4. Henry Charles Keith Petty-Fitz-maurice, 5th Marquess of Lansdowne (1845–1927), whose mother was a daughter of Comte de Flahault, married in 1869 Lady Maud Evelyn Hamilton, daughter of the 1st Duke of Abercorn. Jowett had been his tutor at Balliol.

bright and amiable (with a touch of French blood) she is amiable but not bright. Of course we saw a crowd and some of the crowd very interesting. But on Monday morning about 4, Polly had a recurrence of her kidney attack and for three hours was in great pain. I got her safely home, however, and she is now in bed with a bad headache, but not suffering otherwise. She sends her love to the Ambassadress, and rejoices in her escape from India.

Ever yours truly
G. H. Lewes.

Thanks for '*Roland*.'[5]

VI, 141:16 GHL TO MRS. CHARLES BRAY, LONDON, [8 MAY 1875]

MS: Yale.

The Priory, | 21. North Bank, | Regents Park.

Dear Mrs. Bray

Alas! Marian is in such an uncertain state of health—recovering from another bad attack of her old enemy which came on on Monday morning at 4 o'clock—(and while we were on a visit to Jowett at Oxford and I didn't know where the servants slept, so couldn't get her hot water or any other aid!) that it is only a bare chance she may be well enough to see you on Wednesday. In this case we think the best thing for us to do will be to come to you at the Calls about ¼ to 3 on Wednesday *if* she is well enough and we can drive you in the park if the weather is fine, if not you can have your talk in the drawingroom.[6] This arrangement seems the most feasible under the circumstances though she would like to have you to lunch if she felt sure of herself.

Yours very truly
G. H. Lewes.

If we are not with you by 3 you will know the cause.

5. I cannot find this memorial to his son Rowland.

6. "We went to see Cara at the Calls and drove her in Park." (GHL Diary, 12 May 1875.)

VI, 144:1 HERBERT ARTHUR LEWES TO GHL,
DURBAN, [17 MAY] 1875

MS: Nuneaton Public Library.

Durban 17th | 1875.

Dearest Pater

I arrived a week ago[7] in Durban regular done up. I travelled in my wagon with a Transport Load from Newcastle to P[ieter] M[aritz] Burg. I was ill the whole time and very glad to get to P. M. Burg. I sent the wagon back and came in the Bus from P. M. B. to here. I had the Doctor next day and he has been attending every [day] since. All my glands are swollen and before I left home I got the Mumps. They caused me a great deal of pain. I have not got rid of the swellings yet. The Doctor recomends good living and has given me some medecine. I am at an Hotel, I have a very comfortable room. Just fancy I have got Natal sores[8] I did not think I should get them it is only newcomers that get them. Eliza was confined on the 16th of a fine son[9] so her Granmoder writes me. I have a very bad cold I had it now two months. I hope I shall soon get rid of it. Thanks we have received the Box of Books we have reading now for years. I have not drawn any money on you as I have so far had sufficient, but I shall be very glad of some to pay the doctor and Hotel.

Please excuse such bad writing it is so hot. Did you get my last letter with a penny stamp on it. That was the Postmasters doing.

Love to little Mutter and self from your

Affectionate son
H. A. Lewes.

I will try and write more next time.

7. Herbert reached Durban 16 May and began this letter the 17th, but was too ill to finish it.
8. A kind of boil.

9. George Herbert Lewes, born at Newcastle 16 May 1875, died at Perth, Australia, 10 November 1956.

VI, 144:1   GHL TO J. R. OSGOOD & CO., LONDON, 24 MAY 1875

MS: Yale.

The Priory, | 21. North Bank, | Regents Park.
24 May 75.

Gentlemen

Very shortly I shall send you early sheets of a little book I am to publish on Actors and the Art of Acting which will I dare say have even a better sale in America than in England.[1] If you think it worth republishing on the old royalty terms, I shall be satisfied.

In October or November next also I shall bring out a new edition of my Life and Works of Goethe. In the ten years that have elapsed since the last edition there have been very many works published in Germany from which I shall glean interesting details. Would you also like to issue this? You had the old book.

I presume your remittance promised for this month is on the way.[2]

Believe me

Yours very truly
G. H. Lewes.

Messrs. J. R. Osgood & Co.

VI, 147:19   GE TO FREDERIC HARRISON, LONDON, 28 MAY 1875

MS: University of North Carolina.

The Priory, | 21. North Bank, | Regents Park.
May 28. 75.

Dear Mr. Harrison

I wish very much to ask you a question or two before we leave town. Could you and Mrs. Harrison kindly manage to give me an hour by lunching with us on Sunday?[3]

1. *On Actors and the Art of Acting*, published by Smith & Elder, 1875, was inscribed to Anthony Trollope with a prefatory letter. Osgood did not publish the book nor the revised *Goethe*.

2. A payment of £147.7.9 from Osgood is recorded in June 1875 for "Problems, Poems, etc." (GHL Diary.)

3. They did not come to lunch.

I hope that it will not be difficult to take us in your way from the School, if you are bent in that direction.

Always yours sincerely

M. E. Lewes.

VI, 147:19 JOHN BLACKWOOD TO WM. BLACKWOOD, LONDON, 29 MAY [1875]

MS: National Library of Scotland.

The Burlington, May 29.

Yesterday Molly[4] and I drove up to the Priory where we passed a most charming hour with Mrs. Lewes. She was in great spirits and talked much with Molly enquiring if she ever intended to send her father a M.S. I said writing apparently does not run in the family. She said with empressement, "Writing good letters certainly does." She enquired minutely as to Molly's dress for the reception, from which I learn that it is to be green with orange flowers. . . .

VI, 150:13 GHL TO J. R. OSGOOD & CO., LONDON, 9 JUNE 1875

MS: Princeton.

The Priory, | 21. North Bank, | Regents Park.

June 9th 75.

Messrs. J. R. Osgood & Co.

Gentlemen

Your draft for £147.7.9 is duly come to hand, for which thanks.

I wrote to you a few days ago about a little book, the sheets of which will be sent you, on Actors and the Art of Acting—also about a new edition

---

4. Blackwood's daughter Mary (Mrs. John Porter, 1855–1939) describes the visit: "On one occasion when we were calling on her that summer she said she was very anxious about the safety of the MS. of 'Deronda,' and wanted to have it back, but dared not trust it to the post-office. My father said he could not bring it himself next day, but could send it by a trusty messenger (the footman). At this she quailed. 'Oh, he might stop at a public-house and forget it.' We assured her such a lapse had never been known to occur. 'Then might he not, if he were the sort of high-minded Bayard we described, be very likely to stop and help at a fire?' This was a contingency we had never contemplated, and finally, after much laughter, we promised that some member of the family should place the MS. in her hands, and as a matter of fact I think my mother drove over with it to her the next morning." (*John Blackwood,* pp. 388–389.)

of the Life and Works of Goethe to be published in October or November. No doubt you will have received it.

Yours truly

G. H. Lewes.

VI, 150:13 GHL TO GEORGE SMITH, LONDON [10 JUNE 1875]

MS: National Library of Scotland. *Envelope:* George Smith Esq | 15 Waterloo Place | S.W. *Postmark:* LONDON N.W | 4 | JU 10 | 75.

The Priory, | 21. North Bank, | Regents Park.

Thursday.

Dear Smith

The printers are going on at a satisfactory rate, and I return for press by each post. I don't know whether it is an oversight of theirs or an intention that they make the running head Actors and Acting instead of 'On Actors and the *Art* of Acting'—at any rate that is how I wish the book advertized.[5]

Will you please order proofs when struck off to be addressed to J.R. Osgood and Co., Boston U.S.

Ever yours truly

G. H. Lewes.

VI, 154:5 HERBERT ARTHUR LEWES TO GHL, DURBAN, [24? JUNE 1875]

MS: Nuneaton Public Library.

Durban.

Dearest Pater

I was obliged to draw upon you for £50. I have been here a month and my own money has been down some time. I am better than when I last wrote. All my glands are swollen. My ankels and feet have been swollen so that I could not get my boots on. The Doctor attends me me about every other day. He says I progress too slowly so has changed medecines.

I forgot to thank you in my last for [x] It has been touch and go with me. I feel it will take some time to get back my old strenght. I have been expecting a letter from you every mail. Did you get mine of last month?[6]

5. The book was published 3 July 1875 with the running head as GHL wished it.

6. Unfinished. His letter of [23 May] arrived 4 July 1875.

VI, 154:5 JOHN H. SANDERSON[7] TO GHL,
DURBAN, 2 JULY 1875

MS: Nuneaton Public Library.

D'Urban, Natal, 2nd July 1875.
George Henry Lewes, Esq. | The Priory, | 21 North Bank, | Regents' Park.
Sir,

I fear the latest accounts of his state of health which you may have had
from your son Herbert will hardly have prepared you for the intelligence
of his death which it is my sad duty to communicate. It took place on the
29th June, and to me was very unexpected, as he always represented himself as gaining in flesh and strength.

You may be aware that Thornton used to frequent my house, and
naturally on Herbert's arrival brought him to us. From that time however,
excepting seeing him with Thornton at the house of the Bishop of Natal[8]
shortly after, I had seen nothing of him until quite lately. He arrived in
Durban some weeks ago in the absence of Mrs. Sanderson and myself, but
on our return, hearing accidentally that he was in town, I sent a message
to him, and from that time he paid us a long visit every two or three days,
conversing, reading, getting Mrs. Sanderson to play for him on the piano,
or taking an hour's nap on the couch. The last time he came to us was on
Thursday, the 24th. He appeared weak and tired, and asked Mrs. Sanderson to give him a shake-down. We made him as comfortable as possible
and he retired about nine o'clock. Mrs. Sanderson told him he must not
get up to breakfast, but he did so, having he said, slept well,—a thing he
had not done for two or three nights previously. He left our house about
ten o'clock that day, Friday, and we did not see him again until Monday,
when we called at his quarters. He appeared much worse, very feeble, but
insisted on coming out to the sitting room to see Mrs. Sanderson. He was
apparently in good spirits, but we were shocked at the change in his
appearance. About seven o'clock on the following evening the people of
the house sent to say it would be needful to get some one to sit with him
all night, and we procured a nurse. I immediately went to him myself, a
second messenger coming for me just as I was setting out. I found him
breathing with great difficulty, and almost unable to articulate. He took
my hand two or three times and said it was kind of me to come to see him,

---

7. John H. Sanderson, editor of the
Natal Colonist in Durban, had written
earlier for Glasgow newspapers. (A. F.
Hattersley, *The British Settlement of Natal,*
Cambridge, 1950, p. 184.)
   8. John William Colenso (1814–83),
Bishop of Natal.

and afterward addressed me by name, although I could not quite make out whether he was endeavoring to assure himself of my identity or not. In answer to my questions he said he had no pain. While I was there, Dr. Taylor who had been sent for, for the second time that day, when the attack came on in the afternoon, came in. He told me Herbert could not live many hours. On asking if he had made him aware of this, he said no: it was of no use: he was too far gone.

Excepting for a few minutes I remained till all was over. The Dr. said he would choke if laid down, and so he sat in an arm-chair, with some one of his fellow lodgers or me supporting him. A mustard plaster had been applied three times in succession without effect. A dose of medicine was given him every hour. About half past nine he asked for tea, which was at once made for him and he eagerly swallowed a mouthful or two. As I sat by him, holding his hand, and supporting his head with my left, he seemed to make several attempts to speak without being able to articulate, and my endeavors to help him were of no avail. About five minutes to ten I thought he said something about bread—more probably he meant breath, but his breathing became less violent and as nearly as possible at ten o'clock, with one or two slight gasps he died, so peacefully and without effort or struggle that I continued with his forehead resting in my hand, not sure that he might not yet revive. We at once sent for Dr. Taylor, but he did not think it needful to come; and being assured that all was over, the landlord asked me to take charge of his watch and other property and arrange for the funeral, which I did on the following morning after consulting with Mr. Brickhill, the Manager of the Bank through whom he had lately drawn upon you. I also at once wrote to Mr. Harrison, his father-in-law, to break the news to the poor young wife, who as you are probably aware had been confined of a fine boy since Herbert left home.

I have thought it might be some satisfaction that I should tell you all I could of his last days, and I enclose a note briefly describing the course of his illness since he has been in Durban, which at my request Dr. Taylor has written. I believe he was as comfortable as it was possible for him to be in a public hotel. The people of the house were kind to him, and one or two of his fellow-lodgers he was friendly with, and sat up with him, or did little offices for him. Mrs. Sanderson and I were always glad to see him and he seemed to enjoy coming to us. [*Two lines deleted.*]

Of course he had not many friends or even acquaintances here, but about a dozen followed him to the grave, which is under the shadow of the trees in the beautiful Episcopal Cemetery, the service being read by Archdeacon Lloyd.[9]

9. W. H. C. Lloyd, Archdeacon of St. Peter's Cathedral, Durban.

I must now trouble you with some business matters as you will doubtless be anxious to know how these stand. Pending instructions from Mrs. Lewes or her father, I have taken possession of all Herbert's little belongings, including a gold watch (French), a breast pin with hair encircled by an enameled serpent, and a gold stud. Of cash I found £14.1.4. In his pocketbook I find a memorandum of having drawn upon you for £50 on the— (blank) June, the discount on which 10/–leaves £49.10.–to be accounted for.

I copy the entry verbatim:–

c On the June (*sic*) 1875
Drawn on Pater for
£50 Bank discount 10/
£49.10.0

	£10.	–.	–
Paid Ingle Hotel	8.	–.	–
Eliza	8.	–.	–

I find no receipt for the £10 nor have I yet been able to ascertain what it refers to. Assuming it however to be a payment of some kind hereafter to be accounted for, the above amount with £2. borrowed of a fellow lodger and repaid after drawing upon you, will within a few pence amount to the cash to be accounted for. Thus:

(To be yet explained)	10.	–.	–
Hotel Bill	8.	6.	6
Mrs. H. A. Lewes	8.	–.	–
Loan from Mr. Pardy, repaid	2.	–.	–
Cash paid for a revolver on account of Mr. C. I. Harrison	7.	–.	–
Cash in my hands	14.	1.	4
	£49.	7.	10
deficiency		2.	2
	£49.	10.	–

I hope, through Mr. Harrison, or otherwise, to be able to explain the item of £10. There are certain bills to pay, the hotel bill £14.2.–, the doctor's bill and the funeral expenses, the statements for which have not yet been sent to me. For these, I fear, I shall be under the necessity of drawing upon you, as I know his poor wife is badly off, and was almost without a penny until he sent the little remittance noted above. Her father I presume will at once repay her the £7 advanced by Herbert for him as he had arranged to do: but with two helpless babes she must be in great straits. Herbert seemed very proud of his daughter. The name fixed on for the boy was I believe George Henry Arthur.

On hearing from Mr. Harrison I shall probably write to you further. I enclose a little hair I cut for you. I do not know that I have anything further to say at present. Probably Herbert explained the origin of the illness, which the Doctor told me would in England have taken the form of consumption of the lungs, but here seems to have attacked other organs. He had been exerting himself violently driving his wagon up a long ascent and on reaching the top threw off his coat and took a chill. This was in January. He coughed a good deal, and told me his glands were much swollen. Latterly his feet swelled greatly. He was always hopeful and thought himself improving in health, but his breathing was so difficult that we rather discouraged talking. I cannot think that even up to almost the last he thought his end so near.

I trust that you will not think because I have said nothing about it that I do not feel the deepest sympathy for you in this second sad loss, and will only add that if I can be of any service to you in any way here I beg that you will command me.—Believe me, Sir,

Most faithfully yours,
John Sanderson.

I have reason to hope he had had his likeness taken here, but have made enquiry without success.—The age stated in the paper herewith, 27, is that named by himself to a fellow lodger. I have this moment found an unfinished letter to you which I enclose.—I hope to be able to write with final settlement of everything next mail and tell you something of the poor young widow and her babes. She seems a fine brave girl, most unselfish and entirely devoted to her husband and children, but I fear, delicate. I should dread the effects of this blow upon her.

VI, 154:5 MRS. JOHN H. SANDERSON TO GE, DURBAN, 3 JULY 1875

MS: Nuneaton Public Library.

D'Urban, July 3 /75.

My dear Madam

I write a few hasty lines at my husband's request to give you such little details about dear Herbert as came under my own particular observation though there is but little to add.

It was unfortunate that we were absent during the first month or more of his residence in D'Urban as we might have helped to make it less lonely for him but we were very glad that once having found his way here he seemed quite at home with us and used to come in and stay for a few hours whenever he felt inclined: the last time we had seen him, previous to his last sad visit, was in '66 when Thornton and he dined and slept at Bishopstown where Mr. Sanderson and I were staying at the time—they were both full of life and energy then and we were particularly struck by Herbert's good sense and quiet cheerfulness, which contrasted well with but did not spoil Thornton's gay, good natured, winning manner; you can understand how shocked we were when the latter came down here evidently in the last stages of his fatal disease; he came in to our house, looking like the ghost of his former self, quite suddenly one day and I shall never forget the shock it gave me, but when a few short weeks ago the same thing happened with Herbert I was almost too much overpowered to greet him; he was very cheerful and hopeful about himself and as he said that he had gained flesh since he came down I tried to hope that he was not so bad as he appeared to be—we used to have pleasant talk about different things— Middlemarch for instance—and other interesting matters of that sort in which he seemed much interested but after the first visit I never asked him many questions as his breathing was so difficult at times that I did not encourage him to talk—he said very little about his own affairs, and as I did not know any thing of his wife or her family there was not much scope for conversation on these points: his last visit will ever be one of my saddest recollections; he was so much exhausted when he came in that he fell into a deep sleep while sitting in an easy chair and it was very soon evident that he would not be able to go back to his hotel that day; our own spare room being unoccupied we were able to make him comfortable and the next morning he was much refreshed and made a good breakfast. I was unwilling to let him go and begged him to wait till the afternoon thinking that I should induce him to sleep here again but he would not be persuaded to remain and I did not like to worry him, so he left here to return and I only saw him once afterwards when Mr. Sanderson and I called to see him at the hotel.

For his poor young wife, left with two babies we feel the greatest sympathy and I cannot help thinking of her constantly as I believe she is very weakly and this dreadful shock so soon after her confinement may be very serious, and then the desolation! Poor young creature! I met with a lady the other day who knew Herbert in Newcastle—she told me that he was greatly esteemed and liked in that neighborhood. She also told me that his little girl was a most lovely and engaging child—the most beautiful little girl she ever saw was the expression she used. It was a question with her whether Herbert ought to be told of his danger—the doctor said nothing and before we could decide what seemed the best he sank—for my own part I am inclined to think that it was better not to say anything and so spare him the bitterness of knowing that he was to die far away from those he loved best and who were fondly hoping to see him return to them restored in health and ready to face the struggles of life again. To the last he said he was getting better.

I shall always regret not having been here when he came down and also that my husband's duties as editor of a newspaper did not allow him more time to devote to the invalid.

We shall never forget Herbert. I must now conclude this very sad letter and am

Yours sincerely
Marie Sanderson.

VI, 160:28   MRS. HERBERT ARTHUR LEWES TO GHL, SANDFONTEIN, 6 AUGUST 1875

MS: Nuneaton Public Library.

Sandfontein | August 6th 1875.

Dear Pater

For the last week or two I have been thinking I ought to write to you and tell you what little I can about my beloved Herbert. It is yet an effort for me to write, and to you, but if it meet your approbation I am repaid.

My darling seemed to be getting thiner and thiner after we returned from Utrecht, he felt the cold very much and always went to bed before the sun had set, then he would have a little sleep, then he would have his tea something light a little corn flour or a custard he always eat better during the night of biscuits and raisins or any little thing I could make him, his cough was very troublesome, I was very very anxious about him and sent a Kafer on his horse one night after he had gone to bed, for Mr. Gunner, the man who had been attending him, to come and see him, he came the day after and questioned dear Herbert very much about his cough, his chest and not being able only to sleep on one side he then turned to me and said Herbert must go to Durban for two months to avoid our cold winter and *he assured* to me he would return at the end of that time well and strong. Dear Herbert refused to go. I was not well or strong and could get no one to stay with me and he would not hear of my going too. Mr. G. offered his Kafer woman to come and she did, it was two weeks before I could get him to go, he once said 'I do not think I shall live a month longer in this place' it made me more anxious for him to go, and he believed the change would quite restore him, he left us the 22 of April and he spent a week at a friends in Newcastle, and reached Durban the 16th of May the day his boy was born, he wrote to me once a week in every letter he assured me he was getting stronger faster and better when he had been there two weeks he got weighed he had gained twelve pounds, I was so happy and contented then, I had had a severe confinement. I wrote and told him he had got such a fine big boy—he wrote and said "I always told you I wanted a boy like you is it like you?" No it is a true Lewes like its Father. You do not know how dear we were to each other and what *I* have lost, when he painted his wagon the last thing he did at home, I had to go and admire it. The sail we stitched together the ornaments for our table the cushions for the chairs even the antimacasars we made together. We were rarely apart. You have lost a dear loving son, he always spoke of Pater as *my* Father—and with much depth of affection and the "dear little Mutter"—The very life of my life is gone. I often wonder if it is true and what I can be making the black dresses for. I feel so utterly alone. We had grown so dearly fond of our little Marian. She used to wait on him so nicely, she never let him go to the door without his hat on, without running for Dadda's hat or getting his slippers when he returned home or any thing she saw he wanted. We never told the child to get them. I can see him so plainly now as he would turn from the Piano, lay his hand on her head 'good night god bless you my child.' Had they have let me have known I would have gone to him, but it seems the old Doctor took such a little interest in him, and has given me such unsatisfactory statements about him, and every one says now Mr. Gunner gave him sufficient strychnia and iron to kill any man. He always thought he should soon be all right even in his last letter written only the day before, he said he had walked too far the week before and was ill in a few days he would be better then he would write me a nice long letter, but that was to be the last he would write.

Marian is not old enough to send love but when she is at home she will get on my couch and kiss grandpapa's chair before going in tears because she cannot reach your face.

Love to you and the dear little Mutter.

> Your affectionate Daughter-in-law
> Eliza Lewes.

errors please excuse.

VI, 171:13   GHL TO PAUL LINDAU,[10]
LONDON, 23 SEPTEMBER 1875

MS: Yale.

The Priory, | 21. North Bank, | Regents Park.
23rd September 75.

Dear Sir

Your colleague in the editorship of the 'Gegenwart' has written a friendly letter to me requesting my permission for the publication in your journal of certain chapters from my book on Actors.[1] I cannot decipher his *signature*, and must therefore send my reply through you lest my letter should reach the wrong person.

If there is anything in my trifling little book which you think would interest your public I should have only pleasure in granting the permission asked; and as to honorarium I beg that may be waived altogether. Believe me,

Yours truly
G. H. Lewes.

Dr. Paul Lindau

VI, 180:1   ANTHONY TROLLOPE TO GHL,
LONDON, 1 NOVEMBER 1875

MS: Yale. *Published: The Letters of Anthony Trollope,* ed. B. A. Booth, 1951, pp. 343–344.

39, Montagu Square.
1. November 1875.

My dear Lewes.

I have just completed my second journey round the world, having returned home on Saturday night. I was greeted by your volume on actors and acting and write to say how pleased I am by the book, and by the compliment.[2] I have never studied the science or theory of acting as you have done,—but in almost all that you say you carry me with you. I some-

---

10. Paul Lindau (1839–1919) edited *Die Gegenwart* in Berlin 1872–1901.

1. *Actors and the Art of Acting* was reprinted in Germany by Tauchnitz, 1875.

2. *On Actors and the Art of Acting*, 1875.

GHL's introduction is an "Epistle to Anthony Trollope," who had once "expressed a wish to see some dramatic criticisms which had interested you republished in a more accessible form than the pages of a periodical."

times find myself differing from [you] as to trifles in regard to character. I have always fancied that Shakespeare intended Hamlet to be, not mad, but erratic in the brain, "on and off"—first a little ajar, and then right again, and then again astray. In the scene which you quote[3] as displaying want of reverence it has seemed to me that the language has been intended to ape want of reverence,—to pretend to Horatio and the others that he was at ease etc. etc.

Your admiration of Fechter I cannot understand. To me Macready was a man of supreme intelligence, but with no histronic genius.[4] He never moved me to tears. The greatest actors I ever saw were E. Kean, Rachel, Mars, Got, Lemaitre—a French lady whose name, beginning with B, I forget, and Mrs. Yates,—yes,—and a Frenchman whose name I also forget still alive, beginning with D, and I would add Robson.[5]

I will come up next Sunday, hoping to find you.[6] Yours always with best love to your wife

Most affectionately
A. T.

VI, 185:18 GE TO MME OLGA NOVIKOFF, LONDON, 15 NOVEMBER 1875

MS: Institute of Russian Literature, Academy of Sciences, Leningrad. *Envelope:* Madame Novikoff | Symonds' Hotel | Brook Street | W. *Postmarks:* ST JOHNS WOOD N.W | C 5 | NO 15 | 75; LONDON W | JA | NO 15 | 75.

The Priory, | 21. North Bank, | Regents Park.
November 15. 75.

Dear Madame Novikoff

Many thanks. We are at home now on Sundays from $\frac{1}{2}$ past 2 to $\frac{1}{2}$ past 5, and shall be happy to see you.[7]

Yours very truly
M. E. Lewes.

3. See pp. 137–144.

4. Charles Albert Fechter (1824–79), French actor, whose Hamlet, GHL wrote, "was one of the very best, and his Othello one of the very worst I have ever seen." (p. 131.) William Charles Macready (1793–1873).

5. The actors Trollope lists are Edmund Kean (1787–1833), Elisa Félix Rachel (1820–58), Anne Françoise Hippolyte Mars (1779–1847), Edmond François Jules Gôt (1822–1901), Antoine Louis Prosper Frédérick Lemaître (1800–76), Mrs. Eliza Brunton Yates, and Frederick Robson (1821–64).

6. Trollope and his son Henry called 7 November 1875. (GHL Diary.)

7. In response to this note Mme Novikoff called on 28 November and the first three Sundays in December. (GHL Diary.)

VI, 187:22 GHL TO DAVID MASSON, LONDON, [17? NOVEMBER 1875]

MS: National Library of Scotland.

The Priory, | 21. North Bank, | Regents Park.

My dear Masson

When Williams[8] asked me if I thought he might subscribe to the Carlyle medal[9] (I knowing him to be a devout admirer had told him, not suspecting there was any secrecy preserved) I said he had better apply to you. He will understand if you tell him it is to be restricted to the circle of those *known* to Carlyle.

Mrs. Lewes was very desirous to pay her tribute, but did not suggest it lest women should have been excluded. Herewith her signature.

Yours ever

G. H. Lewes.

I find she has written her signature so badly that I will ask you to send me another prospectus on which she may improve!

VI, 193:12 GHL TO DAVID MASSON, LONDON, [22? NOVEMBER 1875]

MS: National Library of Scotland.

The Priory, | 21. North Bank, | Regents Park.

My dear Masson

Madonna is distressed and 'can't think' what you will think of her stupidity and carelessness when you hear that she has blurred and spoiled the second programe you sent for signature. Enclosed is a clean one on a piece of paper. If that won't do, but if it must be on the programe, forgive the trouble, and send a third! But I suppose this will do as well?[1]

8. Samuel D. Williams, Jr.

9. As Carlyle's 80th birthday approached a group of his friends proposed a tribute. Boehm was commissioned to cut a medallion portrait, cast in gold for Carlyle, in bronze for the subscribers. Masson and John Morley collected 119 signatures to append to an address they composed. On the flap of an envelope, GHL wrote: "A most felicitous idea! Repeats his own tribute to Goethe. GHL" (NLS.) See GHL, *Life and Works of Goethe*, 1854, II, 440–42, Everyman ed., pp. 568–570, for Carlyle's tribute to Goethe in 1831.

1. All the signatures have been cut out and pasted on a single sheet under the address. (Carlyle birthplace, Ecclefechan.)

Williams is a Birmingham Manufacturer—highly cultivated but in no sense distinguished. He wrote a paper on Euthanasia in the Birmingham Essays[2]—and that is all I know of his literary work though I have known him for 20 years. I don't think he has any claim to be admitted unless the circle were a very large one.

Shall we present this memorial in person?[3]

I have been suffering lately from nervous exhaustion which quite incapacitated me for work. But the week before last I was at Cambridge hard at work in the physiological laboratory, and instead of being made worse by it I seem to have recovered something of my old strength (more accurately *feebleness*). I told Blackwood it was another case of Antæus. *He* recovered when he touched the earth—*I* when I handled the frogs.

Ever yours

G. H. L.

VI, 197:20   GHL TO OSCAR BROWNING, LONDON, [13 DECEMBER 1875]

MS: Yale. *Address:* Oscar Browning Esq. | Eton College | Eton. *Postmark:* LONDON N.W | 4 | DE 13 | 75; WINDSOR | C | DE 13 | 75.

Le Prieuré, Lundi.

Nous ferons notre possible—même notre impossible! Envoyez-moi une liste des noms. Nous pensons signer de nos deux noms le même testimonial.[4] Est ce que cela serait convenable?

G. H. L.

2. *Euthanasia*, 1872, in *Essays by Members of the Birmingham Speculative Club*, went through 4 eds. (BM.)

3. GHL was rereading Carlyle's *Heroes and Hero Worship*. (GHL Diary, 24–25 November 1875.)

4. Browning was dismissed from Eton at the end of term 1875. See VI, 127, n. 8.

In April 1876 Sir Edward Knatchbull-Hugessen, whose son the Headmaster Hornby had prevented from entering Browning's house at Eton, introduced the subject in the House of Commons. (H. E. Wortham, *Oscar Browning*, 1927, p. 147.) Browning called at the Priory 19 December 1875.

Daniel Deronda

1876 February 1	*Daniel Deronda*, Book I published.
1876 April 26	GHL on Tennyson's *Queen Mary*.
1876 May 13	GE and GHL meet Rubinstein ("Klesmer") at Lehmanns'.
1876 May 31	GHL presented to King of the Belgians.
1876 June 8	GE finishes writing *Daniel Deronda*.
1876 June–July	Holiday in France and Switzerland.
1876 September 1	*Daniel Deronda*, Book VIII published.
1876 December 6	GE and GHL buy the Heights at Witley.
1876 December 24–28	GE and GHL spend Christmas with Mrs. Cross.
1877 February	GHL has rheumatic gout.
1877 February 18	GE has severe renal attack.
1877 April 17	*Problems*, vol. III, *The Physical Basis Of Mind* published.
1877 May 19–21	GE and GHL visit Jowett at Oxford.
1877 June 12	Harrison asks GE to write for Religion of Humanity.
1877 August 28	John Cross introduces GE and GHL to lawn tennis.
1877 September 29	Pigott and Charles Lewes come to Witley.
1877 October 4	Jowett visits GE and GHL at Witley.
1877 October 7	GHL tells Lady Holland how GE began to write fiction.
1877 October 25–29	GE and GHL visit Halls at Six Mile Bottom.
1877 November 7	GE silent on Edith Simcox's dedication of *Natural Law*.
1877 November 23	Main compiles *The George Eliot Birthday Book*.
1877 December 25	Mrs. Cross seriously ill; GE and GHL alone.

VI, 210:26 GHL TO GEORGE CROOM ROBERTSON, LONDON, [7 JANUARY 1876]

MS: University College, London. *Endorsed:* 7/1/76. Thanks. Glad he is thinking of matter for No. II.

The Priory, | 21. North Bank, | Regents Park.

My dear Robertson

I thought I had given you to understand on learning that Bain was to find the funds,[5] that I should consider all my contributions gratuitous. It is hard enough that he should have to bear the brunt of the inevitable expenses.

No. I seems to me very promising, all the papers are interesting, and that of Pattison[6] a real contribution to the history of our time. Stupendous as the judgment of Prof. Flint seems to be on Brentano[7] I think the review itself quite a pattern of useful notices.

I have one or two things in petto for No. II. When I see you I will consult you about them.

Ever yours truly
G. H. L.

VI, 217:16 GE TO MRS. LAWRENCE RUCK, LONDON, 25 JANUARY 1876

MS: Mrs. Maud Hamer.

The Priory, | 21. North Bank, | Regents Park.

January 25. 76.

Is it not my often remembered friend Mrs. Ruck to whom I am indebted for the lovely white flowers and red berries which are cheering me on my table since yesterday?

5. When *Mind* was established, Professor Alexander Bain undertook all the publishing expenses "on condition that Robertson should be the sole editor." (*DNB, sub* Robertson.) GHL's article was a review 1 (January 1876), 122–125, of F. Lussana and A. Lemoigne, *Fisiologia dei centri nervosi encefalica,* 2 vols., Padua, 1871.

6. Mark Pattison, "Philosophy at Oxford," pp. 82–97.

7. Robert Flint (1838–1910), Professor of Moral Philosophy at St. Andrews 1864–1876, review pp. 116–122 of Franz Brentano's *Psychologie vom empirischen Standpuncte,* Leipzig, 1874.

It is a great encouragement to me to have a sign that I have a place in her thoughts still, and any word from her will always be welcome to

[hers most sincerely
M. E. Lewes].[8]

VI, 221:15   GE TO MRS. RICHARD STRACHEY, LONDON, 16 FEBRUARY 1876

MS: British Museum. *Published:* *TLS*, 16 May 1968, p. 507.

The Priory, | 21. North Bank, | Regents Park.
February 16. 1876.

Dear Mrs. Strachey

It is very sweet and good of you to remember my appeals to your sympathy and to take trouble in consequence. But I am happy to tell you that friends have united in providing for Miss Marks[9] the means of preparation for entering Girton College, and the prospect now before her is altogether hopeful.

If I hear of any other young creature fit and anxious for the excellent office you mention I will send word of her.

My poor husband is in bed with a sharp attack of lumbago, which I hope will be short in proportion to its sharpness.

We miss you. I am rather jealous of the babies, and wish that the "Mitwelt" had a larger share of you.[1]

Mr. Lewes unites with me in kindest regards, and I am always

Truly yours
M. E. Lewes.

8. Signature has been cut away and supplied by Mrs. Ruck.
9. Phoebe Sarah Marks (1854–1923). GHL's charities list for 1875 has "Miss Marks £10."

1. In a note to the *TLS* article Joan Bennett observes that "There were already six Strachey children ranging from sixteen to two years; there were four more to come."

VI, 231:1   GE TO MRS. FREDERICK LEHMANN, LONDON, 5 MARCH [1876]

MS: Princeton

The Priory, | 21. North Bank, | Regents Park.
March 5.

My dear Mrs. Lehmann

I could not send my answer until Mr. Lewes had come in from his walk. He looks very grave and thinks I shall be too much knocked up by the pleasure, but on the whole the temptation is too strong to be withstood and we will be with you next Sunday[2] at 7.30.

I hasten to release your messenger.

Yours always
M. E. Lewes.

VI, 234:13   GE TO GEORGE GROVE, LONDON, 28 MARCH 1876

MS: Royal College of Music, London.

The Priory, | 21. North Bank, | Regents Park.
March 28. 76.

Dear Mr. Grove

Many thanks for your kind letter.[3] I am much cheered and comforted by the encouragement it gives me to hope that some of the purpose which has animated me in writing 'Daniel Deronda' may not be without its fulfilment. I shall know at least that in much of what is to follow I shall have you for a sympathetic reader. Mr. Lewes unites with me in best regards.

Always truly yours
M. E. Lewes.

2. They dined with the Lehmanns Sunday, 12 March 1876. (GHL Diary.)

3. George Grove (1820–1900), author of *The Dictionary of Music and Musicians*, 1878–90, had been instrumental in founding the Palestine Exploration Fund, of which he was Honorary Secretary. Of Mirah he wrote to GE, 27 March [1876]: "You must have thought of our dear Deutsch when you conceived her character.... my memory of him welled up." (Yale.)

VI, 237:7 GHL TO MRS. A. HENRY HUTH, LONDON [? APRIL 1876]

MS: Yale. Watermark: 1875.

The Priory, | 21. North Bank, | Regents Park.
Thursday.
Dear Mrs. Huth
Our rule[4] must be adhered to and we cannot therefore accept your kind invitation.

Yours truly
G. H. Lewes.

VI, 239:1 GHL TO PETER GUTHRIE TAIT, LONDON 16 APRIL [1876]

MS: Miss M. Tait.

The Priory, | 21. North Bank, | Regents Park.
Easter Sunday.
My dear Sir
I have just finished the second reading of your Advances in Science,[5] and although as an outsider my opinion is not worth twopence, you may bear to be told that this outsider found the book instructive and *energetic*. It is indeed alive with energy—kinetic and polemic—and in every chapter the rush drags me along, pushes me on, and sometimes knocks me aside. I only *saw*, I did not *read*. Have you by chance seen Möllner's Cometenlehre, and the drastic passages, about *die Phrase* in Science?
I don't mean you to answer this question.

Ever yours truly
G. H. Lewes.

Prof. P. G. Tait

4. Without GE, GHL "Went to a concert at Mrs. Huth's. . . . Very hot with crowded rooms and a keen cold draught from windows made me quickly depart and drive with Mrs. Benzon and Lily in the Park." (GHL Diary, 30 May 1876.)
5. *Recent Advances in Physical Science,* 1876, printed from shorthand notes of his lecture to the Edinburgh Evening Club, 1874. "Tait, whose religious sentiment was always strong, joined his colleague Balfour Stewart in an endeavour 'to overthrow materialism by a purely scientific argument.'" (*DNB.*)

VI, 242:20   GHL TO THEODORE MARTIN, LONDON [25 APRIL 1876]

MS: University of California Los Angeles.

The Priory, | 21. North Bank, | Regents Park.
Tuesday.

My dear Martin

Thanks for your pleasant letter and enclosure. Your critical friend, however, seems to me not yet to have mastered the a, b, c of the art. I was at Queen Mary the first night[6] and at Hamlet yesterday afternoon. Queen Mary was deplorably acted throughout (of which said "critic" seems to have no *Ahnung*) but although nothing could make it a fine drama, if *Mary* had been played by a certain actress[7] known to us, and prized wherever known, the effect would have been quite other!—As to Rossi[8] it is difficult to say how bad I thought him; but my objections did not like the critic's fall on his costume and his business so unlike that of English Hamlets—nor indeed on his conception that Hamlet was mad—but on the absolute want of expression—facial, vocal, gestural (sit venia verbo!) and emotional. Let him have what conception of the part he pleases, he has no glimmering of expressing human emotion—all the sarcasms were sermons or snivels—all the princely dignity and unbending graciousness were absent—all the reverie was like that of a drunken man. The man has a bull throat, deep chest, and the animal figure which goes therewith; but brains were forgotten in the making of him. Salvini's Hamlet was not what one desired,[9] but it was stupendous compared with Rossi's. It had very fine moments. Rossi was absurd or ineffective throughout. Yet all your critical friend objects to is a certain extravagance and eccentricity of bearing and reading.

6. Tennyson's *Queen Mary* at the Lyceum, 18 April 1876, with Henry Irving as Philip of Spain, Kate Bateman (Mrs. Crowe) as Mary of England, her sisters Virginia Francis as the Princess Elizabeth, and Isabel Bateman (not Ellen) as Alice, one of the Queen's women. George Smalley in one of his London letters to the *New York Tribune* (9 January 1881, p. 5b) wrote: "I chanced to sit next to her [GE] on the first night of Tennyson's 'Queen Mary' at the Lyceum. The acting of the piece did not please her, and she favored me with a running commentary on the perfor-

mance which was incomparably more brilliant than either the play or the acting. Her criticism disclosed a singular talent for sharp pleasantries." No evidence confirms this doubtful account.

7. i.e. Helen Faucit, Mrs. Theodore Martin.

8. Ernesto Fortunato Giovanni Maria Rossi (1827–96) played Hamlet at Drury Lane 24 April 1876.

9. GE and GHL saw Salvini's Othello twice, 7 and 19 April, and his Hamlet, 31 May and 14 June 1875. See GHL, *On Actors and the Art of Acting*, 1875, pp. 264–278.

Just as he says not a word on the horrible declamation of Miss Bateman, her sister, and Ellen—but thinks their acting good enough for the play.

But lunch is served so I must close, with our love to Mrs. Martin.

Ever yours truly
G. H. L.

VI, 245:17   GE TO WILLIAM M. STATHAM,[1] LONDON, 6 MAY 1876

MS: University of California Los Angeles. *Envelope:* Rev. W. M. Statham | 2 West Parade Terrace | Hull. *Postmark:* LONDON N.W | MY 6 | 76.

The Priory, | 21. North Bank, | Regents Park.
May 6. 76.

Dear Sir

As the "Authoress of Middlemarch" I thank you sincerely for sending me the sort of encouragement I most value, namely, a proof that anything I have written has been a help to others in the work of trying to make our life worthier.

Truly yours
M. E. Lewes.

VI, 247:13   GHL TO MRS. FREDERICK LEHMANN, LONDON, [8 MAY 1876]

MS: Yale. *Brief extract published:* G. S. Haight, "George Eliot's Klesmer," *Imagined Worlds*, ed. Maynard Mack and Ian Gregor, 1968, p. 214.

The Priory, | 21. North Bank, | Regents Park.
Monday.

Most delightful Person!

There is no resisting *that* invitation, although Madonna has sternly resolved not to accept any and has I fear given great offence by refusals, still she must give way to you! We shall so like to renew our acquaintance

---

1. William M. Statham had been Vicar of Ellesmere-Port Chester since 1866. The "Authoress of Middlemarch" is clearly a quotation from his letter.

with Klesmer—whom we met at Weimar in 54!² Therefore "whisper it not in Gath"³ but expect us.

Ever your ancient lover
The Matchless.

Couldn't you bring Rubinstein here next Sunday?

VI, 249:20   GHL TO JAMES SULLY, LONDON, [11 MAY 1876]

MS: University College, London. *Envelope:* James Sully Esq | 17 Nicoll Road | Willesden | N.W. *Postmark:* LONDON N.W | MY 11 | 76.

The Priory, | 21. North Bank, | Regents Park.

Wednesday.

My dear Sir

Chapman & Hall have applied to me to direct them to a competent translator for L'Étourneau's *La Biologie*—a book which if you have not seen, I will send you, should your occupations and your inclinations dispose you to undertake the translation. I thought if you were not too busy it might be a bit of work you would like. There is no immediate hurry I fancy, and you would have to fix your own terms. Are you free and disposed? and shall I send you the book?

Yours truly,
G. H. Lewes.

2. Anton Rubinstein (1830–94) was presented to GE at the Erbprinz Hotel, Weimar, 18 September 1854, by Franz Liszt, who was about to produce his opera *The Siberian Huntsmen*. GHL and GE met him at dinner at the Felix Moscheles', 13 May 1876, the other guests being Henri Wieniawski, with whom Rubinstein was to tour the United States, Mr. and Mrs. Tom Taylor, and a Herr Eberstatt. "In the evening a large party: talked with Stansfield, Browning, Liebreich, Mrs. Benzon, Mad. Roche, Mad. Vasella, a Mr. Paton, and several others. Rubinstein and Wieniawski played a sonata of R's for violin and piano. Home at 12." On 15 May they dined with him again at the Lehmanns'. The other guests were Mr. and Mrs. Rudolph Lehmann, Sir Coutts and Lady Lindsay, Ferdinand Heilbutt, and Frederic Leighton. "In the evening a large gathering and Rubinstein played Beethoven, Chopin, Schumann, and his own compositions. Stupendous playing. Home a little after 12." (GHL Diary.)

3. Cf. II Samuel, 1:20.

VI, 261:17 GHL TO MME EUGÈNE BODICHON, LONDON, 6 JUNE 1876

MS: Philip Leigh-Smith

The Priory, | 21. North Bank, | Regents Park.

6 June 76.

Dear Barbara

This is capital news about Miss Marks![4] Madonna is terribly overdone and I should be really anxious about her if we were not going to depart on Thursday; but quiet, new scenes, and her own powerful frame will I hope restore the bloom to her sweet cheek.

On Wednesday I was presented to the King of the Belgians (at *his* request not mine) and had an agreeable interview in German, French, and English, about the Life of Goethe, Italy, Belgium and its relations to England, and the English language as one unpronounceable by foreigners. He is six foot two, not bad looking, with very amiable manners. He had expressed a particular wish to make Madonna's acquaintance but that shy saint wouldn't go.

Àpropos—read the enclosed letter and see if you recognize the handwriting. Is it Miss Blind?[5] The writer called with it herself hoping to be admitted, which was not very ladylike. I wrote to say that I was obliged to keep Mrs. Lewes from every kind of agitation just now, and thought that as you were a friend you were about the best person to whom anyone in trouble might unbosom. On reflection I don't quite like the tone of the letter—either it is that of a morbid gushing and impracticable woman or else it is a disguised way of begging. God bless you!

Ever yours

G. H. L.

4. Mme Bodichon had arranged for Phoebe Sarah Marks to enter Girton College.

5. Mathilde Blind (1841–96) wrote the earliest biography, *George Eliot*, Eminent Women series, 1883. Nothing more is known of this episode.

VI, 264:1 GHL TO JOHN BLACKWOOD, PARIS, [13 JUNE 1876]

Text: Copy by Edwin Mallard Everett.

Paris, Tuesday.

My dear Blackwood

You will be glad to hear that our journey here was effected without fatigue, though the gaieties have been a little too much for our weakness and deposited a headache in both of us—but that's of no consequence and we start tomorrow for Dijon and thence to the quiet of Aix and Chambéry.

Your letter was a great pleasure to her—we read it *in* the post office and then went to the Champs Elysées where I couldn't resist reading the proofs—and made myself icy more than was necessary before entering the Salon. Such a Salon! 4000 frames of theatricality, lubricity, and commonplace, with some score of good pictures—portraits and landscapes.

The weather which was winter when we arrived has become splendid and summery, which also makes Paris so brilliant. Tonight we close our gaieties with L'Étrangère—we were last night at the Français and the night before at the Odéon,[6] but now unless the open air theatres of Italy I don't fancy we shall have any more theatricals.

Madonna sends her very best regards to you and Willie.

Ever yours,
G. H. L.

I send the proofs in duplicate in case one should miss.

VI, 274:28 MRS. HERBERT ARTHUR LEWES TO GE, DURBAN, 26 JULY 1876

MS: Nuneaton Public Library.

D'Urban July 26th, | 1876.

My Dear Mutter

I want to ask you if you think it requisite that our little ones should be Christened, neither of them are, and would you and my Pater be God-

---

6. They began with the Russian Church on Sunday, 11 June; in the evening Nevski's *Les Danicheffs* at the Odéon; on the 12th, when the final proofs of *Daniel Deronda* arrived, they went to the Théâtre Français, where Coquelin played in *Le Luthier de Cremone* and Got in *La Joie fait peur*. After GHL wrote this letter, they went again and saw Coquelin and Sarah Bernhardt in L'Étrangère by Dumas *fils*: "Very much interested both in piece and acting." (GHL Diary.)

parents to them by proxy? If you and My Pater were, Mr. and Mrs. Sanderson would be the others, I think, not that I wish to give any trouble or responsibility to their Godparents, if you think it proper they should be Christened, but it shall be as you decide. Please tell me what you think of the photographs. Wont you and dear Pater send me yours? I should so dearly like to have them, and I should prize them so much and I want your portrait for our new little home when we get one again. You know we have always had one of Dear Pater's to look at but not our Dear Mutter's. The affairs are not wound up yet. Mr. Sanderson was enquiring about them for me, as I was not able, a short time ago. I shall be glad when they are. I enclose you a little piece of the children's hair, perhaps you may like to have it, and you can form a better idea of them I think. I have not been well for some time, I am trying cold water hip baths, and if that does no good the Doctor says I must be examined. I hope you are much better than when My Dear Pater last wrote to me. With much love I am My Dear Mutter

> Your affectionate daughter
> Eliza Lewes.

VI, 274:28 MRS. HERBERT ARTHUR LEWES TO GHL, DURBAN, 26 JULY 1876

MS: Nuneaton Public Library.

D'Urban, July 26th /76.

My Dear Pater

I shall be so glad when I receive a letter again from you and My Dear Mutter, it seems such a long time since I had one, not since I was in Newcastle on my way down here, when you wrote you were going on the Continent. I hope so much the change has been beneficial to you and My Mutter. I should have written before but I have been waiting to have the portraits taken to send to you and My Dear Mutter. Dear little George Herbert was recovering from his illness when I went for a short ride with Mr. Sanderson to look at a place he thought might suit me. When I returned I was obliged to send for the Doctor, and was not able to move about for some time, this morning the artist sent me the ones enclosed. Baby's is a very good portrait I think with the exception of the hair being much too dark the man has just struck a bell and he opened his mouth in astonishment—I think he looks a little frightened. Marian's is not so good she was kept so long in that attitude that she was wearied. She is much brighter and prettier looking. Mine is a fright I think.

Dear Pater I do not like to do it but I fear I must draw the remainder of the money you were so good to say I could if I realy wanted it.[7] I can rent no house that is at all healthy and those that would be are 5 and 6£ a month. I and Mr. Sanderson think my only plan is to buy a small piece of land and have a little house built out at Sydenham it is about four miles from here. I did not think I should have been obliged to stay here so long it is so expensive. Mr. Sanderson does all he can to assist me if I could only get stronger I could do much more to help us. I think if ever you did a good action it was when you and my Mutter did not leave us to the mercy of strangers. Dear Pater if any thing should happen to me will you and my Mutter take our little ones to bring up? I don't think I shall leave them, only when I am not well I am so uncomfortable about them if they were to be left. I know it is a great thing to ask, but I only ask it supposing they should be left.

I hope they won't, they are very very dear to me. I did [not] think they were so dear until the other week Mrs. Ashton Mrs. Sanderson's Sister toke little Marian home with her to stay for a week when I was not well. Marian much enjoyed the change and did not ask to come home because she said poor Mama was not well. Dear little George Herbert grows very nicely I think rubbing the cod liver oil on his chest every night is doing him much good, he runs about now quite alone. I have to keep a Kafer boy to carry him out—I should so like to read My Mutter's last work. Won't you please send it to me, I hope I have not done wrong to ask for it, but I do so much wish for it. With much love

Your affectionate daughter
Eliza Lewes.

Please excuse errors I have Neuralgia in my head and face.

VI, 278:29   GE TO CATHERINE H. SPENCE, LONDON, 4 SEPTEMBER 1876

Text: Melbourne Review, 10 (1885).

The Priory, | **21. North Bank,** | **Regents Park.**
September 4, 1876.

Dear Madam

Owing to an absence of some months, it was only the other day that I read your kind letter of the 17th April, and, although I have long been obliged to give up answering the majority of letters addressed to me, I felt

7. In January 1876 GHL lists under Charities £250 for Eliza. (GHL Diary.)

much pleased that you had given me an opportunity of answering one from you. For I have always remembered your visit with a regretful feeling that I had probably caused you some pain by a rather unwise effort to give you a reception, which the state of my health at the moment made altogether blundering and infelicitous.[8] The mistake was all on my side, and you were not in the least to blame.

I also remember that your studies have been of a serious kind, such as are likely to render a judgement of fiction and poetry—or, as the Germans with better classification say, on 'Dichtung' in general—quite other than the superficial haphazard remark of which reviews are usually made. You will all the better understand that I have made it a rule not to read writing about myself. I am exceptionally sensitive, and liable to discouragement, and to read much remark about my doings would have as depressing an effect on me as staring in a mirror—perhaps I may say—even of defective glass. But my husband looks at all the numerous articles that are forwarded to me, and kindly keeps them out of my way, only on rare occasions reading me a passage which he thinks will comfort me by its evidence of unusual insight or sympathy. Yesterday he read your article in the *Melbourne Review*, and said, at the end, 'This is an excellently written article, which would do credit to any English periodical,' adding the very uncommon testimony 'I shall keep this.' Then he told me of some passages in it which gratified me by that comprehension of my meaning—that laying of the finger on the right spot, which is more precious than praise; and forthwith he went to lay the *Melbourne Review* in the drawer he assigns to any writing about me

8. Catherine Helen Spence (1825–1910) emigrated to South Australia in 1839. Her *Autobiography*, reprinted from the *Register*, Adelaide, 1910, p. 42, gives this account of her call on GE in 1866: "Before I left England Mr. Williams of Smith, Elder & Co. offered me an introduction to George Henry Lewes, and I expressed the hope that it might also include an introduction to George Eliot, whose works I so admired. Mr. Lewes being away from home when I called, I requested that the introductory letter of Mr. Williams should be taken to George Eliot herself. She received me in the big Priory drawing room . . . but she asked me if I had any business relating to the article which Mr. Williams had mentioned, and I had to confess that I had none. For once I felt myself at fault. I did not get on with George Eliot. She said she was not well, and she did not look well. That strong pale face . . . did not soften. . . . The voice, which was singularly musical and impressive, touched me, . . . but no subject that I started seemed to fall in with her ideas, and she started none in which I could follow her lead pleasantly. It was a short interview and it was a failure. I felt I had been looked on as an inquisitive Australian desiring an interview upon any pretext; and, indeed, next day I had a letter from Mr. Williams in which he told me that, but for the idea that I had some business arrangement to speak of, she would not have seen me at all."

that gives him satisfaction. For he feels on my behalf more than I feel on my own—at least, in matters of this kind.

If you should come to England again, when I happen to be in town, I hope that you will give me the pleasure of seeing you under happier auspices than those of your former visit.[9]

Believe me, dear Madam, yours sincerely
M. E. Lewes.

VI, 278:29 GHL TO ALEXANDER MAIN, LONDON, 4 SEPTEMBER [1876]

MS: Harvard. *Address:* Alex. Main Esq | 71 Millgate Loan | Arbroath | N.B. *Postmark:* LONDON N.W | 12 | SP 4 | 76.

The Priory September 4.
Just returned from the mountains of Switzerland after 3 months splendid weather and matchless scenery; but with very varying health. On the whole a decided benefit to both, but less than could have been desired! Three months arrears of correspondence to make up—a perfect Swiss mountain of letters!

G. H. L.

VI, 288:20 GE TO MME EUGÈNE BODICHON, LONDON, [SEPTEMBER 1876]

MS: Berg Collection, New York Public Library.

21 North Bank | Friday.
Dear Barbara
Do you mind telling me what wages you give to Henrietta and to your cook? I ask you especially, because I know that your views of housekeeping and servants are more like mine than those of anyone else I can think of. I shall be grateful if you will send me a *note* by return i.e. for Monday morning.

Yours always affectionately,
M. E. Lewes.

9. GE may have regretted her kindness when another letter from Miss Spence, 23 November 1876, announced that she was about to review *Daniel Deronda* and asked her to receive her brother John Spence with his wife and three girls, who were soon coming to London. (Yale.)

VI, 323:24 GHL TO ALEXANDER MAIN, LONDON, 29 DECEMBER [1876]

MS: Harvard. *Address:* Alexr Main Esq | 71 Millgate Loan | Arbroath | N.B. *Postmark:* ST JOHNS WOOD N.W | A 3 | DE 29 | 76.

The Priory 29th December.

Thanks for your letter. Horribly busy with lawyers and agents as well as correspondents. Bought a place in Surrey. Health tolerable.

I know no *more* of the Meyricks[1] than you do! But we did spend Christmas with our Scotch friends.[2]

G. H. L.

VI, 328:20 GE TO GEORGE SMITH, LONDON, 2 JANUARY 1877

MS: Mr. Gordon N. Ray.

The Priory, | 21. North Bank, | Regents Park.

January 2. 1877.

Dear Mr. Smith

Still better than the beauty of your handsome New Year's gift is the kind remembrance it assures me of. My grateful pleasure in receiving it has only one reserve. Are the bon-bons meant to sweeten your absence from our doorstep for another year?

Mr. Lewes suggests to me a better ground for contentment in the fact that you are residing at Brighton, and this in consequence of Mrs. Smith's health allowing her to remain in England through the winter.

I trust that this comfort will be more and more confirmed and that the gift which the New Year bears in its hand for you may be that supreme one, perfect family happiness.

Believe me, with many pleasant recollections,

Yours always sincerely

M. E. Lewes.

George Smith Esq.

1. The family of Daniel Deronda's friend Hans.
2. GE and GHL went to Weybridge to stay with the Crosses 24 December 1876. The weather was bad, with snow or rain every day; "but we were very jolly—billiards, chat, etc." On Boxing Day Dr. and Mrs. Andrew Clark and Matthew Arnold came to dinner; on the 27th they lunched with the Druces; and on the 28th returned to London. (GHL Diary.)

VI, 328:20   GE TO MRS. GEORGE OTTO TREVELYAN, LONDON, 12 JANUARY 1877

MS: Trevelyan Papers, University of Newcastle.

The Priory, | 21. North Bank, | Regents Park.
12 January.

Dear Mrs. Trevelyan

We shall be very happy to dine with you on Wednesday the 24th at $\frac{1}{4}$ 8.[3]

Sincerely yours

M. E. Lewes.

VI, 335:1   GHL TO [?], LONDON, 25 JANUARY 1877

Text: Boston Commonwealth, 19 February 1881.

The Priory, | 21. North Bank, | Regents Park.
January 25. 1877.

Dear Sir,

Mrs. Lewes never reads articles written about herself. I have read what you were good enough to send, and, in reply to your question, beg to assure you that every single detail in it is imaginary—birth, parentage, education, and history are not distorted or exaggerated, they are totally wide of all resemblance to the facts. The circumstantial history might have had Mrs. Smith or Brown for its subject with equal veracity.

One single point will suffice. Mr. Herbert Spencer is said to have been her instructor, and taught her languages.[4] Had the writer troubled himself to make the slightest inquiry, he would have learned that Mr. Herbert Spencer knows very little of one language besides his own, whereas she, before she knew him, was mistress of seven.

Yours truly

G. H. Lewes.

3. The other guests were Mr. and Mrs. Grenfell, Mr. and Mrs. Brand, Mr. G. Broderick Courtney, and Mr. and Mrs. Frederic Harrison. (GHL Diary.)

4. For this canard, derived from *Men of the Time,* 9th ed., 1875, pp. 382–383, see vi, 68, n. 3.

VI, 336:15   GE TO MRS. ELMA STUART, LONDON, 30 JANUARY [1877]

MS: British Museum.

Monday, January 30.[5]

Better, dearest Elma, than when Gertrude came to ask for her report. The lumbago is departing, but too much like an evil spirit that likes his lodging.[6]

VI, 336:15   GE TO ANDREW CLARK, LONDON, 1 FEBRUARY 1877

MS: Yale.

The Priory, | 21. North Bank, | Regents Park.
February 1. 77.

Dear Dr. Clarke

Mr. Lewes is for the second time suffering from an attack of fierce pain in the left leg, which hinders him from walking and even from getting into a carriage. It is now the third day of this second attack,[7] and he has been suffering also from hemicrania and general malaise. Can you be an angel of mercy to us, and come to Mr. Lewes since he is not able to get to you? Even if there is no prescription but patience, the sight of you and the sound of your voice will strengthen the patience.

Always yours gratefully
M. E. Lewes.

Dr. Andrew Clarke

VI, 339:14   GE TO MRS. WILLIAM ALLINGHAM, LONDON, [6 FEBRUARY 1877]

MS: Private Collection.

The Priory, | 21. North Bank, | Regents Park.
Tuesday Morning.

Dear Mrs. Allingham

If we do not get to you to see your pictures, as Mr. Allingham's letter kindly permitted us to do, conclude that Mr. Lewes is still too unwell for us

5. Monday was 29 January 1877.   January 1877.)
6. "Polly had lumbago and I went   7. See VI, 338, n. 8.
to Concert alone." (GHL Diary, 27

to drive out. He has been ailing for a fortnight, and is now suffering severe pain. If we have the comfort of finding that he is well enough to drive as far as your house tomorrow or Thursday about 3 there is nothing he would like better than to see your Surrey work.

Yours always truly
M. E. Lewes.

VI, 339:14 GE TO MME EUGÈNE BODICHON, [LONDON, 6 FEBRUARY 1877]

MS: Berg Collection, New York Public Library. *Address:* Madame Bodichon | 5 Blanford Square.

Tuesday.

Dear Barbara

Can you use the carriage? If not, this will at least serve to tell you that G's leg is quite easy now so long as he lies still. Movement is painful, but I trust that the utmost quiet will gradually prove curative.

Your affectionate
M.

VI, 341:1 GE TO OSCAR BROWNING, LONDON, 12 FEBRUARY 1877

MS: Yale.

The Priory, | 21. North Bank, | Regents Park.
February 12. 77.

Dear Mr. Browning

Your pleasant letter has come to us while we are sitting in chill shadow and helps our belief in future sunshine.

For the last fortnight Mr. Lewes has been laid up with rheumatic gout. But for the last few days there has been a gradual improvement and your attractive proposal seems to have a sanitary quality, fixing his imagination on something agreeable that may happen to him next month. So we gratefully accept your offer to get us tickets and rooms, and also your kind invitation to join your dinner-party on the Wednesday.[8]

I have several times had news both of you and of Mrs. Julius Browning.[9]

8. The plan to visit Cambridge 7–8 March was abandoned because of GE's illness.

9. Oscar Browning's sister-in-law.

Lately I was talking to a charming girl who spoke warmly of her happiness under their care, and with affectionate admiration of your "duchess-mother."[1]

It would be too melancholy a view of the world for us to think ourselves rash in trusting that Mr. Lewes will be his usual active self again by March 8. It will be very pleasant to us then to have a chat with you once more after so long an interval, and hear more particularly from you of the satisfactory way in which your labours are now appropriated.

Ever sincerely yours
M. E. Lewes.

VI, 345:1   GHL TO MRS. FREDERICK LEHMANN, LONDON, [26 FEBRUARY 1877]

MS: Yale.

The Priory, | 21. North Bank, | Regents Park.
Monday.

Sweet Person!

I am recovering from an attack of rheumatic gout, and Madonna has not left her room for more than a week—(return of her old malady)—so you see there is but a grim prospect of our being able to delight ourselves at your house on the 6th—nevertheless she is decidedly mending, and the attraction of the music (with a corner out of the way of draughts) is so great that we hope to be able to come. Should we not, pity us![2]

Ever yours
G. H. L.

1. Mrs. William Shipton Browning, a merchant's daughter.
2. "Concert at the Lehmanns. Hen-schel sang (finely), Joachim, Piatti, and Krebs. Home at 12." (GHL Diary, 6 March 1877.) GE did not go.

VI, 347:9 GHL TO GEORGE CROOM ROBERTSON, LONDON, [1 MARCH 1877]

MS: University College, London. *Endorsed:* 2.3.77. May not be possible to print all —but 'in his own words.'

The Priory, | 21. North Bank, | Regents Park.
Thursday.

My dear Robertson

Immediately after you left[3] Mrs. Lewes was taken ill with a return of her old painful malady and has not yet left her room, though she now seems decidedly mending and I hope will be out soon.

In consequence I have not been able to write the analysis you asked for, but send you instead a copy of the *preface* which you can introduce with a few words saying the book[4] will appear in a few days.

Last night I read your interesting paper in the XIX Century.[5] Can you give me the titles of the books and essays you seem to refer to as having preceded me in the discovery of the social factor in Psychology—you will see from the preface that I claim it as mine—but if I have been anticipated I must "bate my breath."

Yours truly

G. H. L.

VI, 347:9 GEORGE CROOM ROBERTSON TO GHL, LONDON, 2 MARCH 1877

MS: Draft of letter, University College, London.

6, Lorton Terrace, | Ladbroke Road W.
2. 3. 77.

My Dear Mr. Lewes

We are very sorry to hear about Mrs. Lewes and hope she will soon be quite well again.

3. Robertson called Sunday 18 February 1877. During the night GE's "return of her renal troubles began." (GHL Diary.)

4. Robertson reprinted under "New Books" in *Mind*, 2 (April 1877), 278– 279, extracts from the Preface of *The Physical Basis of Mind*, 1877, pp. v-vi, GHL's "new volume, which will very shortly appear."

5. "How We Come by Our Knowledge," *Nineteenth Century*, 1 (March 1877), 113–121. "It is only in more recent psychological works, like Mr. Lewes's, or as yet in less systematic essays and general literature, that the social influence of man on man is forcing its way to recognition as a condition second to none in the actual process of mental development." (p. 120.)

Many thanks for the preface. It may not be possible to print it in full, but what is given shall be in your own words. You need not be deterred from asserting your claims by anything I have said in the supplement hurriedly tagged to my little paper, read months ago to the Metaphysical Society and which Knowles would have to be printed. In adding the supplementary remarks a short time ago, I had in view, besides odd essays like Clifford's and Pollock's, chiefly Leslie Stephen's new book,[6] which I have read since the paper was written and which has certainly struck me as saturated with the notion of the overshadowing influence of society. Maudsley[7] also has a number of passages (though plainly inspired by Comte) which point the right way. Even in Spencer, I have in the last few days come across a passage which is worth looking at—*Psychology* II. § 493. And for myself I may say that anything there is in this paper—and there is more implied than could be set forth—has been taking shape in my mind for quite a number of years past. But I regret that when it did seem to me in writing, first to remark on Mill etc. and then to mention you, I did not look up your first volume and do more justice to your emphatic statement of the position as fundamental in psychology.

VI, 347:9   GHL TO JOHN WALTER CROSS, [LONDON, 5 MARCH 1877]

MS: Yale.

Monday.

My dear Nephew

Enclosed signed transfer. Your Aunt enjoyed the concert[8] greatly, but I don't know whether it did her any harm. At any rate she had a return of pain on Sunday morning early and it lasted all day. But this morning she is easy again though there are still unpleasant symptoms of irritation.

Why are the Saints to suffer bodily as well as mentally? Voilà une question!

Ever yours truly
[*Unsigned*]

6. *History of English Thought in the Eighteenth Century*, 2 vols., 1876.

7. Henry Maudsley, *Body and Mind*, 1873.

8. "Polly accompanied me to Concert: Joachim, Mad. Schumann. Brahm's new Quartett and Schumann's Quintett." (GHL Diary, 3 March 1877.)

VI, 349:3 GHL TO JOHN WALTER CROSS, LONDON, [16 MARCH 1877]

MS: Yale.

The Priory, | 21. North Bank, | Regents Park.

Friday.

My dear Nephew

What does the enclosed mean? Is the Ry. bankrupt?

Your Aunt continues *very* weak and makes me uneasy by the continuance; but yesterday and today there were better signs. We are going to Leighton's in the afternoon to hear Joachim and in the evening to the concert for the Blind at St. James's Hall[9]—rather a glut of music and a bold defiance to disease!

Ever yours

G. H. L.

VI, 360:27 GHL TO JOHN EVERETT MILLAIS, LONDON, [3 APRIL 1877]

MS: Morgan Library.

The Priory, | 21 North Bank, | Regents Park.

Tuesday.

My dear Millais

Mrs. Lewes and I should much like to see your pictures if it could be done when there were no other visitors—which is what makes her shrink —on Thursday[1] afternoon about 4? A line on a card to say yes or no in answer to the query 'Is it convenient?'

Yours truly

G. H. Lewes.

J. F.[2] Millais, Esq.

9. See VI, 348. At this concert the Princess Louise drew on her program the sketch of GE (reproduced in Haight, *George Eliot*, facing p. 530) owned by Mr. Reginald Allen.

1. "We went to see Millais's pictures." (GHL Diary, Wednesday, 4 April 1877.)

2. F. is clear in MS.

VI, 362:8 GHL TO MRS. FELIX MOSCHELES,
LONDON, 12 APRIL 1877

MS: Yale.

The Priory, | 21. North Bank, | Regents Park.

12 April 77.

Dear Mrs. Moscheles

The 18th is my birthday—my 60th—and will be passed in the bosom of my family, so that your kind invitation cannot be accepted.

Best regards to your husband.[3] I heard he was in the East.

Yours truly

G. H. Lewes.

VI, 373:25 GE TO CATHARINE PAGET,
LONDON, 17 MAY 1877

MS: Yale.

The Priory, | 21. North Bank, | Regents Park.

May 17. 77.

My dear Miss Paget

It will not, I trust, seem strange to you that we should wish to associate ourselves, however slightly, with the greatest event of your life;[4] and that we should have devised no less arrogant a way of asking you to keep a remembrancer of us by you than begging you to accept a complete copy of my rather lengthy books.

My only apology is, that whatever may be their or my worth, they are the best of me. So we venture to offer them as a small sign of the deep interest we both take in your prospect of entering on that marriage state which holds the highest possibilities of our mortal lot.

Believe me, dear Miss Paget,

Yours always sincerely

M. E. Lewes.

3. Felix Stone Moscheles (1833–1917), portrait and genre painter, was a son of Ignaz Moscheles the pianist and a cousin of the Benzons.
4. Catharine, elder daughter of Sir James Paget, was married 30 June 1877 to the Reverend Henry Lewis Thompson, Rector of Iron Acton, Shropshire, later Vicar of St. Mary's, Oxford.

VI, 377:15 GE TO OSCAR BROWNING, LONDON, 26 MAY 1877

MS: Yale.

The Priory, | 21. North Bank, | Regents Park.
May 26. 77.

Dear Mr. Browning

We shall be delighted to lunch with you on Sunday the 3d at 1.30.[5] There are long arrears of talk between us.

I hope you will return from your lecturing like 'a conqueror coming home.'

Yours always sincerely
M. E. Lewes.

VI, 378:18 GE TO NIKOLAUS TRÜBNER, LONDON, 27 MAY 1877

MS: Yale.

The Priory, | 21. North Bank, | Regents Park.
May 27. 77.

Dear Mr. Trübner

I return the precious annotated Hebrew Grammar, lest any accident should happen to it owing to our flight into the country. Also the other books you have been so good as to lend me except two, namely: Sola and Raphall's 'Genesis'[6] and Green's 'Hebrew Grammar.'[7] Many thanks for your kind loans.

When will another *Lieferung* of Hamburger come out?

Yours sincerely,
M. E. Lewes.

5. Browning is not mentioned in GHL's notes of their visit to Cambridge. See VI, 380.

6. Morris Jacob Raphall and D. A. de Sola, *The Sacred Scriptures*. A New Translation with Notes by M. J. Raphall, Hebrew and English, 1844.

7. Samuel Gosnell Green, *A Handbook to Hebrew Grammar*.

VI, 387:6 FREDERIC HARRISON TO GE,
LONDON, 12 JUNE 1877

MS: Brotherton Library, Leeds. *Extract published:* Haight, *George Eliot*, p. 506.

1 Southwick Place W. | June 12. 1877.

Dear Mrs Lewes,

Now that you are in the quiet of the Surrey Hills, I renew a petition which I once began to make at your house. If you cannot accord it, I will not ask for your reasons; and the matter will end with no more than your trouble in reading this.

I told you that at the address at the Positivist School on the newyear's day, Dr. Congreve had used—"Oh may I join the choir invisible"—as his conclusion without comment, and before this Llewellyn Davies[8] had spoken of it as the germ of a new Hymnology.

I now ask you—if you can give us anything further, either in prose or in verse, for public or for private use, by way of collect, hymn, or litany —something I mean to give form to our ideas of sympathy and confidence in Humanity. Positive emotions, whether of the more defined or of the more unsystematic kind, are at present shapeless and rudimentary—cavent quia vate sacro. What effusions there are, are of so dogmatic and pedantic a kind, that they tend to narrow and harden, rather than to enlarge the healthy feeling. As yet it has no poet. You alone can supply this.

Indeed I have often longed that we could have your full estimate of the scheme of the Polity, now it is complete in its English form.[9] I mean especially your judgment of a Religion of Humanity as a possible rallying point for mankind in the future. That you differ very much from the form which Comte has given it in such sharp lines, I know, or suppose that I know. But where you differ, wherein, how far; when you agree, how far —this is what we all want to know, those who accept Comte's ritual in different degrees, and those who reject it but converge to the general idea of Humanity, as the ultimate centre of life and of thought. Your readers are perpetually asking themselves the question—what is your real mind on this subject, and they answer it in different ways. Why, I keep asking myself, should you not quickly answer them, not by way of poetry, but by philosophy; and having asked myself the question so often, I now ask you—though I have no right to expect an answer.

8. John Llewellyn Davies (1826–1916), Rector of Christ Church, Marylebone, a Broad Churchman and a Liberal in politics. His wife was a sister of Henry Crompton, the Positivist.

9. Auguste Comte, *A System of Positive Polity*, tr. by J. H. Bridges *et al.*, 4 vols., 1875–77.

There are some things that Art cannot do, and one is, to tell us what to believe; and there are many who will never be satisfied till they know what you have to say. I am

Yours sincerely

Frederic Harrison.

VI, 388:18 GHL TO ALFRED TENNYSON, WITLEY, 18 JUNE 1877

MS: Tennyson Research Centre, Lincoln. *Mostly published: Alfred Lord Tennyson, A Memoir*, 2 vols., 1898, II, 192.

The Heights, Witley, Godalming.

18 June 1877.

My dear Tennyson

We have just read 'Harold' (for the first time) and 'Mary' (for the fourth) and greatly wished you had been here to read certain scenes, especially that masterly interview between Harold and William,[1] or that most pathetic close of Mary.[2] It is needless for me to say how profound a pleasure both works have given us. They are great contributions, and your wretched critics, who would dissuade you from enriching Literature with such dramas must be forgiven "for they know not what they say."[3]

It is not, however, to carry the coals of applause to your Newcastle that I scribble these lines, but to inquire whether there is a hope of your being at Blackdown this summer and of our seeing you?[4]

We should be glad to hear that Mrs. Tennyson was better—and news of yourself and the "boys" would be welcome to

Yours truly

G. H. Lewes.

1. Tennyson's *Harold*, 1877, II, ii. The play was published in October 1876, dedicated to Lord Lytton.

2. *Queen Mary*, 1875, produced by Henry Irving at the Lyceum 18 April 1876, which GE and GHL attended. See VI, 242.

3. Cf. Luke 23:34.

4. Tennyson replied 27 June 1877 that he would be at Aldworth the following week and gave an invitation to Mr. and Mrs. Lewes. (Sotheby's, 27 June 1923, item 605.)

VI, 404:8   GHL TO HENRY JENNINGS,[5]
WITLEY, 21 SEPTEMBER 1877

Text: Copy by Edwin Mallard Everett.

The Heights, | Witley, Surrey | 21 September 77.

Sir

Mrs. Lewes has an objection to the modern system of applying to living persons for their autograph, and has never acceded to any request for her's. I also object; but as I have weakly consented in some cases I cannot refuse to sign myself

Yours truly

G. H. Lewes.

H. Jennings, Esq.

VI, 404:8   GE TO BENJAMIN JOWETT,
WITLEY, 25 SEPTEMBER 1877

MS: Bodleian.

The Heights | Witley | Godalming | (Telegraph Witley Station)
September 25. 77.

My dear Master

Some awkwardness about our postal arrangements makes me fear the possibility that the letter addressed to you at Oxford may not arrive in time to be in your hands on Wednesday morning (tomorrow).

For security, I write again to assure you that a visit from you either Tuesday or Thursday[6] in next week will be most welcome to us.

Mr. Lewes will await you at our Station, hoping that you will have started by the train which leaves Waterloo at 11.30. We are so barely provided here at present that we have no spare bed—much to our regret since there is a chance that you would have accepted it. But the latest train to town leaves Witley at 8.25. This is too early, but it leaves time to dine comfortably at seven.

We shall look forward to your visit as a pleasure that we should have

---

5. Henry Jennings, barrister, 10 Lincoln's Inn Fields, W. C.

6. He came Thursday, 4 October. "Jowett spent the day with us. After lunch drove him to Chiddingfold and walked on the common and through wood home. We all went in to see the Hollands, where Jowett was to sleep. He stayed with us till 10 and left us knocked up." (GHL Diary includes 3 stories Jowett told.)

chosen, but one made all the more welcome and valuable by the fact that you have chosen it.

Yours very sincerely

M. E. Lewes.

VI, 404:8 GHL TO EDWARD F. S. PIGOTT, WITLEY, [25 SEPTEMBER 1877]

MS: Mr. Gordon N. Ray.

The Heights, Witley | Godalming.

My dear Pigott

So many overhanging engagements have prevented our fixing on a day when we should be free but next Saturday the 29th we shall certainly be free and very glad if you are so likewise, and can run down here. There is a train from Waterloo at 11.30 which arrives here at 12.43—capital time for lunch, and the return train at 8.25 allows due time for dinner as we are only 5 minutes from the station. May we expect you?[7]

Yours ever

G. H. Lewes.

VI, 404:8 LADY HOLLAND'S[8] NOTE ON GE, WITLEY, 7 OCTOBER 1877

MS: Huntington Library.

Pinewood October 7th 1877.

Mr. Lewes came in to see me today. The conversation falling on Mrs. Lewes's writings he said, as far as I recollect, "The extraordinary thing is that I never discovered this power in her—that she never should have written a line till her 35th year. Our friends—Herbert Spencer—and others used to say to me—Why doesn't she write a novel? and I used to reply that she was without the creative power. At last—we were very badly off—I was writing for Blackwood—I said to her 'My dear—try your hand at something. Do not attempt a novel—but try a story. We may get 20 guineas for it from Blackwood and that will be something.'

7. Pigott came down with Charles Lewes Saturday. "Drove them to Hinde Head—lovely day. Tennis before dinner." (GHL Diary, 29 September 1877.)

8. Margaret Jean Trevelyan, daughter of Sir Charles Edward Trevelyan, the 2d wife of Sir Henry Thurstan Holland, lived at Pinewood, next to the Heights, Witley.

"Well she did try, and she began and then she read me the first chapter of 'Amos Barton' (Scenes of CL.) Well, this was all descriptive and I doubted. 'We want something dramatic,' I said to her. She shook her head and seemed to say that was hopeless. The next thing she read to me was the scene in Widow Hackitt's cottage. 'Come' said I 'this will do. Now for the pathos—unless you can manage that we shall not get on.' But she seemed to think that quite hopeless, that there was no power of pathos in her. However one day when I was going to town she said 'I wish you would dine in London today.' I was all astonishment to hear such an extraordinary wish expressed as that we should be apart and eagerly enquired the reason—but she would not answer. Presently she said again 'I *wish* you would stay and dine in town today.' And then on my pressing for a reason, it came out. She said she felt she had something she must write that evening. And I always objected to her working at night. But so it was this time—she said she felt she *must*. And that evening she produced the scene of Milly's death. Then I felt all was right—no one could doubt success was secured.

"When it was finished I sent it to Blackwood saying it was written by a friend of mine who intended it to be one of a series—and that the author must make the condition of retaining the copyright and of the whole series being published. Blackwood was enchanted—carried away."

VI, 413:19 GE TO MRS. EDWARD ATKINSON, LONDON, 29 OCTOBER 1877

MS: Princeton. *Envelope:* Mrs. Edward Atkinson | care of Mr. Edward Atkinson | 40 State Street | Boston | Mass. | U.S.A. *Postmarks:* st johns wood n.w | c 2 | oc 30 | 77; boston | nov 14 | paid. *Endorsed:* Mrs. Lewes (George Eliot) Care of Messrs Blackwood & Sons, Publishers, London, England. *Extract published:* vi, 413–414.

The Priory, | 21. North Bank, | Regents Park.

October 29. 77.

Dear Mrs. Atkinson[9]

I remember very well the interesting party which the name 'Frothingham'[1] recals to me, notwithstanding the many eventful years that now divide me from our meeting at Mr. Chapman's in the Strand. Many kind letters come to me from your side of the Atlantic which want of time and

9. Mary Caroline Heath was married in 1855 to Edward Atkinson (1827 –1905), industrialist, economist, and advocate of the safe construction of factories.

1. In 1853 Miss Heath stayed at 142 Strand with Octavius Brooks Frothingham (1822–95) and his wife. He was a Unitarian clergyman, a founder of the Free Religion Association of Boston.

strength for unnecessary correspondence obliges me to leave unanswered, but I cannot allow you to imagine me discourteously indifferent to your friendly recollection of our interviews in old days. That you are the mother of grown-up children is one of the many reminders I am constantly receiving that the larger part of life's journey lies behind me. I trust that the waymarks with you are signs of long-continued happiness, in spite of that infirmity of the eyes to which you refer.

Of Dr. and Mrs. Chapman I rarely hear anything, and the news of his death must I imagine be mistaken, since no public announcement of it has fallen under our notice.

Your request for my photograph[2] it is impossible for me to fulfil, as I have had no such image of myself taken. Requests for autographs and photographs are too numerous for me to answer them without great discomfort, and a sacrifice of time that would hardly be warranted by the value of the result. Hence I resign myself to being pronounced rather churlish by numerous 'unknown friends.'

With best wishes for you and yours, I remain, dear Mrs. Atkinson,

Sincerely yours
M. E. Lewes.

VI, 416:19 EDITH SIMCOX, AUTOBIOGRAPHY, 7–9 NOVEMBER 1877

MS: Bodleian. *Extract published:* McKenzie, pp. 90–91.

Wednesday 7 November 1877

November 7, 1877. My whole soul is a longing question.[3] I am going to see her. It rained this morning; now the sun is coming out. I feel as if that were a bad omen. She will be pre-engaged.

Friday 9 November 1877

9th. I was ushered in without hesitation. They were together sitting reading; he was at the second day of a headache. I tried to say something easy—that it was her fate not to get rid of me. She—that it seemed rather hard on me on Sundays. I—was she afraid of my poisoning Johnny's shirts? (Mr.

2. For a similar attempt to secure a photograph of GE in behalf of Frothingham see IV, 413.

3. Since 4 June 1877 GE had been at Witley, where Edith sent the copy of her *Natural Law. An Essay in Ethics,* inscribed and with a passionate colophon. GE's only comment on it was "eloquent silence."

Lewes had invited me to come early on Sunday, before other people; but I only contrive to get a few minutes start of J.C.) which she seemed inclined to parry by saying many other people came. They had tried battledore and shuttlecock as a substitute for the exercise of lawn tennis which had done her so much good. He had had a letter from a young Cambridge man[4] who had dreamt so vividly and repeatedly that she was ill that he couldn't help writing to ask—enclosing a directed card for reply "Only a dream" or something of the sort to prove that he wasn't in quest of an autograph. She said perhaps that would make me more charitable to menfolk. I protested I wasn't otherwise, and she said she had always owed me a grudge for not being grateful enough to the Italian officer who was kind to me when the train was snowed up beyond Foggia. She said unlike most people she believed I should have thought more of the adventure if a woman had been kind to me. I said I might have if I had had the opportunity of being kind to a woman. But that I had no prejudice whatever against man. He and she said as they have before that among chance acquaintances men are more appreciative and courteous to her than women. I said that I had found women kinder than men, which she was "glad to hear," as showing they could be kind to each other—and I didn't explain either that I had always taken their kindness as a sign that I was half a man—and they knew it; or that I thought it rather hard she should visit, as a fault, my constitutional want of charm for men.

I did not stay long and she only said—Are you going so soon? I spent an hour afterwards in hunting for a book[5] she wanted in the Holborn bookstalls, then attended a Shirtmakers' Committee and walked home— crossing Hyde Park for the first time in the dark. I have been very wretched since, and even more perplexed. Clearly she has nothing to say to me about the book; and it is hardly for me to open the subject now. I have seldom been more entirely at a loss what to do. I know they would be annoyed if I simply asked Trübner to withdraw the book when it had covered his expenses, and yet I daren't, and to tell the truth, hardly feel a wish to dare—to ask her counsel again. It is not pride, because if I could ask, it would be more humbly than ever. I shall wait, dragging out useless days as heretofore till some irresistible impulse declares itself.

4. The letter was from Leonard A. Montefiore, 17 October 1877. (Yale.) He was not a Cambridge man. See vi, 413, n. 8.

5. William Cobbett, *Rural Rides*, 1830.

VI, 421:6 GE TO FREDERIC W. H. MYERS, LONDON, 16 NOVEMBER 1877

MS: Trinity College, Cambridge. *Envelope:* Frederic W.H. Myers Esq. | Brandon House | Cheltenham. *Postmarks:* LONDON N.W | B 5 | NO 16 | 77; CHELTENHAM | A | NO 17 | 77.

The Priory, | 21. North Bank, | Regents Park.
November 16. 77.

My dear Mr. Myers

I am very grateful to you for your confidence. Indefinable impressions had convinced me that since we began to know something of each other a blight had passed over your energies and it was painful to me to feel in the dark about one of whom I had from the first thought with that hopeful interest which the elder mind, dissatisfied with itself, delights to entertain with regard to the younger, whose years and powers hold a larger measure of unspoiled life.

What you have disclosed to me affects me too deeply for me to say more about it just now than that my sympathy nullifies to my mind that difference which we were trying to explain on Sunday. When you write—"My own mournful present and solemn past seem sometimes to show me as it were, for a moment, by direct revelation the whole world's love and woe, and I seem to have drawn closer to other lives in that I have lost my own"—you express that spiritual result which seems to me the fount of real betterness for poor mankind. I have no controversy with a sorrowing love which has wrought such a result, no controversy with the faith that cries out and clings from the depths of man's need. I only long, if it were possible to me, to help in satisfying the need of those who want a reason for living in the absence of what has been called consolatory belief.

But all the while I gather a sort of strength from the certainty that there must be limits or negations in my own moral powers and life-experience which may screen from me many possibilities of blessedness for our suffering human nature. The most melancholy thought surely would be that we in our own persons had measured and exhausted the sources of spiritual good. But we know how the poor help the poor.

The poems you have sent me I have read several times already and they will be treasured by me as a sacred memorial of your confidence. I feel as if some foggy obstruction had been cleared away from my mind and feel strangely the more contented because I know of your great sadness —as if I had seen and joined hands with one whom I had envied in the procession of reverential mourners. Believe me always

Yours most faithfully
M. E. Lewes.

VI, 421:6 EDITH SIMCOX, AUTOBIOGRAPHY, 17 NOVEMBER 1877

MS: Bodleian. *Extract published:* McKenzie, pp. 91–92.

Saturday 17 November 1877

November 17. Last Sunday—the 11th—it rained with such preternatural violence and constancy that very slowly and diffidently I came round to the conclusion—that I had better go to the Priory! I arrived at a quarter to 3. My only terror was lest they should have had people to luncheon by invitation. My spirits rose when I saw the hall innocent of hats and cloaks, and when I found them alone together, the world began to smile again. I laid the blame deprecatingly on the rain—thought if I didn't come there would be nobody to ask after Mr. Lewes's headache; and they said, well, I should have the afternoon to myself and we had better sit down, which I proceeded to do on the rug at her feet, which I kissed; while observing that Lady Paget[6] had adopted the same seat, she intimated a preference for my taking another, which of course I also did.

She gave me a book of Miss Phelps to read "Avis," which the writer had sent her,[7] seeming to think that her promise to read the book when she could might be supplemented by any charitable judgment I could give more promptly. She said Miss Phelps would know my name from Trübner's series[8] being published in America. Before that, apropos of bonnets, she said her recollections of people's clothes was a part of her general mental image of them, and that she suffered much when worthy men were unfortunate in their choice of trouserings. Herbert Spencer had improved in that particular—but improvement had been needed. This led to the mention of his having been one of the visitors the Sunday before, his companion was an American admirer.[9] Everyone, Mr. Lewes observed, had an American admirer.

I suggested there might be a few books that didn't get even as far as across the Atlantic, to which he replied with the story of two books, both

6. A few weeks after GE's death Lady Paget wrote to her son: "The more one thinks of her and her deep affection for your father, the more one feels how she stood alone, amid the many friends he has won. I never can think of her without a strange feeling of jealousy over her, a kind of true regard and admiration I can't describe. She was so gentle, so generous, so affectionate, so charitable in her spirit towards others." (Stephen Paget, ed., *Memoirs and Letters of Sir James Paget*, 1901, p. 402.)

7. See vi, 417, n. 5.

8. Trübner's English and Foreign Philosophical Library, vol. 4.

9. Edward Livingston Youmans.

of which were puffed in 4 or 5 leading papers, of which one did not sell
a single copy and the other only 50 copies taken on speculation by the
trade. I can't recal in what context it was that Mr Lewes spoke of the
unreasonableness of people who ask your advice when the last thing they
would think of would be to take it "if it didn't fall in with their intention."
Then I said, I should have asked his advice, if I hadn't known it would
not fall in with my intention—about Trübner. She said, of course, what
business had I to have the book printed if I didn't mean it to sell and to
be read, that anyway the edition had to take its chance, that there would
be no second edition unless it were all sold off pretty quickly, and he
suggested that the only thing to be done if one were dissatisfied with a
written book was to write a better. I intimated that that was not exactly
my difficulty, I don't know what I succeeded in saying at last. I kissed
her hand—I guard my own—I implied that her approval or blame ended
everything for me. I think she said, Why should I have supposed she—not
disapproved—that was too arrogant a word, but failed to sympathize?
Then as by an effort of recollection: "I think I never told you what I
thought of the book after the first chapters?"[1]—I could not say, that was
just why I despaired. I did say that these were stern judgments she had
pronounced, which I had been loth to think deserved—though of course
she must know best—that I had reason to despair if the book gave her
no reason to modify those. Of course she has never known how every word
of hers enters into my flesh, but this much at least she said to me now:
That there had been nothing that jarred on her in reading the book—if
there had she would have remembered it, of course she did not always
agree, but the general impression was of sympathy, there were no passages
that struck her as cynical—she had been somewhat uneasily on the lookout
for them; she thought what I said of religion was good,—barring the
somewhat too impersonal, unconcerned or hypothetical way of saying it;
—it rather confirmed what she had thought before that I might write a

---

1. Spurred by GE's inspiration,
Edith wrote *Natural Law* to demonstrate her devotion. On the half-title of
the copy she gave to GE (now in Dr.
Williams's Library) Edith wrote: "Ma-
rian Evans Lewes | June 21. 1877—."
The final sentence of the book (p. 361)
reads: "Heaven and hell are names or
visions; the earth is ours—here a hell of
sensuality and hardened cruelty, there
a heaven of love and wisdom, with a
tender smile upon her gracious lips, and
yearning prophecy in the melting depths
of her unfathomable eyes." Edith changed the final period to a comma and added: "—to whom with idolatrous love
this book is dedicated." Whether GE
failed to notice the addition or was embarrassed by it, she never mentioned
the dedication to Edith. On the opposite page [362] Edith wrote: "Schwarzer
schatten ist über dem Staube | Der
Geliebten Gefährte; | Ich machte mich
zum Staube | Aber der Schatten ging
über mich hin." (Goethe, *West-östlicher
Divan, Goethes Werke,* Weimar, VI, 286.)

history of religious thought or a natural history of Christianity! I said I had been glad the book gave no scandal: she, that it could not, its tone was perfectly reverent. I told her that I had had the fear—or rather the love, of her before my eyes and had struck out any of the little malicious tails to a sentence I thought she might not like, but explained that theology had always been so uninteresting and meaningless to me that I should not care to have to get up its history. She said that Charles Lewes had read some of the book with interest, and appealed to Mr. Lewes if he himself had not sympathized with its spirit—to which he in a somewhat uninviting tone—oh yes, what I read of it.—In my desperation I had just utterly ignored his presence, which is perhaps hardly the way to a man's tender mercies. She used the words "sound and wholesome" and thought it would be useful. I did not deserve to be told this, but she had had serious thought of recommending the book to a lady who had "difficulties"—one who would be flattered by the argumentative apparatus and the rigidly meagre assumptions of the first page. She had not done so on the whole because the said lady would have known I was a friend of hers and so might either I suppose have identified us too much, or have attached less weight to the supposed echo. In all she said there was nothing to flatter any author's vanity —rather the contrary in tone and implication —so I have the more respect for my spiritual sincerity seeing that I can write that the clouds of misery and despair lifted themselves from my heart. I walked back through the pelting rain with inward sunshine, and I have been soberly glad and happily loving ever since.

I had a note from her yesterday, referring to the remainder of the conversation. I had been more than an hour alone with them. Locker and his daughter came and afterwards Myers; the former was talking to them about some unpublished poems of Tennyson—whose dramas, by the way, they admire. On Thursday I was fortunately able to get her a copy of Cobbett's "Rural Rides" which she had expressed a wish for.

VI, 425:1 GHL TO ALEXANDER MAIN, LONDON, [23 NOVEMBER 1877]

MS: Harvard. *Address:* A. Main Esq. | 71 Millgate Loan | Arbroath | N.B. *Postmark:* LONDON N.W | C 12 | NO 23 | 77.

The Priory, Friday.

Dear M

B[lackwood] has written to Mrs. L. about the book[2] and she referred the decision to him. She is quite well. But when you consider the arduous correspondence which is necessary, and her weak health, you really must give up the idea of her writing merely to say you are not "forgotten"! When there is anything needful to be said be sure you will hear.

G. H. L.

VI, 430:1 EDITH SIMCOX, AUTOBIOGRAPHY, 1 DECEMBER 1877

MS: Bodleian.

Sunday 1 December 1877

December 1. On Wednesday saw Trübner, who hadn't much to say; about 170 copies of the book appeared to have been sold in England. I went through some unprofitably strong emotions about a thing he told me. He has got leave to reprint her translation of Feuerbach,[3] and he was so ill-advised as to suggest to Mr. Lewes that some raison d'être for a second edition would be advisable and to propose that I should write an introduction on the life and writings of Feuerbach. I was annoyed at my name having been used so without my knowledge, because of course *I* knew beforehand how unhesitatingly Mr. Lewes would negative such a proposition on her account. But the thrill that went through me when Trübner was telling his story gave me a rather sad intimation of all the happiness that might be possible—where such relations were possible.

VI, 432:27 EDITH SIMCOX, AUTOBIOGRAPHY, 8–12 DECEMBER 1877

MS: Bodleian. *Brief extract published:* McKenzie, p. 43.

Saturday 8 December 1877

December 8. If things are less pleasant today I can scarcely blame myself. It is nothing—a trifle—but then the wise agree that trifles are much. It is a card from Lewes, asking me if I was coming today not to arrive early as they had some business matters to discuss. As it happens today was the anniversary of the day—5 years ago—when I first saw her hand-

2. *The George Eliot Birthday Book*, 1878, blank spaces for each day in the year faced with quotations from GE's works. Main's name does not appear in it.

3. *The Essence of Christianity*, 1854, was reissued in Trübner's English and Foreign Philosophical Library, 1881.

writing[4]—of the day three years ago when I dined with them and she read her "Symposium" to me.[5] What a singularly complete ass I must be to remain even more of a stranger to her now than three years ago. But I have renounced. I will not "thirst" again. I hardly do. My heart has ached, a few tears have come, but the pain is passive.

Wednesday 12 December 1877

December 12. At 5 o'clock next day i.e. the Monday 5 years of her first letter, a note came asking me to go and see her one day this week. Of course I went yesterday. She kissed me at length. Lewes also was kind. I forget what was spoken of first—no I don't—it was the state of the shop,[6] trade in general, French politics and the fall of Plevna.[7] Then I said Mary Hamilton was gone to Scotland and that her mother was getting tired of not going up the Nile, and mentioned casually that she was unhappy at her daughter's not marrying. Mr. Lewes seemed to think there was no hurry, and I said at 27 there was not much time to lose. She said marriages had seemed to be getting later and later and she was—of course—rather wroth with me for expressing a prejudice against late marriages; she thought that people who go on developing may have a much better chance of happiness in marrying after thirty than at 20; she was so beautiful and I was so fond of her that I wasn't angry when she proceeded to affirm that I had never been so fit to marry as now—I answered "that wasn't saying much" —to which with a sweet laugh and a still sweeter gesticulation—that brought her hand within reach of my lips—that she didn't pretend that her speeches amounted to much—it was enough if they came to a little. At which I laughed resignedly.

Then she asked what I had been doing, and I said nothing—I had been reading Wilhelm Meister; she was curious to know how it impressed me: she had much disliked Lotharo, his special objection was the *beteutende Mariana* and the Macaria business:[8] she thought it strange that with such

4. A note inviting her to call 13 December 1872.

5. GHL's Diary notes it, 9 December 1874.

6. In 1875 Edith had joined with Mary Hamilton in a co-operative shirt-making company called Hamilton & Co. at 83 Dean Street, Soho. See McKenzie, p. 27.

7. Plevna fell to the Russians in 1877 after having been defended by the Bulgarians for three months.

8. Wilhelm Meister's first love, the protesting but unfaithful actress Mariana. The mysterious Baron Lothario, head of a secret society into which Wilhelm is initiated, marries Theresa after discovering that she is not, as was thought, the daughter of his old lover. To eke out a second volume Goethe got Eckermann to patch together a group of isolated tales found in Makaria's house. See GHL's *Life and Works of Goethe*, 1855, II, 410–413.

perfectly finished dramatic passages all Goethe's prose works should be so unequal and without finished unity; was grateful to me for quoting the phrase *Vielen das Erwunschte.*

Then I made the confession I wished—that I had shaken hands with Bradlaugh and Mrs. Besant.[9] Of course she asked how that might be— and of course, on the whole, all things well weighed, she wished me not to have my name printed in the same list with theirs or Mrs. Harriet Law's.[1] She gave full weight to the dread of Pharisaism, and said incidentally some kindly sounding things of my qualifications for useful influence, suggested that I should lecture to these friends and brothers.

VI, 434:12 ISAAC EVANS TO EDWARD CLARKE, GRIFF, 20 DECEMBER 1877

MS: Mrs. Michael Womersley.

Griff, Nuneaton | December 20th 1877.

Dear Edward

I have received your letter announcing your arrival at Brighton.[2] I heard from Emily that she had received a telegram saying you were at Liverpool.

In consequence of which I wrote to her to say it will be out of our power to receive you here. We wish you well but cannot renew your acquaintance. It would be painful for all to do so. I am glad you are doing well in America. Your sister has been very good and exemplary in her conduct, having worked hard to maintain a good position and has succeeded in doing so. All who know her respect her and admire her perseverance. I am sorry her health is very delicate and requires great care.

If you have anything to communicate to me, I shall be glad to hear from you by *letter only.* I remain,

Yours faithfully
Isaac P. Evans.

Mr. E. Clarke
7, Gladstone Terrace
Brighton

9. Charles Bradlaugh (1833–91) and Mrs. Annie Besant (1847–1933), joint editors of the *National Reformer*, were active in the movement to revive the International Working Men's Association.

1. Mrs. Harriet Law (1832–97), notorious champion of atheism.

2. Edward was staying with his sister at Brighton when he wrote to his uncle Isaac, perhaps hoping to be invited to Griff for Christmas.

Lewes's Death

VII, 3:1 GHL TO GEORGE CROOM ROBERTSON, LONDON, 2 JANUARY 1878

MS: University College, London.

The Priory, | 21. North Bank, | Regents Park.

2 January 78.

My dear Robertson

I must tell you how very much your review[3] has gratified both of us by its sympathetic insight and its penetrating though sparing objections —I could have wished there had been more objections for me to profit by as I do by those you have made.

I have to thank you also for the reply to Jevons[4] which is calmly crushing —I had thoughts of sending you a more angry answer to him, but your tone is far better.

Yours truly

G. H. Lewes.

VII, 3:21 EDITH SIMCOX, AUTOBIOGRAPHY, 7–16 JANUARY 1878

MS: Bodleian. *Brief extract published:* McKenzie, p. 90.

Monday 7 January 1878

January 7. Went today to see her—after looking again at certain of her letters last night. Arrived about 5, stooped and only kissed her hand. Lewes stooped to kiss me, and I said I wasn't to kiss any one because I had kissed Mary[5] who thought she was going to have the mumps. He said they weren't catching, and she that it was an awful complaint but she must risk it. She asked what news? if my people[6] had come back? said they had expected

3. At the end of his long review of *The Physical Basis of Mind* Robertson wrote: "And, returning to Mr. Lewes, who has shown himself among the first—who claims indeed in his present preface to have been quite the first—to understand Psychology as the science of Mind in its wider implications, I cannot but venture the opinion that he has not now made all the use that might have been expected of his insight in dealing with the fallacy of 'Animal Automatism.'" (*Mind*, 3 [Jan-

uary 1878], 24–43).

4. William Stanley Jevons published in the *Contemporary Review* for December 1877 the first of three attacks entitled "John Stuart Mill's Philosophy Tested." Robertson replied in *Mind*, 3 (January 1878), 141–144.

5. Mary Hamilton.

6. Her mother Mrs. George Price Simcox and her brother George Augustus Simcox lived with Edith at 1 Douro Place, Victoria Road.

me to come and wish them a happy new year—in a sceptical way—; she had lost her cold, he had had a headache, but both were in a tolerable state of preservation. She said, apropos of the shop that she kept hearing fresh people say in a matter of course way that they were going to "Hamiltons," and mentioned somebody who was coming to us in the wake of a certain Hennell, of whom I knew nothing but wondered if he might be a relative of Sara. Mention of Oxford men who wear shirts brought up the Pattisons; they said he was so interesting in conversation if he once got launched; and Mrs. Lewes thought she had been getting up her book ever since she had known her.[7]

All this took but a few minutes, and I had hardly begun to despair of reaching more interesting topics when the fatal Johnny[8] came in, he had missed his train yesterday and had a book to return by way of pretext. Mrs. Cross[9] was mending; apropos of a sister going to see a married sister, something was said concerning the comparative wickedness of husbands and wives to each other. They thought there were extenuating circumstances for Dickens because his sister-in-law did everything for the family and for him, and his wife did nothing. From such conjugal trials it was a step to an absurdly circumstantial dream of Lewes',—that the archangel was in love with a humpbacked nobleman in holy orders—which he persisted was a most plausible combination of her three weak points! He was exercised how to make her realize the extent of her delinquencies against him, and thought of going away for a night—again in reference to her real dread of such an event, but he decided that would be so great a punishment to him that he would try the effect of a reproachful scene instead— at which point he woke. This she capped with a rather ludicrous dream of Stanleys—who thought he was elected Pope; then they talked of FitzJames Stephen on Bright about Indian irrigation—I not remembering till I was on my way home the objections to the former's answer which had occurred to me. I stayed about half an hour all told and left the field for Johnny. . . .

7. Mrs. Mark Pattison, *The Renaissance of Art in France*, 1879.

8. John Walter Cross.

9. His mother Mrs. William Cross.

VII, 5:21   EDITH SIMCOX, AUTOBIOGRAPHY, 16 JANUARY 1878

MS: Bodleian. *Extract published:* McKenzie, p. 94.

Wednesday 16 January 1878

16. After hesitating "to go or not to go" Monday and yesterday, a kind providence took me N.W. today. Mr. Lewes had gone to see a man with an artificial larynx[1] "could anything be more delightful?"—and she was alone. *Could* anything be more delightful? First she took me to task again about Cobbett and said she wanted me to get her another book and wouldn't tell me what unless I confessed the price of the Rural Rides. So I had to own to 10/6 and then it appeared she wanted our old friend "The Child's Own Book."[2] That I was delightedly able to promise anyway to lend her. She said they had laughed at the fatality of my crossing with Johnny last week; I said I knew I should poison his shirts some day, and she hoped I wouldn't, he saved them a great deal of trouble about money affairs, besides being the best of sons and brothers—I said of course, that was just why; I was jealous.

Then I told her of Mary's departure, and tried to explain why I thought I might do more work in consequence. I talked of a German dictionary— she was not enthusiastic, but said Sander's German one (like Littré's) would be a good foundation; but it would be useless unless one were employed by a publisher. I also mentioned as possible themes folklore and a history of property. She wanted a book made out of all the nice stories of ancient and modern history—the stories that all modern writers leave out to make room for characters etc. quite as mythical as the stories and much less entertaining. She also wished I could get one of the new primers, like Macmillan's, to do. Otherwise she encouraged the folk lore—she was much interested in the subject—the history of property likewise, though with rather more latent doubt as to my making the most of it. She thought it was a failing of mine to want to make my work impracticably complete—instancing "Natural Law" as well as what I said now of the unsatisfactoriness of the folklore investigation unless one could reach a satisfactory theory.

She also urged me to say and make people feel what she, as an author had a scruple about saying critically, that authorship should not be regarded in the same light as other professions, that every writer was *ipso facto* a teacher,—an educational influence—on his readers—and the

1. See VII, 12–13.
2. *The Child's Own Book*, 13th ed., 1869.

lightest poetaster could not escape the weight of attendant responsibility. She wished me to write because she thought the root of the matter was in me—concerning the moral relations of life—and whatever one wrote about, the work would be "informed" with one's fundamental views. She wished people would think more of the real matter of life—even the word "right" had come to have a dangerous metaphysical use—people would say you ought to do a thing, not for the real present reason, but because it is "right" to do it.

I stayed nearly two hours, and talked round and round, sometimes getting out something that I wanted to say, sometimes feeling helpless, as when she laughed at me again for being like Mr. Sidgwick[3]—talking as if what "bad people" might do was out of the question: . . . then she went on speaking of our fundamental agreement and of the extent to which one's character was in one's own hands; this apropos of my reference to the old difficulty. I said, did she not believe that it depended on the strength of a man's own inborn inclination whether he ever did anything to count in the world; she first said I was perverting her doctrine, and then agreed to my statement of it and quoted a definition of genius "God's gift, a man's own exertion, and circumstances to suit." But she added what was true, that it is suicidal to stop one's life in the middle by the application of a formula— that might cease to apply if from then onwards one gave one's mind to making the application cease. She insisted on calling the cooperative scheme "admirable" and on being glad that I had taken up some practical work besides authorship. I said after all the root of the evil was idleness.

I spoke of the creeping onwards of middle-aged content—or resignation—which I refused to call a progress when the evils were unaltered, only grown tolerable by use. I said, and she agreed that it was evil when people can do no more than—as in Mary Cross's story[4]—"find life possible and even bearable without any happiness in particular." She said no one could take a sadder view of life than she did—sometimes not on account of her own experience, that had been, but she had gone beyond it,—she lay back in her chair, and I said caressingly, it would be ungrateful if she did not like to live when she made so many people happy—I kissed her again and again and wondered meditatively how it was that one should be so glad just

3. Henry Sidgwick in *The Methods of Ethics*, 1874, argued that egoistic hedonism determines volition, "since to conscientious persons the pleasure in conduct is more or less dependent on its righteousness." In 1877 he published a supplement to the first edition in which ch. 1 and the first section of ch. 2 were almost entirely rewritten, and the view

on hedonism was retracted in ch. 4.

4. Mary Cross, "Marie of Villefranche," *Macmillan's*, 24 (August 1871), 297–303. Heinrich, billeted in Marie's house after the German occupation, loved her, but goes away when her husband, long thought dead, returns with one leg.

because somebody else was what she was. She wondered why I was so fond of her and I didn't know unless it was because she was herself and not somebody else, whereto she, that was no merit of hers, and I—No I gave providence the glory.

On the whole I was very happy, and came away consoled and resigned —to not being resigned just yet to final, fatal failure. She said once that I was wiser than I used to be—I talked less discontent—I hinted one might think the more. She admitted that there might be cases—though in frequently—of people to whom opportunities do not come, and said in answer to my charge that she believed in providence that she had never risked her influence more than by breaking out to a young woman who was sobbing to her—"I know it must be all for my good"—"it" being a trial proceeding from somebody's wrong doing—"Nay, but a great many things happen to people that are not at all good for them." Altogether she is a darling, and I shall proceed to write.

VII, 7:9 GE TO JAMES HARWOOD, LONDON, 18 JANUARY 1878

Text: Copy from Mrs. C. Humphry Trevelyan.

The Priory, | 21. North Bank, | Regents Park.
January 18. 1878.

Mr. James Harwood
Dear Sir
   In reply to your question concerning the name Romola, I would beg to say that the correct pronunciation according to the Italian usage is Rŏmŏla.
I remain

Yours faithfully
M. E. Lewes.

VII, 10:1 EDITH SIMCOX, AUTOBIOGRAPHY, 20–22 JANUARY 1878

MS: Bodleian.

Sunday 20 January 1878

20. And today though it is Sunday (I have not been since November 25) I will take "The Child's Own Book" with me and just see her and make wild attempts to talk to somebody the few minutes I stay—then come back and go on if I can with my scribbling.

Tuesday 22 January 1878

22. There were few visitors, so if I had not been stupidly modest I might have had "good times." Lewes was affectionate. I took her the book and talked mostly—for 20 minutes to him and W. Cross. He said Herbert Spencer was preparing autobiographical materials[5]—it will be entertainingly wooden and arrogant.

VII, 13:15   EDITH SIMCOX, AUTOBIOGRAPHY, 6–13 FEBRUARY 1878

MS: Bodleian. *Extract published:* McKenzie, p. 105.

Wednesday 6 February 1878

6. Yesterday I went to see her, and have been in a calm glow of happiness since:—for no special reason, only that to have been near her happens to have that effect on me. She had had headaches and was in a somewhat despondent mood, so I did nothing but make reckless love to her. I told her about the International[6] (how I withheld my name from the council and then in remorse offered to lend Dean St.[7] for a council chamber!) and she seemed to think me well out of it. I brought her two of the least spoilt of my valentines, which she humanely forebore to read in my presence. She said it was a pity my letters could not be kept some 5 centuries to show a more sober posterity what hyperbole had once been possible. I asked if she took so gloomy a view of the future as to think 5 centuries hence there would be no one as adorable as herself:—of that, said Lewes, you may be sure. I agreed and she professed to be silenced in confusion. I had told her of my ambition to be allowed to lie silently at her feet as she pursued her occupations, and that made her refer to my last letter. She also said—as she once wrote that I "knew all the craft of fyne loving,"[8] as she also tells her husband; he and I pelted her with a little loving chaff about her own unamiableness, and when he affected to agree with her I said it was a mean attempt to curry favour with divinity—I could be no party to such hypo-

5. See VI, 310, n. 1.
6. The International Working Men's Association. Edith had represented the Shirt and Collar Makers at the Trade Union Congress in Glasgow in October 1875 and at Newcastle-upon-Tyne in September 1876, and was interested in the efforts to revive the International.

See K.A. McKenzie, *Edith Simcox and George Eliot*, 1961, pp. 36–51.
7. Hamilton & Co., 68 Dean Street, Soho.
8. Chaucer's Alceste "taughte al the craft of fyn lovinge." (*Legend of Good Women*, Prologue, line 544.)

crisy—unless I had as much as he to gain! I tore myself away with difficulty, choked with tears in the passages—and so came away.

Wednesday 13 February 1878

13. Heard from Trübner that a second edition of "Natural Law" would be wanted soon. Today wrote a little "Competition" and—just before 3—a visitor was announced!—Came forward and lo! in the middle of the room was my goddess! I threw my arms round her—she had on a spotted net veil that could have grieved me but for the angelic way in which she took it off at my prayer. Apropos of the second edition we got onto high problems of ethics. I said I was in doubt whether to give any explanation about Utilitarianism; she thought the misunderstandings of reviewers hardly amounted to a presumption that one was wrong. She thought the weak point of Utilitarianism, in Sidgwick and others, lay not in their taking human welfare as the standard of right but in their trying to find in it the moral *motive*. We agreed I think in substance there, and they assented to my objection to Huxley's last article, evening Darwin's Origin of Species with Harvey's circulation of the blood.[1] I proposed to add a paragraph in the sense of what she had said to me, of the dangerousness of making "right" into a metaphysical abstraction, severed from the intuitions which constitute its nature, and said that I felt myself that that might be a snare. She was rather slow to believe that it could be a snare to me to take anything for granted, and I said she didn't know, I was always very much of my own opinion. Then (there had been some professional transactions[2] first of all) they arose to go; I should say that for the last few minutes I had been kneeling by her, looking up into her face with my cheek resting against a bit of fur round her wrist,—we went down stairs and at the door Maria was admitting a man, he advanced to the foot of the stairs and lo! The Rector of Lincoln[3]—tableau! They turned back and there was more conversation, concerning Jevons on Mill and the rising school in Oxford which follows Green and Caird to think English philosophy nowhere, Kant and Hegel on the right track, but they themselves in some unexplained way, many leagues in advance even of them—She thought there was a dangerous tendency among 2nd and 3rd rate thinkers to go on inventing something that shall catch disciples without any strong preliminary conviction. She instanced

1. For the tercentenary of William Harvey's birth Huxley gave a lecture at the Royal Institution, 25 January 1878, published in the *Fortnightly*, 23 (February 1878), 167–190. The comparison with Darwin, p. 183, comments on the general acceptance of evolution within 20 years while Harvey's discovery took much longer.

2. Cuffs GE had come to order.

3. Mark Pattison.

Schopenhauer and a man for whom she had a great respect—I guessed Herbert Spencer. The Rector thought professional jealousies were not officially to blame for this, but quoted Pusey on the other side. Then they really went, but I got yet another kiss and am considerably consoled.

VII, 14:6 EDITH SIMCOX, AUTOBIOGRAPHY, 26 FEBRUARY 1878

MS: Bodleian.

Tuesday 26 February 1878

26. . . . When the last entry was made I had been working over "Natural Law" and was rather disgusted with it—at least it failed to interest me and I seemed to understand that she could not care for it. On the next Tuesday [19 February] I went to the Priory to take her the cuffs she had ordered at the office and to tell her I didn't want to have a 2nd edition. However he had a headache and she, I thought was tired with her drive, so I said nothing. I forget what we spoke of, besides the Rector of Lincoln and Pierre Leroux—they were gratified at my remembering his "Il ne s'agit que d'y arriver" (quoted by Lewes who forgot having done so). Stayed only a short time—returned to the shop and tailoresses. Two days after saw Trübner, and felt it would not be possible to withdraw the book as it was in his series.

VII, 14:6 GHL TO MME EUGÈNE BODICHON, LONDON, [27 FEBRUARY 1878]

MS: Yale.

The Priory, | 21. North Bank, | Regents Park.

Dear Bar

No! it was no inspiration of mine that prompted the good Hall[4] but his own thoughtful heart. All I did was to give him your address.

Your niece says nothing of your health so we take the 'no news good news' interpretation as most pleasant to us.

We are shaky. Madonna has been suffering from colds and sore throat and I from constant headaches. For all that we have been gay and gadding and "the cry is still they come."[4a]

4. W.H.B. Hall lunched at the Priory 10 February 1878. He had been looking   for a governess for his son.
4a. *Macbeth*, v, v, 2.

On the 6th we dined with Lady Colvile,[5] on the 7th I dined with Sir H. Thompson (one of his octave dinners—Trollope, Alma Tadema, Burton, Jeaffreson,[6] Leslie Stephen, and Sir F. Pollock). On the 9th at the concert the Princess Louise, having first bowed to us, told the Princess of Wales and the Princess Christian,[7] who all the rest of the time were carefully inspecting her; and the next Saturday while I was speaking to Neruda[8] Mrs. Baring[9] came and told me the Princess Christian desired I should be presented to her. This was done. We had a brief and trivial talk, mainly about George Eliot. On the 12 we lunched at Lord Houghtons—present Kinglake, Browning, Morris, the Bruces, Lady Galway, Sir C. Dilke and Mrs. Moulton, an American poetess.[1]—capital stories!

On the 16th we had a small dinner party—present Lady Claud Hamilton, the Tyndalls, the Bowens, and Sir Lewis Pelly—went off capitally.

On the 20th a 'drum' at Hamilton Aidés—at which Fanny Kemble and Lady Salisbury were the two to whom we mostly talked, but there were also others—old and new—and some good recitation by Miss Geneviève Ward, who also talks very well.

On Sunday our new acquaintance Moritz[2] the Hungarian tragedian gave us a scene from Othello—(I reading Iago) and last Monday evening he went through the part with us alone, to see whether we approved of his conception and execution. He is a very interesting fellow as you may imagine from this exclamation at the end of our long rehearsal—"Oh I feel I know so little—but in 10 years I shall be able to play Othello"—He is to give a performance on Saturday morning at the Queen's—I hope it will be a success.

The great event is to come off tomorrow—the marriage of Lionel Tennyson to Eleanor Locker at Westminter Abbey. I tremble somewhat at the prospect of the cold Abbey with Madonna's throat in its present state—otherwise the scene will be very interesting.

Much love is sent to you

Ever yours
G. H. L.

5. Lord Houghton, Mrs. Richard Strachey, and Professor George James Allman were the other guests.

6. John Cordy Jeaffreson (1831–1901) was Inspector of Manuscripts for the Royal Historical Manuscripts Commission.

7. Helena, Queen Victoria's third daughter, was married to Prince Christian of Schleswig-Holstein. The *her* is GE.

8. Wilma Norman-Neruda (1839–1911), violinist.

9. The Hon. Mrs. R. Bruce Baring.

1. See VII, 19.

2. Neville Moritz. "In performing Othello in English he accomplishes a remarkable feat. His English is far better than that of Mr. Fechter, a fact for which a long residence in America may account." (*Athenæum*, 9 March 1878, p. 326.)

VII, 14:17   GHL TO ALBERT GEORGE DEW-SMITH, LONDON, [? MARCH 1878]

MS: Yale.

The Priory, | 21. North Bank, | Regents Park.
My dear Sir

Though I think *Cambridge* ought to honor itself with Darwin's Portrait and not allow outsiders to participate I gladly send my mite.[3]

Yours truly

G. H. Lewes.

VII, 16:8   EDITH SIMCOX, AUTOBIOGRAPHY, 17–18 MARCH 1878

MS: Bodleian.

Sunday 17 March 1878

March 17. On the 11th after 3 weeks all but a day, ventured again. She had been poorly, with a cold and thought I was never coming again. She was alone when I got there, but all is gone from me of what passed except that I found myself being scolded by both of them at once for unresponsive, cold and apparently supercilious manners.

Oh yes! I asked about the Lifted Veil. Lewes said it came out in Blackwood[4] without name soon after Adam Bede. He asked what I thought of it. I was embarrassed and said—as he did—that it was not at all like her other writings, wherefrom she differed; she said it was "schauderhaft" was it, and I yes; but I was put out by things that I didn't quite know what to do with —it was a shame to give such things a moral, but—: He Oh, but the moral is plain enough—it is only an exaggeration of what happens—the one-sided knowing of things in relation to the self—not whole knowledge because "tout comprehendre est tout pardonner." She said he wasn't in the habit of asking people before her what they thought of her books—which was rather hard on the people—I was at least unnecessary then since she must know. She said she didn't at all, and she had never felt with me as she had with many people what it was in her books that worked on me; she had never felt that I had been influenced either by what she wrote or what

---

3. GHL's account shows a contribution of £1.1 for the Darwin portrait, now at Darwin College, Cambridge.

4. *Blackwood's*, 86 (July 1859), 24–48.

she said. I looked protests and then they both went on. Lewes said that it was months before I so much as looked at, let alone spoke to him; his amour propre was not hurt but he observed it. She said—if he was not sensitive in that way, she was. I hardly said anything in self defence. I quoted George Sand "On n'aime pas ceux qui ne s'aiment pas eux-mêmes et qui par consequent ne tâchent pas de plaire." She said but I had wanted to please her —and the sentence finished itself "and you see you did not succeed"—in the same breath she said—"I don't mean that"—But it was something to know that all my tears and agony had not been for nothing. I was as miserable as ever I had believed.

Monday 18 March 1878

March 18. I went today again as I had meant—All the more though for a letter that came this morning—she had been cheered by a letter I wrote last Thursday (about the effect of her books on me) after an abortive attempt to see her, baffled by the sight of a pony carriage at the door. Today Lewes was unhappy about a friend, a self-taught correspondent for whom he had got a clerkship, who is threatened with blindness.[5] I stayed a long hour, yet have not much to record. I got out most of what I meant to say about my general social demeanour. Lewes laid it down as a principle that a man would much rather forgive you for boring him than for letting him imagine he bored you. He said he was not speaking for himself, for there was nothing he was so impatient of as being bored. When reviewers were spoken of I said I hoped they sometimes spoke the truth by mistake and quoted the Athenaeum;[6] she seemed interested but surprised and said "No doubt he had a nasty meaning"—which Lewes said was hard on both him and me. She is a darling. I told her I was going to do Hartmann and she wanted me to make notes of my dissent as I went along and publish an independent criticism. Lewes would not hear of the idea of a dissentient preface. She is a darling.—I feel as if I was going to be good for a long time on end.

---

5. Robert Ripley.
6. Reviewing *Natural Law* in the *Athenæum*, 13 October 1877, pp. 460–461, [Henderson] wrote: "The author, however, to whom we should say Miss Simcox has been most deeply indebted, and from whom she has learned most, is George Eliot. There is the same stoicism, tinged occasionally by the same hues of tragic sadness, which are prominent in our greatest living novelist." GE is mentioned only once in the book with three lines quoted from "Armgart" (p. 138). GHL is also referred to: "And just as we find Mr. Lewes speak of the world and the system of things which constitutes what we call reality as being still the same, though all our theories about them are nought, so is Miss Simcox contented to accept things as they are. . . ."

VII, 16:8 GHL TO JABEZ HOGG, LONDON, [? APRIL 1878]

MS: Berg Collection, New York Public Library.

The Priory, | 21 North Bank, | Regents Park.

Tuesday.

My dear Mr. Hogg[7]

Your view of Ripley's case is sadder than I expected. Poor fellow! His story is most interesting as you will hear on the 1st when I hope to have the pleasure of thanking you in person for your kindness to him.

Yours truly

G. H. Lewes.

VII, 19:5 GHL TO MRS. EDWIN LANKESTER, LONDON, [? APRIL 1878]

Text: Transcript by Mr. J. Lester.

The Priory, | 21. North Bank, | Regents Park.

Wednesday.

Dear Mrs. Lankester[8]

I am sure that you desire that I should be perfectly open with you. Mrs. Lewes's strength and time are already so severely tasked by visitors that we have constantly to decline proposals of friends to introduce their relatives and friends, and of strangers to introduce themselves—it is our only safeguard; without it our rooms would not contain the visitors. From all she had heard of you she had formed such a respect for you that she at once acceded to your desire to see her; but you will understand why I beg you not to extend the invitation beyond yourself; and I am sure you would rather be frankly told the reason.

Yours truly

G. H. Lewes.

7. Jabez Hogg (1817–99), ophthalmologist, wrote *Impairment of Vision*, 1876, and *The Cure of Cataract*, 1878. GHL chatted with him at the Royal Society soirée, 1 May 1878. (GHL Diary.)

8. Phebe Pope Lankester (1845–1900), widow of Edwin Lankester, by whom she had 8 children, was the daughter of a Manchester mill owner. She wrote *British Ferns*, 1858, *Wild Flowers*, 1861, and *Talks about Health*, 1874. She was an energetic campaigner for reforms, contributing to many country papers under the pseudonym "Penelope."

VII, 19:5 EDITH SIMCOX, AUTOBIOGRAPHY, 1–10 APRIL 1878

MS: Bodleian

Monday 1 April 1878

April 1. Last Wednesday I went again; stayed only a few minutes as she was reading the Ms. of his book,[1] but I got a kiss or two and the chance of be-moaning myself at the coming summer; I said I wished her house[2] ready betimes and so on for her sake but *not* for my own. She said she liked people to be a little unhappy when she went—did not care for a too disinterested affection. I had a commission which will give me an excuse for going again this week and today I have written to her—what I hope will not be dis-pleasing—oh! I love her dearly dearly.

Saturday 6 April 1878

April 6. Yesterday I had a few lines bidding me come on Wednesday [10 April] at 3.30 for an hour to "hear and say more than can be written." I am anxious and yet content, I feel that nothing that she can say will fail to touch me.

Wednesday 10 April 1878

10. Arrived to the moment. Began with little talk about cuffs and hand-kerchiefs. Elizabeth brought tea. Presently she said: she knew so well the state of mind in which I had written when there seemed no inducements to choose one kind of work rather than another. She had nothing to suggest as to ways of determining oneself, only thought it a pity to feel bound to produce; I tried to explain that production—or the inclination thereto —came of itself if I took up any subject—but I was blankly idle now. She could not understand the want of natural interest without ulterior purpose, but said Mr Lewes also, unlike her, only cared for lines of enquiry etc. in view of a particular end, she sometimes wished he had more hobbies —Could I not take up a language or a science? I had referred to an old taste for teaching, she thought it was a pity I should not have pupils. She said once, more as an assertion than a question that I was sincere in wishing to do and would take any opportunity that came even if it was rather hard. She called the shirtmaking an excellent bit of work, only had hoped that the idea might have spread more rapidly. Mr. Lewes was dining out

1. *Problems of Life and Mind*, 3d series, *The Study of Psychology*, published   in May 1879.
    2. The Heights, Witley.

and I prayed to be allowed to stay without talking till he came in. She said she couldn't read with me there. I complained a little at such evidence that one did not belong to her and she spoke of her complete dependence on his society and unreasonable anxiety when he was away. This was all on the 10th.

VII, 19:5 GE TO WILLIAM R. SHEDDEN-RALSTON, LONDON, 4 APRIL 1878

MS: Pennsylvania State University.

The Priory, | 21. North Bank, | Regents Park.
April 4. 78.

My dear Mr. Ralston

We knew of your illness while you were still laid low in Paris, and were so far comforted about you as to learn that you had a mother's tendance.[3] We saw the announcement of your return, and though I remembered well your pretty project about Switzerland and did not like thinking that you had been obliged to renounce it, I hoped and imagined that your health was restored. It is a sad disappointment to learn that you are still a sufferer—and from a complaint which we too, between us, have had enough bodily hints of, to experience a lively fellow-feeling with a friend who is more severely afflicted.

It is some relief for you that you are able to write, but I feel that your days must be trying—I hope the nights are less so.

Your letter is a welcome assurance at least that you believe in our caring about any good or evil that befals you, and we are both heartily wishing that we may soon hear of the good after this smart visitation of evil.

Always, dear Mr. Ralston,

Yours very truly
M. E. Lewes.

3. After his retirement from the British Museum, where he had served as the authority on Russian books 1853– 75, Ralston, who never married, suffered periodically from acute mental depression. (*DNB.*)

VII, 23:1 LORD ACTON TO GE, LONDON, 15 APRIL 1878

MS: University of Virginia.

72, Princes Gate.

April 15 1878.

Dear Mrs. Lewes

As Mr. Lewes has the flair of a Dominican for the detection and exposure of heresy, allow me to confess mine in secret. In pursuing the topic of awkward and misdirected admiration, Mr. Lewes said[4] that both Wordsworth and yourself write in reality for a chosen audience and are shut out from intelligent appreciation by many schools of men.

To me who do not rate Wordsworth next to Shakespeare among modern writers there was a flavour of heresy in the juxtaposition and I was going on to say that no intelligent man or woman of any school seems to me shut out from sympathy with your writings or enjoyment of them. For myself who come to them from afar the perpetual wonder next to your supreme faculty of prose is the gift of penetrating and dwelling in regions not your own. I suppose it must be as difficult an art as that of thinking according to mood or subject in different languages and I never knew anybody who thought in more than three.

But I am persuaded that if you chose you could make not only characters of men reveal their secrets to the world more fully than they are known to themselves, but all manner of doctrines and persuasions display themselves in their strength and attraction more faithfully and more vividly than they appear to their own exponents.

That was the argument that was on my lips during the short freedom of my tête à tête with Mr. Lewes and if I bore to look foolish and even disrespectful rather than deliver it before you, it was from a selfish fear that I should forfeit your gracious farewell, bidding me come again. Believe me, Dear Mrs. Lewes,

Most truly yours

Acton.

4. Lord Acton met GHL and GE at dinner at Tennyson's 12 April 1878. The conversation described here occurred during his first call at the Priory, 14 April. He came again 19 and 26 May 1878.

VII, 23:1   GHL TO [?],
LONDON, 19 APRIL [1878]

MS: Yale.

The Priory, | 21. North Bank, | Regents Park.

19 April.

Dear Sir

Mr. Trübner had arranged to look in here yesterday to see if Mrs. Lewes approved of the Bookcase—he either forgot or was unable to keep this engagement, and as he is now, no doubt, on his journey I write to you to say that Mrs. Lewes finds the *size* of the Bookcase sent her inconveniently large, and would be glad if you could send her in exchange one of the smaller size—with only two rows. If there should not be one ready she can wait. Meanwhile the one now here will not be used.

Yours truly

G. H. Lewes.

VII, 23:1   GE TO JOHN WALTER CROSS,
LONDON, 29 APRIL 1878

MS: Yale.

The Priory, | 21. North Bank, | Regents Park.

April 29. 78.

Dearest Nephew

I had no opportunity yesterday[5] of thanking you for my transcendantly beautiful basket of flowers, which not only cheered me as a sign of your valued affection, but made our table cheerful and supplied some deficit of vivacity in the hostess.

It is a precious thought to me that you care for that part of me which will live when the 'Auntship' is gone—'Non omnis moriar'[6] is a keen hope with me. Yet I like to be loved in this faulty, frail (yet venerable) flesh.

My master insists that I shall go out to walk with him. So I have had only three minutes to scribble in.

Always your affectionate

Aunt.

5. Cross and his sister Florence were among the guests at lunch Sunday, 28 April.
6. Horace, *Odes,* III, xxx, 6.

VII, 24:14 BENJAMIN JOWETT TO GE, OXFORD, 7 MAY 1878

MS: University of Virginia.

Oxford May 7, 1878.

Dear Mrs. Lewes

Will you and Mr. Lewes give me the great pleasure of a visit this year? The servants asked me today "When is Mrs. Lewes coming?" and I venture to think with them that I have a vested interest or am beginning to acquire one. Shall I propose Saturday June 8th or would any other day suit you better?

I remember with great interest our walks and talks in the country.[7] I once thought of writing to you about this but feared I should take up your time to no purpose. It seemed to me that you were sometimes troubled with the want of seriousness in the public and indisposed to write because in this babble of voices nothing was heard. One certainly does feel in this age that a book is not made to be understood or appreciated, but to be criticized. But all this endless superficial criticism does not prevent a work of genius and character finding its way to the hearts of mankind. And though it is a queer age in which we live I suppose we should school ourselves to take the world of literature as it is in order that we may exert our whole strength in trying to rise above it. Almost anything worth writing must provoke a good deal of resentment in antipathetic minds which is very often the measure of its excellence and success.

The more I think of it the more I agree in what you said that the really great and abiding interest of philosophy is human motive. I can never go along with Mr. Herbert Spencer in system-making nor meet my friend Professor Green[8] and others in attempting to bring back the antiquated philosophies of Germany. But about human motive there is a great deal which might be taught mankind and has never been taught them, to their great loss. It is the natural way of supplying the religious want which is so deeply felt just now.

With best regards to Mr. Lewes, I remain, Dear Mrs. Lewes,

Yours most truly

B. Jowett.

I was very sorry to hear of the calamity which has befallen your friends the Hollands.

7. At Witley, 4 October 1877. GE may have confessed her discouragement at the reception of *Daniel Deronda*.

8. Thomas Hill Green (1836–82), Fellow of Balliol College and Professor of Moral Philosophy at Oxford.

VII, 28:28 EDITH SIMCOX, AUTOBIOGRAPHY, 26 MAY 1878

MS: Bodleian.

Sunday 26 May 1878

May 26. On Monday next (20th) Mary came back from Egypt and just as she was leaving with her mother, the carriage drove up (I was in the doorway with Mrs. Hamilton and their cab had just drawn up so that the Lewes's carriage stopped further down the street). I rushed down the muddy pavement to greet them and then beckoned Mary, who was kindly welcomed—then Mrs. Hamilton came and begged to introduce herself. Then they (the Lewes) drove off. We spoke for a few moments about silks, then the vision was lost. On Friday [24th] I went with fresh patterns of silk; Johnny was there and she asked me to come some other day, Sunday or Monday or Tuesday. Returning home through Kensington Gardens, if the truth must be told I sat down under a spreading tree and cried. By the next day I was ashamed and on Sunday [26th], rather than write to her, I resolved to go.—Arrived just after 5, found Miss Helps and a lady, Lord Acton, (I think) Pauli the historian, another German,[9] Mark Pattison, later Kegan Paul and his wife. Talk was of Shakespere's generic superiority to other dramatists.

After the first set had left (I was going but she bade me stay) talk was of translations, ignorance in print and the unprincipledness of even good people like Mrs. Oliphant who write of that whereof they know nothing. I asked Lewes if the poem announced in Macmillan was the "Symposium"[1] as I supposed and he said yes. I am keeping back the sheets of Natural Law so as to get a motto thence. A note concerning silks was posted on Sunday, which got at the shop on the 28th. I answering half apologized for my appearance on Sunday—a living refutation of the charge of misanthropy she brought in Johnny's presence. On Wednesday was in doubt whether to take or send another variety of silk—at last resolved to take it and leave the parcel at the door if need were. The servant made me come in; she was very tired, but as I kissed her, her cheek pressed caressingly against

9. The lady was Henrietta Rintoul and the other German her friend Paul Friedmann.

1. "The College Breakfast-Party." Frederic Chapman came 10 May and offered £250 for permission to print the poem. GHL told him that "Macmillan must have the first refusal. He lunched with us. Then went to Macmillan, who is 'to consider,' " and wrote the next day "to accept with delight." (GHL Diary.) It was published in *Macmillan's*, 38 (July 1878), 161–179. MS Yale.

mine. Then threw the folds of the silk round sleeves to see the effect in a mass, and as her hand passed near him, he seized it, even as I do, and left a kiss thereon; one of the things for which I am thankful through every jealous pain is the perfectness of the love binding those two together.

VII, 29:11   GHL TO MME EUGÈNE BODICHON, LONDON, [5 JUNE 1878]

MS: Yale.

The Priory, | 21. North Bank, | Regents Park.

Dear Barbara

Before you leave town please send me the French novels, I shall want them in the country.

If you have a laugh at disposal these stories claim it. They have just arrived from Lytton.

In a recent number of the *Hindu Patriot* this sentence occurs. "Sir G. Campbell[2] set up as a great authority in England but House of Commons soon stripped him to pieces and exposed his cui bono in all its naked hideousness"—

A Hindoo suspecting that during his absence his wife might be imitating Lady Potiphar, asked leave, went home, and found my lady in the arms of her unreluctant Joseph. Narrating the event he said "Think, Sahib, what a *magnificent* spectacle!"

We have not yet finished our furniture troubles, nor our dissipations. On Friday we dined with the Crown Prince and Princess. They were extremely gracious, reproaching us for not having let them know when we were in Berlin and on taking leave both Prince and Princess made Madonna promise that we would not again visit Berlin without reporting ourselves. —"I believe you know my sister Louise" were the Princess's first words to Madonna. "I have long wanted to know you"—etc.

When she was complimenting me, I got over the awkwardness by saying that I should excuse myself as Dr. Johnson did for accepting the flatteries of George III: "Sir, it was not for me to bandy words with my sovereign."[3]—and I told her that one of her future subjects would have an extra *groll* against her if he heard of the notice she was taking of me.

---

2. Sir George Campbell (1824–92), Indian administrator during the Mutiny.

3. Boswell, *Life of Johnson*, ed. L.F. Powell, 6 vols., Oxford, 1934–40, II, 35: "bandy Civilities."

She opened her wide eyes and asked "Who? Werder?"[4]—I could not *name* him, but I told her the alarm some one felt about her coming to the throne lest she should introduce *English laxity* in Religion! This amused her and then dropping her voice she said seriously "I know why it is. It is because Strauss was a dear friend of mine." It was a delightful party—every man present (except Lord Ripon) being distinguished, and except the necessity of *standing* so long everything was pleasant.

Tonight we go to Lord Carnarvon's, on Saturday[5] to Jowett at Oxford —on Monday to music party at Sir H. Thompson's, on Tuesday to music party at Hamilton Aïdé's—and then I hope to Witley.

Ever yours affectionately

G. H. L.

VII, 29:11   GE TO LADY THOMPSON, LONDON, 5 JUNE 1878

MS: Private collection.

The Priory, | 21. North Bank, | Regents Park.

June 5. 78.

Dear Lady Thompson

We shall be happy to dine with you on the 10th (Monday next) and will remember the ruling as to the hour 7.15 for 7.30.

Yours always truly

M. E. Lewes.

4. Karl Wilhelm Friedrich Werder (1806–93), poet and philosopher, a friend of the Princess Royal, who wrote to Queen Victoria (20 March 1858), that she was greatly pleased by his interest in English literature.

5. "At 10.30 went to a large gathering at Lord Carnarvon's. Talked with Browning, Lady Portsmouth, her daughter Camilla, Adams the astronomer, Richardson, and long and delightfully with Lady Amory, who begged to be allowed to call on our return to town. Home at 12.15." (GHL Diary, 5 June 1878.)

VII, 32:3　GHL TO EDWARD DOWDEN, LONDON, [12 JUNE 1878]

MS: Berg Collection, New York Public Library.

The Priory, | **21. North Bank,** | **Regents Park.**
Wednesday.

Dear Mr. Dowden

A very welcome present saluted me today on my return home—your capital Studies in Literature—I am already familiar with them—with two of them, *very* familiar—and it is on this account that I am so glad to have them all together in a handsome volume.[6]

Are we never to have the pleasure of seeing you in London again?[7] We flit at the end of this month and shall not return till December.

Yours truly
G. H. Lewes.

VII, 32:3　GHL TO SIR HENRY THOMPSON, LONDON, [12 JUNE 1878]

MS: Yale.

The Priory, | **21. North Bank,** | **Regents Park.**

Dear Sir Henry

Montalba's address is R. A. Montalba, 20 Stanley Crescent, Kensington Park Gardens.

He and his daughters[8] not only *can* but will be *delighted* to give you all information artistic and sanitary about Venice which they know so well. As brother artists[9] you ought to be acquainted and I am sorry we shall not be in town to make our house the place of meeting. You need no other introduction than your name.

We trust lady Thompson still has good effects from the Henschel Kur[1] —so delightful an evening ought to have nothing but delightful results.

6. Edward Dowden (1843–1913), *Studies in Literature 1789–1877*, 1878. GE's works are surveyed in two chapters, pp. 240–272 and 273–310.
7. He called 9 April 1876. (GHL Diary.)
8. Anthony Rubens Montalba, R.A. had four daughters. Clara (1842–1929) was known for her watercolors of Venice; Henrietta Skerrett (1856–93) had studied there at the Belle Arti.
9. Sir Henry Thompson (1820–1904), a surgeon, exhibited his paintings at the Royal Academy 1865–85.
1. After the Thompsons' dinner Henschel "played and sang till 11.30." (GHL Diary, 10 June 1878.)

Though I am sorry to say *I* had an agonizing attack of cramps which almost made me faint. That I should suffer thus for a lifelong abstemiousness!

Yours truly
G. H. Lewes.

VII, 32:3 EDITH SIMCOX, AUTOBIOGRAPHY, 16–22 JUNE 1878

MS: Bodleian.

Sunday 16 June 1878

June 16. I told her (on the 29th) that my idea of happiness was to buy her slop-pails for her.—whereto she—"They are all bought now"—I wrote in sending the desired bill for the silks,[2] that that completed the definition in a tragic fashion, and rashly committed myself by a promise to leave her alone for a space. The next week I took holiday from the shop and for the last fortnight have been trying the experiment of living like other people —gardening, visiting, shopping, reading, sewing, carpentering and so on. I have not minded it for a change—but the fortnight has not been short. Last Sunday—only 10 long days after my rash promise I wrote to·her again—partly about Daniel Deronda that I had read through in the first days of my holiday. After luncheon on Wednesday I went to take some syringa, not knowing whether she would be back from Oxford. They were out driving. Last night came one of those sweet envelopes, bidding me come tomorrow for the dreaded farewell: after which life becomes a blank for alas! nearly 5 months.

Saturday 22 June 1878

22. I went on Monday "towards 6 o'clock." She was alone and very beautiful. The travelling book case was in the hall and general signs of discomfort; they were going down on Wednesday. Elizabeth is going to be married. I just remember exchanging a few words about these things and then—I cannot in the very least recal the transition, she said it was a shame to find fault with me the last day but she wanted to give me a parting exhortation.—The old story: she said I was uncivil to Johnny the other day—my unlucky "only Mr. Cross" I suppose that really was supercilious and indifferent, that she herself even now had a difficulty sometimes

2. GHL's account for June shows Hamilton & Co., £6. 12. 6.

in realizing that I was not feeling superciliously towards her. She said perhaps one reason was that I "did not like men"—against which I protested as usual—perhaps as usual in vain, and then by way of diversion I related my last attempts at sociability. At half past six Lewes came in and asked me if I had prayed for him for his goodness in staying away: as usual I was unready with the answer. Then I had to go; they left the room with me. She said to him she had been finding fault with me—I think but am not sure adding it was good if I did not mind, anyway adding that she did not like people to find fault with her.

VII, 35:9 GHL TO JABEZ HOGG, WITLEY, 28 JUNE 1878

MS: University of California Los Angeles.

The Heights, Witley, | Nr. Godalming.
28 June 78.

My dear Mr. Hogg

It was very kind of you to think of me and had I been in town I should for your sake have gone to hear your protégé, but the concerts to which alone I am seductible by now are those of my own wood—nightingales at night, finches, thrushes, blackbirds by day. The roar of London is happily distant now and the heat of society exchanged for the delicious warmth of nature!

We were both knocked up by London gaieties and Royalties and have said adieu to all for another five months.

Yours very truly
G. H. Lewes.

When last I heard from Ripley his sight had almost recovered its healthy state.

VII, 37:1 GE TO MME EUGÈNE BODICHON, WITLEY, 8 JULY 1878

MS: Berg Collection, New York Public Library.

The Heights, Witley, | Nr. Godalming.
July 8. 78.

Dearest Barbara

I received this morning the carefully packed fan, which I feel renewed compunction for having teazed you about. I imagine poor Miss Marks having made explorations for it in your drawers or boxes and feel myself ignobly indebted as one who has been more considerate of her own small wants than of others' trouble. By post I return the beautiful Sandalwood Fan which was a too valuable object of barter for my old trumpery, the sole attraction of this latter being that it has the telescope structure now difficult to find and especially convenient to one of my dropping-all-things-from-hands-and-lap propensity, because it passes easily into my pocket.

Is it not a comfort for each of us separately and the country generally that the sunshine is come back? Mr. Lewes has been gouty and I bilious, so I dare say you have had the advantage of us lately and will soon make us look, as usual, pitiable by the side of you. With best love

Yours ever
Marian.

VII, 44:6   GHL TO PHILIP GILBERT HAMERTON, [WITLEY, 18? JULY 1878]

Text: Philip Gilbert Hamerton, *An Autobiography and a Memoir*, London, 1897, pp. 459–60.

We left London before your book[3] arrived, but I sent for it, and Mrs. Lewes has been reading it aloud to me the last few evenings. It has charmed us both, and we regret that so good a scheme, so well carried out, should in the nature of case be one doomed to meet with small public response. No reader worth having can read it without interest and profit, but *il s'agit de trouver des lecteurs*. My son writes in great delight with it, and I have recommended it to the *one* person we have seen in our solitude,[4] but I fear you will find the deaf adder of a public deafer than usual to your charming. A volume of biographies of well-known Frenchmen would have but a slender chance of success—and a volume on the unknown would need to be spiced with religion or politics—*et fortement épicé*—to attract more than a reader here and there.

We are here for five weeks in our Paradise *without* the serpent (symbol of visitors!); but alas! without the health which would make the long peace one filled with work. As for me, I vegetate mostly. I get up at six to stroll out for an hour before breakfast, leaving Madonna in bed with Dante or Homer, and quite insensible to the attractions of before-breakfast walks.

---

3. Hamerton's *Modern Frenchmen,* 1878, is mentioned several times in GHL's Diary, 10–18 July 1878.

4. Perhaps John Cross, who came to lunch 14 July.

With my cigar I get a little reading done, and sometimes write a little; but the forenoon is usually sauntered and pottered away. When Madonna has satisfied her inexhaustible craving for knowledge till nearly lunchtime, we play at lawn-tennis. Then drive out for two or three hours. Music and books till dinner. After cigar and nap, she reads to me till ten, and I finish by some light work till eleven. But I hope in a week or two to get stronger and able to work again, the more so as 'the night in which no man can work'[5] is fast approaching.

VII, 57:1 EDITH SIMCOX, AUTOBIOGRAPHY, 11 AUGUST 1878

MS: Bodleian. *Extracts published:* McKenzie, pp. 105–106.

Sunday 11 August 1878

11. A wet morning; took Beccaria "Des délits et des peines"[6] to read in the train—which was moderately punctual at first. I knew the line as far as Woking, it seemed long between that and Guildford; then by some mental confusion I began to expect Witley as the next station—we reached that at last and lo! it was Godalming—a very pretty place, pine woods beyond, a pretty line but the very longest $4\frac{1}{2}$ miles I ever went by rail. Witley at last! I have hardly time to look and leap out when I see Mr. Lewes, dear fellow, they have sent the carriage; as we drive round to the house he tells me I am their first visitor; and they have heard from Elma. The only drawback is that he is unwell; his face made me rather unhappy by the looks of ill-health without a shade of ill-temper, which beautifies it in a melancholy kind of way. I flew across the drawing room into her arms; then Elizabeth's successor[7] took me upstairs to take off my things and then we sat in the drawing room till luncheon.

She read me part of Elma's letter and said—which I was heartily delighted to hear—that on some old man's death she would have £20,000.[8] They scolded me for bringing rain, and I said there could not be two suns in one firmament; he said that was his name for her, and began seriously enumerating the points of resemblance; but he identifies the two and calls

5. John 9:4.
6. Cesare Bonesano, Marchese di Beccaria (1735–94), published *Dei Delitti e delle pene,* his famous essay on crimes and punishments, in 1764. Edith was reading a French translation by Faustin Hélie, Paris, 1856.
7. Brett, the new housemaid.

8. Elma Stuart's stepfather Sir James Coxe, M.D. of Kinellan left Elma £3,000 for life-rent use (afterwards to her son Roland), and a third share in the residuary estate. The will is dated 8 March 1875. Sir James died 9 May 1878. See VII, 54, n. 8.

the Sun "Polly"—which was an ingenious way of meeting any metaphysical difficulty of two suns at once for him. After luncheon, we walked round the garden, which is quite perfect, then drove round and about between fir woods and heathy commons and shady lanes with quaint tiled cottages, and I thought the country was very worthy of its happiness in harbouring her. She told me about Browning and his wife's Portuguese sonnets,[9] and she said once more that she wished my letters could be printed in the same veiled way—"the Newest Heloise."

After dinner I talked about retiring from the shirts and she was strongly against complete retirement and the loss of such humanizing influence as we might be supposed to exercise, but agreed that such supervision as one could exercise by coming in once a week was enough. I was particularly touched by the little commonplaces of hospitality, coming from them,—when I was going she came up with me to the bedroom, and he insisted on walking with me to the station, and in driving, though with much remonstrance I was allowed to sit opposite them at starting, he made me change afterwards that I might see the view better.

The return journey was as marvellously short as the outward one was long. I thought of her and the happy hours all the way,—and laughed at myself for the thousand sensible things I had meant to say not one of which I had remembered.

VII, 60:1   GHL TO ALFRED TENNYSON, WITLEY, [17 AUGUST 1878]

MS: Tennyson Research Centre.

The Heights, Witley, | Nr. Godalming.
Saturday.

Mi caro Poeta

On Wednesday Tom Trollope and his wife are coming to stay ⟨a couple of days⟩ till Friday morning with us. If not disagreeable to you, and if you are not otherwise engaged we should like to give them the treat of seeing you. We could come *on Thursday*[1] after your snooze, and if you were perfectly amiable you might read one or two short poems to us—but *that* is a suggestion not to be whispered to any one else!

Yours truly

G. H. Lewes.

9. The "Sonnets from the Portuguese" were first published in *Poems of*   *Elizabeth Barrett Browning*, 2 vols., 1850.
1. "After lunch we went to Tennyson

VII, 65:25   GE TO MRS. THOMAS A. TROLLOPE, WITLEY, 27 AUGUST 1878

MS: Princeton.

The Heights, Witley, | Nr. Godalming.
August 27. 78.

My dear Mrs. Trollope

Mr. Trollope's letter has been a great comfort to us this morning, clearing up painful doubts.

And O thanks for the trouble you took—when you had the headache too—to get me the impossible Hat! Headache makes me selfish, but in you apparently it only adds more merit to your good nature. I blame myself for not having reflected that my request might cause you to make an otherwise unnecessary loop in your journey.

The cheering effect of your visit remains in my mind, notwithstanding a further drop in my health and the barometer. We value very much that new fastening of mutual memories, and hope that we may live to have another little epoch of the same sort.

I feel sure that Tennyson was highly gratified by the sympathetic audience you made for him. I saw an expression in his face that always reminds me of a large dog laying down its ears and wagging its tail on being stroked and patted.

Perhaps Mr. Lewes is writing to Mr. Trollope and saying what he feels on his own behalf. Anyhow we are one in all friendly remembrances.

I am still "all of a tremble"[2] with my foolish, feeble agitation about this servant business, and my hand straggles at its own will. Good weather and all other possible good attend you in the rest of your journey.

Yours always affectionately
M. E. Lewes.

who took us to the spring and then read two of his new poems; most interesting visit." (GHL Diary, 22 August 1878.) The Trollopes left at 11 Friday, 23 August.

2. Henry Brooke, *The Fool of Quality* (1809), II, 151.

VII, 68:1   GHL TO EDWARD F. S. PIGOTT, WITLEY, [25 SEPTEMBER 1878]

MS: Mr. Gordon N. Ray.

The Heights, Witley, | Nr. Godalming.

Dear Pigott

We shall be delighted to see you as proposed on Saturday.

I do *not* think you can safely license Les Lionnes Pauvres.[3] It is *really* a very moral piece but the situations are too scabreuse, and the public is so stupid that it will fasten on them.

Adultery is one thing—but adultery furnishing rooms and dressing ladies in the fashion! In haste

Yours ever

G. H. L.

VII, 68:1   GE TO MRS. RICHARD GREVILLE, WITLEY, 26 SEPTEMBER 1878

MS: Yale.

The Heights, Witley, | Nr Godalming.

September 26. 78.

My dear Mrs. Greville

I should have called again long ago to ask about you, but that our Horse has fallen lame, and we have been confined to a narrow home circuit of walks.[3a] I was glad to have the assurance that you were so far better as to be able to drive out. When my imprisonment is at an end I shall call to know more about you.

Always yours affectionately

M. E. Lewes.

3. Pigott was Examiner of Plays for the Lord Chamberlain from 25 August 1874 until his death in 1895. I can find no record of *Les Lionnes Pauvres* among the plays or in the day book of the Lord Chamberlain's MSS in the British Museum. Pigott and Alice Helps spent Saturday at Witley 28 September 1878.

3a. They had been taking long drives every day until 23 September, when GHL wrote in his Diary: "*Horse lame* so Polly and I had a walk on Hambledon Common." James wrote to Elizabeth Boott, 30 October: "Tomorrow I go to lunch with George Eliot who also lives near; so you see I am in good company." (*Letters*, 2 vols., ed. Leon Edel, [1974], II, 190.)

VII, 74:21 IVAN TURGENEV TO GHL, BOUGIVAL, 1 NOVEMBER 1878

MS: Balliol College, Oxford.

Bougival Les Frênes.
Friday November 1st 78.

Dear Mr. Lewes

I have received the two volumes and thank you very much indeed for this gift. My own books will, I hope it, reach your hands before the 9th of November; and the box with the pills (capsules de F. Joseph[4]) will leave Paris to morrow. Try them—and may they be as useful to you as they are to me.

I need not repeat you how happy I have been to meet Mrs. Lewes and you at our friends residence[5]—and with what pleasure I remember those three days—cela s'entend de soi-même. But be so kind and tell George Eliot how much I admire in her the poet and the woman—and believe me

Yours very sincerely
Ivan Tourgueneff.

VII, 74:21 EDITH SIMCOX, AUTOBIOGRAPHY, 5 NOVEMBER 1878

MS: Bodleian.

Tuesday 5 November 1878

5. At last! The dear fellow has sent a card (and I hope it was she who corrected its reading)—within 13 days from now I shall be happy. I was disappointed at first to find they were coming so late, but I guess they only arrive the end of the week before, and I am glad not to be asked to come on Sunday.

4. Capsules de François-Joseph, étant un remède contre la goutte et les rhumatismes.
5. At the Halls' in Six Mile Bottom. See VII, 73, n. 6. A detailed account of the conversation 22 October is given by Oscar Browning, *Life of George Eliot*, 1890, pp. 128–130. At dinner when GHL proposed Turgenev's health "in an admirable speech, as the greatest living novelist," Turgenev repudiated the compliment, transferring it to GE.

VII, 78:1   GE TO [THOMAS HENDERSON[6]], LONDON, 16 NOVEMBER 1878

MS: National Library, Canberra, New South Wales.

The Priory, | 21. North Bank, | Regents Park.
November 16. 78.

Dear Sir

I return by to-day's post the two last batches of proof.[7] Perhaps owing to our absence the earlier batch may have lain here a day or two before I saw it, but I have always been careful to return them speedily. I hope to have the proofs of "Jubal" etc. next week.

Yours faithfully

M. E. Lewes.

VII, 78:20   MRS. HERBERT ARTHUR LEWES TO GHL, SYDENHAM, 18 NOVEMBER 1878

MS: Nuneaton Public Library.

Sydenham, | 18 November 78.

My Dear Pater

We this evening had the delight of receiving your dear letter of October 7th. little Marian at once said oh I know whose letter this is it is from *my* Grandpa, what does he say now Mamy read me it *all*. Why I am not a chick does not my Grandpa know I've not got a sharp beak and feathers! Shall not I often laugh to myself when I think how funny my Grandpa is! Then dear little George Herbert came from his evening bath, tell my Grandpa me is only a little boy not a chick! If me was there me would not let my Grandma get hurt. That was when he heard about the accident. I am truly thankful my Pater and Mutter were not in the carriage at the time. . . .

Oh dear Pater I was so deceived in every way with the Ladys help. I think I told you I felt timid being alone now the country is so unsettled and many of the houses have been broken into by Kafirs. The help had been with me but a fortnight when a suspicious Kafir came one day. Some nights after, some one was round the house all the evening trying doors windows and even trying the Iron roofing that night and the three following ones.

---

6. Thomas Henderson succeeded George Simpson as manager of Blackwood's printing office.

7. Of the Cabinet edition of *Daniel Deronda* and *The Legend of Jubal, and Other Poems, Old and New.*

We were up till morning, once I fired at him from the window he had with him a bright long cane knife. I dare not go out. The fifth night some neighbour's boys came. We were very tired and did not sit up. The boys watched the fellow file a key for hours fit it to the door and they did not like to fire at him. I fancy they were frightened too. Two nights he opened the door with his key but the iron bolt our Miner here kindly put on for me saved us—I went to the Magistrate in Durban. I found the boys fathers had also. for more than a week we had three Kafir police watching in the sitting room. Then if I did not stay there too they all went to sleep and plainly let the fellow know that he was not to come, and just fancy dear Pater these nasty dirty black creatures each occupying two little slight made cane chairs creaking with their heavy weight, and their appetites were dreadful, and so I got so nervous and ill I told them not to come again. Since then the white constable comes up at odd times, and has cleared off all Kafirs not able to give a good account of themselves. The help I sent away at the end of the month. The Magistrate sent me word she had lived in his family for a short time etc. and glad I was when she went. We have now a little girl from the village. She does help me a little. . . . One day this week I want to try and take the little ones on the beach, I have been frightened to take them even through Durban, the fever there has been so bad. There has been such mortality among little children.

We have more than two miles to walk before we get to the first buss. The little ones would have so many more messages to send in the morning, still I think I had better send this off the first thing in the morning. I know I ought to have written before indeed each day I told myself I would, and so let it go by—and yet it is not for want of love for my Pater we know only too well in this large world we have only our good loving Pater and Mutter that cares for us and love us. Good night and God bless you Dear Pater and Mutter is always our prayers each night.

Your affectionate daughter
Eliza Lewes.

Please forgive errors.

VII, 80:18 EDITH SIMCOX, AUTOBIOGRAPHY, 22 NOVEMBER 1878

MS: Bodleian. *Published:* McKenzie, pp. 93–94.

Friday 22 November 1878

22. Monday came at last, but hardly the greeting I had dreamt of; the first thing I saw was Lewes stretched upon the sofa, and in concern for him I lost

something of the sight of her. He was affectionate, and when I said I wanted to kiss her feet he said he would let me do it as much as I liked—or—correcting himself—as much as she liked. He could enter into the desire though she couldn't. I did in spite of her protests lie down before the fire and for one short moment give the passionate kisses that filled my eyes with tears:— and for the rest of the evening her feet avoided the footstool where I had found them then.—Still though I would rather have had the kisses un- grudged—I would rather have the memory of them thus than not at all. She was unhappy about him, I cried all the way back—at the intense pain of her anxiety—which I was tempted to share. I was sorry for myself too: all one's gladness turned to pain; and the hopes lost of pleasing her for a moment with loving sense and nonsense. At first I felt hopeless, what could one do but shut oneself up with ones grief?

VII, 84:10 EDITH SIMCOX, AUTOBIOGRAPHY, 26–30 NOVEMBER 1878

MS: Bodleian. *Partly published:* Haight, *George Eliot*, p. 515.

Tuesday 26 November 1878

26. On Monday the doctors were there and he was very ill. Today I went in the morning and the answer was the same. In the afternoon I went again; trying to hope she would let me be with him in the night. I sent up a written line with the prayer. It came down I think unread in the servant's hand— she could not attend to anything. "Mr. Charles" would write to me! I could not expect anything else, and yet her intense excitement and distress —the servant said she could do nothing but cry and fret—make it cruelly unfit for her to be alone. God forgive me! I feel as if I would give my mother's life for his!

Saturday 30 November 1878

30. Yesterday the answer was "just the same"—Charles Lewes and Johnny Cross were with him. She had written to the latter—whom he wished to see—and who came from his mother's death bed.[8] Today I reached the house about half-past 3, a private cab was driving up and down slowly before it, I waited till that was gone and then rang at the gate. Brett with a white face and dark eyes answered me: "He is very ill—" then "there are no hopes."—I stood stupefied, without word or sign, without feeling, and

8. Mrs. William Cross died 9 December 1878.

so turned away. It was as if something quite different from my fears had come.

I could not leave the place and walked up and down, and almost immediately a carriage like a doctor's drove up fast and two men got out. I hastened after them and they entered the gate; the other carriages followed and the two, with their 4 sleek horses stood a few paces back. The coachmen talked and laughed, cabs and coal carts and men and women on foot passed by as I stood behind the carriages, watching the gate down the fogbound road. Then—in about 20 minutes, the 2 figures came in sight. I strode towards them and as they stood speaking together, I asked was there no hope. A tall man—probably Sir James Paget—answered kindly: "None: he is dying—dying quickly." Then again I could not speak, but the tears rushed up and shading my face with a hand, I came here with this worst of griefs.

She cannot bear it. There have been unendurable sorrows, but I do not see how any can equal hers—who can feel as she does, who could have so much to love?—I am dimly thankful that I parted from him with a kiss— I feel the touch of his hand as I held it at Witley—but oh! what does anything matter—would God the grief might kill her even now. But whether she lives or dies—there is no comfort for her left on earth but this, to know that their love and life have not been in vain for others, that the happiness which is dead and the sorrow that endures bind us for evermore to love and service of the sorrowing and the glad.—But oh! to think of that sweet frame shaken with the unconsolable anguish!

VII, 84:10   CHARLES LEWES TO IVAN TURGENEV, LONDON, 29 NOVEMBER 1878

MS: Bibliothèque Nationale.

The Priory, | 21. North Bank, | Regents Park.
29 November 78.

Dear Mr. Tourguenieff

My mother asks me to write to let you know that my Father is very dangerously ill, and she is unable therefore to answer any letters herself but she wishes me to tell you with their thanks that all the things which you have sent have safely arrived, and also a photograph from Mme. Viardot. You will I know be grieved to hear of my Father's state. Since Friday last he has been in bed in a constant state of pain and prostration. He has some inflammatory disorder of the stomach.

Yours very truly
C. L. Lewes.

VII, 84:10 CHARLES LEWES TO E. F. S. PIGOTT, LONDON, 1 DECEMBER 1878

MS: University of Iowa.

The Priory, | 21. North Bank, | Regents Park.

1 December 1878.

My dear Pigott

You will I know be terribly grieved to hear that my Father after an illness of eight days has been taken away from us. He died last night at about 6 o'clock having been sinking all through the day. He died quite peacefully and was conscious up to quite a few moments of the end. We have the consolation of knowing that if he had lived he would have suffered from an internal malady which would have gradually become more and more painful and would have carried him off within six months. But you will know what a terrible blow his death is to us, and to my Mother of course quite inexpressible. The Funeral will I expect take place on Wednesday. I do not ask you to come to it, but if as one of my Father's oldest intimate friends you would wish to do so let me know and I will send you word of the exact time fixed.

Yours ever

C. L. Lewes.

VII, 86:25 EMILY SUSANNAH CLARKE TO GE, BRIGHTON, 2 DECEMBER 1878

MS: Yale.

7 Gladstone Terrace, Brighton | December 2. 78.

Dearest Aunt Polly

Words fail me to say how grieved I am. He whom you have lost was so loving and tender hearted—to me ever kind.

God help you to bear it, I know nothing I can do but to pray you may have comfort, if there be anything do tell me. With heartfelt sympathy

Your loving niece

Emily S. Clarke.

VII, 86:25 EDITH SIMCOX TO CHARLES LEE LEWES, LONDON, [2 DECEMBER 1878]

MS: Yale.

1 Douro Place. Monday.

Dear Mr. Lewes

Thank you for your note. It is a sad comfort that both have been spared longer pain, and we can only pray that some of the strength she has given to others may be with her now. But there was never grief like hers. One can think of no other loss beside that, but yours too—and ours—he was all generous loving kindness—God comfort her!

I saw the doctors when they left the house on Saturday, and wrote a line to Mrs. Stuart to prepare her for the worst.

It is a mercy that she has something to live for in doing what he wished. I know all other love must be unbearable because it is not his, and she will know it is not for want of love I do not write to her: it must be best to leave her alone with the blessed memory of his perfect goodness.

Thanks again for your kindness in writing. With deep sympathy,

Yours ever

Edith J. Simcox.

Please burn if you see a foolish note of mine trying to speak of hope a week ago.

VII, 86:25 CHARLES LEWES TO E. F. S. PIGOTT, LONDON, 3 DECEMBER 1878

MS: Mr. Gordon N. Ray.

The Priory | 3 December 78.

Thank you very much, my dear Pigott, for your most kind and affectionate letter. The funeral will be at Highgate and we shall leave here at 11.15; but please do not think of coming in your state of health unless you should be really *safe* to come and the weather fine. I cannot bear to think of your running any risks. *He* would not have wished it. So unless it is absolutely safe you will know that by staying away you are doing what he would prefer.

Ever affectionately yours

C. L. Lewes.

VII, 86:25 BENJAMIN JOWETT TO GE, OXFORD, 3 DECEMBER 1878

MS: Balliol College, Oxford.

Oxford | December 3/78.

Dear Mrs. Lewes

I hardly know how either to write to you or not to write to you after the sad news which I read in this morning's paper. I am afraid that the blow must be to you an overwhelming one, and that for years you will feel the dreariness and isolation caused by it.

I am so glad that I knew him and was able to appreciate him. He was so very kind and disinterested and he was one of the first literary men of the day: His life of Goethe to say nothing of his other works was the second best biography in the English language, and as you have told me that it was by his encouragement you were induced to write we are indebted to him for a great deal more than this.

And now as a duty to his memory you must bear up under the greatest trial of life, and make the most of the years which remain to you. It would not be worthy of you who have done so much for others just to pine away because your best friend is taken from you. Dear Mrs. Lewes, it seems hard to say this to you just now, but you know that I deeply feel with you.

I should like to come and see you some time when it is suitable and pleasant to you. If there is anything I can by any possibility do for you, will you let me know?

I remain (if I may venture to call myself)

Your sincere friend
B. Jowett.

You kindly wrote to me, about seven weeks ago. But I am sorry to say through some strange accident the letter was mislaid and could never be found.

Do you remember my secretary—a most remarkable youth—I grieve to say that he is dying.[9]

9. Matthew Knight (1853?–95), son of Jowett's manservant, outlived his master by two years.

VII, 87:1   IVAN TURGENEV TO GE, PARIS, 3 DECEMBER 1878

MS: Balliol College, Oxford.

50, Rue de Douai, | Paris.
December 3d 1878.

My dear Mrs. Lewes,

An hour ago I received from your daughter[1] a letter telling me of the very dangerous illness of her father, and just now I read in the newspapers a telegramme relating the fatal termination of this illness! I don't dare to trouble the very deep grief you must feel; I only ask the permission to send you the expression of my heartfelt and sincere sympathy. May you find in your own great mind the necessary fortitude to sustain such a loss! All your friends, all learned Europe mourn with you. Believe me, my dear Mrs. Lewes

Yours very truly
Iv. Tourgueneff.

VII, 87:17   MRS. ISAAC PEARSON EVANS TO GE, GRIFF, 5 DECEMBER [1878]

MS: Yale. *Endorsed:* ack[nowledge]d [by Charles Lee Lewes].

My dear Marianne

My heart aches for you in your sad bereavement.

Your affectionate sister
Sarah Evans.

December 5th.

VII, 87:1   EDITH SIMCOX, AUTOBIOGRAPHY, 5 DECEMBER 1878

MS: Bodleian.

Thursday 5 December 1878

5. Yesterday went to see Elma; she grieves as much as I—and yet—she is able to go to shops, to visit strangers, rail at things and people, and even

1. Mrs. Charles Lee Lewes.

half jest—I wonder as of old whether the strong feeling is *as* strong there
where it does not always rule. Today I went to Highgate—I learnt incidentally from her that he was buried there yesterday. It was hard to have
to ask where the grave was—of cheerful officials who look it out in a
book like house agents—No. 84 "in the dissenters' portion." I ask a
gardener—with half-a-crown—to find it for me and he got a relenting
clerk to come—then at last I was close by the desolate new mound. Two
white wreaths were on the grave and I laid mine of heather between them.
Then I lay on the grass just beyond, and after a while the spot did not
seem so hideous; it is there, not to the ghostly portal of buried hope and
joy that I must go now to pray. Oh it is strange to see the crowded streets.
I asked the man how many graves they made each day—he said 5 or 6,
sometimes 2, sometimes 10. I thought that was hardly enough to make
them care so little. A funeral came while I was there—with nodding horse-
plumes, the clergyman went away jovially before me—tapes were hanging
down from the sleeves of his surplice. As I was lying on the grass a grave-
digger came to me. He said he had put forked sticks to keep the white
wreaths from the wet; he had been told the lady was coming to see it this
afternoon and he had tried to make it "look nice." I gave him a shilling
and hoped—perhaps in vain—that the next comer might be spared his talk.
He promised soothingly to turf it over soon—I asked when and he didn't
know. "You see the ground may sink a little, we have some more earth at
the side to put on if it does." Then he went and I think I cried, till looking
up I saw two dark figures I thought were Elma and her friend;[2] I rushed
back behind the shelter of an evergreen clump—a withered azalea bloom
still hung on the branch. Then I sobbed bitterly, and when I rose after a
while no one was there. Visitors are many—it was probably not.

Then I walked across to Hampstead and passed hesitatingly their
son's gate; as I turned back some one in black (? 'Octavia') was going
in. I had hardly meant to go today, but somehow the aspect of the house
was not forbidding, and I thought I might dare to go tomorrow. . . . It is
a cruel thing to say of so good a mother, but if she only *had* children of her
own to comfort her now—perhaps Johnny does, but one feels now without
selfishness what one used to grudge at wickedly that none of the gladness
from another's being, which is still my note of love, that none of that—
or not enough to count—ever came to her from us.

2. Catharine Thurlow, daughter of   After his death in 1867 she lived much
the 17th Lord Saltoun of Abernethy,   with her cousin Elma Stuart.
married in 1860 John Stewart Menzies.

VII, 87:17 JOHN MORLEY TO GE, BRIGHTON, 5 DECEMBER 1878

MS: Balliol College.

4 Chesham Place, | Brighton | December 5. 78.

Dear Mrs. Lewes

I cannot help writing to say to you how deeply I sympathise with you in the sorrow that has fallen upon you. It is very grievous and irreparable. We must all feel that we have lost one of the most vivid, helpful, and encouraging of our friends; but to you it is very different from this—a loss for which there can be no words.

I have often thought of that night when you bade farewell to the Lyttons, saying how little likely it was that we should all five of us ever meet again.[3] And now we never shall meet again.

The last time that I heard from him was when—some weeks ago—he wrote me a friendly and encouraging word about a book of mine.[4] It is indeed sorrowful to think that the light of so gifted and brilliant a spirit should have gone out, while there still remained such power of ever fresh illumination. His gifts can at least never be forgotten by any who knew him, and his ideas and influence will continue among thousands who never knew him. With sincere sorrow and sympathy in your grief, believe me,

Always yours most faithfully,

John Morley.

VII, 90:28 EDWARD BURNE-JONES TO C. L. LONDON, [18? DECEMBER 1878]

MS: Balliol College, Oxford.

The Grange. Northend | Fulham.

My dear Mr. Lewes

Will you say I accept them and with gratitude for being so affectionately remembered.[5] Even the little word in your note that tells us how he could be mindful at the last of kind thoughts for his friends is inexpressibly touching and sweet to us. We do want to know about your mother—we

3. "We went to dine with the Lyttons and say good-bye before they start for India. Morley there. Very pleasant. Home at 12." (GHL Diary, 26 February 1876)

4. *Diderot and the Encyclopaedists*, 2 vols., 1878.

5. Charles had offered some of GHL's cigars.

need not say how day and night she is in our thoughts and how hard it feels to be so useless. And we will depend upon you for giving us any little intelligence that you may have time to send. I speak for both of us that we wait with anxiety for some sign that the love of friends may comfort her a little.

Yours very truly and gratefully
E. Burne-Jones.

VII, 90:28 EDITH SIMCOX, AUTOBIOGRAPHY, 12–29 DECEMBER 1878

MS: Bodleian.

Thursday 12 December 1878

12. Yesterday I saw Charles Lewes. He is good to her and I never liked him so well,—he has no thought of sparing himself in caring for her. For her my instinct has not been wrong. She proposes to live on as she is,—he says, she is able to live alone, and cannot bear to have, even a niece she is fond of with her. She has but the one thought to make his wishes her law; the rest of the world she would have think of her "as a dead friend." It is not strange, knowing her and loving and worshipping as I did, it is not strange that my instinct should have discerned this; Elma said—That is hard for her friends—I have hardly ventured to think so more than if she were dead indeed. I said she had no duties left. He said, after a long time perhaps she might make a new life with new interests, she was so full of sympathy she could hardly fail to do so, but her feeling now is that no one can give her any comfort and she has a right to avoid the agitation which might hinder her work. Charles said, she can speak of nothing but him, and she can only speak of him to me. Mrs. Cross died on Monday. I sat up writing a few lines of sympathy to Johnny—uneasily though with complete sincerity—through blinding tears. I have not said how hard it was to go to the house for the first time after that evening of death—and yet it was a common duty to go and ask how she was. At last I went—without wish, as a duty. I took a cab, I couldn't bear to traverse the so well known track. The maid said she was better than she had been yet, "seemed more cheerful"—God help her! If anything could be harder it was to enter the house, to wait in the dining room—Charles was out and had left word for me to wait: I had never been in the dining room but with him, and usually it was for some kind purpose that he called me there. There he showed me all her manuscripts. There he gave me "The Spanish Gipsy," there he had

come to answer my questions about her. Is it disloyal to say—He was kinder to me while I thought of him as a stranger than she when I had given all my love? I waited half an hour, standing on the rug looking at her portrait[6] and finding more sweetness in it than before. Lying on the chimney piece under my eyes was an open bill—1 widow's cap—7/6— and something else—that is how I see her—with a set, worn, white face. —My poor darling—it is too hard—I think of meeting her—it seems years hence, with a mere hand clasp and a sad, silent look.

Saturday 28 December 1878

28. On Christmas day, with great hesitation I wrote a few lines to her, —of his divine presence—which I enclosed in an open envelope to Charles Lewes asking him to give it to her or not as he thought best. He returns it, with a note that tells me nothing new, only makes the silence, which seems heartless, a plain necessity. Am I nearer or not than Johnny and Elma, since I cannot wish to see her again—if she offered to see me, it would be a pain to endure—like the first revisiting of the dark doorway, only harder.

Sunday 29 December 1878

29. . . . . Charles Lewes said in his letter that she would never be able to endure any caress—I knew that—and so was not specially hurt by his saying it—though I cried behind my veil all the way across the Park yesterday. But there is an inexhaustible tragedy in the thought of that last visit and the last stolen passionate kisses—it is pain to think that it may be one more hurt to her, as well as a fresh stone on the barrier between us, yet in my inmost heart I cannot repent—even if I had not stolen, the barrier would be impassible now. Let us take what good is left—Charles will gain from her dependence and the close intercourse with the higher nature. It is better to feel that than to say that Johnny would have been more worthy of the son's privileges.

VII, 90:28 CHARLES LEWES TO E. F. S. PIGOTT, LONDON, 22 DECEMBER 1878

MS: Mr. Gordon N. Ray.

The Priory | 22 December 1878.

My dear Pigott
    I am sorry that I cannot give you altogether a favourable report of my Mother. She seems as time goes on to find it more difficult rather than

6. By F. W. Burton.

less difficult to bear her sorrow. Still I think her frame and heart are so strong that she will weather it. She is not worse in health but perhaps a shade better. It is only mentally that she is worse—seeming to realise more intensely the terrible *fact*. But in her work she to a great extent rights herself and there are many hours each day that she can work.

I have got three or four boxes of my Father's cigarettes for you, when I can find time to put them up. He had meant to send them to you in addition to the cigars but as they are the only things you can now smoke they will come to you alone.

Yours ever
C. L. Lewes.

Theophrastus Such and *Problems*

VII, 90:28 JOHN BLACKWOOD TO CHARLES LEE LEWES, EDINBURGH, 31 DECEMBER 1878

Text: Blackwood Letter Book, National Library of Scotland.

45 George St. | Edinburgh December 31/78.

My Dear Charles Lewes

You should have heard from me sooner had I not been confined to the house partly from the weather and more from a confounded pain in the back which made anything but sitting in an easy chair at the fire irksome. However it is nothing and I seem all right now.

I enclose a formal note which will I doubt not enable you to settle any enquiries as to succession duty on Physiology of Common Life and Seaside Studies. Among your father's papers you will probably find an elaborate statement as to the Physiology of Common Life rendered on 10th April 1876.

I was greatly troubled to see by your letter that Mrs. Lewes was still so very poorly and it will be a real relief if you can give me a more favourable account of her. The Weather here has been very trying but now it is soft and mild and I hope she may be able to get into the Garden.

Will you give her my wife and daughter's warm regards as well as my own and with full wishes to yourself in the new Year I am

Always yours truly
John Blackwood.

Charles Lewes Esq.

P.S. I have got the bulk of Theophrastus and send you a proof.[7]

VII, 90:28 BLACKWOOD & SONS TO CHARLES LEWES, EDINBURGH, 31 DECEMBER 1878

Text: Blackwood Letter Book, National Library of Scotland.

45 George St. | Edinburgh December 31/78.

Dear Mr. Lewes

Your father's "Sea Side Studies" has been out of print since 1869 so no copyright value can be put upon it.

The same must be said in regard to the Physiology of Common Life as we see our last payment was on 10th April 1876 when some £66 was

7. In the Cabinet edition.

paid for reprint of odd numbers or sheets to complete sets of the book. There is an occasional dropping sale but it would take years to clear out the 400 stock on hand and until after these are sold there is nothing payable to your father's representatives and it would then be a question whether to reprint. We are, Dear Sir

Yours truly

Wm. Blackwood and Sons.

Charles Lewes Esq.

VII, 93:1 EDITH SIMCOX, AUTOBIOGRAPHY, 6 JANUARY 1879

MS: Bodleian. *Extract published:* Haight, *George Eliot,* pp. 518–519.

Monday 6 January 1879

January 6. After luncheon I went up there: I had rung the bell and was looking vacantly eastward when I saw a tall reddish bearded man coming up, I stared without moving and when he had come within two or three paces he made some sign of recognition, and I knew it was Johnny. I had thought we should never meet so again. It was an intensely painful moment; there is nothing much more pathetic than a look of set gravity on a habitually cheerful face. We went in together and I asked him to question Brett. She had been out that morning in the garden for a little and felt the better. Johnny said "Give her our love." I listened and came away without speaking but was faintly pleased at the strange chance which brought us there together, because I thought, servant-like, Brett would tell her of the fact and I hoped it would please her to think of our meeting as friends. On leaving the house we adjusted our directions so as to cross Regent's Park together. The anxiety was less after Brett's report—he only felt that the life of isolation could not last, that it might be the only possibility for her at first, but that it would be fatal if prolonged too far. He comforted himself that perhaps she felt if she saw one person, there would be so many who would be just a little hurt if she did not see them too. But clearly he looked forward to a time when she would receive again a few constant visitors. His sober, earthly sense cheered me a little, and though I cried most of the way it was with the quiet sadness that can break no peaceful slumber.

VII, 96:15 MARK PATTISON TO GE, LONDON, 18 JANUARY 1879

MS: Balliol College, Oxford.

Athenaeum Club | Pall Mall.
S.W. 18 January | 1879.

Dear Mrs. Lewes

I have forborne to intrude upon your sorrow with a letter, hitherto, because, under such circumstances, anything which one can write has an air of formality and conventionalism, even when the sympathy is most sincere.

I cannot, however, bear that you should think that I have been unmindful of you all this time. I may safely say not a day passes, but a thought of you comes across me.

Nor am I myself without a special share in the common loss of all of us. For the last few years no one's word of approval has been more to me than Mr. Lewes'—I have had the feeling that however others might miss the point of any allusion, there was one friendly house in which every word would be taken in as it was meant.[8]

I hear you see no one; so that I will not attempt to call. I only send this sheet in the hope that you may receive a momentary satisfaction from such assurance of remembrance and sympathy as can be offered by one who is

Your sincere friend
Mark Pattison.

VII, 97:20 EDITH SIMCOX, AUTOBIOGRAPHY, 19 JANUARY 1879

MS: Bodleian.

Sunday 19 January 1879

19th. Yesterday Eleanor Cross came here. She is a good girl, and I was fed by her mention of her last visit to the Heights with Johnny; they went over for a call one day in October[9] when they were able to leave their

8. GHL read Pattison's *Isaac Casaubon* as soon as it appeared in February 1875, noting it in his Diary 7–13, 18, 20, 24 February, and 1 March. It was doubt-less discussed when Mr. and Mrs. Pattison came to lunch at the Priory 14 February.
9. 13 October 1878. (GHL Diary.)

mother for a few hours, and were made to stay to luncheon and dinner. In the afternoon they went a long lovely drive; they had never had a happier day and she quoted from Dante (a passage she asked me to find) that they would never see the Dawn of such a day again. "The dear little man" as she calls him, laid himself out for their amusement, sang to them in the evening, was if possible more actively kind than usual.—When he was dying he told them to give his cigars to Willy Cross—who is a great smoker.

VII, 100:12   EDITH SIMCOX, AUTOBIOGRAPHY, 30 JANUARY 1879

MS: Bodleian.

Thursday 30 January 1879

30. . . . Went to the Priory to enquire: just the same. Then walked on to Hampstead, with some trepidation, meaning and fearing to call on Mrs. Charles Lewes.—Rang and the door was some time in being answered, was ushered in and waited some time in the pretty little cottage drawing room; then Mrs. Charles came in with her things on and explained her children were spending the afternoon with friends and she had to fetch them home before dark, would I walk with her—I assented gladly and soon began my enquiries. She said there seemed little to tell; her health was fairly good—for her; the hysterical fits recur, but she says though she is weaker after them, they relieve the brain. There are times when she cannot shed a tear and then the physical oppression is terrible. I asked a little how she occupied herself and learnt that besides reading and looking over Ms for his book, she is also reading through old letters and journals of his, going back to quite early years.

It was strange to find her daughter-in-law complaining, with even a little jealous bitterness, of never having been taken into the "familiarity" of intercourse—to use the word pedantically. She said He was glad—it added to his happiness that she should exist, but she had never been able to feel it was so with Her. I hardly ventured to suggest qualifying consolations—it would only make matters worse if I knew better than she if she was dear to her husband's mother. She said she thought even Charlie was only valued because he was his father's son. She took credit to herself for having proposed that he should go and stay there, feeling that all *she* could do was to give up her claims to him.

It is not like me to find pleasure in the woes of others, and yet I cannot

quite help feeling relieved when others make such complaints, and I feel
how I indeed have not—have never had any ground for complaining—I
have been exacting, troublesome, and she patient and generous. I wonder
whether they will come—I have asked Elma, Miss Helps and Johnny and
Miss Cross to luncheon on Sunday—shall we succeed if so in making the
meeting a service of commemoration?[10] Dear one—will it comfort you
by and bye to know what comfort you have given—how, for me your
teaching has made all the world anew. A little cheque for a review came
in today—I am promising myself to take some flowers to Highgate on
Saturday.

VII, 110:5 EDITH SIMCOX, AUTOBIOGRAPHY, 27 FEBRUARY 1879

MS: Bodleian.

Thursday 27 February 1879

27. On Tuesday I got to the Priory later, saw Brett who said Mrs. Lewes
wanted her to order 6 shirts made like Mrs. Stuart's; when could I come
and see about them? She was better and had been out for an hour and a
half. Brett looked more like herself and I too was comforted. Yesterday
morning I called about 11 and was taken into the drawing room.—While
Brett left me I looked round—wondering with tears how she was able to
live at all:—the room looked bright and pretty—the only change long
white curtains to the front windows, like a veil making it impossible for
people to see in: the sofa was not against the wall, but out in front of the
fire as it was the last time I had been in the room, when he was lying there.
Brett said she was already down in the dining room,—much stronger,
"quite cheerful this morning." It was almost as hard as seeing her to pass
outside the room with but a door between us. Cards from Herbert Spencer,
Trübner and George Smith were lying on the table. She has offered to see
Mrs. Charles Lewes and the children on Saturday.

10. "Miss Helps and Mrs. Menzies
came to luncheon on Sunday, Elma
being not so well." (Autobiography,
4 February 1879.)

VII, 117:17 EDITH SIMCOX, AUTOBIOGRAPHY, 19 MARCH 1879

MS: Bodleian.

Wednesday 19 March 1879

19. This afternoon Eleanor Cross came again. Johnny saw her on Tuesday and thought her better, but I grieve to hear she is dissatisfied about her work—if that anxiety begins I fear neither peace nor health can be looked for. If one could only help and comfort her in that—but no possible changes in the past could have made that less impossible than now. She was going to see Mrs. Congreve yesterday. She told Johnny she shrank from seeing people—also that she was going to see Mrs. Stuart.—I think that must be my doing—on Monday [17 March] at the end of the short note acknowledging hers about the shirts, I said Elma was better, going to leave town in 2 or 3 weeks, and "as she talked of wintering in a warm climate it might be a year before she was in England again."—I feared whether this was saying too much—seeming to make a suggestion, and yet I feared for Elma's soul if she had to leave England without a word. My dread of seeing Her grows more and more intense and yet—if one only might, there are so many ways in which I could serve her more easily and gladly than perhaps anyone else—if she could feel it possible. Johnny said she seemed better. Yet whatever happens there is always in my ears as it were her voice silencing every half-rising murmur "Am I then upon a bed of roses?" Dearest—I would be content to live forever outside your love if my endurance could spare you but a moment of the scorching pain.

VII, 120:15 EDITH SIMCOX, AUTOBIOGRAPHY, 23 MARCH 1879

MS: Bodleian.

Sunday 23 March 1879

23. On Friday as I was going there, I met Charles coming away and turned and went with him to the station. She has sent to the printer the first "Problem"—about 200 pages, and is going to publish them in that way singly, not in large volumes. He rather negatived her being discouraged, but said it was well that it should be out of her hands, otherwise she only read it through and through, wondering if it was yet complete. He said

she was always much exhausted after seeing anyone and he never went himself the day anyone else did: also that she had been much interested in arranging for a memorial endowment at Cambridge, about which she had been seeing two or 3 people,—Sidgwick, Foster, etc., besides Johnny about changing investments—it was such a comfort being able to trust that to him as both a friend and so excellent a man of business. She is going to try living at Witley this summer, and let it if she cannot bear it. I fear whether she will, since the only idea of breaking her loneliness is that "Gertrude and the children should stay there for a week at a time." Elma is still a difficulty to me—to know how to help a mind so ingenious in remembering things its own way.

VII, 134:12   EDITH SIMCOX, AUTOBIOGRAPHY, 12 APRIL 1879

MS: Bodleian. *Extracts published:* McKenzie, pp. 95–96; Haight, *George Eliot*, pp. 523–524.

Saturday 12 April 1879

12. There are days when one seems taken care of from above. I was kept at the shop till after 4 writing letters etc.; sleet and rain were falling heavily —I was in two minds whether to carry out my purpose of going round by the Priory—but I had not been since Wednesday and I did not like letting so many days pass, besides, I had almost made up my mind to write to her on Easterday, but I couldn't risk doing so unless I knew how she was—so I went. Brett exclaimed at my being out such a day and said—Would I come in for a little? I said—Oh no! and then she, perhaps I was too wet to stop now, but Mrs. Lewes had said she would like to see me the next time I came. Fortunately I had on a long jacket and had fastened up my dress, so that when one was off and the other down I was not apparently drenched, and she went to ask Mrs. Lewes if I should come in, presently the answer came, she would be glad to see me.

I came in with my veil down—she received me almost as usual and but for the veil which she made me take off would have received me with a kiss of welcome.—I spoke with effort of the long cold, and the danger of inclement holiday times. She said the coffee palaces seemed the only resource—had I seen much of them? I spoke of my lecturing for the working men's clubs. She had in her hands some of his Ms and proof and said she would leave me for a moment to put it in a place of safety. I tried to force back the tears, and stooped as she came back to move the footstool out of her way. She called me a thoughtful child and presently as another easy subject I spoke of Mrs. Stuart. She was sorry for her without blaming the boy,[1] and said she had begun to defend him a little, when Mrs. Stuart was overcome and apparently they spoke of other things. She said she had seen no one but men about the Studentship, Mrs. Congreve, and Elma. She spoke about the foundation and the volume she was bringing out, and when she found I knew of both, she touched my cheek almost playfully and asked me how I came to know so much. Before this I had risen to go, fearing to weary her, but instead, she made me sit down on her footstool, and she took my hand in hers. I told her how I had met Charlie and that Eleanor Cross had been to see me and given me news of her from Johnny. She said the latter told her he had seen me—and he praised me for unselfishness—said I never seemed to think of myself. She spoke, to my delight, freely and often of her husband, and said at first she had an intense repulsion from everyone—it seemed wicked—but she could hardly bear even Charlie—who was as good as a son could be, but so different. She said the studentship had made it easier to her to see people—she was going tomorrow to see Mr. and Mrs. Harrison who had been so kind; but other people she could not attempt. She spoke of the servants, of the comfort of human kindness without companionship when any nearer sympathy would be intolerable—nothing could be further from morbid sensibility than her whole manner and words. She said she did not know how she could have lived if she had not had his Ms. and the Studentship to think about,—she could read nothing else and went over that again and again till her brain went round, but she was comforted in reading the proofs after an interval. She had always identified herself with his Ms. so that he said she found more fault with them than she would if they had belonged to anyone else, and now she had a dread of any light words that might be said in forgetfulness of the unfinished state of the work:—which was foolish, since he would not have cared,—he was the only man who really delighted in adverse criticism—in a fair spirit as a means of reaching truth. Her pleasure in the endowment is that he would delight to live in a series of lives—he had always looked to the younger students and been patient of the unreceptiveness of others—who if they accepted his views did not own to doing so,—which was the rarer merit since he delighted so much in any sympathy that came,—only the week after their return from Brighton he had been pleased by receiving from some young men's reading club at Liverpool notice that the book they were going to discuss this winter was

1. Roland Stuart.

his. I was inexpressibly thankful to find that one might speak freely of the dear one. It had seemed to me cruel to be shut out from that, and yet I had the intense feeling of gratitude for an unexpected, unmerited boon when I found myself received as near to her as ever—the delight of receiving as a gift what one had made up one's mind not to claim.—She is so good she will find comfort yet in the blessedness she sheds on her children.

Elma is really very good: she sends me double thanks for my letter, she will not answer but will *think* about it. This is very generous. I said something to Mrs. Lewes about her having an unhappy nature—setting her heart on things—being cast down from a height when they failed her— which She translated better—she does things under an impulse and then feels they give her a claim. I said I had told her when she spoke of Roland as ungrateful that by asking for gratitude one ceased to deserve it. Mrs. Lewes said "How did she take it?"—and all that I wrote on Friday must have been to the full as hard—though doubtless she was helped by having seen Mrs. Lewes, and perhaps, such is human nature—by the thought that she had seen her and I had not! One smiles at those little jealous promptings, and yet I cannot but own to a selfish joy at finding that she places me only after Johnny and one of her oldest friends for I feel no jealousy of the Cambridge men or Elma, who owed something to my intercession:—"such is human nature"—I mean such as to prompt that last clause. I am unspeakably thankful for her goodness—for the future hope that she will accept a daughter's duty at one's hands. The African daughter-in-law has sailed to England with her children, and as soon as they arrive she will go down to Witley. I hope Mrs. Congreve will be in the neighbourhood[2] still; otherwise one fears as her strength increases the complete solitude will have its risks, in letting her labour too exclusively at the Ms.

VII, 138:20 GE TO HARRIS (THE BUILDER), LONDON, 19 APRIL 1879

MS: Colorado College, Colorado Springs, Colorado.

21 North Bank | April 19. 79.

In reply to Mr. Harris's letter on the subject of the coal cellar Mrs. Lewes begs to say that she is exceedingly annoyed to find an alteration of an expensive kind, made after an examination and estimate, turn out to be

2. The Congreves and Mrs. Geddes were living at Guildford.

quite ineffectual.[3] She would have thought, however, that an extension of the concrete at both ends might be a sufficient safeguard, without carrying the stone paving all along the path. She is naturally reluctant to incur a much greater expense after being disappointed in a plan which was before proposed as complete and effectual. She is now informed that the cellar is in a worse state than before the alteration.

She requests Mr. Harris to consider fully whether an extension of the concrete (with covering pavement) a certain distance beyond the cellar walls will not suffice.

VII, 143:1   EDITH SIMCOX, AUTOBIOGRAPHY, 25–29 APRIL 1879

MS: Bodleian.

Friday 25 April 1879

25. . . . At last I reached the cemetery; men were at work again; I doubt if the grave had been visited since I was there; the white wreath was withered to a brown skeleton; the fir twigs of mine were still just green— and in the centre of it I laid a bunch of fresh primroses: then I fled from the workmen with their well meaning assurances the slab would look better when it was cleaned up a bit; it was a flat marble slab with his name and the date of birth and death. I roamed about and then turned to the Church of England portion, where the slope of the hill is steeper, the trees shadier, and the whole aspect less like that of new built suburb. Then I came back and passed near the workmen again—then, a little before 3 I turned to leave; as I was walking down the lane below the cemetery, I saw a carriage half open—and a well known face—set and sad she was looking straight before her and did not see me and my first impulse was to look away as an intruder; my heart was wrung for her and I walked up and down long, but it was some time before I began to feel what I have felt with bitter regret ever since,—that I might have turned and tried to overtake her— have met her at the gate and let her lean on me as she walked and perhaps

---

3. GHL employed Harris to make the alterations in the Priory when he bought it in August 1863. In December 1873 there was a disagreement over some work, which was settled by Harris's taking £5. A brief note dated 24 January 1879 reads: "Mrs. Lewes has received Mr. Harris's estimate of the expense of laying concrete over the coal cellar and wishes to have the work done when the weather permits." (*MS:* Mr. Oliver R. Barrett.) Again the daughter of Robert Evans found the work unsatisfactory. There were many builders named Harris in London at this time.

come between her and the workmen. I lost this chance and had only the comfort of hoping that she would be glad to find the fresh flowers as a sign he was not quite forgotten. I have regretted my cowardice ever since, all the more because I think if I had thought first of her only, my impulse must have been to fly to her side—and yet one hardly knows—could she have borne for any one to be near? Since then I have longed to write to her, but all words seem a profanation.

Tuesday 29 April 1879

29. On Saturday I saw Brett, who said she had just returned from her drive. I was resolute in not expecting anything more, but on Sunday, with much hesitation I wrote to her—saying what had happened, and then speaking of his book. Today I called as usual; Brett was out and "Mary" answered my questions. Mrs. Herbert Lewes and the children had arrived, on Saturday, and had been to see Mrs. Lewes, and she had just driven them back and was still out. Mary was full of the beauty of the children. Sometimes one is forced to believe in a Providence. I was hardly outside the gate when I saw the carriage driving up—this time there could be no hesitation and I darted up to open the door for her and give my hand; she asked me to turn back and come in with her.

There is something infinitely touching to me in what one sees as a resolve to throw off the overmastering sense of grief and "live for others in a living world."[4] She spoke of the loveliness of the children and said, though it wasn't right or reasonable, she could never care for a plain child, though with dogs or any other kind of creature ugliness appealed to all her sympathies. She was tired with the children, who were full of life and restlessness and said she was glad she had not even attempted to have them with her. She smiled compassionately at the good friends who think these children will be a comfort and interest to her—of course she is glad to be able to provide for them, but they cannot enter into her life. And yet she said, if the girl[5] had been alone in the world, it would have been a temptation to her; but it was best as it was; she always became a slave to the child or whatever else she lived with. Her sister had a little girl, since dead,[6] who used to stay with her, and notwithstanding the biting things she has written since about maternal follies, she used every night long before bedtime to undress this child and rock her to sleep in her arms, feeling a sort of rapture in the mere presence, even though she might want the time for reading.

4. "We must bury our dead joys | And live above them with a living world." ("Armgart," *The Legend of Jubal*, 1874, p. 147.)

5. Herbert Lewes's daughter Marian.

6. Clara Christiana Clarke (1842–49). See I, 301, n. 2.

She spoke half in self-reproach of the people who live in so many relations that their life must be always full, whereas she always sent the strength of her feeling in the channel which absorbed it all. It had been so with her father. And then she said something that I cannot quite repeat —a reference to the step they had taken, which, without injuring, perhaps favouring the work they could do best for other people, forced them to live for each other and in such complete independence of the outer world that the world could be nothing for them. She said it seemed a sort of dual egoism: but then again that it must surely be best to make the nearest relation perfect: it was sad to see husbands and wives running away from each other after philanthropic works while the true life was left unblessed.

I asked about her nephew Vivian,[7] who is to be married at Christmas. I tried to say I had been interested in that love story because he spoke of it to me, but I broke down, swallowed the last of my tea and said I must go. She said she was tired, and that I must not cry: she could not bear it: she was obliged to turn herself by force from the passion of grief. That she had the comfort of knowing his life was perfect to the last, that mind and character suffered no falling off, and she—here she broke down into sobs, that she must live while she could—as he would have wished for her. —I knelt and kissed her, reproaching myself inwardly for having brought on the painful outbreak, but she recovered herself again. Said she was anxious to be at Witley and free from disturbance.—That what she missed most was the moral support—that she ended once—she was glad now to think she had—a summary of a year's journal[8] by saying his presence was a check on all that was evil, an encouragement to all that was good in her: her feeling was of rest and freedom from all difficulty because her pleasure was to do what he wished and he never wished anything but the right. Her one pleasure now was to read appreciation of him. She mentioned a letter from Peter Bayne[9]—a man she had only seen once, but who had written her a letter of such just estimate of what was most characteristic of his criticism that she had been truly grateful. He mentioned his reluctance to give pain and she quoted as a fresh and precious memory how some 3 and 20 years before when she was, for a short time, writing reviews, she had referred to some inadequate translation with a strong and appropriate adjective—and he asked her to leave out the adjective—why should she make a poor man miserable unnecessarily? She spoke of having

7. Vivian Byam Lewes married 21 August 1879 Constance, daughter of Thomas R. Abraham. (*Pall Mall Budget*, 5 September 1879, p. 898.)

8. "In each other, we are happier than ever; I am more grateful to my dear husband for his perfect love, which helps me in all good and checks me in all evil—more conscious that in him I have the greatest of blessings." (GE Journal, 1 January 1865, Yale.)

9. Peter Bayne (1830–96) called at the Priory 9 December 1877. His letter 3 December 1878 is at Yale.

the perfect life to look back on—which might have been a hell: death would be welcome when it came—the path that he had trod.—At least, she said, she had more duties, she could do hard things now—he had kept all difficulties far from her. I said her duty would be to let other people do all they could for her, but she clung to the scourge and called herself self indulgent.

Then she referred to the time when they were poor and how then and since they laughed at all their troubles and how he exaggerated hers— which would have been quite intolerable to her—who had had a very luxurious life—but for the happy love,—which reconciled her to having nothing but a very hard chair covered with moreen to sit on when her head ached badly. I said I had read all that between the lines about Lydgate and Rosamond. At 6, after $\frac{3}{4}$ of an hour, I left, gathering up her things, and she came with me to the door and I put my arms around her for a last kiss. Nearly the first thing she said was that [the] morbid time of repulsion was over for ever—that it was a strange and horrible experience to her to feel the springs of affection dried up, but it was over, and love and tenderness were as precious—or more precious—than ever. She said she had written to me and this evening the sweet lines came. If the mere thought of her pain seemed to me to make discontent at one's own small ills impossible, how much more the thought of the pain not merely suffered but endured as she endures with upright loving courage?

VII, 147:1 EDITH SIMCOX, AUTOBIOGRAPHY, 10 MAY 1879

MS: Bodleian.

Saturday 10 May 1879

10. Yesterday I had a sweet line from her at the shop, sending a cheque and the promising of a goodbye before she left. Today after the shop and a brief visit to Westminster, I hesitated whether to go to the Priory or no—was a little selfishly afraid of going and failing to get any clue as to when she would like to see me, but decided, since the hesitation was only selfish, to go and enquire, as of old and take my chance. Brett asked if I could wait—Mrs. Lewes had said she would like to see me if I came. She is anxious to get to Witley—there are so many people she feels she must see, lest they should be hurt, and one tells another—they do not all understand—she spoke of there being perhaps 150 people to whom she owed some debt of gratitude. Mrs. Ritchie, Mrs. Burne Jones, Herbert Spencer and Leslie Stephen happened to be mentioned as people whom

she had seen. She asked what I was doing—if I did not mind being asked—
she did. I said no—I wished she would ask that I might be ashamed of
saying "Nothing." I talked a little about the Westminster concern, Workmen's Clubs etc.,[1] and she accused herself of having spoken ill of philan-
thropists when she said some went far afield after mechanical work in the
name of benevolence leaving the nearest need unsupplied; I said I had
not misunderstood her. I asked about the children—she had been to buy
them toys—the first time she had been into London—to the din of Oxford
St. I asked about the Scholarship and she said there was some delay, a
difference of opinion among the trustees,[2] and there was no real hurry,
but she was impatient, always wanted things settled and had written to
ask Mr. Sidgwick about it.

I had not said anything that I wanted when Mr. Pigott was announced.
I offered to go at once, but she said, Sit down, and so I exerted myself to
make conversation with him, wondering all the while whether he came on
business or as an old friend,—he referred to a former visit. Then he turned
his back to look at some flowers and I rose with a questioning look; she
assented and said hurriedly as she kissed me—'Go into the dining room,
there is something you will like to see.'—An enlarged photograph of him,
framed and put over the chimney piece where her portrait used to be.

VII, 147:1   GE TO ANDREW CLARK, LONDON, 11 MAY 1879

MS: Yale.

The Priory, | 21. North Bank, | Regents Park.
May 11. 79.

My dear Physician

I am going into the country in a week or so, and if you happened to be
driving near enough to me to give me ten minutes of your precious time
I should value the gift greatly. Not that I am in the least ailing physically,
but I venture to ask for a 'Goodbye' for his sake who esteemed you so
highly.[3]

Ever yours gratefully
M. E. Lewes.

1. The men of the Westminster
Democratic Club suggested that Edith
stand for election to the London School
Board. See K. A. McKenzie, *Edith
Simcox and George Eliot*, 1961, pp. 37–38.

2. See vii, 177.

3. "Dr. Andrew Clarke came and
gave me important suggestions about
the Studentship of which I wrote to Mr.
Sidgwick, Dr. C. having promised to
see Huxley tomorrow." (GE Diary, 13
May 1879.)

VII, 151:21   EDITH SIMCOX, AUTOBIOGRAPHY
22 MAY 1879

MS: Bodleian.

Thursday 22 May 1879

22. I went on Sunday [18 May]: she looked ill and answered my anxious
question by saying she was very ill. I must not stay long. Her face was like
Watts' Paolo[4] with a deathlike expression of overpast pain. She had exhausted her powers of endurance in the attempt to do too much for—I
imagined—the daughters-in-law: they weary her and she does not like to
say so—she said to me—"One cannot enjoy vicariously"—and then she
checked herself and said she ought not to grumble. She leant back in her
chair exhausted but told me to wait while she tried to remember what she
had to say to me.—It was to ask about the plan of shareholders for H. & Co.
—I answered very shortly and took my leave; before—through all the grief
for her grief and pain, selfish comfort came to me because she was able to
bear my nearness; her hand rested in mine and when I kissed her in farewell,
the dear cheek pressed itself caressingly on my lips. It is so sweet of her to
endure to be loved.

On Monday [19 May] I went to ask and was told she was better, had
been for a drive in the morning. Wednesday I wanted much to go but was
hindered. I had settled mentally she would leave town on Thursday and
thought to find out when or dreamt of lurking at Waterloo to meet her
carriage by each possible train and press her hand once more—risking
the dread that she would as soon be alone. But it was not to be. She had
left this morning, an hour or so before I called. I tried in vain to find a
secret place in Regent's Park where to lie on the grass and sob out one's
first bitter grief. It was a warm shady May day and strollers and children
were everywhere—also my moans were choked by the awful thought—her
desolation is even more complete than this.

4. *Dante's "Paolo and Francesca"* by George Frederick Watts, now in Melbourne,
Australia.

VII, 172:25   GE TO HERBERT SPENCER,
WITLEY, 27 JUNE 1879

MS: University of London. *Partly published:* vii, 172–173.

The Heights, Witley, | Nr. Godalming.

June 27. 79.

Dear Friend

Thank you for your kind present.[5] I am now at the end of the "Criticisms and Explanations" and am carrying on my reading with an interest which you will infer to be rather strong when I tell you that I have for the last 12 days been going through rather a sharp illness. My reading as well as my correspondence have been chiefly done in bed.

I rejoice not in the cause, but in the fact of your having broken the contemplated order of your series for the sake of securing this portion of your Ethics, and if I did not believe it to be an impertinence to tell an author what one would wish him to do, I should say a little more of the value that many would attach to a continuation of this weft as something more needed than even the completion of the Sociological portion.[6] Of course, as you predict, you will be partly misunderstood and misrepresented. That is destiny unshunnable.[7] All one must care about is that some grains of corrective knowledge or useful stimulus will be here and there swallowed and digested.

I have an evil pleasure in observing that you have as good a crop of little misprints as I should have left myself.

Yours always sincerely

M. E. Lewes.

VII, 186:9   EDITH SIMCOX, AUTOBIOGRAPHY,
23–26 JULY 1879

MS: Bodleian.

Wednesday 23 July 1879

23. Yesterday the longed for letter came at last, with the expected dreaded news, of her continuous ill health. I had not the heart to write, besides I

---

5. *The Data of Ethics,* published separately 17 June 1879, was the first part of *The Principles of Ethics,* which Spencer completed in 1893.

6. *The Principles of Sociology,* begun in 1876, was completed in 1896.

7. *Othello,* iii, iii, 275.

feel she would have opened the letter with just a little dread of a despairing outcry, so I sent a card with 2 lines in German: now she knows it seems easier to bury oneself in books; what was wearing me out was the double anxiety—lest she should be more ill than one knew or lest one should in any way unwittingly have jarred upon her in anything said or left unsaid.

Saturday 26 July 1879

26. Yesterday went to Hampstead: walked up the heath with Mrs. Charles Lewes who was good in telling me of her: the news are very anxious, the internal irritation having set up inflammation: the doctors trust to the strength and soundness of her constitution, but Mrs. Charles said she was fearfully thin, and I doubt her having much power now to throw off any serious illness. I remember what he told me and there remains the possibility behind of terrible pain: perhaps an operation—one can only live from week to week. She was downstairs with Charles on Sunday, but had a very bad night and they dreaded another relapse, but since then she has written to say she is better and to urge them to make no change in their summer plans on her account and to start without any haunting fears of a telegram.

VII, 195:1 GE TO JAMES SULLY, WITLEY, 19 AUGUST 1879

MS: University College, London. *Envelope:* James Sully Esq | care of Prof. Alexander Bain | Aberdeen | N.B. *Postmark:* GODALMING | C | AU 19 | 79; ABERDEEN | A | AU 21 | 79. *Endorsed:* on a possible miscarriage of her letter.

The Heights, Witley, | Nr. Godalming.

August 19. 79.

Dear Mr. Sully

Excuse my teasing you, but you are usually so punctual that I cannot help being anxious to know whether my letter addressed to Aberdeen actually reached you. Do not write to say "Yes"; the proofs, when they come, will be satisfactory evidence.

Always yours truly,

M. E. Lewes.

VII, 198:1 GE TO JAMES SULLY,
WITLEY, 10 SEPTEMBER 1879

MS: University College, London. *Envelope:* James Sully Esq | 57 Tideswell Road |
Eastbourne. *Postmark:* GODALMING | C | SP 10 | 79. *Endorsed:* On GHL's work (cor-
recting my article). Success of Life of Goethe in Germany. *Partly published:* VII, 198.

The Heights, Witley, | Nr. Godalming.

September 10. 79.

Dear Mr. Sully

I have read the article with very grateful feelings. I think that he would
himself have regarded it as a generally just estimate. And I am much obliged
to you for sending it to me in proof.[8] In addition to what, in compliance with
your kind request, I have pencilled in the margin, there are one or two
suggestions which may be the more easily carried out because some omissions are required by the Editor.

I think that his acting in 1841 at Whitehall was merely incidental. At
least I always understood from him, that his idea of becoming an actor
arose out of ⟨events⟩ conditions which were subsequent to his acting with
Dickens's amateur company.[9]

I think he would have strongly desired the omission of the passage
which I have marked on page 3,[10] and in the case of your being obliged
to make further excisions, he would have felt that the account of the plot of
'Rose, Blanche and Violet' might best be spared. I have ventured to put
some pencil marks here, but they are merely for you to exercise your judgment on.

But I beg you in his name and my own to omit the paragraph about the
article on "Robert Browning and the Poetry of the Age."[11] I know that he

8. The proof of [Sully's] "George
Henry Lewes," *New Quarterly Magazine*,
N.S., 2 (October 1879), 356–376, with
GE's pencil notes is at University
College, London.

9. Sully wrote: "In the year 1841 we
find him playing at the Whitehall
Theatre in Garrick's comedy The
Guardian." (p. 357.) Charles Hennell
reported that Swynfen Jervis "called
and invited him to their Comédie de
Famille, when *The Guardian* was produced." (S. S. Hennell, *A Memoir of
Charles Christian Hennell*, privately
printed, 1899, p. 115.) With Dickens's
company in 1847 GHL played the Host
in *The Merry Wives of Windsor* and Old

Knowell in *Every Man in His Humour*;
in 1848 he played Sir Hugh Evans and
Wellbred in the same plays.

10. Sully glossed this: "A reference
to an article 'The Miseries of a Dramatic
Author' in the *Cornhill* [8 (August 1863),
498–512], supposed to be autobiographical."

11. *British Quarterly Review*, 6 (November 1847), 490–509, a review of
Bells and Pomegranates. In the proof
Sully wrote: "Tennyson is here spoken
of as probably the only living writer
who deserves the name of poet. The
estimate of Browning corresponds to
that of most later critics. Lewes had no
patience with the poet's obscurity."

would have objected to have attention called to his early observations on two living poets—observations which his later mind would have considerably modified.

This [is] all that I have to ask or suggest, beyond the remainder of my pencilings. Your selection of subjects for remark and the remarks themselves are in accordance with my feeling to a comforting extent, and I shall always remain your debtor for writing the article.

I trust you will not be forced to omit anything about his scientific and philosophical work, because that is the part of his life's labour which he most valued.

Perhaps you a little underrate the (original) effect of his Life of Goethe in Germany. It was received with enthusiasm and an immense number of copies in both the English and German form have been sold in Germany since its appearance in 1855.

I return the proof at once, that your kindness in sending it to me may not be the occasion of inconvenient delay. Believe me, dear Mr. Sully,

Yours most sincerely

M. E. Lewes.

I wish you were allowed to put your name to the article.

VII, 198:18 GE TO ALBERT GEORGE DEW-SMITH, WITLEY, 11 SEPTEMBER 1879

MS: Yale. *Envelope:* A.G. Dew-Smith, Esq. | Trinity College | Cambridge. *Postmarks:* GODALMING | C | SP 12 | 79; CAMBRIDGE | 2 | SP 13 | 79.

The Heights, Witley, | Godalming.

September 11. 79.

Dear Sir

Having Dr. Foster's warrant for troubling you on the subject of the paper sent to me yesterday, I venture to ask that you will oblige me by making a correction which I omitted, namely—in the heading instead of '*by Mary Ann Evans Lewes*' simply '*by M. E. Lewes*' known as an author etc.[1]

Yours faithfully

M. E. Lewes.

1. The original wording of the name was taken from the deed transferring £5,000 to the trustees for the George Henry Lewes Studentship in Physiology. The revised form appears in the announcement and invitation for applicants. Dew-Smith (1848–1903), B.A. 1873, who was connected with the Cambridge Scientific Instrument Co. and the Cambridge Engraving Co., was seeing the announcement through the press. GHL lunched at his house, Chesterton Hall, while visiting Michael Foster at Cambridge, 10 November 1875.

VII, 202:10   GE TO JAMES SULLY,
WITLEY, 21 SEPTEMBER 1879

MS: University College, London. *Envelope:* James Sully Esq | Savile Club | 15 Savile Row | London | W. *Postmarks:* GODALMING | B | SP 22 | 79; LONDON N.W | M 3 | SP 22 | 79. *Endorsed:* Asking me to let her make acknowledgment of indebtedness to me.

The Heights, Witley, | Nr. Godalming.

September 21. 79.

Dear Mr. Sully

You are almost at the end of your kind labours for me. I have five proofs by me awaiting your and Dr. Foster's notes and I think there are only about three more to come.

Do you object to my mentioning your name with Dr. Foster's in a brief prefatory note?[2]

Always yours truly

M. E. Lewes.

VII, 206:1   GE TO MME EUGÈNE BODICHON,
WITLEY, 4 OCTOBER 1879

MS: Berg Collection, New York Public Library. *Envelope:* Madame Bodichon | Scalands Gate | Robertsbridge. *Postmark:* GODALMING | C | OC 4 | 79.

Saturday morning.

Dearest Barbara

Delighted to hear that you got home safely without too much fatigue.[3] Thanks for the enclosed letter. I think it is very reasonable.

Your loving

Marian.

2. "In correcting the proof-sheets of this volume the Editor has been generously aided by Dr. Michael Foster and Mr. James Sully." (*Problems of Life* and *Mind. Mind as a Function of the Organism*, 1879, p. [v].)

3. Mme Bodichon stayed at Witley 29 September–2 October.

VII, 210:1 GE TO W. L. BICKNELL, WITLEY, 9 OCTOBER 1879

MS: Professor Blake Nevius.

The Heights, Witley, | Nr. Godalming.
October 9. 79.

Dear Sir

You will no doubt on reflection appreciate as well as imagine the reasons that must prevent a writer who cares much about his writings from willingly allowing them to be modified and in any way 'adapted' by another mind than his own.

And with regard to 'Romola,' the state of our stage would make me shudder at the prospect of its characters' being represented there. I need not enter into the question whether there would be the slightest probability of a play founded on that work meeting acceptance from a manager. I remain,

Yours faithfully
M. E. Lewes.
(George Eliot)

VII, 219:13 EDITH SIMCOX, AUTOBIOGRAPHY, 29 OCTOBER 1879

MS: Bodleian.

Wednesday 29 October 1879

29. I have been reading Daniel Deronda through. It is strange that with all the intensity of my love for her, I never cease to feel as if the physical part of our conscious nature was more than remote—opposite. Somehow it is a more depressing book to me than her others, perhaps because it is a faithful transcript of the coexistence of unreconciled tendencies. I am more struck by the pathos of Gwendolen's rejection than by the healing power of Daniel's virtuous conduct and counsel. As in the passage of Theophrastus which hurt me one is reminded at once of the solitude of eminence, "the impossibility of reciprocating confidences with one who looks up to us" and the double solitude when the confidence we wish to make is suppressed, or one we wish to receive is withheld. She speaks of the scepticism which people call "Knowledge of the world and which is

really disappointment in you and me." Is not the world made of yous and mes, and if it falls into these 2 classes with a minority in whom are answering needs—to bestow and to receive—is the "Knowledge of the world" a hopeful science? I know with me faith, hope and charity remain unhurt because I live outside the world, which is of a nature to make those virtues difficult.

VII, 219:13   GE TO WILLIAM BLACKWOOD, WITLEY, 30 OCTOBER 1879

MS: National Library of Scotland.

The Heights, Witley, | Nr. Godalming.
October 30. 79.
My dear Mr. William

Your letter of yesterday[4] has not yet reached me but the Times tells me its purport. I am mourning with you our irreparable loss. Perhaps none outside your family will feel it more than I do.

I cannot intrude on such sorrow as Mrs. Blackwood's, but she and all of you, whenever you have leisure to think of me, will know that I am a sharer in all grief for the friend who is lost to me—except in the memory of his goodness.

Yours always truly,
M. E. Lewes.

VII, 224:1   EDITH SIMCOX, AUTOBIOGRAPHY, 9 NOVEMBER 1879

MS: Bodleian.

Sunday 9 November 1879

November 9. . . . I wrote to Her a report of the election proceedings[5] up to Friday and last night had a word of thanks to say it had amused her. I saw her on Tuesday having settled to leave Sunday and Monday for

4. To Joseph Langford, William Blackwood wrote 26 October 1879: "I have written to George Eliot a private note, as we have not written to her for three weeks." (NLS.) Neither his note, nor GE's "beautiful letter of 28th," nor his letter announcing John Blackwood's death 29 October has been found.

5. Edith was elected to the London School Board. See McKenzie, pp. 30–36.

rest. She was looking much better and said the constant care of the local doctor had been much in her favour. She had not seen or heard much in detail about Dr. Roy[6] yet. She had been to the Cemetery that day and was disappointed with the ivy and the place of the grave. She had been vexed, as I feared at the well-meant blundering way of the article in the New Quarterly—which she said was written by a clever man and a friend.[7] "Don Garcia in England" had been sent her with an inscription, she thought because of one sentence about him. She spoke of the difficulty, after living an ideal life—thinking of things and people as they might be— to come back into the real world and exercise the virtues one had been dreaming about; and she assented without demur to my remark as above, that one's charity was warmest when least tried. But I must try not to let her worry herself with the thought she ought to do more than she likes or can. I shall go again—if possible on Wednesday straight after the nomination if there is any contest.

VII, 226:8   EDITH SIMCOX, AUTOBIOGRAPHY, 23 NOVEMBER 1879

MS: Bodleian. *Extract published:* McKenzie, p. 105; Haight, *George Eliot*, p. 531.

Sunday 23 November 1879

23. I was not able to get to her till the Saturday afternoon and then Lady Paget was there, so I only left my love. On the 19th I saw her, for about half an hour; she protested against the time and mental force spent in writing to her—another long report.—Spoke of the wearisomeness of business and letters—a man called sending in an impertinent note—"My dear George Eliot" which she answered by a message, she was not able to receive strangers: said he used to tease her for not being content with dispatching a letter unless it was a composition—his own notes were scribbled off with ease and he comforted himself that no one would ever wish to print them. She added life wasn't long enough to read up old productions of the penny post, then looked at me to make an exception and when I said 'those least of all' she denied—thought if my letters could be printed anonymously, they would make a very pretty complete romance. Then she went on to say how horrid it was to hear indirectly that some letters, even of sympathy, were only dictated by the hope of an autograph. On the other hand some perfectly beautiful letters came unsigned—she

6. See vii, 213, n. 5.   7. James Sully.

had one such from a gentleman in New Zealand lately, and they were the most precious tribute: Johnny came in and I could have kissed him for he kissed her hand when he came in.

VII, 227:23 GE TO MRS. RICHARD STRACHEY, LONDON, 2 DECEMBER 1879

MS: British Museum. *Envelope:* Mrs Strachey | Stowey House | Clapham Common, *Postmarks:* ST JOHNS WOOD N.W | DE 2 | 79; LONDON S.W | DE 4 | 79. *Published: TLS*, 16 May 1968, p. 507.

The Priory, | 21. North Bank, | Regents Park.
December 2. 79.
My dear Mrs. Strachey

I shall be in town for the next few months. Your letter to me long ago is still in my mind and makes me trust that it is in yours also. Will you come and see me? Any day after 4.30.[8]

Yours always affectionately
M. E. Lewes.

VII, 228:7 GE TO JAMES A. H. MURRAY, LONDON, 5 DECEMBER 1879

MS: Girton College.

The Priory, | 21. North Bank, | Regents Park.
December 5. 79.
Dear Sir

I am obliged by your communication of the 3d. So far as I can answer for the self of seventeen years ago, I believe that I was determined in the choice of *adust*[9] rather than *dusty* partly by the feeling of rhythm which accompanies my prose writing and partly by the (perhaps fallacious) impression that by adust the imagination was less restricted and could

---

8. Mrs. Strachey called 10 December. (GE Diary.)

9. James Augustus Henry Murray (1837–1915), lexicographer, a master at the Mill Hill School in London 1870–85, was appointed editor of the *New English Dictionary on Historical Principles* (*OED*) in 1879. In his first section (1884) Murray defines *adust* as "In a dusty condition, affected by dust," derived after analogy with *a-blaze*, *a-sleep*, adding the note "[So explained by the author quoted.]" and giving as the only quotation "He was tired and adust with long riding" from George Eliot, *Romola*, *Cornhill Mag.* 7 (March 1863), 297 [Ch. 45].

be led to include other conditions of which dustiness is one sign. But I did not intend to represent the latin *adustus*. I dared to form my word analogically.

I wish always to be quoted as George Eliot. Thanking you for your courteous solicitude on this point, I remain

Yours very truly
M. E. Lewes.

VII, 228:17 JAMES A. H. MURRAY TO GE, LONDON, 6 DECEMBER 1879

MS: Brotherton Library, Leeds.

Mill Hill, Middlesex, N.W. | 6 December 1879.

Dear Madam

Many thanks for your obliging note, and for the 'slip' now returned.

Your 'instinct'—shall I call it?—was quite correct as to *adust*, which, in strictest analogy, means *in a dusty state*, i.e. not merely *dusty* but "affected by dust," in every way that it could affect clothes, skin, eyes, or throat. It really differs from *dusty*, as *a-fire* does from *fiery*, or *a-cold* "poor Tom's a-cold"[10] from "cold" merely. It is of course by such extension of analogy, —instinctive most of it—that language is made; not by conscious synthesis of roots and particles which ⟨live⟩ have independent existence only on paper, but exist in living speech in the concrete, and by analogy produce other living words "living creatures after their kind."[1]

I am happy to have had, so to say, a peep at such a genius, and am, Dear Madam,

Yours very truly
James A. H. Murray.

VII, 228:17 EDITH SIMCOX, AUTOBIOGRAPHY, 10 DECEMBER 1879

MS: Bodleian.

Wednesday 10 December 1879

December 10. On Wednesday (26th) I went to the Priory, she was engaged. Wrote to her to ask what I should do about the offer of divers people to

---

10. *King Lear*, II, iv, 152.   1. Genesis, 1:24.

subscribe to the election expenses. She answered accept, and so I ceased to refuse. Then came the election and on Sunday, the 30th I forgot everything except that day last year, and the sadness of her maimed life and the grief that one may share but cannot lessen. I could not bring myself to write to her though I had her note of counsel to acknowledge. The next day brought me a card of affectionate congratulations, and then I went to see her on Wednesday—after writing what I could. I was shown in at once, Leslie Stephen was there, Mr. and Mrs. Beesly came. The talk was of Pope, Gladstone, James Payn,[2] on educating authors, Afghanistan and Secocoeni.[3] My heart ached for her—it was like the Sunday afternoons, without the one who could always shield her from fatigue and come to the rescue in endless ways. I talked, not badly, but I did not see her alone. Last Friday I had one of her remorseful afterthoughts by post, she was afraid she had spoken with needless severity of Overton's[4] literary shortcomings, and this gave me the opportunity of delivering *my* remorseful afterthought. There are so many for her to see—is it kind to make one more?

VII, 231:20   EDITH SIMCOX, AUTOBIOGRAPHY,
21 DECEMBER 1879

MS: Bodleian.

Sunday 21 December 1879

21. Last Thursday between a day at the shop and an evening at the Craven school, I made up my mind to seek her. She was alone and we were uninterrupted. She was looking and feeling well in health—surprisingly so to herself—she was sweet and dear, showed me bits of letters about him— one from a German who said how few writers either German or English understood equally the philosophy—or even the philosophical languages of the 2 countries as he did. I asked about Mrs. Stuart, she had not heard from her since she went south, but thought she was at Alassio. She had thought her much changed by her illness—I suggested that she had only seen her before in a happy mood. I stayed an hour and hardly know what we spoke of—School Board, Delboeuf on double consciousness in dreams,

2. James Payn (1830–98) published more than fifty novels, some of them serialized in *Chambers's Edinburgh Journal*, which he edited.
3. Secocoeni (or Sikukini), a powerful native chief on whom the Dutch settlers of the Transvaal made war in 1876.
4. John Henry Overton (1835–1903) published *The English Church in the Eighteenth Century*, 2 vols., 1878.

Cabul,[5] and Ireland, Dr. Roy, who is full of delightful young enthusiasm about the heart and pulse, and has sent her his published Memoirs and a letter from Leipzig where he was studying to say Ludwig[6] knew all about the Studentship, thought the arrangements admirable and hoped it would tend to raise the *status* of physiological research in England. I mentioned what had struck me as curious in walking there—a waggon came close behind me as I was crossing a side road up which the waggon was turning out of the main road. I had a dim vision of it out of the corners of my eyes as dangerously near and had to control the first irrational impulse to start back right under the shafts. I took this first as an explanation of why horses wear blinkers and then reflected that one habitually sees what is in front and therefore in the case of danger one habitually starts back and it seems, does so still when the danger is seen at an unaccustomed angle. This led her to say she had an exceptional power of seeing out of the corners of her eyes and used to dispute with him about the dictum of physiologists that you can only see colours with a certain part of the retina and that what is behind is *seen* black and only judged to be coloured. She was very beautiful and let me give her dear cheek long clinging kisses. I said, looking at the letters she was writing—did she not want a Secretary—she said Charlie was unhappy because she would let him do so little for her and would break his heart (I doubt it) if she let anyone else do anything. She said she must keep her faculties from stupefying and met my half uttered prayers by saying I had quite enough to do, I should attend to my own business— whereto I, Yes, but one coveted a little pleasure too—it was human nature. She owned human nature did crave (in reference to our mention before of the dangers of Boxing day) its taste of gin—I said and kissed her crape— was not mine of an innocent sort, and then went away. She asked me about Mr. Overton and said he had elected Mrs. Congreve as his director after 5 minutes discourse and had shown the Ms. of his book to her first of any one: it represented I heard elsewhere the work 3 years Sundays. I left her cheered and comforted.

VII, 235:18 EDITH SIMCOX, AUTOBIOGRAPHY, 26 DECEMBER 1879

MS: Bodleian. *Extract published:* Haight, *George Eliot,* p. 533.

26th. She was alone; said it was rare for her to see no one all day as was the case the day before. She was reading, or rather cutting a new book.

5. Or Kabul, capital of Afghanistan, captured by the British and held for a time in the second Afghan war.

6. Karl Friedrich Wilhelm Ludwig (1816–95), German physiologist, inventor of the sphygmometer.

I apologized for coming so soon again, that I felt always guilty because instead of bringing her useful or entertaining information my own ideal was just to hold my tongue and be comfortable, she deprecated the useful information and the silence alike: then reflected she had not returned my kiss, and did so—she thought it such a horrid habit of people to put their cheek and make no return, the little niece from Natal does so (and she is called Marian!) while the little boy puts up his lips. I said should I go, having had the kiss I came for. She said she wasn't so easily tired. She had heard from Elma, who had been ill and was sorry, not surprised that Roland had not passed;[7] I failed to explain myself about the absence of the maternal instinct in Elma. She said with all her admirable generosity and so on she was a strange person and quoted some one, perhaps Mrs. Charles Lewes, who found it difficult to get on with her. I was vexed with myself for seeming to be judging her, though Mrs. Lewes was doing so also by her regrets that Elma had planned everything in such detail to her own mind that she could not but have been disappointed. Then we got on to politics—Lady Strangford and her Bulgarians, whom she doesn't think half as wise and good as the Turks. Disraeli—she scolded me much for calling him un-principled—she was disgusted with the venom of the Liberal speeches from Gladstone downwards. I tried to justify my use of the term as a slowly formed sincere belief, referred to his books, which she thought wonderfully clever; ·I said look at the Truck System in Sybil[8] and his indifference to the obscure useful acts upon the subject. She admitted that was a real charge and implored me only to make *such* real concrete doings or omissions the ground of attack and to refrain from judgments on the whole man. Then we mixed in the Cornhill on Tennyson, which she got to refer to the one parallel passage which showed a really interesting resemblance (a poem of Lord Herbert of Cherbury to In Memoriam).[9]

She said men's characters were as mixed as the origins of mythology. We went back more than once to the question of "principle." I said I used to hate L. N.[1] and she said Yes—one was tempted to call the author of the Coup d'Etat a *bad* man, but she believed he was only willing to do one bad action as a means, and then meant to do good ones. Dizzy was [a politician?] therefore ambitious, not a fool, and so he must care for a place

7. Examinations for military college.

8. In depicting the miners in *Sybil* Disraeli, who depended on the Blue Book reports of the employment of women and children, passed lightly over the horrors of their drawing trucks of coal through the mines. See Book III, ch. 1.

9. In "A New Study of Tennyson (Part I)," *Cornhill* 41 (January 1880), 36–50, J. Churton Collins compares six stanzas from "An Ode upon the Quest-ion, Whether Love Should Continue Forever" with stanzas of *In Memoriam*.

1. Louis Napoleon executed the coup d'état in 1851.

in history and how could he expect to win that by doing harm? I said he would be satisfied with such a place as Wolsey or Richelieu—whereto She "And the Positivists are setting to work to idealize Richelieu, so what then?[2] But here she stopped, it was enough not to idealize the evil, she did wish to idealize the good out of knowledge. I said no, because hero worship was an indulgence, there was self-denial in not insisting on it, and then I lapsed into some of the fond folly which always provokes her. She had never known anyone perfect and worshipped none the less.

Then for the twentieth time I prepared to go and said she had been scolding me for the nearest approach to good points I had—I thought she believed me to be at least charitable and veracious, she startled me by some little outcry at the last word—had she ever said I was veracious— that was a rash thing to say of any one, it was so very difficult to attain perfect truth—nay more, it was a virtue that might be overdone and on the whole she elected to scold me rather for imperfect veiling of unpleasant truths, as when I didn't like any one—here I burst in that I never did dislike any one, and she quoted my letter from Dinan, as if I had said their love-making bored me. Still she didn't deny I was indifferent honest. I said, she must tell me if she ever thought otherwise.

She said, after half a pause, would I really rather she said anything she thought—would it hurt me—my heart sank fathoms underground and tears came into my eyes—if she said she did not like for me to call her 'Mother'—I gave a sigh of relief, if that was all. She went on, she knew it was her fault, she had begun, she was apt to be rash and commit herself in one mood to what was irksome to her in another—not with her own mother, but her associations otherwise with the name were as of a task and it was a fact that her feeling for me was *not* at all a mother's—any other name she didn't mind, she had much more "respect and admiration" for me now than when she knew me first, but etc.—she hoped I was not hurt.[3] I tried to say that the only name natural to me was darling, and that I took the other as being less greedy and more dutiful. I sat up late last night writing (to post tomorrow) a short reassurance that I am not hurt.

2. Note GE's detachment from the Positivists.
3. Elma Stuart's tombstone is in-
scribed: "whom for $8\frac{1}{2}$ blessed years George Eliot called by the sweet name of 'Daughter.'"

VII, 237:7 BENJAMIN JOWETT TO GE,
WEST MALVERN, 30 DECEMBER 1879

MS: Brotherton Library, Leeds.

West Malvern | December 30. 1879.

Dear Mrs. Lewes,

Will you think me forward if I send you good wishes on New Year's day?

The only good wish which I can offer is that you may have health and strength to make the most of life: my faith is that more may be done by us in our later than in our earlier years (if the faculties remain) because we have more experience and are more humanized by trials and sufferings of many kinds: I like your notion of the duty of 'diffusing ourselves,' making the most of the one life for the good of many:—that is a phrase of yours which often comes into my mind: and, especially in the case of a great sorrow the first thing is to bear it and to feel it; and the next thing is to convert the particular sorrow into a wider and deeper sympathy for men and women everywhere, and having suffered ourselves, to lighten the hearts and minds of others: I hardly think you are aware how great a good and comfort your writings have been to numberless persons; how they have really been made better by Dinah and Milly and Romola and the Garths and many of our other friends, and how much knowledge of life they have gained from your writings which is one of the best sorts of knowledge. I know that it is not the writer of fiction's direct business to preach morality and truth, but it is a great blessing to the world when he can teach this indirectly by his own natural sense of them pervading his creations. Therefore I was delighted to hear you say that you did not give up the idea of writing; and I would not ask you to hurry in this: It might be well to have rest and a time for study; and a good deal of thought may be required to fix upon the precise form which is most suited to your own genius—I would have you sometimes think that you may yet attain better and higher things in writing (that is my New Year's wish for you and I believe it to be the true spirit in which to write)

> For every gift of noble origin
> Is breathed upon by hope's perpetual breath.[4]

(Do you remember quoting this to me?)

I have been reading through 1) Pattison's Milton[5]—a good book with many interesting remarks, but written too much in the spirit of the litera-

4. Wordsworth, "These times strike monied worldlings with dismay," October 1803, *Poems Dedicated to National* *Independence*, Part I, no. 20.
5. Mark Pattison, *Milton*, 1879, English Men of Letters series.

teur, who estimates all men and books by their purely literary merit. He is a man of genius but he is wanting in the sense of proportion and lets little things get the better of great ones. 2) Another book which I have been reading is M. Arnold's Selections from Wordsworth[6]: I love and value Wordsworth more as I get older. He makes you better and he expresses your own best thoughts and wishes in the best words. Yet he is a warning against being didactic which has taken from more than half his writings the true value and grace. He also seems to me wanting in logic or coherence. Stories such as Ruth or Margaret or Michael though extremely beautiful have no point: I suppose that Wordsworth would have defended this by saying that 'real life has no point.' But I think that in poetry it ought to have; for poetry or fiction is a selected piece of life, or like the composition of a picture.

I have also been reading more books about Homer lately and am more inclined than I used to be to give up Wolfe's[7] theory of the Homeric poems:

I. Wolfe's authorities if you examine them are really worthless. It may be truly said 'that absolutely nothing is known about the history of the Homeric poems from tradition or scholia including the Venetus scholia.' And nothing more was known to the Alexandrian Critics than to ourselves.

II. If you examine the Iliad and Odyssey from within you will find that there is no possibility of breaking either poem up into lays, because every part refers to every other part and the separate lays such as Lachmann[8] imagined are quite motiveless and inconsistent.

III. The Iliad and Odyssey were not sound [?] books: But they were as carefully defined and preserved as if they had been. There are no traces of other readings, other versions. But is not this best accounted for by supposing a single genius who (of course out of preexisting materials and beliefs, and in a certain stage of the language and of poetry) composed both the Iliad and Odyssey? I do not believe in the Separatists when I see how closely the two poems hang together.

Wolfe and Niebuhr[9] have been two of the greatest influences on Criticism: And yet probably the theories of both are the failure of a vision.

I see that I am running on with my own thoughts and studies. Once more let me come back to the New Year. These divisions of time always produce an effect on my mind: "I will begin again" "I will resolve" and though this is illusion I think one does keep oneself at a somewhat higher mark by the help of them. We all of us need more strength than we have

6. Matthew Arnold, *Poems of Wordsworth*, 1879, Golden Treasury series.
7. I.e. Friedrich August Wolf. See v, 124, n. 6.
8. Karl K. F. W. Lachmann, *Betrach-* *tungen über Homers Ilias*, Berlin, 1874.
9. Barthold Georg Niebuhr, *Römische Geschichte*, new ed., 3 vols., Berlin, 1873–74.

for the tasks of life—we must go on, never hasting, never resting, to the end. We are often tired and discouraged, and we think of the days that are past and of those who are gone. We must journey alone and finish our work (something like Milton in his blindness if we may venture to appropriate so great an example). There is probably no one now living in England, who could do as much for literature and for the world as you could by writing, and you must not throw this precious trust away, or let yourself be overpowered by the thought of it, and give way to any paralyzing sensitiveness about the opinion of others: As I said before, I would not have you hurry. Great things of this kind are not realized in a day or in a year: they require health and strength and peace of mind: Believe me | Dear Mrs. Lewes,

Yours most truly
B. Jowett.

I shall be careful not to speak of your writing to any one.

VII, 243:11   GE TO FREDERIC W. H. MYERS, LONDON, 9 JANUARY 1880

MS: Trinity College, Cambridge. *Envelope:* F.W.H. Myers Esq. | Hôtel Meurice | 228 Rue de Rivoli | Paris. *Postmark:* st johns-wood n.w | c 5 | ja 9 | 80.

The Priory, | 21. North Bank, | Regents Park.

January 9. 80.

My dear Mr. Myers

I do rejoice in this new blossoming of joy for you,[4] and I thank you for telling me of it. What I like best is to hear of some gladness in this difficult world.

You will both come and see me, will you not?—and with this steady light of a thoroughly sanctioned affection you will do better and better things of the same sort as those you have already done so well.

With the wishes of sincerest friendship

Always yours truly
M. E. Lewes.

4. Myers's engagement. He married 13 March 1880 Eveleen, youngest daughter of Charles Tennant of Cadoxton Lodge, Neath. Before her marriage she had posed for Millais, and her portrait was hung in the Royal Academy. "On seeing it Mr. Myers, founder of the Society for Psychical Research, turned to George Eliot, saying: 'I have fallen in love with the girl in that picture.' In a few days Mr. Myers had found and married her." (*N. Y. Times,* obituary of Mrs. Myers, 14 March 1937.) There is no evidence that Myers was ever at the Academy with GE. Millais's portrait was painted in 1874 and exhibited in 1875.

VII, 246:13 EDITH SIMCOX, AUTOBIOGRAPHY, 21–24 JANUARY 1880

MS: Bodleian.

Wednesday 21 January 1880

21. I did go on the Friday (16th) with the pretext that Mme Bodichon would like to have the latest news of her. Somehow I was stupid and bothered her, I think with long silences; and then made things worse by raising the to her painful question—would she reprint any of his Articles? She was able to a certain extent to discuss the question freely—that his early papers had an historical interest from the precocious justness of his appreciations, but still they were so different from his later writings, the best of him was in these—anyway she could do nothing now; she had no word or hint from him to guide her, and then in a tone of distress, she must judge for herself. I must not speak to her again about it. She said too that I was speaking for myself only, not thinking of the general public, and it was hard for me to explain that it was just for the more careless readers who will not approach his Problems that I thought miscellanies might form an attractive introduction. Her strongest feeling was, I think, dislike for a publication that she did not herself desire and which was only likely, in her apprehension, to elicit "something nasty in the Athenaeum." I was painfully affected by an impression of half-formed gestures, deprecating a near approach, and yet how can I have anything but sympathy for much stronger repulsion or irritability than she ever allows herself to feel or show?

Saturday 24 January 1880

24. I did write and shall call the end of next week. The foolish feeling will have worn off by then, and with it the longing to bother her with foolish talk. My poor darling! it is strange that since she said that I have often had to check myself on the verge of the forbidden address—I hardly knew how natural and dear the name had become. I liked to hear and speak of her at Scalands. "Barbara" sympathised with what I said of the delight of not having to make allowances for her; said Charles had been good to her but he couldn't understand; agreed with my half-spoken regret that no one could be any comfort to her—she asked if Mrs. Congreve was or Johnny Cross. Tennyson, and Johnny and some one else came to the Heights while she was there.[5] She herself spoke of a neighbour having

5. While Mme Bodichon stayed with GE at Witley, Tennyson and his son Hallam called 26 September 1879; Cross dined with them 30 September. (GE Diary.)

introduced Kate Greenaway. It is only by thinking of her lot that I compel myself not to say—I cannot bear the distance—. Mme Bodichon told me how she said to "Marian" in the earlier days "I do not like Mr. Lewes" and was answered "You do not know him": but, she went on to me, he was not then as we knew him later, her influence, all agree, improved his character, though she must have seen in advance all that was to be—and was her justification. . . . The only thing that makes me doubt if it would have been good for me to know her sooner is the doubt whether she would still have given the same advice—for it is barely conceivable that had I loved her at 20 and been referred by her to other possibilities of love it is barely conceivable that I might have accomplished an unhappy marriage. She would ask, why not a happy one, to which the answer is that it is not given to me to inspire the true ideal passion in anyone for whom I can feel it.

VII, 246:25   GE TO SYDNEY M. SAMUEL, LONDON, 1 FEBRUARY 1880

MS: Mr. Christopher Beauman.

The Priory, | 21. North Bank, | Regents Park.

February 1. 80.

Dear Sir

As our talk yesterday wandered considerably from the object of your visit I fear that you may not have carried away a clear impression of what I intended to say. To prevent any misunderstanding which may lead to disappointment on your part it will perhaps be well for me to write my conclusions more definitely than I may have been able to express them in conversation.

With all obligation to you for your deference to my wishes, I must repeat that I can have nothing whatever to do with the adaptation of my work[6] to the stage, and I must decline to have my name connected with such adaptation.

It is unnecessary for me to enter into my reasons which are too many

6. Sydney M. Samuel wrote to William Hunter Kendal (1843–1917), who (with John Hare) was managing the St. James's Theatre, offering his version of *Daniel Deronda*. Kendal replied 20 February 1880 that, though he had never read the novel, he would "be delighted to read your dramatic version of 'Daniel Deronda' when done." (MS: Beauman.)

and various to be overcome. I am only anxious to save you from any waste of time and energy which might be due to my want of explicitness. Believe me dear Sir,

Yours faithfully
M. E. Lewes.

Mrs. John Walter Cross

VII, 246:25 EDITH SIMCOX, AUTOBIOGRAPHY,
1 FEBRUARY 1880

MS: Bodleian.

Sunday 1 February 1880

February 1. I had meant to call last Friday, but by ill luck forgot a school engagement that had determined me and went instead on Thursday. Young Johnny and Eleanor Cross were there when I arrived and out-stayed me. I listened while the latter talked Music, and looked at her,[7] she was well and beautiful. She had been to the Old Masters and the Grosvenor[8] (with whom?)—she said "we"—I don't know why I should have been surprised. I had thought she would never go to the Saturday concerts again, perhaps she will. I suppose I should have been pleased enough if she had proposed to go to the Grosvenor with me—but it was probably the Burne Jones, as she spoke of his reluctance to sell his drawings. They being there I could not ask about the girl. I think perhaps what wearies her least is the ardour of a single-minded youth—with which she has some natural sympathy and at all events can feel a dramatic interest. I was fool enough to come away in tears again, shall I never reach the end of this disappointed covetousness? It is here I can always silence the craving of my own soul by thinking of her solitude but she has a spring of vitality within which makes her winter less barren than my prime. She told little Marks[9] that she was doing conic sections every morning because "she didn't want to lose the power of learning" . . . It is something known, lived through and unalterable that my life has flung itself at her feet—and not been picked up—only told to rise and make itself a serviceable place elsewhere—So be it—so it is.

7. i.e. GE.
8. "To the Grosvenor Gallery with Mrs. Burne Jones." (GE Diary, 26 January 1880.) "Went to the Grosvenor Gallery again." (29 January), with Cross? The Old Masters exhibition was at the Royal Academy.
9. Phoebe Sarah Marks.

VII, 249:1 GE TO MARY A. EWART, LONDON, 7 FEBRUARY 1880

MS: Yale. *Endorsed:* "Miss North"—Pol and I went next Sunday to shew Mrs. Lewes some of the Indian paintings, and spent a delightful hour and a half. Mary A. Ewart.

The Priory | 21 North Bank | February 7. 80.

Dear Miss Ewart[1]

Madame Bodichon assures me that you would like to come and see me with your friend Miss North,[2] and that Miss North herself would have some kind pleasure in showing me her admirable drawings.

If Madame Bodichon's benevolent imagination has not misled her, pray carry out this pleasant plan. I am at home every day after 4.30, but the light would then hardly suffice for seeing drawings. I have ceased to make Sunday a special day of reception, but I am then always at home between 2 o'clock and 7. If Sunday is not a convenient day for you and Miss North, I will arrange to be at home on any other day that you are able to fix for so generous a purpose, at an hour when we may expect light.

Of course it may have happened that you and Miss North have hindrances unknown to our friend Mde Bodichon, and I am quite prepared to hear that the visit must be postponed.

Believe me, dear Miss Ewart,

Yours very sincerely

M. E. Lewes.

VII, 250:7 GE TO GEORGE SMITH, LONDON, 11 FEBRUARY 1880

MS: National Library of Scotland.

21 North Bank | February 11. 80.

My dear Sir

Pray excuse a superstitious distrust of the Post Office arising from the fact that some time ago a letter of mine was lost in transmission.

I was unable to send an answer to your kind letter by your messenger, and now an uneasiness has taken hold of me lest the answer which I posted a few hours after may have missed delivery.

1. See VI, 70, n. 8.   2. See VII, 248, n. 1.

It is a hard test of human charity to ask for an unnecessary letter, but I dislike so much the possibility of having seemed indifferent to your delicate consideration of my wishes that I venture on that test, while feeling a little ashamed of myself for doing so. Two lines to say that my answer reached you will set my nervous fidgets at rest.[3]

Yours very truly
M. E. Lewes.

VII, 253:23   EDITH SIMCOX, AUTOBIOGRAPHY, 17 FEBRUARY 1880

MS: Bodleian.

Tuesday 17 February 1880

17th. Last Saturday I went rather too early, but was told she was in; had a headache and the day was too damp for her to drive. Johnny was there—and she said to me, how did I guess she would be in. I said I had expected her to be out, but called just to know how she was because I foreboded being unable to call all the next week. I did not stay long, or outstay Johnny, but ventured to kiss her cheek in farewell and wrote on Sunday before speaking to a very few Radicals about "Common Ground."

VII, 253:23   LORD LYTTON TO GE, CALCUTTA, 22 FEBRUARY 1880

MS: Lady Hermione Cobbold. It was sent to Lady Lytton by Mrs. C.L. Lewes, 30 September 1892.

Calcutta | 22 February 1880.

My very dear Friend

It is a failure, not of affection, but of courage, that has witheld me from writing to you sooner. We grow familiar with our dearest friends by light approaches, and a careless interchange of life's commonest trifles. And then suddenly—without warning—the grave opens between us and them. We see them caught within an awful circle—the dear familiar presences have grown supernatural. Yearn as we may toward them, what

---

3. "Mr. George Smith called—about Romola." (GE Diary, 13 February 1880.)

can we do? I have hushed and hidden myself till now. I know that this is not always best. When I lost my dear father, I felt so stunned that it was not sympathy but distraction that I craved, and even a tradesman's letter was a relief. But I *dared* not write to you, dared not speak of what I felt; still less, of what I knew you were feeling. Turn which way I will the shadow of your sorrow still lies darkly on me. I measure it by my knowledge of the magnitude of your own great nature, and his worth, who was the last of the few friends wiser than myself, to whom from boyhood I have looked up. I shall honour his memory, and mourn his loss, and love and thank him as long as I live. But I cannot offer consolations I have never found, and do not feel. Your strength, your wisdom, and insight are immeasurably greater than mine. I am comforted by the consciousness that fine souls like yours know how to turn great griefs to best account. But I cannot comfort *you*. If there be any personal compensation for the death of those we love—and need—it is unknown to me. The only mitigating consequence of such bereavements that I have ever experienced is one which you yourself once predicted to me, and which I therefore know you will not miss. Certainly, since my dear father died I have been in closer and more constant intercourse with him, and have seemed to understand him better than when he was alive. But even this comes slowly. And Oh, the difference! All intercourse with the dead is so shadowy, so indistinct—so like twilight—after daylight.

I have for months been longing to write to you, but lacked the encouragement now taken from two recent stimulants. First a line I had a few weeks ago from Mrs. Richard Strachey, telling me she had seen and talked with you. I cannot bear that I, who feel bound to you by that long chain of memories which links my childhood with your widowhood, should be the only one of your friends whose intercourse with you still awaits renewal. And next, the perusal of Theophrastus Such. There is so much that I wished to say to you about that book—and would have said had I ventured to write sooner—but cannot well say now. Partly because I have left the book behind me—at Simla—and cannot refer to the particular parts and passages which have most impressed or delighted me— partly too because, since I began this letter I have been interrupted twenty times, and I fear that if I do not finish it quickly I may never finish it at all.

Theophrastus is a great book, eminently wise. I wonder how many of the exquisite subtleties have by this time penetrated the coarse cuticle of that snorting Behemoth the British public. To me it is a tantalising book only from what is perhaps one of its chief merits—as a work of art. It opens and indicates so many avenues of reflection which one would wish to penetrate further in the company of and under the guidance of its Author. The chapter I most value is on the debasement of the moral currency. I would have it, if I could, written in letters of gold—or better, fire—over Downing Street, Westminster Hall, all the newspaper offices— and every provincial hustings. The chapter of which I most enjoy the humour is on How we treat original research.

But I must bring this letter to an end. My Edith sends you her lovingest love. We have, as a lesser evil than sending them to England left our children at Simla, where they are snowed up, and we are impatient to rejoin them. But I must bring out our budget before I can close the Calcutta Session. It will be an astonishingly satisfactory budget—and for that reason I suppose the Liberals will denounce it as "another of Lord Lytton's lies."

I know not what more I can tell you of myself that is in any wise worth telling. My life now is one of unceasing activity nor could my chronicling keep pace with the movements of it, even were I your 'special correspondent.' But when I look into myself I know not what has become of my ego—my individuality—if it ever existed. I seem to find in that self, when inspected, an incongruous assemblage of different beings—one who thinks, another who feels, a third who acts, a fourth who eats and drinks etc. Many who are now put upon the shelf and are at present out of employment,—like other discharged functionaries pertinaciously craving compensations and personal allowances which cannot be given them. Some who have quite lately come into the Science of my Existence, and are still quite raw to their work. In the midst of all these, an idle nondescript sort of Gentleman, who pretends to be at home, and calls himself 'I.' His function, or raison d'etre, I am unable to discover. He seems to be a rather tired, and quite useless spectator of all the others and their doings. He yawns more and more and snores frequently. Latterly I find him constantly pulling out his watch, and glancing at the door, like a gentleman who is waiting for the carriage he has ordered round to take him . . . Where? Has he anywhere a home? I wish I knew the address . . . or even 'What the devil he is doing here.'[4]

Adieu Dear and great friend

Your affectionate
Lytton.

As I am not sure of your present address I send this to the care of Mrs. Strachey.

4. Cf. Pope, *Epistle to Dr. Arbuthnot*, line 172.

VII, 253:23   GE TO MRS. EDWIN LANKESTER,
LONDON, 28 FEBRUARY 1880

MS: Princeton.

The Priory, | 21. North Bank, | Regents Park.

February 28. 80.

Dear Mrs. Lankester

I am at home on all days at 5 o'clock and shall be glad to see you.
Believe me

Yours very truly

M. E. Lewes.

VII, 254:23   EDITH SIMCOX, AUTOBIOGRAPHY,
9 MARCH 1880

MS: Bodleian. *Extract published:* McKenzie, p. 97; Haight, *George Eliot,* pp. 535–
536.

Tuesday 9 March 1880

March 9. . . . I got there a little before 5; she had just come in from her
drive and came down after a few minutes. She was looking well and I
began to talk about the Bretts' children[5]—her recollection of them was
as "fit to eat." Then Mrs. Lankester[6] and a daughter were announced.
The former was appallingly voluble and I felt for my darling, and indeed
did her some service later, when she turned to me, *apropos* of a mention
of Miss Bevington—the latter was said to take a melancholy view of life
and Mrs. Lewes referred to me as despising all prospective consolations
as "a gambling speculation." It was questioned whether Miss Bevington
would be consoled by marriage or if it was too late. Mrs. Lankester was
comparatively reserved while the conversation wandered among abstract
themes—they stayed a good while, then the daughter moved slightly
and I rose to encourage them, but the darling said graciously to me to
wait a little longer.

5. Not GE's housemaid, but John
Brett (1831–1902), landscape painter
and astronomer. He exhibited *Cornish
Lions* (1878) and *Britannia's Realm*
(1880), painted with minute scientific
detail. He was introduced to GHL at
the Physiological Society dinner, 26
May 1876, and called at the Priory
with his two children 28 May. GE and
GHL went to his studio to see his
paintings 1 April 1878. (GHL Diary.)
6. Mrs. Edwin Lankester had eight
children, the eldest son Edwin Ray
Lankester, later Director of the Natural
History Musem, South Kensington.

I said presently it was hard at the end of 7 years to feel I had not yet explained what I meant by the "gambling speculation." I recurred to what I had meant by the "danger" of referring young people to the satisfaction of emotional affections—I said all ones normal appetites were sane and lawful in themselves, but just as she insists on the danger of seeking for pleasantness in the outer life—I hold it to be a danger to seek first for pleasantness in the inner life. She said one could not empty oneself of all desires and impulses. I said, was it not better to attack the objective sources of evil, rather than await in patience their possible diversion or drying up. At last she was content to leave it as a matter of temperament— that some may be more cheered by words of fortitude than hope.

She moved to a low chair opposite the fire to warm her feet and I ventured to kneel by her side. She was a little tired by the discussion and said I had taken it up too seriously, she only spoke in play. I said it was ungrateful to complain of one thing she had said when all the rest had been full of consolation. She answered, Nay, she had given up all thought of consoling me. I kissed her again and again and murmured broken words of love. She bade me not exaggerate. I said I didn't—nor could, and then scolded her for not being satisfied with letting me love her as I did—as in present reality—and proposing instead that I should save my love for some imaginary he. She said—expressly what she has often before implied to my distress—that the love of men and women for each other must always be more and better than any other and bade me not wish to be wiser than "God who made me"—in pious phrase. I hung over her caressingly and she bade me not think too much of her;—she knew all her own frailty and if I went on, she would have to confess some of it to me. Then she said—Perhaps it would shock me—she had never all her life cared very much for women—it must seem monstrous to me. I said I had always known it. She went on to say, what I also knew, that she cared for the womanly ideal, sympathised with women and liked for them to come to her in their troubles, but while feeling near to them in one way, she felt far off in another; the friendship and intimacy of men was more to her. Then she tried to add what I had already imagined in explanation, that when she was young, girls and women seemed to look on her as somehow "uncanny" while men were always kind. I kissed her again, and said I did not mind—if she did not mind having holes kissed in her cheek. She said I gave her a very beautiful affection.—and then again she called me a silly child, and I asked if she would never say anything kind to me. I asked her to kiss me. Let a trembling lover tell of the intense consciousness of the first deliberate touch of the dear one's lips. I returned the kiss to the lips that gave it and started to go—she waved me a farewell.

VII, 255:1   GE TO ROBERT RIPLEY,
LONDON, [15 MARCH 1880]

Text: Maggs Bros. Catalogue, 322 (March–April 1914), item 962.

Regents Park.

The money is already yours in prospect and shall be so in reality, if you will send me word to that effect.[7]

M. E. Lewes.

VII, 255:1   GE TO MISS BENEKE,
LONDON, 19 MARCH 1880

MS: Yale.

The Priory, | 21. North Bank, | Regents Park.

March 19. 80.

Dear Miss Beneke[8]

So far as I am able to judge in a case quite away from my observation, I should say that you would do well—no duties opposing—to have a course of Mathematics.

Allow me, as an elder person, to caution you against taking life too eagerly and looking at all things as means, instead of regarding each good, pure, beautiful exercise of faculty as a sufficient end.

I am just now much oppressed with difficulties and trials in my own inward life, and much claimed by others. This will be an explanation to you of my brevity in answering your confidential letter. Believe me, with sincere wishes for your welfare

Yours very truly
M. E. Lewes.

7. Under "Old and New Engagements to pay" GE's Diary for 1880 lists "Ripley £20," and in the Cash Account for January, "Ripley £10."

8. GE notes in her Diary, 19 March, "Long letter from Miss Beneke." I cannot identify her.

VII, 255:1   GE TO JAMES SULLY, LONDON, 20 MARCH 1880

MS: University College, London. *Envelope:* James Sully Esq | Holyrood House | Windmill Hill | Hampstead | N.W. *Postmark:* ST JOHNS-WOOD N.W | C X | MR 20 | 80. *Endorsed:* Again thanks.

The Priory, | 21. North Bank, | Regents Park.
March 20. 80.

Dear Mr. Sully

I am greatly obliged to you for sending me your notes of errata.

When your article appears in the Academy,[9] will you kindly send me a copy?—as I do not ordinarily see that paper.

Always yours most truly

M. E. Lewes.

VII, 255:1   GE TO MRS. RICHARD STRACHEY, LONDON, 21 MARCH 1880

MS: British Museum. *Envelope:* Mrs. Strachey | Stowey House | Clapham Common | S.W. *Postmarks:* LONDON | C 6 | MR 23 | 80; LONDON S-W. | KB | MR 22 | 80. *Published:* TLS, 16 May 1968, p. 507.

The Priory, | 21. North Bank, | Regents Park.
March 21. 80.

Dear Mrs. Strachey

Thank you for sending me on Lord Lytton's letter. I had been glad to hear from Lady Colvile the other day that "the Monotony" '(to be continued in our next)' had been safely produced[10] and that you were going on well.

It will be a welcome proof that you are able to go about, when you can manage to get as far as my corner.

Always yours affectionately

M. E. Lewes.

9. See VII. 265.

10. Lytton Strachey (1 March 1880–1932), the 8th of Mrs. Strachey's 10 children. GE heard of his birth from her sister Lady Colvile at the Priory Sunday, 19 March. (GE Diary.)

VII, 256:1   EDITH SIMCOX, AUTOBIOGRAPHY,
26 MARCH 1880

MS: Bodleian. *Extract published:* McKenzie, p. 107.

Friday 26 March 1880

26. I went yesterday and had 5 minutes alone with her, enough to hear she had not been well, was tired, and thought "she had done her duty" and might leave town the end of April or beginning of May. Then the bell rang, and before the new visitors were announced I kissed her and left. She said I should go to the Channel Islands—I was looking pale and overdone.

VII, 258:1   GE TO ALICE HELPS,
LONDON, 28 MARCH 1880

MS: Yale.

The Priory, | 21. North Bank, | Regents Park.
March 28. 80.

Dearest Alice

I shall be away tomorrow.[11] Any day after Wednesday, come without notice.

Thine affectionately
M. E. L.

VII, 258:1   EDITH SIMCOX TO GE,[1]
LONDON, [28 MARCH 1880]

MS: Bodleian. *Published:* McKenzie, pp. 107–109.

1 Douro Place, | Victoria Road W. | Sunday.
My own Darling,

There are no frosts in particular at Sark and as I am going there especially to be out of temptation to torment you, I want, as a reward, leave for one more last caress. For, my own, you *have* 'done your duty' to us, and as I can't forget how hard that is I can't help loving you more

---

11. At Weybridge, with the Crosses. She came Friday, 2 April. (GE Diary.)

1. Of the scores of letters between them, this is the only one of Edith's known to have survived. It was probably never sent. Professor McKenzie comments: "Perhaps it is as well that no more of this rather wordy sentimentality has been preserved." (p. 109.)

and more dearly for the sake of the sweet patience that bears and does what is so hard. And therefore, darling, I do want you to leave us before you are quite outworn, and I ought to be able to let you go without moaning, that it is like dying once a year, and that each year it is harder than the last.

It seems horrible that I should be better off than you, and yet while you are here, I cannot help being happy for every moment in your presence. A word you let fall on Thursday makes me want to say one thing—you said some people wrote to you more freely from thinking you were alone. Darling, just because my love for you is the one great joy and blessing of my life, I should like you to know that if you had been alone seven years ago, I should not have ventured to let the love I felt have all its way. I tried to love you like this and to tell you so because he liked for you to be told, and all one's love couldn't be more than he thought due, than he liked to have poured out at your feet. He delighted in sharing the blessedness of loving you and but for the sweet memory of his generous welcome I could not bear to be glad in feeling your dearness now. All my little bits of good fortune seemed to come through him, and the thought of him is never more vividly present than when I am happiest in your love. If it were not so it would seem a disloyalty—as it is I often half hate myself because your happiness is dead and mine because of yours must live while you do.

One more little confession: it does not hurt me in the least not to say it, but 'Sweet Mother' has come a hundred times to the tip of my pen since it was told not. Do you see darling that I can only love you three lawful ways, idolatrously as Faber the Virgin Mary,[2] in romance wise as Petrarch, Laura, or with a child's fondness for the mother one leans on notwithstanding the irreverence of one's longing to pet and take care of her. Sober friendship seems to make the ugliest claim to a kind of equality: friendship is a precious thing indeed but between friends I think if there is love at all it must be equal, and whichever way we take it, our relation is between unequals.—It is a quite impractical trifle but I am impelled to say this because any change in one's speech seems to imply a change of feeling and there has been none in my feeling for you except a growing desire not to make any burdensome claim, not even to weary you with the boundless, grateful love that must still and always be yours—as I am.

Edith

7 kisses are launched upon the foggy air. Goodbye darling.

2. Frederick William Faber (1814–63), one of John Henry Newman's followers at Oxford, became a Roman Catholic in 1845 and head of the London Oratory in 1849. Among his many books was *The Foot of the Cross; or the Sorrows of Mary*, 1858.

VII, 258:1   EDITH SIMCOX, AUTOBIOGRAPHY, 28 MARCH 1880

MS: Bodleian. *Extract published:* McKenzie, pp. 61–62.

Sunday 28 March 1880

28. This is my real Easter holiday. . . . Yesterday I read through my private journal from May 74 to the fatal March—I don't admire myself on the retrospect and I can understand the "exasperating" effect on her mind of my alternations from the tone of rapturous delighted adoration and devotion to still unsatisfied questioning. . . .

I have thought, the last few days, of writing a little book of "Vignettes";[3] I shall sound the boys and Annie[4] at Sark, as, if it were written, I should not like my own people to guess quite how much autobiography there might be in it, and also I could imagine the boys each contributing a scene or two that would increase one's dramatic range. On the other hand, it would be nothing if not finished into very classical perfection and it is hard to be sure. As to ulterior motives, I should be glad of a chance of delivering myself aloud as to divers conclusions upon life and morals, and I want before giving up the ghost of ambition to have one—or two—more shots at my neighbours' ears. It is still a question whether one is to write for money or antiquity.

VII, 265:19   GE TO LADY HOLLAND, LONDON, 26 APRIL 1880

MS: Fales Collection, New York University.

The Priory, | 21. North Bank, | Regents Park.

April 26. 80.

My dear Lady Holland

I felt that I was unfortunate when I found that it was you and Sir Henry whom I had missed seeing on Saturday.

3. Autobiographical sketches, by fictional authors, eleven of which were published as *Episodes in the Lives of Men, Women, and Lovers*, 1882. Five of them appeared in *Fraser's* in 1881: "Consolations," 23 (June), 771–782; "A Diptych," 24 (July), 42–56; "Midsummer Noon," (August), 204–211; "Love and Friendship," (October), 448–461; and "At Anchor," (November), 624–

629. See McKenzie, pp. 62–75, for an excellent analysis of the "Vignettes."
    4. Edith's brothers George Augustus Simcox (1841–1905), who lived with her in Douro Place, and William Henry Simcox (1843–89), who married in 1876 Annie Ludlum, and was Vicar of Harlaxton, Lincolnshire. They were on holiday together on Sark.

I was just getting ready to go to Weybridge, and the servant took it for granted that I could not see any one, but if I had known who was at the door I should have begged you to let me see you only for five minutes. It is rather hard that one should see many whom one does not care about seeing and should twice miss those who would be most welcome.

As our visiting is not of the formal sort I do not add one more to the multitude of formalities you are obliged to attend to, by calling at Rutland Gate[5] when you are sure to be preoccupied.

I have a wretched cold in the head which almost blinds me, after winning through the terrible winter without any such effect. I like to think you and Sir Henry gave me a proof that you are both well.

Yours most sincerely
M. E. Lewes.

VII, 267:10   EDITH SIMCOX, AUTOBIOGRAPHY, 2 MAY 1880

MS: Bodleian. *Published:* McKenzie, p. 98.

Sunday 2 May 1880

May 2. Last Monday I left the Works Committee early and got to the Priory a quarter or half past five. Asked how she was and Brett said she had a very bad cold, would ask if she was well enough to see me. She was lying down and rather miserable with violent influenza cold. I had only been with her 2 or 3 minutes when Mr. Pigott was announced—she said, to ask him to wait 5 minutes in the dining room, she had not seen me for so long, but he was such an old friend she did not like to refuse him though she wasn't fit to see any one. Before this she had taken away my breath when I spoke of her leaving London by saying she was going abroad for 2 or 3 months—she would write to me about her plans—she was not going to Witley before. I was rather stunned—glad in a way, as of every sign that she has not done with life and only hurt in an unavoidable way by the feeling how far away all the determining conditions of her life are from me, and a rapid thought that it was an irksome task to her to feel bound to give so much account of her doings, because my love was covetous. I wrote a few lines that night to excuse my silence at the news.

5. GE's Address Book lists Lady Holland, 65 Rutland Gate S.W. and Pinewood, Witley, Surrey. (Yale.)

VII, 271:18   EMILY SUSANNAH CLARKE TO GE, LEIPZIG, 6 MAY 1880

MS: Yale.

Frau Krieg, | Turnerstrasse 12. III | Leipzig | May 6. 80.

Dear Aunt Polly

Your letter was a welcome surprize. I am sure you would marry no one who is not worthy of you and one so thoughtful for others as you are is worthy of the best. Could you only have all the happiness I wish you! It is a great comfort to know that you are no longer leading a lonely life, but have someone who will love and care for you.

Will you give a kindly greeting to my new Uncle from me, and when you have a few spare minutes I should like to know a little more about him, and where you intend to live.

Thank you for thinking of me at such a busy time. I shall be only too pleased to stay here and I feel sure Uncle Isaac will be glad for me to have another six months rest. The £25 in August—and the other £25 later on will be all that is necessary so far as I can calculate.

And for the rest of your letter[6] there is so much for which I ought to thank you—the words I use sound so cold but I think dear Aunt Polly you will understand what I would wish to say.

With loving wishes for a peaceful happy life Believe me ever

Your affectionate and grateful niece

Emily S. Clarke.

VII, 271:18   ELEANOR CROSS TO E. F. S. PIGOTT, WEYBRIDGE, 6 MAY [1880]

MS: Yale.

Weybridge Heath, | Surrey.

May 6th.

Dear Mr. Pigott

I cannot let the day pass without writing a line to give you John's message which is that he would have called to tell you himself of his marriage to Mrs. Lewes had he not been immersed in business up to the last

---

6. GE's Diary under "Old and New Engagements to pay" lists £25 for Emily, and in the Cash account £25 in February and August 1880. GE left her £5,000 in her will.

moment. I do not know if you have known of his long devotion to and adoration of our dear friend, but if you have you will sympathise with our happiness and will I hope feel with us that it is the best thing for them both. Feeling sure of your good wishes and with affectionate remembrances from all Believe me

> Very sincerely yours
> Eleanor Cross.

VII, 272:27   E. F. S. PIGOTT TO JOHN W. CROSS, LONDON, 7 MAY 1880

MS: Yale.

126 Oxford Street W | May 7. 1880.

My dear John Cross

When I found your card on my table the other evening, I had, as you may suppose, not the faintest idea of the news you had come to tell me! Imagine how the paragraph in this morning's D[aily] N[ews] startled me! It was a shock of surprise, but of very delightful surprise, such as one feels on the very rare occasions in this burdened world, when a great man's love has found its happy haven in a noble woman's heart. Surely it is all that her truest friends, and all that yours, could have desired for both! It will crown her life with peace and contentment, inspire her genius afresh, comfort and sustain her future, without doing violence to the tender memories of the past, and consecrate your own beautiful example of devotedness and fidelity of affection.

Heartiest congratulations, then, my dear fellow, and all best wishes for many years of happy and perfect union, for you both! You will always believe me your affectionate friend

> Edward F. S. Pigott.

VII, 272:27   THOMAS V. HOLBECHE TO ISAAC EVANS, SUTTON COLDFIELD, 7 MAY 1880

MS: British Museum.

Sutton Coldfield | Holbeche & Addenbrooke | Solicitors.
7th May 1880.

Dear Mr. Evans

We have this morning received from Messrs Duncan Warren & Gardner, Solicitors, 45 Bloomsbury Square, London, [a letter] stating that they have been requested by Mrs. Mary Ann Evans Lewes to inform us that she was yesterday married to Mr. John Walter Cross of 38 Cornhill. With kindest regards to all at Griff, and hoping that Mrs. Evans is better,

Yours sincerely

Thomas V. Holbeche.

I. P. Evans Esqre

VII, 272:27   EDITH SIMCOX, AUTOBIOGRAPHY, 7 MAY 1880

MS: Bodleian. *Published:* McKenzie, p. 99.

Friday 7 May 1880

7. Yesterday morning She was married to Johnny Cross and they went abroad. Charles Lewes came immediately after to tell me, and made an appointment for this morning. He tried to "break it to me" and then to explain and reason. I said I was not surprised. I could hardly say anywhere but here that the conception had in some dim form or other crossed my mind. I need not explain to myself how it was. Of course she suffered much —Charles said she had twice broken it off as impossible—had thought of all the difficulties—the effect upon her influence and all the rest: then she had consulted Sir James Paget, as a friend, her physician and impartial. He said there was no reason why she should not. Charles thought it would be well for the world, as she might write again now. He had told Mrs. Peter Taylor and dreaded telling Mrs. Congreve—Harrison and Beesly had been told. Mr. Hall was to delay the announcement in the Times till Monday. She herself had not been able even to tell Charles, she had made Mr. Cross do so.

VII, 275:28   LORD HOUGHTON TO GE, LONDON, 10 MAY [1880]

MS: University of Virginia.

7 Clifford Str. | May 10th.

My dear Madam

I have some hesitation in writing to you, but the balance of my thoughts is in favour of my doing so. Our personal intercourse would hardly authorise me, but associated as it is with the moral sympathy existing between yourself and so many minds, it offers a plausible excuse. I have condoled with you so sincerely that I can congratulate you, in the deep consciousness of the wonderful weft of pain and pleasure that makes up our emotional existence, and in the assurance that whatever of happiness you have taken up is just as duteous and honest as your sorrow. I have met Mr. Cross at your house and hope to know more of him; from those who do, I hear of nothing but good. My daughters desire their remembrances and hope to call on you soon.

Believe me yours very sincerely

Houghton.

VII, 280:13 HENRY JAMES TO JOHN W. CROSS, FLORENCE, 14 MAY 1880

MS: Mr. Richard L. Purdy.

Florence, May 14th 1880.

My dear Cross.

I have just heard of your marriage, and I must give myself the satisfaction of sending you a word of very friendly sympathy on the occasion —which I beg you to communicate, in the most deferential form, to your illustrious wife. Receive my heartiest congratulations and good wishes, and try and fancy that they have hovering about them the perfume and promise of a Florentine May-time. I have congratulated friends before on their approaching, or accomplished, nuptials; but I have never had the privilege of doing so in a case in which I felt (as to-day) all the cordiality of mankind mingling with my individual voice. Don't let this mighty murmur drown my feeble note, by the way; but remember that I am what the newspapers call a "distinct factor" in any sense of the good-will of your fellow-mortals that you may now enjoy. Don't on the other hand dream of answering this hasty note—you have probably so many letters to write. I am on the point of returning to England and I shall see you then. I wish I could fold into this sheet a glimpse of the yellow Arno, the blue-grey hills, the old brown city, which your wife knows so well and which she has helped to make me know.—But I will only attempt to insert again, a friendly handshake from yours very faithfully,

Henry James Jr.

VII, 284:27   EDITH SIMCOX, AUTOBIOGRAPHY, 23 MAY 1880

MS: Bodleian.

Sunday 23 May 1880

23. Have been scribbling off and on at "Vignettes." Hardly know whether they will come to anything. Am positive not to publish unless they are likely to be really good. Have not been unhappy about her, only just a little uneasy as to whether I may have said a thought too much in answer to her unspoken doubt about our feeling—mine with that of others. It was honest not to ignore the existence of the question, but was it possible to answer it in a way that should save the fact of its having been asked from causing any pain? I love her just as before: involuntary kisses form themselves and it is an unmixed pleasure to me to think of her as having life made easier again. But this has come of the repeated checks on such close dependence as my soul desired,—the help I might not have has been done without, and the impulse to seek it is almost extinct. I feel now as if it would not be too costly a risk to ask her, if the need arose, whether it would be for her happiness to let our intercourse drop into casual and rarer shape.

VII, 291:32   JOHN W. CROSS TO MARY F. CROSS, VERONA, 1 JUNE 1880

MS: Yale.

Verona 1 June 1880.

My Dearest Marly

I do believe you are the only one of my sweet sisters to whom I have not written since I entered into the holy state of matrimony and as I know the pleasure my autograph will be to you—le voici! This is *the* most delicious town you can conceive—molto molto pittoresquo e sympatico— a very proper place for Romeo and Juliet. The Capulets palace is within a few doors of this hotel and one can see the balcony cette chère creature leaned out of. Also the stairs of Cangrande's palace where poor Dante found how salt was the bread of another as you will no doubt remember in your Purgatorio[7]—I would give you the exact reference if Murray were handy! but it isn't. Also there is a Duomo with a wondrous portico and

7. *Paradiso*, xvii, 58.

bronze gates of the 9th Century and a Church of Sta Anastasia with a notable roof and a charming picture by Andrea Mantegna and a sweet thing in the way of a porch which has been the joy of many architectural minds. My knowledge of early art is becoming surprising to myself! Imbued with the spirit of Cimabue and Giotto I come to my Mantegna and find him adequate and can understand the force he has been in the development of art—a fact which will no doubt be well known to you my dear sister— and if not let me refer you to Kugler[8]—a worthy man though dry.

The best things here to my mind are the Piazzi de Erbe (the market place) and dei Signori (where Cangrande's palace is) and the Roman remains Amphitheatre etc. Yesterday we took a charming drive to a hill behind the town where we saw the whole Lombard plain stretched out at our feet with the Euganean Hills between us and Padua and on the other side Mantua, Solferino, Villafranca—all names well known in ancient or in modern story. The view was as our Italian coachman—an excellent fellow—remarked "stupendo"—this beautiful city with its purple roofs and graceful Campanile nestling itself in a great bend of the swiftly flowing Adige, over which there are 5 very picturesque bridges and the sense that our dear Dante might have been there, and no doubt often was—musing on the hardness of his lot as an exile.

Murray says there are more balconies in Verona than in any other city in the world and I believe him: though as mia Donna aptly remarked she wondered if he had counted the balconies in the other Italian cities! But if ever one were to become blasé of balconies it would be here.[9] But that is not possible for balconies are a chief joy in life when you have a sun and thank God we have seen a good deal of that almost forgotten luminary since we have been out! In fact we have only had rain on 2 days: once at Lyons, and on Sunday when we left Milan it was pouring. It has never yet become quite unclouded since Sunday but though a little over- cast the temperature is very pleasant sitting with the windows open. Mia Donna continues in excellent form and surprises me by the amount of fatigue she can go through in seeing churches pictures etc. and she looks all the better of it. We have not talked to another soul since we left England and if I don't become very wise with Cotanta Amante, guide, philosopher, and friend—well I ought to!

8. Franz Theodor Kugler, *Handbuch der Kunstgeschichte*, 1841–42.
9. On 16 June Cross jumped from a balcony into the Grand Canal in Venice. See Haight, *George Eliot*, p. 544. Lord Acton's note must be based on personal inquiry: "At Venice she thought him mad, and she never recovered the dreadful depression that followed. Sent for Richetti, told him that Cross had a mad brother. Told her fears. Just then, heard that he had jumped into the Canal." (Cambridge University Library, MS 5019, item 1571.)

This afternoon we go on to Padua. I had half expected a letter here as I gave Nelly this address—but no doubt we will find letters at Venice where we will arrive on Thursday and will probably remain some 10 days as there are so many pictures to see. I don't know what people generally complain so much of in their wedding journeys—ours has certainly been very full of delight and it goes on increasing and I hope will go on jusqu'à la fin—she is a very inexhaustible storehouse.

We hope to hear at Venice that you have found the right house and I am also anxious to hear from Willy how things are going on at No. 4 Cheyne Walk. I very often feel as if the whole thing were a dream! It is so very curious when I think of her as Mrs. Cross! Do you remember how we heard of Billy Druce's birth at Venice? How much has happened since then and how long ago it seems. I will write Anna from Venice in memoriam of the great event. Give her and Albert my best love when you see them also Emmy and all the children of light. Write soon and tell us all about yourselves. Love to Will and Henry and Dottie

Thine
J. W. C.

VII, 291:32   EDITH SIMCOX, AUTOBIOGRAPHY, 29 MAY–5 JUNE 1880

MS: Bodleian.

Tuesday 29 May 1880

29. Yesterday came in—with my mind full of her—to find a dear letter from Milan. I had said nothing unwelcome, she was well and grateful—to me and others: there is something very touching in the way in which her lovingness disarms the pride that would resent external judgments.

Saturday 5 June 1880

5. . . . Am a little anxious about "Vignettes" lest I should anywhere let slip what might be too plain a confession to her, if she saw it: but I suppose there is little danger. The one I call "At Anchor" is pure reminiscence— of the Solent from the Needles the summer after "Natural Law" came out, but I don't think she will guess this.[1] Augustus thinks there is great

---

1. Reuben, the imaginary author of "At Anchor," an unsuccessful painter in love with "a pretty rich young woman of the gay world," has gone off to the Isle of Wight to meditate on her failure to recognize that "every line and every tint was born directly of her influence, was inspired by her gracious smile." It was not published till after GE's death.

"force and distinction" about the bits he has seen, but feels them to be queer and does not know what people will make of them. A fair criticism is that the intense and vivid feeling is all *apropos* of something off the general track. . . . Have been reading her early letters through on end and I seem to see daylight now. What seemed to me a hard inconsistency—perhaps I might tell her so some day—was that she began by telling me to let feeling have its way and trust myself to love. I did love her—who could help it? and then once again I struggled with my covetousness and tried to be reasonable, but there was a heartache left for me to struggle with, and it was more than I could bear that while I was trying to do without what I wanted most, she should be always ready to congratulate me on getting what I didn't want or to scold me for not wanting something else that I could get as little as what I wanted. I think this was the key to all that happened till her stern letter.[2] Then I was thrown back upon myself. I might neither live with her nor without her, so I held my life in suspense —it was a period of suicide. Then came her eloquent silence about the book—and I have never wished passionately for anything for myself since.

VII, 302:12   EDITH SIMCOX, AUTOBIOGRAPHY, 30 JUNE 1880

MS: Bodleian.

Wednesday 30 June 1880

30. I hear today at second hand that they have taken a house in Cheyne Walk. I hope it may be true. I had a horrible dread of having to welcome Johnny in the place where I had known Lewes. And yet I feel robbed—as if I had lost something irreplaceable—now I shall never see that room again—it is taken from me without so much as a moment's farewell. She wrote to Mrs. Burne Jones and to Blackwood the night before. The things that are said of her hurt me. They go back to the old story. I cannot believe that she built her happiness upon a separation,[3] that but for her need not have come. No doubt she lets her own feeling count for something, but I am sure the controlling motive was the thought for him. The only difference this has made in my feeling is to give me courage to blame myself less where she has been apt to blame me for not being like herself.

2. In March 1876. See McKenzie, p. 88.
3. The gossip of 1854 that GHL had "run away from his wife and family." See GE to John Chapman, [15 October 1854].

VII, 303:12   EDITH SIMCOX, AUTOBIOGRAPHY, 11–12 JULY 1880

MS: Bodleian.

Sunday 11 July 1880

11. Yesterday I was startled by the question "Is Mr. Cross any better?" and then a rumour that he was ill—or like to die—of typhoid fever at Venice.[4] It seemed too horrible to be true and yet I hardly dared to doubt it. It was bad enough at best to think of her alarm if he was ill at all. I tried to harden myself shiveringly, as I went up to Hampstead to seek news from Charley. He had gone to join his wife and children at Witley—I asked the servant if she knew how Mr. Cross was and she said getting better, when she heard them speak of it last—they were talking of coming back to England. This did not tell me what the worst had been and I tried again at the Priory where the woman in charge had heard nothing. It seemed the first report was exaggerated but I could not help feeling besides the anxiety for her a dull pain at the thought that her anxiety might have come and gone without my knowing. Shall I run down to Weybridge this afternoon and see if it was true his sisters had been telegraphed for—the servants there at least will know all about it.

Monday 12 July 1880

12. On the whole, after some hesitation I went. I took a 3rd class return from Clapham Junction and arrived just before 6. Eleanor and Florence were alone at home. Three weeks or more he had been taken ill, she telegraphed at once and Willy Cross went out; for a week he was ill—if not in danger, and then, very weak, they carried him by slow stages out of Venice. Munich did not suit him, but he was out of danger now, had written one letter himself, they were going to Wildbad and likely to be back as proposed the end of this month. I was very glad I went. Eleanor spoke a little about the marriage, hoped I was glad for her as well as him and said, as Charles Lewes had, that they had been very anxious before the marriage, he was so worn and ill. He had to continue all his business to the last because she would not let anyone be told and he shrank from the responsibility, if her friends were likely to take it as she thought they would, of coming between her and them. She had said to them—"Edith would disapprove." I was glad I went.

4. See Haight, *George Eliot*, pp. 544–545.

VII, 307:1   EDITH SIMCOX, AUTOBIOGRAPHY, 24–29 JULY 1880

MS: Bodleian.

Saturday 24 July 1880

24. I have been thinking lately of that day in March 73—three years before the fatal March. She said to me then, when I tried to tell her of the strange feeling of "conversion," "Why should one expect the truth to be consoling?" Why indeed?

Thursday 29 July 1880

29. A letter came last night and pleased me by some—*freilich* rather scant —concessions in reply to my letter sent to Venice. They think of staying at Witley till November. Since the 9th of March I have only seen her twice for a short 5 minutes—that makes full 8 months out of the 12 an utter, barren blank. Yet I am cheered by her letter—even while I smile at myself for being nourished by such slender consolations. She is very dear—I must not tell her how much she has herself done to kill the ambitions to which she now appeals. If I were to tell her I am less at my ease with her than any one else because no one else thinks so ill of me (with reason). Is there any one else she loves of whom her good opinion is in proportion to the reserve shown? Well, well,—it is over now; I have answered her letter and it is likely shall feel no impulse to write again.

VII, 308:25   GE TO MRS. RICHARD STRACHEY, WITLEY, 2 AUGUST 1880

MS: British Museum. *Envelope:* Mrs. Strachey | c | 2 au | 80. *Postmarks:* GODAL-MING | c | 2 au | 80; az | LONDON EC | au 2 | 80. *Published:* TLS, 16 May 1968, p. 507.

The Heights, Witley, | Nr. Godalming.
August 2. 80.

Dear Mrs. Strachey

Your letter, very sweet to me to read, written on the 14th of May, has lain awaiting me all the long time till last Wednesday when it was brought me from the Priory. Thank you, dear friend, for your cordial words.

We arrived here on the 26th, glad to be at home on all accounts except the weather, which is sadly in contrast with our three months of continental warmth and sunshine. In writing to you after so long an interval I half think you will be farther away from London than Stowey House, but some time this note will meet your eyes to assure you how much I like being remembered by you.

We shall probably not be in London till the beginning of November, but then I hope you will come and see me at 4 Cheyne Walk, Chelsea, which perhaps will not lie very much out of your usual tracks. Mr. Cross, I am sure, would feel it an advantage to know you better.

The General is probably yearning for a needed holiday. Please commend me to him, and believe me always,

Yours with affectionate regard

M. A. Cross.

VII, 321:16 EDITH SIMCOX, AUTOBIOGRAPHY, 9 SEPTEMBER 1880

MS: Bodleian.

Thursday 9 September 1880

September 9. On Monday I heard from her, in prompt reply to my last which had only just reached her. She speaks of love and tenderness that do not prevent her feeling sometimes as if she had woke in an unremembered state of existence and almost wished she were dead. One felt all the difficulty; she will miss the active intellectual companionship. The "family" is all very dear and good, but of old she did not depend on them alone. Then before the marriage between her and Johnny I think the sympathy must have been complete: now he cannot in any way lighten her feeling of a divided duty; she must remember what is lost, and yet for his sake it would be well if she could sometimes forget.

VII, 332:9 GE TO MRS. ALFRED TENNYSON, WITLEY, 5 NOVEMBER 1880

MS: Tennyson Research Centre, Lincoln.

The Heights, Witley, | Nr. Godalming.

November 5. 80.

Dear Mrs. Tennyson

The regret I felt on finding your cards that my drive had happened when I might have had the pleasure of seeing you has been deepened by my inability to get to Aldworth.

I have been rather seriously ill, and am not allowed to be out in the open air for more than an hour in the scant sunshine. One seems to be making too much of such facts by writing about them; but I cannot bear to seem unmindful of any friendly sign made to me by you and yours.

Our friend Mrs. Greville has told me—I hope quite correctly—that you are in some respects better in health than you were last year, and that Mr. Tennyson is as energetic and bright as usual. You and he will I trust always believe in the high regard with which I am

Yours most sincerely
M. A. Cross.

Mr. Cross feels himself a loser, that he has missed this year's opportunity of making your and Mr. Tennyson's acquaintance. I am hoping that Mr. Hallam may find his way to us when we are in town at 4 Cheyne Walk, Chelsea.

VII, 337:6   EDITH SIMCOX, AUTOBIOGRAPHY, 19 NOVEMBER 1880

MS: Bodleian.

Friday 19 November 1880

19. Again last Tuesday I went to Cheyne Walk, driven by growing anxiety. The house was not ready or furnished; the man in charge wished to show me over and said Mr. Cross was coming up with furniture mid-day. I wrote to her in the evening and last night heard in reply that she was better, but not to be in town till the end of the month. The physical alienation makes some way. An absence of 9 months, which she could have abridged by a cheap word, makes it impossible to ignore one's fate—to live a long way off.

VII, 338:1   WILLIAM BLACKWOOD TO GE, EDINBURGH, [? NOVEMBER 1880]

Text: Blackwood Letter Book.

My dear Mrs. Cross

It is a long time since we have heard from one another and I feel the fault lies on my side but it is not from my not thinking of you as I have daily intended for weeks past to write you but some matter of business more urgent than another seemed to crop up day after day and made me postpone my letter to you. When I last heard from you you had not been very well and had gone to Brighton for some bracing air which, I was glad to learn from a letter you wrote to either Mr. Langford or Mr. Henderson shortly after, had done you much good and I trust the improvement continued and that this finds you strong for the short and sunless winter days. I suppose you will have left Witley and are now settled in Cheyne Walk for the winter and I hope are liking it.

Your kind words and sympathy with us in our heavy sorrow were very comforting and gratifying and sorely have I felt my gallant and warm hearted brother's death.[5] Every mail continues to bring us fresh particulars of how he was wounded and killed and how much he was valued which keeps opening up the wound although it makes the memory of him a proud satisfaction to us. Poor fellow he was wounded early in the fight in the inside of the thigh which disabled him from riding as the day wore on, then in the ankle and finally a sabre cut on the head killed him when fighting with the brave 66th in the garden enclosures. But I must not inflict you with more harrowing details of the sad disaster and our grief.

Now to business matters. I am very happy to tell you that although business in general has been terribly dull your books have been selling capitally and I enclose you memo of last month's London sales which will interest you. Mr. Langford also writes me that they have been doing equally well during this month. Theophrastus in the 5/– form has not however started as well as I expected and the London subscription was 620 and between Glasgow and Dublin and here we disposed of about another hundred I daresay. But I have no doubt there will be a continuous dropping sale which should we have any new work from you to bring out is sure to give it a fresh impetus and I hope I may soon hear from you that there is something on the stocks.

You will I expect be deeply interested in Laurence Oliphant's forth-coming work "The Land of Gilead,"[6] and your acceptance of a presenta-tion copy will give me pleasure. I shall also be sending you the first Volume of our Philosophical Classics next week and I hope you will be pleased with the way Mr. Mahaffy has done Cervantes.[7] The series will not I fear be so

5. George Frederick Blackwood (1838–80) sailed for India on Christmas Eve 1879, a Major in the Royal Horse Artillery. In July 1880 at Maiwand, the battery "fought until only eleven of them remained; then holding their colours aloft they went forward and perished." (F. D. Tredrey, *The House of Blackwood 1804–1954*, Edinburgh and London, 1954, p. 160.)

6. *The Land of Gilead, with Excursions in the Lebanon*, Edinburgh, 1880.

7. *Cervantes* in Blackwood's Philoso-phical Classics series was edited by Mrs. Oliphant, not Mahaffy. It was adver-tised as "now ready" in the *Athenaeum*, 27 November 1880, p. 720.

popular as our Ancient Classics but yet I hope it will do fairly well. I
wonder if you will read Endymion.[8] I have read the first volume and it
amused me greatly and I long to get at the second this evening.

Looking forward to a letter from you soon and hoping this finds both
you and Mr. Cross well believe me

Always yours sincerely
William Blackwood.

VII, 347:19 GE TO WILLIAM BLACKWOOD, LONDON, 14 DECEMBER 1880

MS: National Library of Scotland.

4. Cheyne Walk, | Chelsea, S.W.
December 14. 1880.

My dear Mr. William

I thank you with much feeling for sending me the well-judged volume
in memory of your dear Uncle.[9] I have read through it this morning, and
I should not have believed beforehand that a selection of Obituary Notices
would give me so much satisfaction. They are sober and truthful and, I
imagine, only inexact in some minor details. It is really to the credit of
our press that such a volume would be a trustworthy authority to a writer
who wished to give a full history of our literature and its *personnel* in the
last quarter of a century.

My experience and affection say a hearty amen to all the praise of
your Uncle's character contained in this volume. I feel that his death was
an irreparable loss to my mental life, for nowhere else is it possible that
I can find the same long-tried genuineness of sympathy and unmixed
impartial gladness in anything I might happen to do well. To have had
a publisher who was in the fullest sense of the word a gentleman and at
the same time a man of excellent moral judgment, has been an invaluable
stimulus and comfort to me. Your Uncle had retained that fruit of experience which makes a man of the world as opposed to the narrow man
of literature. He judged well of writing because he had learned to judge
well of men and things, not merely through quickness of observation and
insight, but with the illumination of a heart in the right place—a thorough
integrity and rare tenderness of feeling.

8. Benjamin Disraeli, *Endymion. By the Author of Lothair*, 3 vols., 1880.
9. *A Selection from the Obituary Notices of the Late John Blackwood*, ed. William Blackwood, Edinburgh, 1880.

When you write to me again I should be very glad to hear news about your Uncle's family, especially his son. I finish hurriedly in order to send this to the post.

Yours always sincerely,
M. A. Cross.

VII, 349:18   GE TO MRS. RICHARD STRACHEY, LONDON, 19 DECEMBER 1880

MS: British Museum. *Published:* Cross, III, 438; facsimile in *TLS*, 16 May 1968, p. 507.

4, Cheyne Walk, | Chelsea, S.W.
December 19. 1880.

Dear Mrs. Strachey

I have been thinking so much of Lady Colvile, and yet I shrank from troubling even your more indirect and sympathetic sorrow with a letter.[1] I am wondering how far her health is in a state to endure this loss—a loss which extends even to me who only occasionally saw, but was always cheered by, the expression of a wise and sweet nature which clearly shone in Sir James Colvile's manner and conversation. One great comfort I believe she has—that of a sister's affection.[2]

VII, 350:1   EDITH SIMCOX, AUTOBIOGRAPHY, 19–23 DECEMBER 1880

MS: Bodleian. *Extract published:* Haight, *George Eliot*, p. 547.

Sunday 19 December 1880

19. A short and sweet—quite sweet—note came last night asking me to go this afternoon, she hoped no one else would be there. I don't think it likely that no one will but of course would rather go invited than not.

Thursday 23 December 1880

23rd. She was alone when I arrived. I was too shy to ask for any special greeting—only kissed her again and again as she sat. Mr. Cross came in

1. Sir James William Colvile died suddenly 6 December 1880. Lady Colvile was Mrs. Strachey's sister.
2. "Here the letter is broken off. The pen which had carried delight and comfort to so many minds and hearts, here made its last mark. The spring, which had broadened out into so wide a river of speech, ceased to flow." (Cross, III, 438.)

soon and I noticed his countenance was transfigured, a calm look of pure *beatitude* had succeeded the ordinary good nature.—Poor fellow! She was complaining of a slight sore throat; when he came in and touched her hand, said she felt the reverse of better. I only stayed half an hour therefore; she said Do not go, but I gave as a reason that she should not tire her throat and then she asked me to come in again and tell them the news. He came down to the door with me and I only asked after his health. She had spoken before of being quite well and I thought it was only a passing cold—she thought it was caught at the Agamemnon. I meant to call again tomorrow and take her some snowdrops. This morning I hear from Johnny—she died at 10 last night!

VII, 350:1 JOHN W. CROSS TO ISAAC P. EVANS, LONDON, 22 DECEMBER 1880

MS: British Museum.

4, Cheyne Walk, | Chelsea, S.W.
22 December 1880.

My dear Mr. Evans,

I scarcely know how to write and tell you that your noble sister and my wife died this night a little before 10 o'clock. I can scarcely realize yet that the crown of my life is gone. It has all been so very sudden. She was very ill this summer with a renal complaint of some standing but had quite recovered and we had just got into our new house here. On Friday last she went with me to St. George's Hall Langham Place to see the Agamemnon acted: on Saturday we were at the Popular Concert where I think she must have caught a chill for on Sunday evening she complained of a little sore throat and on Monday morning her throat being rather worse I went up for Dr. Andrew Clark who has been her chief medical attendant for some years. He was unable to come to see her that day but gave me a letter to a friend and old pupil of his Mr. W. G. Mackenzie who lives near here. Mr. Mackenzie came on Monday afternoon and again in the evening but thought there was nothing worse than a violent affection of the larynx causing great difficulty in swallowing. She had a wretched night on Monday but on Tuesday morning the pulse was down to 80 @ 90 and temperature to 99. Mr. Mackenzie came to see her twice on Tuesday and was not at all anxious about her state. When he came again on Wednesday (this) morning he found a great change for the worse—the pulse having got much quicker and the breathing disturbed. She was also suffering from great pain over the right kidney. He came back at 2 and found her worse again and when Dr. Andrew Clark arrived at 6 o'clock he at once declared there was little or no hope and at 10 o'clock she passed away without any pain—the cold had travelled down to the pericardium and complete loss of power of the heart supervened. I cannot write anything more tonight. I do not at all realize yet what has happened. It has all been so frightfully sudden. We have only been married a little over 7 months and one of the most gratifying collateral incidents of our marriage was that it broke the long silence that had existed between you and your sister.

I will write you again when a day has been fixed for the funeral. I am quite dazed tonight but I feel that you should be written to first of all. The Brother "who leaned soft cheeks together"[3] with her in the old old days.

In great woe,

Yours very truly,
J. W. Cross.

VII, 352:1   J. W. CROSS TO MRS. R. STRACHEY, LONDON, 26 DECEMBER 1880

MS: British Museum. *Envelope:* Mrs. Strachey | Stowey House | Clapham Common | S.W. *Postmark:* LONDON-S.W | DE 27 | 80. Published: *TLS*, 16 May 1968, p. 507.

4 Cheyne Walk, Chelsea | 26 December 1880.

Dear Mrs. Strachey,

In turning over my wife's writing portfolio I found the enclosed. It is the last thing written by her hand on that fatal last Sunday. I fancy she must have been interrupted by Mr. Herbert Spencer's visit. I can scarcely bear to part with it but it belongs to you.

I hope you will come and see me some day soon. She was very fond of you and Lady Colvile. I think the funeral will be on Wednesday at Highgate Cemetery at $\frac{1}{2}$ past 12 but the holidays intervening make all arrangements difficult. I will have notices inserted in the newspapers as soon as we can fix the day absolutely.

Believe me

Yours sincerely
J. W. Cross.

3. "Two Lovers," in *The Legend of Jubal*, 1874, p. 232. Cross may have thought the line occurred in "Brother and Sister."

VII, 352:1   EDITH SIMCOX, AUTOBIOGRAPHY, 26–29 DECEMBER 1880

MS: Bodleian. *Published:* Haight, *George Eliot*, pp. 550–551.

Sunday 26 December 1880

26. This morning I ventured to look again at some of her letters—all dear and gracious and full of sweet acknowledgment of all my love. Mrs. Anderson[4] came to see me this morning—was very kind: wished to know when the funeral would be—spoke of people having spoken of Westminster Abbey; she seemed to understand about the dear one—thought she must have had Bright's disease and would have suffered more if she had lived. She asked if I was going to the house today, and on that instance I did—hoping for some chance to save me from ringing that bell again. I met Florence coming from the house: she could hardly speak; her brother had gone out for a walk with Mr. Druce. He loved the house where she had lived just 3 weeks. I turned back with her—we exchanged few words—I learnt their address (3 Percy Villas)—later Miss Helps called to ask Charles Lewes's address and also about the funeral. This reminded me to write to Charles.

Wednesday 29 December 1880

29. This day stands alone. I am not afraid of forgetting, but as heretofore I record her teaching while the sound is still fresh in my soul's ears. This morning at 10 when the wreath I had ordered—white flowers bordered with laurel leaves—came, I drove with it to Cheyne Walk, giving it silently to the silent cook. Then, instinct guiding—it seemed to guide one right all day—I went to Highgate, stopping on the way to get some violets—I was not sure for what purpose. In the cemetery I found the new grave was in the place I had feebly coveted—nearer the path than his and one step further south.[5] Then I laid my violets at the head of Mr. Lewes's solitary grave and left the already gathering crowd to ask which way the entrance would be. Then I drifted towards the chapel—standing first for a while under the colonnade where a child asked me "Was it the late George Eliot's wife was going to be buried?"—I think I said Yes. Then I waited on the skirts of the group gathered in the porch between the church and chapel sanctuaries. Then some one claimed a passage through the thicken-

4. Dr. Elizabeth Garrett Anderson.
5. Elma Stuart was buried in the next grave to the south 28 January 1903, more than two years after Edith died.

ing crowd and I followed in his wake and found myself without effort in a sort of vestibule past the door which kept back the crowd. Mrs. Lankester was next the chapel—I cannot forget that she offered me her place. I took it and presently every one else was made to stand back, then the solemn procession passed me. The coffin bearers paused in the very doorway, I pressed a kiss upon the pall and trembled violently as I stood motionless else, in the still silence with nothing to mar the realization of that intense moment's awe. Then—it was hard to tell the invited mourners from the other waiting friends—men many of whose faces I knew—and so I passed among them into the chapel, entering a forward pew. White wreaths lay thick upon the velvet pall—it was not painful to think of her last sleep so guarded. I saw her husband's face, pale and still; he forced himself aloof from the unbearable world in sight. The service was so like our own I did not know it apart till afterwards when I could not trace the outlines that had seemed so almost entirely in harmony with her faith. Dr. Sadler quoted —how could he help?—her words of aspiration,[6] but what moved me most was the passage—in the Church Service lesson—it moved me like the voice of God—of Her: "But some man will say, How are the dead raised up? and with what body do they come? . . . As we left the chapel Miss Helps put her arm in mine, but I left her at the door, to make my way alone across the road to the other part where the grave was. I shook hands silently with Mrs. Anderson and waited at the corner where the hearse stopped and the coffin was brought up again. Again I followed near, on the skirts of the procession, a man—Champneys[7] I thought—had a white wreath he wished to lay upon the coffin and as he pressed forward those behind bore me on, till I was standing between his grave and hers and heard the last words said: the grave was deep and narrow—the flowers filled all the level space. I turned away with the first—Charles Lewes pressed my hand as we gave the last look. Then I turned up the hill and walked through the rain by a road unknown before to Hampstead and a station. Then through the twilight I cried and moaned aloud.

6. Thomas Sadler (1822–91), Minister of the Rosslyn Hill Unitarian Chapel at Hampstead, had also conducted GHL's funeral service. In quoting from "O May I Join the Choir Invisible" he changed "immortal dead who live again" to "who still live on." His address is given in the *Daily News*, 30 December 1880, [by W. H. Hall?].

7. Basil Champneys, the architect who oversaw the alterations and decoration of the Priory in 1875.

VII, 352:1 J. W. CROSS TO MRS. R. STRACHEY, LONDON, 30 DECEMBER 1880

MS: British Museum. *Published: TLS*, 16 May 1968, p. 508.

4 Cheyne Walk Chelsea | 30 December 1880.

My dear Mrs. Strachey,

I must write you one line to say that you must never let me see again that half finished note I sent to you. It is yours and I want you to have it and to keep it and to treasure it as I know you will do. If I saw it again I could not part with it. You must not let me see it. I mean what I say.[8]

I hope to see you very soon. I am going to Sevenoaks this afternoon and thence to Lincolnshire and Six Mile Bottom to visit my sisters and brothers in law. I expect to be back in London tomorrow week.

I do trust that you and Lady Colvile took no cold yesterday. I am very anxious that the trouble should spread no further. My very kind remembrances to your sister—smitten almost simultaneously. I cannot say more now.

Yours sincerely
J. W. Cross.

VII, 352:1 JOHN W. CROSS TO MME BODICHON, LONDON, 13 JANUARY 1881

MS: Yale.

4. Cheyne Walk, | **Chelsea, S.W.**
13 January 1881.

Dear Madame Bodichon,

I am glad to have your letter—It was very good of you to write at a time when I am afraid you are not very strong—I had an opportunity the same evening of giving Charles Lewes your message.

Yes it is indeed desolation and I have so often used the words you use "this world is so much poorer." Amongst all her intimate friends I know there was none she valued more or who was more to her than yourself.

She talked to me a great deal about you. In fact a great deal of our talk during our short married life was about old days and I think I know all her

8. But 1 April 1897 Mrs. (then Lady) Strachey wrote to her daughter Philippa: "Mr. Cross has asked me to let him have George Eliot's last letter to exhibit at the Victorian Exhibition, so I have had to let it go very unwillingly." (BM.)

feelings to her friends very thoroughly. Knowing her as intimately as you did you can imagine what the loss is to me of such a companion. During the last few months especially when she was so ill from the end of September till we left Witley at end of November I was scarcely ever away more than an hour or two from her. We did everything together; and if it were not that there has been a great deal to do since her death, I don't know what I should do in this house alone by myself. I should like very much indeed to come to see you some day when you feel strong enough and we can talk over the olden times. She and I were to have come together were we not this spring? "Oh the little more, and how much it is and the little less, and what worlds away!"[9]

Surely I will always remember thankfully that you feel for me—and I can feel for you too. Believe me always

Yours sincerely
J. W. Cross.

VII, 352:1 JOHN W. CROSS TO MME BODICHON, LONDON, 9 JULY 1881

MS: Yale. *Extracts published:* Haight, *George Eliot.* pp. 516–517.

4, Cheyne Walk, | Chelsea, S. W.,
9 July 1881.

My dear Madame Bodichon,

I have had a great hunt for Donne's poems[1] which had got pushed in behind some other books and I was in mortal fear the volume had got lost stolen or strayed. However here it is and I hope it will reach you safely. I will send you the Fraser in a day or two as my sisters want to read the article and I think you said you were in no hurry.

The Donne is very precious with her neat little index of favorite pieces and many markings. On p. 165 you will see what we were trying to recall:

> "For love all love of other sights controls
> And makes one little room an everywhere."

I am so glad that it will be in your appreciative possession—for you having sought the book out with much trouble it is very meet and proper that it should go back to you and remain a constant and delightful memory of her.

---

9. Browning, "By the Fireside," stanza 39.

1. Mme Bodichon had lent GE

Donne's *Poems*, 1633. The lines marked on p. 165 read "controules," "roome," and "every where."

It was a real pleasure to me to be with you and to hear about old days and I hope I may come down again later on in the year and find you equally well in your charming country place and delightfully simple life.

With best regards to Dr. Bodichon and to Mrs. Moore[2]

Believe me always

Very truly yours

J. W. Cross.

Many thanks for my sister's volume of Poems[3] which came safely.

2. Mme Bodichon's niece Amy Leigh Smith Ludlow was married in 1880 to Norman Moore, M.D. (1847–1922).

3. Elizabeth Dennistoun Cross, *An Old Story and Other Poems*, 1868.

ADDENDA AND CORRIGENDA

VOLUME I

xi:n7	*after* 1940 *add* , 2d ed., Archon Books, 1969.
xxiii:35	*for* engaged to *read* proposed to by
xxiii:36	*for* the engagement *read* off the correspondence
xxvi:38	*for* £2000 *read* £3000
xxxiv:2	*for* III *read* IV
xxxvii:5	*insert* BM British Museum, now British Library.
xxxviii:21	*insert* Haight, *George Eliot* Gordon S. Haight, *George Eliot. A Biography*. Oxford, Clarendon Press; New York, Oxford University Press, 1968.
xxxviii:30	*insert* McKenzie K. A. McKenzie, *Edith Simcox and George Eliot*, with an introduction by G. S. Haight, London, Oxford University Press, 1961.
xxxix:7	*for* 1831–32 *read* 1831–33
xxxix:8	*insert* Simcox, Autobiography Edith Jemima Simcox, Autobiography of a Shirt Maker (Bodleian, Eng. misc. d. 494).
xlv:12	*after* *Wesen* insert *des*. GE's copy is in Dr. Williams's Library.
xlix:18	*after* terms. *insert* GE wrote in her Journal, 25 August 1859: "Another pleasant incident was a letter from my old friend and schoolfellow Martha Jackson, asking if the author of Adam Bede was *her* Marian Evans."
l:35	*after* GE *insert* , who had met her once at Rosehill in 1850,
lii:12	*for* John *read* John Alexander
lviii:13	*after* peace *read* on the subject and wrote GE few letters. She did not see
lix:n8	*for* 1848 *read* 23 April 1847
lxii:15	*for* Laffite *read* Laffitte
lxii:38	*after* William *insert* Chalmers
lxiii:12	*for* Weybridge *read* St. George's Hill, Weybridge,
lxiii:24	*after* Rugby *insert* (1855–57)
lxv:10	*for* two *read* three
lxv:12	*after* Attenborough *insert* (1815–81)
lxv:14	*after* Isaac *insert* (1831–1912)
lxv:18	*insert* III. Harriet (1809–bur. 20 January 1810).
lxv:19	*after* (2) *insert* 8 February 1813 Christiana Pearson (1787–
lxv:24	*for* (1838–55) *read* (1839–55)
lxv:36	*for* 1923 *read* 1922
lxv:38	*insert* IV, V. William and Thomas, twins (bap. 26 March 1821–bur. 6 April 1821).
lxv:25	*for* —— Walker *read* William Walker
lxviii:5	*for* Laffite *read* Laffitte
lxviii:21	*after* Hunt, *insert* Carlyle,
lxviii:22	*for* the autumn *read* July
lxiv:15	*after* The Leweses had *insert* a daughter, born 22 December 1841, who lived only two days, and

lxix:16   *for* in *read* on 16
lxix:19   *after* registered *insert* (perhaps with a glance at the bastard in *King Lear*)
lxx:26   *read* (9 October 1853–28 February 1939)
lxx:28   *for* 21 *read* 26
lxxi:6–9   *read* Blanche Southwood Lewes (Mrs. Reginald John Edward Hanson, 18 July 1872–15 February 1964); Maud Southwood Lewes (Mrs. John Rowland Hopwood, 30 March 1874–16 August 1942); and Elinor Southwood Lewes (Mrs. Ernest Carrington Ouvry, 24 June 1877–3 November 1974).
lxxi:12   *for* April *read* February
lxxiv:15   *after* him *read* twenty-seven by GHL are at Harvard, others by GE are at Yale and Princeton.
lxxv:3   *after* but *insert* most of
lxxv:4   *after* disappeared. *insert* Five letters from GE to Spencer, deposited in the British Museum in 1935 with the reservation that they be kept sealed for fifty years, were released in March 1975 to Professor Richard Schoenwald, who published them in the wrong order and with a number of misreadings in the Communication section of the *Bulletin of the New York Public Library*, 79 (Spring 1976), 362–371. A sixth letter was acquired by the British Library in 1976.
lxxvi:18   *for* Elvorinda *read* Evorilda *The name is so spelled in the will of her step-father Sir James Coxe.*
3:n4   *for* 1785 *read* 1787
7:n3   *add* He married Amelia Gould Harper (b. 11 January 1814), daughter of Joseph and Maria Harper (later Harpur) of Chilvers Coton.
7:n7   *read* Mary (1800–67) and Rebecca (1803–73)
8:21   *for* [4] SEPTEMBER 1838 *read* 9 [OCTOBER] 1838
9:7   *for* G——— *read* Gobions.
9:n2   *add* The Coventry oratorio was given 3 October 1838.
14:34   *after* strength." *insert note* 3a. Cf. *Comus*, lines 328–329.
15:n5   *for* 1827–32 *read* 1828–32
21:n8   *add* The friend was Maria Congreve. GE said that Scott "was healthy and historical—'it would not fit on to her creed.'" (Simcox, Autobiography, 16 February 1885.
23:4   *after* growth; *insert note* 2a. Cf. Dryden, *All for Love*, IV, i, 43.
26:n1   *for* 18 May *read* 30 March
29:7   *after* lady" *insert note* 1a. Quiz [Edward Caswall], *Sketches of Young Ladies*, 1837, pp. 16–18. The book, illustrated by Phiz, was mistakenly attributed to Dickens.
31:17   *after* ear, *insert note* 6a. *Il Penseroso*, line 120.
33:18   *after* prospect *insert note* 1a. With her father, 25–30 November 1839. (Robert Evans's Journal.)
34:2   *after* hay, *add note* 1a. *Spectator*, No. 191.
35:21   insert *MS:* Mr. Gordon N. Ray.
35:25   *for* words" *read* words!"
35:34   *for* heavy *read* heavy
36:10   *after* dressing. *read* (You of course know that beautiful ode, if not get an introduction to it.) Newspaper lore at breakfast. Item:

36:13   *for* further *read* farther
36:17–18   *for* liberalising, philosophising *read* liberalizing, philosophizing
36:37   *for* lingered over *read* lingered on
37:5   *for* sheds on *read* sheds over *and insert note* 5a. Pope, *Essay on Man*, IV, 168.
37:8   *for* good gift. *read* good and perfect gift. *and insert note* 5b. "A Prayer for the Clergy and People." In the American revision of the *Book of Common Prayer* (1790), "from whom cometh every good and perfect gift"; the English text still reads "who alone workest great marvels."
37:8   *after* gift. *add* I cannot write more for my hand is sufficiently illegible without crossing, though I must, nathless, tell you I am too hardened by habit to feel compunction for untidy letter writing or I should apologize for this. So send me word when you can most conveniently come and pay me a visit. I tell you beforehand, all here is as uninteresting as I am, but if you have a mind to breathe the bracing air of self-denial, come to Griff.
39:27   *for* breeches *read* breaches
40:n1   *for* uncle *read* great uncle
44:n3   *add* and in *Felix Holt*, Introduction, I, 7.
47:22   *for* [6? APRIL 1840] read [6–7 APRIL 1840]
47:23   insert *MS:* Mr. Gordon N. Ray.
47:26   *after* Patty *insert* You must certainly have been looking through a Camera obscura when you imagined the time that had elapsed since my writing to you a short one; had you been in any danger of my ire, it would have arisen from an opposite view of the matter. And now to dispatch my pill first that all the sweets may come after I must tell you dear Patty, that we are going immediately to have a considerable alteration made in our house, which will consequently I fear, be quite unfit for the reception of visitors, at least till the close of May, so that our meeting must be postponed till the following month if no more pleasant "*lark*" should be offered you nor any less desirable occurrence to either of us render the time inconvenient. | Pity
48:1   *after* contemplation *insert* for mundifying the temple within and trimming the fire there in readiness for actual worship, and though
48:13   *for* some use *read* some little use
48:29   *for* trail [treat?] *read* hail
48:33   *after* arrangement. *insert* Many thanks for the first deep blue violet of your Aunt's garden, and a hearty amen to Sarah's wish. I should as you conjecture, like to know
49:4   *after* extremely *insert*, a declaration that will bring to your recollection a morçeau of school philosophy, a copy book aphorism—La nouveauté plaît." And now my dear Patty, I have tried your patience sufficiently. Talk no more of untidy writing—I challenge you to produce some equally aristocratic in illegibility with this specimen of my penmanship. I began to deface this sheet yesterday and am too late for the letter bag tonight, or you would have had the precious present tomorrow morning. My Father comes and claims my undivided attention.
49:9   *after* Museum. *delete rest of headnote.*

49:27   *after* show *insert note* 2. Psalms 39:6.
49:27   *after* bell *insert note* 3. John Keble, *The Christian Year*, "Advent Sunday," stanza 12.
51:4   *after* name. *insert note* 3a. *Midsummer Night's Dream*, v, i, 17.
53:n3   *for* Diary *read* Journal
57:8   *after* helm" *insert note* 6a. "Our Father's at the Helm," by Miss M. L. Boyle, *Annual Register*, 79 (1837), 405.
60:13   insert *MS:* Mr. Gordon N. Ray.
60:14   insert *Address:* Miss Martha Jackson | Gobions | near Hertford | Prepaid. *Postmark:* COVENTRY | JY 31 | 1840.
60:25   *after* week. *insert* A Leicester coach will carry you to our gate so that no anxiety will befall you as to your journey from Coventry. There is
60:26   *for* dear *read* my
60:28   *delete* that
60:30   *for* Ivy *read Ivy*
61:1   *after* epithalamium? *insert* Do secure me the office. Trèves de badinage! says my Patty, looking as sedate as becomes an "engaged young lady." Be it so. I confess I have need to remind you that I am your junior. However as Cowper wrote John Gilpin under a fit of mental depression, I may be believed when I say that malgré my attempt to sing to the tune of "Begone dull care" I am quite ready to slide into a minor key, and though I send you an awkward apology for a jet d'eau, my current really runs without one frisky ripple.
65:1   *for* [AUGUST? 1840] *read* [14 AUGUST 1840]
65:2   insert *MS:* Mr. Gordon N. Ray. *Address:* Miss Martha Jackson | No. 58 Bread Street | Cheapside | London | Free. *Postmarks:* COVENTRY | AUG 14 | 1840; A | PAID | 15 AUG 15 | 1840.
65:13   *after* joy *insert* on Wednesday next. Thick ink and a real desire for despatch make me say au revoir! which I can happily do without assigning myself a lengthened period of anticipation.
66:n1   *add:* Cf. Wordsworth, "And oh! dear soother," Eversley ed., VIII (1896), 301: "begets strange themes."
70:1   insert *MS:* Mr. Gordon N. Ray. *Address:* Miss Martha Jackson | Gobions | near Hertford | Free.
70:6   *after* friends. *insert* and I am threatened with excision from Jessie's list for I have not heard from her since you dear Martha left me. I will for once repress my imaginative faculty and forbid it to conjure up raven like *un*realities to croak in my mind's ear—you are forgotten or you have wounded or disgusted her whom you love. Is it possible that you did not receive my last hasty note acknowledging your charming execution of my troublesome commissions, and containing an earnest request that you would write to me as soon as possible? I know it has the appearance of selfishness to send such a request without attempting to deserve that you should accord it me, but you know my situation, you know that I am entrammelled in meshes material and aerial and that I really need the solace that an assurance of your affection can give me. I am very
70:11   *for durissimo cor read* durissimo cor *and add* I have heard of your writing to Miss Franklin—the same of Jessie, and I cannot prevent a certain

swelling of heart when the idea suggests itself that you have both determined to treat me after my deserts. Every

70:17   *after* curse." *insert* Time only will prove the prophetic character of my presentiment. In the meantime my dear Ivy (prove your claim to the name) I will not whine about a destiny that is unquestionably right, and though I be left *gourd*less, the leaves of that tree of life planted for the healing of the nations [2a] will be left without a rival in my desires. Would it were so now!

2a. Jonah 4:7 and Revelation 22:2.

70:24   *after* universe."[4] *add* By the bye Mr. Brezzi lent me Aimé Martin's work whence Woman's Mission is drawn—I have been charmed by its stirring eloquence and its assertion of neglected truths, *but* the author is not an orthodox Christian. I use this term to imply that he saps the Gospel of all mystery, of all spirituality, if I rightly apprehend him, and probably it is this that has given rise to the notion that Woman's Mission is the work of a Socinian. Martin's opinions have been attributed to her. || I am culling Mrs. Hemans's beauties, and am specially pleased with her "Forest Sanctuary." What think you of these lines? (perhaps already known to you). The husband, a Spanish exile in the woods of North America, is recalling the death of his wife among other painful events, to his memory.

"And I am he that look'd and saw decay | Steal o'er the fair of earth, th'adored too much!— | It is a fearful thing to love what death may touch. || A fearful thing that love and death may dwell | In the same world! [...] Then sank her head | Against my bursting heart—what did I clasp?—The dead! || I call'd—to call what answers not our cries, | By what we loved to stand unseen, unheard, | With the loud passion of our tears and sighs, | To see but some cold glittering ringlet stirred | And in the quench'd eye's fixedness to gaze | All vainly searching for the parted rays; | This is what waits us! Dead! with that chill word | To link our bosom-names! For this we pour | Our souls upon the dust—nor tremble to adore!"[4a]

I am preparing an unwelcome task for you dear Martha in scribbling so much that is scarcely legible—pardon it on the plea of real indisposition and believe me even though discarded | Your true and affectionate | Clematis.

4a. Felicia Hemans, *The Forest Sanctuary: with Other Poems*, 22d ed., Edinburgh and London, 1829, stanzas 50, 51, 55, 56.

70:n4   *substitute* "Influence of Natural Objects," later *Prelude*, i, 401.

72:29   *for* soi-distant *read* soi-disant

77:n4   *substitute* The College for the Poor, College Street, Chilvers Coton. See Dorothy Dodds, *The George Eliot Country*, 2d ed., Nuneaton, [1966], p. 22.

83:21   *for* Belsser *read* Belper

91:4   *for* incubation *read* inculcation

93:38   *after* God." *insert note* 1a. John Keble, *The Christian Year*, "Morning," stanza 14.

101:29   *after* money *insert note* 3a. According to Edith Simcox it was £20. (Autobiography, 12 June 1885.)

109:6   *for* [SEPTEMBER 1841] *read* 7 SEPTEMBER 1841
109:7   insert *MS:* Mr. Gordon N. Ray.
109:8   *after* Coventry *insert* ⟨Aug⟩ September 7/41.
109:9   *for* My dear Ivy *read* My very dear Martha | To a delinquent who has
          so frequently occasion to confess that her errors are underrated as has
          your humble servant, it is really a treat to be unjustly suspected; ac-
          cordingly I rather exult in being able to tell you that I have a much
          larger stock of the friendship that thinks no evil than your anxiety to
          vindicate yourself from the charge of indifference supposes. I had
          attributed your silence to the right cause—one in which I rejoiced,
          your enjoyment of Brighton pleasures, the being *entwined* among its
          choice flowerets. And now, child of life's sunny clime that you are!
          you have Jessie all to yourself. Shall I begin
109:21   *for* such *read* rich
109:30   *after* turned. *read* | Thank you my dear Ivy for enquiring about *me*,
          that touching monosyllable—which by the bye a process of logic
          something like the Eton youth's might be demonstrated a *Polly's* syl-
          lable. And again thank you for the willingness to welcome me at your
          happy home. *Another* year, peradventure, I may put your patience to
          the test but *this* with its train of engagements requires me to deny
          myself the treat. In these
110:7   *for* the idea *read* this idea
110:11   *after* Geology;[3] *insert* which I think you know. There
110:14   *after* topics. *insert* | What are the London sorrows to which you alluded?
          I suspect you of some *mal*version, you ruthless man-slayer! remem-
          ber your destiny—"revenge will come" say the sybilline leaves you
          gave me. | I have written in extreme haste, which I rather regret.
          Think of what the four materia, time, paper, pen and ink have effected
          for the world! and here have I consumed some of all four in what is of
          very dubious value. This by way of moralizing—a bad actress's
          attempt to bow a graceful parting—but I am secure from hissing. Love
          much love of the warmest kind to Jessie and yourself. | I have had an
          interview to-day with Mr. Mark Wilks[3a] of Paris who has paid a
          transient visit to Coventry. He is a most interesting man. Tell Jessie
          too that I have seen the *Leslie* Group at Miss Franklins'. Those dear
          friends are exemplifying the growing brightness of the path of the just.
          Give my kind regards to your friends, well known to my imagination
          though in a way that will enable me to write a parody on "And is this
          Yarrow?"[3b] if I should ever behold them in propria persona. When
          will the courtship of patriarchal duration reach the "consummation
          devoutly to be wished"?[3c] When will one of the triad of graces leave
          her home? 'More last words'! I hope to see you at Foleshill, my Patty,
          before many more months have fled. Why could we not meet (Jessie
          and ourselves) as we did in London?[3d] I must at last say good night.
          3a. Mark Wilks wrote *Précis de l'histoire de l'église d'Écosse*, Paris,
          1844, and *Tahiti,* ... *Character and Progress of French Roman Catholic
          Efforts for the Destruction of English Protestant Missions in the South
          Seas*, 1844.
          3b. Wordsworth, "Yarrow Revisited," line 1.

3c. *Hamlet*, iii, i, 63–64.

3d. GE spent five days with Jessie Barclay in London, November 1839.

118:2	*for* [OCTOBER 1841] *read* 8 JULY 1841 *and transpose letter to* i, 99.
118:3	*insert MS:* Mr. Gordon N. Ray.
118:4	*for* Coventry 1841 *read* Foleshill Road, Coventry, July 8. 1841.
118:8	*for* professing *read* possessing
118:11	*for* honourable *read* honoured
118:16	*after* engaged. *insert* and my time has of late been lavishly given to laboriously doing the 'nothings' of visits which are often visitations. But that this kind of employment brings so little wholesome fruit is rather attributable to my own lack of anxiety to do and get good than to any other cause. I have been
118:33	*after* Let us *insert* my dear Patty,
119:2	*after* received. *insert*	I am going out almost immediately and have not time to say more. I have written altogether hurriedly, but you will forgive this. I venture to offer my respectful and kind regards to all yours, whom I have learned to love without seeing them. I hope to hear from you soon.
121:n9	*add* GE's copy, 2d ed., inscribed "Mary Ann Evans	Jany 1st 1842" is in Dr. Williams's Library.
126:n5	*for* 16 *read* 14
129:n3	*add* Adam Bede quotes *Poor Richard's Almanac* in chs. 4 and 20.
135:16	*after* good, *insert note* 10. Pope, *Essay on Man*, i, 292.
141:1	*read* FOLESHILL, [7 JUNE 1842]
141:2	*insert MS:* Mr. Gordon N. Ray. *Endorsed:* June 7 1842.
141:5	*after* enabling me *insert* to sympathize with you, and I shall anxiously hope to hear that she is better.
141:6	*after* adversity *insert note* 4a. *As You Like It*, ii, i, 12.
141:7	*after* pleasure of *insert* receiving
141:9	*after* myself; *add* for the last week or I should have answered your kind note before. Even to-night I am too nervous to write with any comfort, but I could not let the post-bag (*your* post-bag) go away again without bearing you and Jessie an assurance of my love.	The servant is waiting for my note. I will soon send you a longer one. Till then let this meagre affair be a proof that I am still	Your affectionate	Mary Ann.	Foleshill	Tuesday evening
147:n2	*delete last sentence.*
151:24	*insert MS:* Mr. Gordon N. Ray. *Endorsed:* Signature given away many years ago.
151:29	*after* ken. *insert* and I should have told you so on the very day I received it but that I was in arrear with another friend and my hour for letter-writing was exhausted in writing to her.
152:2	*after* welcome. *insert*	It is among my real joys to think of you as healthy and happy, and how truly should I delight to have you with me again, to see those merry smiles, and receive those unmatched caresses that are quite unique in my experience. Your
152:9	*after* comfort. *add*	I forget nothing belonging to you dear Patty; not anything I know of your home, your friends or your own mind and

body. I am enough initiated into your family affairs to imagine your pleasant anxieties at this season, and I can offer my earnest wishes that your sum of happiness will be increased by witnessing that of your sister, good and interesting as she must be. When you write to Jessie give my fervent love to her, and assure her of my grateful remembrance of all her affection. | This is but a message-like letter, but you have no time just now to read long epistles, nor I to write them. I shall hope when your bustle has subsided to hear of you again—Interrupted by the arrival of Father and Brother. Good bye—a blessing like Joseph's upon you.

155:n9   *add* Cf. *Martin Chuzzlewit*, ch. 3.

164:12   *after* country' *insert note* 3a. Cf. *Martin Chuzzlewit*, ch. 16.

166:17   *after* pen *insert note* 8a. The missing portion of this letter may have contained the passage Edith Simcox reported about the Brabants: "apparently it was a very ugly family—she wrote of them as being 'almost as ugly as I am.'" (Autobigraphy, 14 July 1885.)

168:n4   *add* and Eliza Lynn Linton, *Autobiography of Christopher Kirkland*, 3 vols., 1885, I, 288–289.

169:4   *for* engaged to *read* proposed to by

169:5   *for* the engagement *read* off the correspondence

169:6   for *April* read *May*

177:11   *after* trifles *insert note* 8a. *Winter's Tale*, IV, iii, 26.

181:29   *for* degre *read* degree

183:3   insert *MS:* Mr. Gordon N. Ray.

183:7   *for* was afraid you would *read* am afraid you may

183:13   *after* feel *insert* very

183:15   *after* love *delete* and

183:15   *after* fear. *add* I have just written a few lines to Jessie, and have supposed you to be at Gobions. I hope your dear Mamma's health is better than when Jessie was staying at Coventry. I was deeply concerned to hear that she was ill enough to give you great anxiety. And how have you borne the office of tending Jessie? Not so as to look pale after it, I hope. I shall be more at liberty than I am now by the end of November and I trust I have perpetrated my last sins of omission with respect to correspondence. Do you suppose I love you a whit less, dear Pattie? Think no such thing. I have not a pleasanter image in my mind than you and your love. Give my kind remembrances to your sister Sara, whose little visit has given me the rights of an acquaintance. I allow you to scold me as much as you please so that you will only believe me, | Your true and affectionate | Mary Ann.

184:n2   *add* In reply to an inquiry from Herbert Spencer Mrs. Bray wrote, 27 January 1886: "All that we can recollect of this so-called 'engagement' of George Eliot, is, that in the early days of our friendship with her, she told us of having met a young artist of Leamington who had interested her—that he often came to see her at her father's house at Foleshill, and that by and bye she signified to us that there was likely to be an engagement between them. We never saw him, and we *cannot* recollect his name. Their acquaintance lasted, I believe, only a month or two, and if I remember rightly, she did not seem very happy about it—did not speak much of him to us. One morning, Mrs. Cash tells us, when she went in to Marian, she found her in much distress of mind, for she said she had done wrong in giving too much encouragement to this young man, and feared she had led him to form expectations which she could not fulfil. (We understood afterwards that she had perceived, as she thought, indications of insanity, and their last interview had decided her, to her sorrow, to end their intercourse.) She told Mrs. Cash that she had written to him to tell him this decision, but that in the meantime he had written to her father, making a formal proposal of marriage, saying that although he was poor, he hoped to be able to earn enough to support his wife. The 2 letters had crossed, and hence her distress. But however, it was broken off, and I think we heard that he sometime afterwards had become insane. We told this to Mr. Cross, who did not seem to have heard it before." (BM, Reserve MS 49.)

197:21	*after* nod *insert note* 5a. Horace, *Ars Poetica*, line 359.
209:21	*after* time *insert note* 7a. *As You Like It*, I, i, 124.
217:n8	*for* The Life *read* The | Life
221:2	*insert* 1846 *October* 21 Professor Bücherwurm letter.
	1846 *October* 30 Reviews Michelet and Quinet.
221:3	*for* à Becket's *read* À Beckett's
226:n3	*for* Büchermann *read* Bücherwurm; *for* fictitious authors *read* authors the fictitious
234:31	*for* Mendlessohn *read* Mendelssohn
234:n8	*substitute* The annual May Meetings of the Church of England Missionary Society at Exeter Hall, 372 Strand.
245:25	*for* now *read* meo
247:n4	*substitute* The winged males and females in Robert Paltock's *Peter Wilkins*, 1751.
249:5	*after* Salvador *insert note* 10. J. Salvador, *Jésus Christ et ses doctrines*, 2 vols., 1838. GE's copy is in Dr. Williams's Library.
251:11	*for* servant's *read* serpent's
251:12	*after* bruised *insert note* 7a. Genesis 3:15.
253:30	*after* newspaper *insert note* 4a. *Illustrated London News*, 4 March 1848, p. 151.
255:1	*after* kind. *insert note* la. *Martin Chuzzlewit*, ch. 21.
256:12	*after* eye' *insert note* 4a. Milton, "Ode on Christ's Nativity," line 59. In his Journal Emerson wrote: "Miss Hennell said at Edward Street to Carlyle, 'Do you think, if we should stand on our heads, we should understand better?'" (VII, 1912, p. 478.)
259:n8	*for* Büchermann *read* Bücherwurm
264:17	*after* deep *insert note* 3a. Genesis 7:11.
276:11	*insert Text:* Typed copy made for Miss Elsie Druce, Yale.
276:12	*insert* My dear Fanny
276:13	*for* harmony, without *read* harmony within by entering
276:26	*for* satirise *read* satirize
276:31	*after* there. *add* Father is middling. | With love, from Mary Ann.
289:15	*for* give your *read* give you
295:34	*after* Cornelius *insert note* 6a. MS is clear. Perhaps GE misunderstood

	the name of Peter Carl Grunelius, a banker at Frankfurt-am-Main.
302:29	*for* Odien *read* Odier
303:28	insert *Text:* Typed copy made for Miss Elsie Druce, Yale.
303:29	*insert* Plongeon, Genève	September 6th.	My dear Fanny	
304:1	*for* Mr. Bray *read* Mrs. Bray
304:7	*after* being *insert* note 7a. See I, 301, n. 2.
304:18	*after* heart. *insert* Sara has written to me once and I answered her

immediately. I hoped to hear again from Isaac before this, but I find
I must moderate my expectations.

| 304:21 | *after* me. *insert* I hope Henry's complaints have left him. Tell him |

Willenhall looks pretty to the imagination even at Geneva. So he
will do well not to despise present good. Is young Robert yet with
you? How are Robert and Jane and all their family? I shall be most
glad to know something of them all.

304:27	*after* healthy. *insert* It is either humid or bleak—
304:30	*after* do. *add* Your affectionate	Mary Ann.
312:31	*for* Vaudeuvres *read* Vandeuvres
318:n6	*delete the last sentence.*
328:7	*insert* 107 Rue des Chanoines.	My dear Fanny	
328:33	*after* sins. *insert* Chrissey writes me word of herself now and then, the

dear creature says how sad a Christmas it has been to her. She has
felt her losses more than ever. Your account of Jane and Robert is
quite sad—I fear poor Robert is likely to suffer much from ill health.
Give my love to them when you write. Tell Jane I am always warmly
interested in any news of her. I hear

| 329:2 | *after* Rive. *insert* He is giving a Cours on the subject. |
| 329:6 | *after* horrors. *add* | It will amuse you to know that M. D'Albert is |

painting my portrait—at his request, not mine, as you may suppose. |
Give my love to Henry. Tell him it is just as possible to be out of
spirits on the continent as on an island—under one degree of latitude
as another. A brave heart is the only guarantee all the world over. |
I have not another minute. | Good-bye dear Fanny. | Ever your affec-
tionate | Mary Ann.

332:n5	*for* Alps *read* Jura
336:2	*for* [1 MAY 1850] *read* [24 APRIL 1850]
338:n11	*add* The answer was written by Dr. Brabant. See I, 342, n. 9.
341:n2	*for* library *read* Library
344:12	*for* [JANUARY 1851] *read* [27 FEBRUARY 1851] *and transpose letter to*

I, 346.

| 344:13 | insert *MS:* Yale. *Envelope:* Miss Sibree | The Grange | Stroud. *Post-* |

marks: FE 27 | 1851 | E; STROUD | FE 28 | 1851 | A. (Nuneaton Public
Library.)

| 346:1 | *for* Wesminster *read* Westminster |
| 346:n4 | *add* Geraldine Jewsbury wrote to Jane Carlyle: "She has published |

it at her own expense, so that says much for her sincerity, but the book
makes one feel 'trailed in the mud.' Nightmares are realities—but
hardly real life. Yet the book is clever." (*Selections from the Letters of
Geraldine Endsor Jewsbury*, ed. Mrs. Alexander Ireland, 1892, p. 405.)

| 347:n1 | *substitute* Alfred Hyman Louis (1829?–1915), born in Birmingham, |

was converted to Christianity and baptized by Charles Kingsley. In America in the 1870s he sometimes posed as GHL and pretended intimacy with him and GE, declaring that he was her model for Daniel Deronda. See R. B. Martin, *The Dust of Combat*, 1959, p. 43.

351:20   *insert* Rosehill | June 15.

355:n2   *for* them *read* the Chapmans

369:21   *after* 'extrumpery' *insert note* 6a. In Isaac Bickerstaffe's *The Hypocrite* Mawworm preaches "extrumpery" because he cannot write.

377:n3   *for* 15 *read* 8

VOLUME II

9:n9   *for* had been seeing *read* was soon to see

10:n5   add *Hamlet*, IV, iv, 37.

20:n3   *for* Whateley *read* Whately

21:13   *after* jolly. *insert note* 5a. Mark Tapley in *Martin Chuzzlewit*, ch. 13.

35:n7   *for* 1848 *read* 1847

38:17   insert GE TO BESSIE RAYNER PARKES, LONDON, 25 JUNE 1852. *Envelope:* Berg Collection, New York Public Library. *Address:* Miss Parkes | Saville Row | *Postmark:* 4 EC 4 | JU 25 | 1852 | A. No letter has been found.

43:n3   *insert* Byron, *Don Juan*, Canto I, Dedication, stanza 2.

48:11   *for* S. Brown *read* J. Brown

50:n8   *add* The Albion Hotel, 37 Albion St.

51:19   *after* sinking," *insert note* 9a. Pope, "Peri Bathous, or the Art of Sinking in Poetry."

52:20   insert *Text:* Typed copy made for Miss Elsie Druce, Yale. | Broadstairs | August 22nd. | My dear Fanny

52:27   *for* to old loves *read* to the old loves

52:31   *after* you. *insert* I have been here for nearly two months, but I shall return to town in a few days, so if you are good enough to write, address to me 142 Strand, as usual. All is well

53:2   *after* number. *add* Ever dear Fanny, | Your affectionate You see I have left no room for my name—but it is unnecessary. Such a scribble could come from no one else. Love to Henry.

55:n6   *for* It might be *read* I no longer believe that GE reviewed

59:12   *after* possibles" *insert note* 3a. Voltaire, *Candide*, ch.6.

61:7   *after* darkly *insert note* 8a. I Corinthians 13:12.

61   *delete note* 2.

64:n1   *for* probably by *read* not by GE. *and add* The "History of Belief" was perhaps also to include Edward Miall's *Bases of Belief*, 1853, which is cut up in the Contemporary Literature section, 59 (April 1853), 585–586.

69:n2   *for* 114 *read* 1114.

70:n3   *add* The *Conventry Herald*, 26 November 1852, reports the dinner on 23 November of the Labourers' and Artizans' Friend Society with Charles Bray in the chair. Among the toasts was "Success to the Cooperative Societies of Foleshill."

71:5   *after* saws *add note* 5a. *As You Like It*, II, vii, 156.
73:1   *for* 20 DECEMBER *read* 19 DECEMBER
81:12   *after* stakes *insert note* 3a. Isaiah 54:2.
84:n1   *add* Cf. *Dombey and Son*, ch. 8, "gashliness."
92:n8   *substitute* August Theodor Stamm, author of *Die Religion der That*,
            Hamburg, 1852, boarded at 142 Strand. See Wilfred Stone, *Religion
            and Art of William Hale White*, Stanford [1954], p. 51.
99:14   *for* [APRIL? 1853] *read* [5 MARCH 1853] *and transpose letter to* II, 91.
100:18   *for* [LONDON] *read* [COVENTRY]
102:2   *for* 28 MAY 1853] *read* 19 MARCH 1853] *and transpose letter to* II, 94.
107:n4   *delete last sentence.*
110:n3   *substitute* Bessie Parkes and her friends.
116:7   *for* [4 SEPTEMBER 1853] *read* [21 AUGUST 1853] *and transpose
            letter to* II, 115.
116:n2   *substitute* The record shows rain 16–18 and fair weather 19–20 August
            1853. Sunday was the 21st.
118:n8   *substitute* Robert Vaughan (1795–1868), D. D. Glasgow 1836, Pres-
            ident of the Lancashire Independent College, Manchester, 1843–57,
            edited the *British Quarterly Review* 1845–65. (*DNB*.) He was the
            father of R. A. Vaughan.
124:3   *insert* Typed copy made for Miss Elsie Druce, Yale. | 21 Cambridge
            Street | Hyde Park. | November 7th 1853. | My dear Fanny
124:4   *for* a letter *read* Henry's letter
124:13   *after* you. *insert* I hope Henry will soon be able to send us word that
            you are regaining some of your strength.
124:15   *after* letter. *add* With love to Henry, I am ever, dear Fanny, | Your
            affectionate sister | Marian Evans.
126:2   *for* disprobation *read* disapprobation
126:n3   *for* 2d ed., 2 vols., 1852. *read* 2d issue, 4 vols. in 2, 1852–53.
126:n4   *for* n.3 *read* n.5.
129:17   *for* cense[a]s *read* censes
129:18   *after* grammar *insert note* 1a. *Eton Latin Grammar*, 24th ed., 1850, p. 166.
132:7   *for* 17? *read* 15?
134:n4   *for* 21 July *read* 20 July
138:27   *read* [LONDON, 17 JANUARY 1854]
139:13   *for* "Development" *read* "Developement"
144:n2   *for* uberweltlichen *read* überweltlichen
149:1   *after* make *insert* new
153:n4   *after* closely *add* but omits the end of §7.
156:n3   *add* Keble reads "range apart."
169:n6   *substitute* Peter Cornelius (1824–74), composer of *The Barber of
            Bagdad*, produced by Liszt at Weimar in 1858.
172:15   *after* hand *insert note* 1a. I Kings 18:44.
172:21   *for* 341 *read* 241
173:18   *after* letter *insert note* 5a. GE Journal, 19 August 1854, notes "Letter
            from Miss Parkes."
176:16   *for* shock *read* shock
176:20   *for* honoured *read* honored
176:n6   *for* 13 October *read* 12 October

177:26   *for* honour *read* honor
178:9   *for* 23 OCTOBER 1854 *read* [16 OCTOBER 1854] *and transpose letter to* II, 176
179:20   *for* Mr. and Mrs. *read* You and Mr. Chapman
179:21   *for* position and *read* position or
181:n9   *substitute* At the end of her lost letter to Bray [23 October 1854], quoted in his letter to Combe, 28 October 1854.
183:n1   *for* 16 *read* 23
184:14–15   *for* generally sent *read* always sent me
184:26   *for* are *read* have
186:n1   *for* "Le *read* "La; *for* grand *read* grande
186:n4   *add* Sara's was the 23rd.
197:5   *for* H. M. *read* F. M.
198:3   *insert* GE TO JOHN CHAPMAN, DOVER, 10 APRIL 1855. *MS:* Not found. Maggs Bros. Catalogue 299 (November 1912), item 3872, "concerning her writing of 'Belles Lettres' for the 'Contemporary Literature' and on other matters."
199:13   *for* banks *read* bank
201:10   *for* Miss Fanny West. *read* Mr. Raymond M. Bennett.
202:11   *for* Miss Fanny West. *read* Mr. Gordon N. Ray.
205:n6   *for* Broughman's *read* Brougham's
214:n9   *add* Mrs. Bray wrote to Frances Power Cobbe, 21 May 1895: "The case of her union with Mr. Lewes was quite an exceptional one. . . . Her ⟨mar⟩ union with Lewes was marriage in the highest sense, and her own marriage ring was a more sacred symbol than are many wedding rings. After Lewes's death she spoke of their 'life together of 25 years of ever-growing affection.' And the fruits of that 'life' were, her own works, Lewes's Philosophical works, a home to himself and his sons, who always called her 'Mother,' excellent education, and settlement for them in life; comfortable provision for Mrs. Lewes, who had refused to return to her husband, and expressed the wish that he 'could marry Miss Evans,' although divorce from herself was for many reasons impracticable." (Huntington Library.)
215:14   *after* before," *insert note* 10 Cf. Philippians 3:13.
216:n3   *after* Lewes *insert* a poet and actor
218:11   after *woman* insert ⟨were known to be the writer⟩
218:n9   *for* "regular *read* "other
222:n8   *substitute* The play was *The Fox Who Got the Grapes*, adapted by GHL at Weimar from *Alexandre chez Apelles*, by Bayard and Dupin, produced in Paris 27 December 1852. GHL rewrote it as a story, "Mrs. Beauchamp's Vengeance," *Blackwood's*, 89 (May 1861), 537–554. MS of the play at Yale. See Edgar Hirshberg, *George Henry Lewes*, New York, 1970, pp. 51–52.
225:8   *after* stakes," *insert note* 8a. Isaiah 54:2.
228:22   *after* clergyman" *insert note* 4a. Tennyson, "The May Queen," Conclusion, line 12.
228:n9   *for* 1851 *read* 1941.
232:n5   *substitute* GE always wrote Croft; the directories read Craft.
242:35   *after* blackberries," *add note* 7a. *I Henry IV*, II, iv, 235.

243:31   *for* Broderie *read* Broderip *and add note* 9a. William John Broderip
            (1789–1859), lawyer and naturalist. His collection of shells was
            deposited in the British Museum.
243:36   *for* thus *read* this
244:21   *after* weeds," *insert note* 10. "Call us not weeds—we are flow'rs of the
            sea." E. L. Aveline, *The Mother's Fables in Verse*, new ed., [1861], p.
            157.
258:n8   *add* See "Silly Novels by Lady Novelists," *Westminster Review*, 66
            (October 1856), p. 446.
298:13   *after* Gwythir *add note* 8a. John Gwyther (1801?–73), born in Bristol,
            admitted pensioner at St. John's College, Cambridge, 1823. From
            1831–41 he was Curate at Chilvers Coton, where his first wife Emma
            died 4 November 1836.
299:n9   *for* 1st ed. *read* publication in *Blackwood's*.
300:15   *for* [in] *read* [for]
300:16–17   *for* [RICHMOND, 24 FEBRUARY 1857] read [GOREY, 30 JUNE
            1857] *and transpose letter to* ii, 359.
301:7   *after* copy *add note* 3a. GE's copy of *Christianity and Infidelity*, 1857, is in
            Dr. Williams's Library, inscribed "Dr. Pollian ab Achate suo fido |
            Feb. 22nd 1857."
304:n2   *add* Though GHL's Literary Receipts lists a payment to him in
            February 1857, GE may have written this notice.
307:16   *for* 9 *read* 2 *and transpose letter to* ii, 304.
317:33   *for* please give *read* please to give
317:n3   *delete*.
319:n7   *for* the Rev. Henry Bristow Wilson . . . (*DNB*) *read* Mark Pattison.
            (*DNB*.)
322:n4   *substitute* The description occurs in ch. 1.
331:28   *for* GHL's *read* Cross's
333:23   *for* honor *read* honour
335:6   *after* Oaks *insert note* 4a. The Derby was run at Epsom Downs 28 May,
            the Oaks, 30 May 1859. Blink Bonny won both races.
345:n9   *substitute* Edward Henry Stanley, 15th Earl of Derby (1826–93).
349:12   *for* GHL's *read* Cross's
349:13   *for* "truly" instead of "faithfully" *read* "faithfully" instead of "truly"
349:30   *for* at present unable *read* unable at present
350:22   *for* circumstances *read* circumstance
352:29   *after* Town" *insert note* 8a. Pope, "A Farewell to London," line 1.
357:10   *for* Trescaid *read* Trescaw [i.e. Tresco]
358:32   *for* Jenne's *read* Jeune's
364:13   *for* [14 JULY *read* [16 JUNE *and transpose letter to* ii, 353.
369:n6   *add* GHL reviewed it in the *Leader*, 4 July 1857, p. 641.
376:n4   *delete last sentence and add* In his *Charge Delivered to the Clergy of the
            London Diocese*, 14 *October* 1842, Blomfield noted that candles "have
            always been retained in our chapels royal, in cathedrals, and in col-
            lege chapels; and I see no objection to them, provided that the candles
            are not burning, except when the church is lighted up for evening
            service." (p. 33.)
378:2   *for* [23? AUGUST ? *read* [9? AUGUST *and transpose letter to* ii, 373.

382:12   *for* revising *read* reviewing
385:n4   *for* 6 May *read* 8 May
391:2   insert *1857 December 6* "How I Came to Write Fiction"
397:15   *after* out *insert note* 8a. Cf. Horace, *Epistles*, i, x, 24.
412:n6   *read* letter to GHL, 7 December 1857, at McGill University.
417:25   *after* Mudie *insert note* 3a. Joseph Langford wrote to John Blackwood,
            4 January 1858: "Mudie thinks the book in a reprint ought to have
            been 2 vols. *fscap* like the Heir of Redclyffe. I agree with him that such
            would have been the better form as I think the book would then have
            got beyond the libraries into the hands of private purchasers, which
            would have done more to get up a reputation for George Eliot. As it
            is however I think the result will leave us with just enough copies to
            enable us to see what sort of hold the book has got upon the public
            before we are called upon to reprint." (NLS.)
420:3   *after* Moore. *insert* Now at Hollins College.
426:27   insert *MS:* Mr. Gordon N. Ray. *Endorsed:* Marianne Evans. |
            Richmond | January 26.58 | Dear Friend | Plenty of time for you to
            come and see us (more than once, I hope,) for we shall not go to
            Germany till we are secure from frost and snow. I sent
427:2   *after* nothing *insert* I hope, now Wilson is going to write the section 1.
            for April,[6a] that he may forget the present sources of repulsion and
            continue to be a contributor. | It is
            6a. Henry Bristow Wilson had reconsidered and agreed to write
            "Theology and Philosophy," section 1 of the Contemporary
            Literature reviews, *Westminster Review*, 69 (April 1858), 557–577.
427:13   *for* parole [puerile?] *read* harsh
427:14   *after* error *add* But my pen has taken to scratching and warns me that
            I am writing quite gratuitously—perhaps obtrusively. | Ever yours
            truly | M. E.
427:n7   *add* See G. S. Haight, "George Meredith and the *Westminster Review*,"
            Modern Language Review, 53 (January 1958), 1–16.
434:n1   *read* John William Parker, Jr. (1820–61).
438:n2   *add* She was a friend of Charlotte Cushman, to whose Romeo she once
            played Juliet.
440:n5   *for* 4 *read* 5
443:n3   *after* GE *insert* and GHL
447:n7   *delete 1st sentence; for* 11th *read* 12th.
453:24   *for* Bodenstadt *read* Bodenstedt
456:n7   *substitute* Call's generally sympathetic account ends at p. 324 with a
            note: "This article being the production of two authors, we indicate
            the point of division by the blank space above." Chapman then adds
            a longer attack (pp. 324–350) on Comte's Religion of Humanity
            from a Theist's point of view. With his article "Medical Reform"
            (pp. 478–530), an attack on the monopoly held by the Royal Colleges
            of Physicians and Surgeons, Chapman wrote more than 75 pages of
            the April number.
457:13   *for* [them] *read* well
462:n3   *for* 1859 *read* 1858
475:n3   for *Kleinen* read *Kleine*

485:2   *for* [OCTOBER 1858] *read* [27 SEPTEMBER 1858] *and transpose letter to* ii, 482.
491:14   *for* [OCTOBER 1858] *read* [1 NOVEMBER 1858]
491:n7   for *littéraire* read *littéraires*
492:10   for *MS:* read *Text:* Copy in Blackwood's Letter Book.
494:3   read *MS:* National Library of Scotland.
494:8   *MS omits* namely
502:15   *after* girl *insert note* 2a. Mary Voce. See *Adam Bede*, ed. G. S. Haight, New York, 1948, p. vii, for the account from the *Nottingham Journal*, 20 March 1802.
504:27   *after* Dinah, *add note* 9. Ch. 52.
504:n8   *for* 27 *read* 48.

VOLUME III

1:14   for *20* read *10*
1:15   insert *1859 June 20   Adam Bede*, 4th ed., 2 vols.
1:20   *for* 3d *read* 4th
1:24   *for* 3d *read* 4th
4:6   *for* WANDSWORTH *read* RICHMOND
10:n6   after *Bede* insert by [Caroline E. S. Norton]
12:1   *for* RICHMOND *read* WANDSWORTH
12:n2   *for* GHL *read* GE
18:21   *after* promiscuously," *add note* 8a. Cf. Samuel Rowlands, *Knave of Clubbes*, line 37.
21:n9   *for* Edbell *read* Ebdell
23:n5   *add* The critic was E. B. Hamley.
39:7   *after* indeed. *insert note* 8a. In the debate 8 March 1859 on the case of the slaving vessel *Charles et Georges* Charles Buxton remarked that no doubt the Earl of Malmsbury "would wish that his conduct, as the farmer's wife said in *Adam Bede*, could be 'hatched over again and hatched different.'" (*Hansard's Parliamentary Debates*, 3d ser., 152 (1859), 1507.
45:18   *for* [11 APRIL 1859] *read* [9 APRIL 1859] *and transpose letter to* ii, 43.
47:30   *for* grl *read* girl
57:19   *after* Sarah. *insert note* 9a. See iii, 117.
58:n1   *add* and in the *Leader*, 23 April 1859, p. 524.
60:n2   *after* 1859, *insert* i, 67,
64:10   *for* manuscripts *read* manuscript
72:2   *for* [21 MAY 1859] *read* [14 MAY 1859] *and transpose letter to* iii, 67.
74:10   *for* I really *read* really I
79:8   *after* Luzern *insert note* 7a. Cf. Wordsworth, "Yarrow Unvisited," line 56.
107:n4   add *Blackwood's* 81 (March 1857), 322, *reads* "milk the geese; yer silly!"
107:n6   *substitute* Kept during her travels with Dr. Bodichon in America 1857–58. Portions published in *English Woman's Journal*, 2 (October

1858), 5 (March 1860), and 8 (October–December 1861). See Hester
Burton, *Barbara Bodichon*, [1949], pp. 115–131. Edited from MS
(Yale) by Joseph W. Reed Jr., in *Barbara Leigh Smith Bodichon. An
American Diary 1857–8*, [1972].

113:29   *after* dive *insert note* 10. The earliest use of the word noted in the *OED*
           is 1882.
117:n7   *for* Lady Saba *read* [Saba], Lady Holland
118:n6   *add* ; 4th ed., I, 398.
120:n9   *for* yet *read* set
121:n3   *add* But my friend Alan Bell informs me that the house, which is on
           Lord Crawford's Balcarres estate, is properly spelled Gibliston.
128:n7   *for* Frederick *read* Frederic
133:18   *for* look *read* looks
137:n3   *for* 2d *read* 3d
139:7   insert *1859 September 26*
139:10   *for* 3d *read* 4th
139:28   *delete*
141:25   *for* Abergile *read* Abergele
148:n7   *add* See 25 November [1859].
149:n1   *substitute* Jacob Lodewijk Coenraad Schroeder van der Kolk, whose
           Bau und Functionen der Medulla Spinalis, tr. from the Dutch by F. W.
           Theile, Braunschweig, 1859, is quoted in GHL's *Physiology*, II, 85 et al.
151:3   *insert* GE's 1st draft at Princeton has many minor variants and omits
           the final sentence about writing *only* for money.
162:34   *for* letter *read* letters
165:16   *after* morning, *insert note* 10. "Since the last entry there has been much
           that might profitably have been chronicled had I not been too busy
           and too lazy. We took a trip to Newark and Gainsboro, on artistic
           grounds, Polly wanting to lay the scene of her new novel on the Trent.
           This little expedition we enjoyed very much, and she found fruitful.
           We took a boat from Gainsboro and rowed down the Idle, which we
           ascended on foot some way and walked back to Gainsboro." (GHL
           Journal, November 1859.)
177:16   *for* weary *read* heavy
179:8   *after* Charlie!" *add note* 8a. A Jacobite song quoted in *Redgauntlet*, ch. 11.
182:n7   *for* 3d *read* 4th
188:n8   *transpose last two lines.*
195:n10   *add* The baby was Agnes's daughter Mildred (b. 21 May 1857).
           Vivian Byam Lewes (1852–1915) was the son of GHL's brother
           Edward.
196:21   *after* Burke." *insert note* 11. After one of Burke's speeches Mr. Cruger
           "exclaimed earnestly, in the language of the counting-house, 'I say
           ditto to Mr. Burke!'" (Sir James Prior, *Life of Burke*, 1824, ch. 5.)
197:23   *for* fool *read* goose
197:n4   *add* In "German Wit: Heinrich Heine" GE wrote, "'consider what
           her flattery was worth before she choked him with it.'" (*Westminster
           Review*, 65 (January 1856), 14.
198:1   *for* Porters *read* Portico
198:18   *for* You *read* You

198:n6   *for* 1849 *read* 1848
210:n3   *add* It was by Miss Elizabeth Julia Hasell (1830–87) of Dalemain, near Penrith.
211:11   insert *MS:* Berg Collection, New York Public Library.
213:n6b   *add* Simpson wrote, 27 January 1879: "Poor George Eliot, how the thought of her haunts me! I heard that she had to appear in Court to prove Lewes's will and to sign 'Marian Evans.' Could not the possibility of such a trial have been provided against?" (F. D. Tredrey, *The House of Blackwood*, 1954, p. 202.)
213:n7   *add* It was by Ann Mozley (1809–91). See her *Essays from Blackwood's*, 1892, pp. 304–344.
214:n10   *substitute* Scott, *Marmion*, Canto VI, stanza 32.
218:17   *for* perecive *read* perceive
233:n9   *add* for *Once a Week.*
236:17   insert *MS:* The late Mr. W. E. Stockhausen. | Holly Lodge, South Fields | December 20. 59 | My dear Sir |
236:25   *add* John Blackwood Esq.
237:18   *for* plently *read* plenty
245:3   *for* opportunty *read* opportunity
247:n2   *add* John Craig, *A New . . . Dictionary*, 2 vols., 1849.
254:12   *after* Despair, *add note* 8a. "I am reading old Bunyan again after the long lapse of years, and am profoundly struck with the true genius manifested in the simple, vigorous, rhythmic style." (GE Journal, 25 November 1859.)
256:n6   *substitute* In the penultimate paragraph of Ch. 2 GE changed "lymphatic fretfulness" to "feeble fretfulness."
260:n4   *for* a thick *read* as thick
274:n6   *add* Martha Baker, born at Brighton 18 May 1814, is described in the 1851 Census return as nurse, unmarried servant. I have found no record of her marriage.
277:23   *after* 22 *add note* 8a. The date is clear. Blackwood may have meant 24.
284:30   *after* unvisited." *add note* 3a. Cf. Wordsworth, "Yarrow Unvisited."
287:6   *after* air" *insert note* 5a. Shakespeare, *Sonnet* 70.
298:n8   *for* 4th impression *read* 5th
304:27   *after* Martha, *insert note* 10. "Since last week we have been in great discomfort with our servant, detecting all kinds of dishonesty and disagreeables. Today we went into town after the character of our new servant, Martha Bunn, which being satisfactory, we engaged her to come tonight." (GHL Journal, 15 June 1859.)
307:n6   *for* 5 March *read* 4 March
308:17   *for* Carney's [?] *read* Canning's
308:18   *after* story. *insert note* 7a. George Canning, "The Friend of Humanity and the Knife-Grinder": "Story! God bless you! I have none to tell, Sir."
310:n2   *add* GE's copy in Dr. Williams's Library is inscribed "Marian Evans Lewes. To the dearly-beloved Translator of Feuerbach's 'Essence of Christianity'—in grateful remembrance of how much I owed to her during the season of happy intercourse which formed the 'German' period of our lives. S.S.H. May 22nd 1860."

314:n1   *for* 4 May *read* 14 March
317:n9   *for* 4 May *read* 14 March
329:12   *On the verso Mme Bodichon wrote:* Miss B. Edwards | Care of A. Betham
          Esq. | 65 Englefield Road | London N.
344:17   *after* "contrairiness" *insert note* 3a. Mrs. Gummidge in *David Copper-
          field*, ch. 3.
349:25   *for* 26 *read* 27
358:13   *for* find *read* finds
372:14   *after* Saturday *insert note* 1a. Miss Hennell came on Saturday, bringing
          a copy of her *The Early Christian Anticipation of an Approaching End of
          the World*, 1860, inscribed "Marian Evans Lewes with S.S.H.'s love.
          Jany 19th 1861." (Dr. Williams's Library.)
373:n4   *add* Owen's book with title page dated 1860, is inscribed "To the
          Author of Adam Bede, from an obliged friend." (Dr. Williams's
          Library.)
379:14   *add* My love is often visiting you. Entertain it well.
387:5   insert *MS:* Yale.
387:9   *for* anxious *read* dubious
387:12   *for* recall *read* recal
387:13   *after* again. *insert* Herewith Spon[taneous] Comb[ustion]. I shall
          finish Petherick in time for this number, and you can use it if you are
          in want of it, or let it stand over. I intend to give myself a holiday as
          soon as the book is over.
388:n1   *add* Mrs. Hay painted a scene in Florence when Savonarola during
          the carnival was preaching a crusade against vanities, but omitted
          him, finding no record that he walked in these processions. (Charles
          R. Weld, *Florence the New Capital*, 1867, pp. 228–229.)
393:n9   *add* See also G. S. Haight, "Dickens and Lewes on Spontaneous Com-
          bustion," *Nineteenth-Century Fiction*, 10 (June 1955), 53–63.
398:8   *for* come *read* comes
401:n1   *for* [in London] *read* [in Edinburgh]
414:25   *for* inutilies *read* inutiles
424:n1   *add* He wrote: "Inglese—grateful for the hospitable attention of these
          benevolent monks and pleased with that courtesy which from the
          severity of their order might not have been expected. 1837 *May* 29th."
          (GHL's Travel Notebook, Yale.)
427:n8   Blackwood wrote to his wife: "George Eliot was extremely delighted
          with the whole affair, which she caused others to enjoy so much. The
          Gunner [Sir Edward B. Hamley] was at his best, which cannot be
          easily beat." (*John Blackwood*, p. 65.)
431:2   *for* [JUNE 1861] *read* [30 MAY 1862] *and transpose letter to* IV, 40.
431:3   insert *MS:* The John Work Garrett Library, the Johns Hopkins
          University.
431:4   *read* **16, Blandford Square,** | **N.W.** | Friday Evening.
431:10   *after* disqualification *insert* , together with what I supposed was the
          etymology of the phrase.
431:12   for *Commune* read *Comune*
431:16   for *piccolo* read *picciolo*
431:18   for *Manelli* read *Manuelli*

431:n4   *add* The phrase occurs in *Romola*, ch. 1.

432:1   *for* phrase[s] *read* phrases

432:4   *for* Macchiavelli *read* Machiavelli

432:9   *for* recognised *read* recognized

432:n8   add *Romola*, ch. 5.

435:18   insert *MS:* The John Work Garrett Library, the Johns Hopkins University, on the same sheet with GHL to T. A. Trollope, 5 July 1861.

435:19   *delete*

435:20   *for* Dear *read* My dear

436:3   *for* this world *read* the world

436:8   *for* off that spine *read* off the effects of that spring

436:11   *for* our own home *read* our home

440:22   *after* influences. insert note 6a. *Measure for Measure*, iii, i, 9.

443:2   *for* [1861] *read* [1862] *and transpose letter to* iv, 52.

451:11   *after* Apennines insert note 4a. Cf. *King John*, i, 1, 202.

451:22   *after* sycamores," insert note 4b. Tennyson, "Audley Court," line 16.

453:n9   *delete*

456:13   *for* Penmæmawr *read* Penmænmawr

457:19   *for* Editor? *read* Editor"

458:n1   *delete 1st sentence*

470:19   *after* people." insert note 10. *Macbeth*, i, vii, 33.

471:15   *for* MRS. *read* MR. AND MRS.

471:24–25   *transpose to follow line 14*

472:n7   *add* Also a believer in spiritualism, Gully testified to D. D. Home's floating about the room. See the *Spiritualist Magazine*, 2 (1861), 63–66.

473:30   *after* toe *insert note* 2a. Thackeray's *Roundabout Papers*, No. 16, *Cornhill*, 4 (November 1861), p. 384, describes the slaves as well treated. No. 17 (pp. 754–760) gives a humorously exaggerated account of his journey from New Orleans to St. Louis.

474:n5   *for* Ferguson *read* Fergusson

485:n9   *add* In "Shadows of the Coming Race," *Theophrastus Such*, ch. 17, p. 303, GE refers to "the ancient edge-tool . . . which we already at Sheffield see paring thick iron as if it were mellow cheese."

VOLUME IV

5:n4   *read* Count Carlo Arrivabene Valenti Gonzaga (1824–74).

12:16   *after* Music *insert note* 7a. Henry Purcell's music (1690) for the Dryden-Davenant adaptation of *The Tempest* (1667).

17:n2   *for* latter *read* former

33:4   *after* "blacks" *insert note* 3a. Flakes of soot.

34:20   add *MS:* National Library of Scotland shows only three minor variants from the copy.

33:12   *for* 1862 *read* [1863]. *MS is clear; watermark 1863; transpose to* iv, 85.

36:n7   *add* Langford wrote to William Blackwood 26 July 1877: "George Eliot's books sell more like Halloway's Pies [Pills] than like books, and it pays to keep them before the public by advertising. I often think that not one out of a thousand would have kept up this connection as your Uncle did when there was such ground for discontent at her being taken away from us." (F. D. Tredrey, *The House of Blackwood*, 1954, p. 262.)

40:n10   *add* In a letter to Alfred W. Johnston, 10 August 1882, Leighton wrote: "In answer to your letter I write to say that G. Eliot, though I saw her often while I was illustrating her book, never to my recollection offered any suggestion as to the appearance of the characters in *Romola*. It may interest you to know that she never could tell me of a subject or a situation a number or two *ahead*. The detail was evolved as she went on and imposed itself on her as fact." (Yale.)

56:21   *after* analysis of *insert* [analogous?]

56:23   *after* least *insert* [last?]

60:7   *after* dinner. *insert note* 3a. "Mr. Spencer lunched with us and we walked with him to the Zoo to see the Catfish and the Limulus." (GE Journal, 13 October 1862.)

94:n1   *for Robi read Roba*

102:n3   *for* Esther *read* Jane Esther

112:4   *for* Wilson, *read* Williams [?],

125:n2   *after* 19. *add* Princeton.)

129:n8   *for* Milne's *read* Milnes's

132:20   *for* [FEBRUARY? 1864?] *read* [AUGUST? 1871] *and transpose to* v, 182.

132:n3a   *substitute* GHL wrote this scenario after reading Carl Dietrich Ludwig Felix von Rumohr's "Der letzte Savello," 1834, reprinted in *Deutscher Novellenschatz*, ed. P. Heyse and H. Kurz, Munich, II (1871), 125–209. (GHL Diary 2 August 1871.) The Savello-Cassandra episode is on pp. 194–209. GHL has invented the melodramatic plot of Act II; in the original Giustiniano flees and Cassandra lives on. The MS is written in pencil by GHL and traced over in ink by GE. Charles Lewes told Edith Simcox that the play was to be written some day if they went to Sicily (Autobiography, 6 April 1884.)

134:33   *after* influences *insert note* 5a. *Measure for Measure*, III, i, 9.

143:18   *after* holiday *insert* ⟨and our beloved tête à tête existence is at an end. We are fond of that dear good boy, but we can't help being fond of his absence. This is in the nature of things.⟩ *and add note* 5a. Edith Simcox copied the passage in her Autobiography, December 1881, when Mme Bodichon lent her the letters.

163:2   *for* [20? *read* [18

185:24   *for* days *read* doings

185:n2   *for* Milne's *read* Milnes's

186:6   *for* vomiting *read* vomissement

186:13   *after* Mutter *insert note* 6. "Mutter" is written by GE.

201:22   *after* truths." *insert note* 1a. Keats, *Hyperion*, II, 203.

213:n4   *read* was a granddaughter of Dr.

227:n9   *substitute* Auguste Comte, *Synthèse subjective, ou systeme universel des conceptions propres à l'état normal de l'humanité*, Vol. I, Paris, 1856.

227:30   *after* heart *insert note* 10. Cf. Charles Dibdin, "Poor Jack": "For they say there's a Providence sits up aloft | To keep watch for the life of poor Jack!"

232:11   *after* influences. *add note* 4a. *Measure for Measure*, III, i, 9.

233:21   *for* resquest *read* request

251:22   *after* 31. *insert note* 8a. MS is clear. Cross corrects to 30.

273:24   *after* hideous." *insert note* 2a. *Hamlet*, I, iv, 54.

281:n8   *add* It was by E. S. Dallas.

289:n7   *add* and Harrison's comment on his proposal in his article on Leslie
           Stephen's *George Eliot*, *Positivist Review*, 10 (August 1902), 161–162.

321:n5   *delete 1st sentence.*

321:n6   *add Charlie Thornhill*, 3 vols., 1863, was by Charles Clarke.

322:n7   *add* The MS of "Brother Jacob" is at Yale; that of "The Lifted Veil"
           has disappeared.

330:13   *after* day, *insert note* 1. *Twelfth Night*, v, i, 401.

333:4   *after* Brownings *insert note* 5a. Oscar Browning and his mother.

363:37   *after* lived *insert note* 8a. *Hamlet*, III, iv, 135.

367:16   *after* thee *insert note* 5a. John 21:17

368:17   *after* shall *insert* [should?]

369:17   *substitute MS:* Mr. Arthur Carrington Ouvry. and add *Envelope:*
           Mrs. Lewes | 25 Church Row | Hampstead | London N.W. *Postmarks:*
           GODSHILL | C | JY 5 | 67; SOUTHAMPTON | JY 6 | 67; LONDON N.W | S7
           | JY 6 | 67.

375:8   *for* Thornton *read* Taunton *and add note* 3. William Frederick Taunton,
           printer in Conventry.

379:11   *insert* GE TO MRS. FREDERICK LEHMANN, LONDON, 15
           JULY 1867 | *MS:* W. & R. Chambers Ltd., Edinburgh. *Envelope:*
           Mrs. F. Lehmann | The Woodlands | Highgate | N. *Postmark:* LONDON
           N.W | 5 | JY 15 | 67. *The letter has not been found.*

395:19   *after* nécessaire" *add note* 4. Voltaire, *Le Mondain*, line 21.

397:n4   *read* published November 1868–February 1869,

401:19   *for* [22? NOVEMBER 1867] *read* 20 NOVEMBER 1867; *add MS:*
           Girton College. *Envelope:* Miss Davies | 17 Cunningham Place | N.W.
           Postmark: LONDON N.W | NOV 20 | 68. | My dear Miss Davies

401:26   *add* Yours sincerely | M. E. Lewes. | Miss Davies.

440:16   *for* 10 MAY 1868 *read* [17 MAY 1868] *and transpose letter to* IV, 442.

441:n4   *for* 20 *read* 21.

453:n3   *substitute* Clifford Harrison wrote to GHL 1 May [1877] recom-
           mending Arthur Thomas to write an opera on *The Spanish Gypsy*. "He
           is good enough to wish me to write a libretto for him—but this I have
           not time or skill for." (Yale.) A dramatization by Garrita Barry Nash
           is in the theater collection at Harvard.

453:18   *after* back *insert note* 5b. A copy in the Jerome Kern sale, 1929, item
           500, inscribed on the half-title "To Mr. Deutsch with the best wishes
           of his friend George Eliot" is in the original blue cloth binding.

466:23   *for* session *read* season

467:19   add *MS:* Girton College. *Envelope:* Miss Davies | 17 Cunningham
           Place | N.W. *Postmark:* LONDON N.W | 2 | AU 8 | 68. | **The Priory,21.
           North Bank, Regents Park.** | August 8.68. | My dear Miss Davies

467:23   *after* eye' *insert note* 7a. Coleridge, *The Ancient Mariner*, stanza 1.

468:35   *add* Yours sincerely | M. E. Lewes.

476:n5   *read* Henry Edger (1820?–88).
489:n4   *for* before 1840 *read* between 1826 and 1840.
494:7   *for* me *read* us.

VOLUME V

4:22   for [14? JANUARY 1869] *read* [7 JANUARY 1869] *and transpose.*
16:17   *after* Rhone *insert note* 6. Byron, *Childe Harold*, III, 71.
21:11   insert *Envelope* (Nuneaton Public Library): Mrs. Trollope | Villa
          Trollope | Florence. *Postmarks:* NAPOLI | 1 APR | 69 | 11M; FIRENZE | 3
          APR | 69 | 6M. *Endorsed.* H. G. Lewes | 1869.
21:n6   *for* Moriz *read* Moritz
24:33   *for* be *read* lie
26:n9   *after* Comte," *substitute* 11 (April 1869), 407–418. Huxley's reply,
32:8   *for* the two *read* two
32:13   *for* gypsy *read* Gypsy
32:14   *for* gypsies *read* Gypsies
32:20   *for* die *read* Die
32:24   *for* the other *read* in the other
32:25   *after* brain *insert* generally
32:n8   *add* Lytton to John Forster, San Juan de Luz, 5 August 1868: "I have
          written to Reeve offering to review the Spanish Gypsy for the Edin-
          burgh. I fancy that if he intends to review it, he will long ere this have
          made other arrangements, and I am not very eager to be taken at my
          word. The book has strongly interested me, but I have not either time
          or space to talk about it now. The faults are obvious I think—its
          genius still more so. I think it a magnificent failure, better than many
          small successes."
              Forster replied, 14 August 1868: "I hope you won't write on the
          Spanish Gipsy for Edinburgh or anything else. I too think it a failure
          but (I suspect) a more pretentious one than you think it. Such an
          enormous break-down both of character and purpose in a piece of so
          much ambition I am indeed not acquainted with in literature."
          (MSS Lady Hermione Cobbold.)
32:n9   *for* 3d *read* 5th
33:11   *for* Gitanélla" *read* Gitanilla"
33:14   *for* error *read* errors
37:n2   *after* Druce. *insert* Now at Yale.)
38:1   GE TO FREDERICK LOCKER, LONDON, 19 MAY 1869 | *En-
          velope:* F. Locker Esqure | 91 Victoria Street. *Postmark:* LONDON N.W |
          5 | MY 19 | 69. (Harvard.) *Letter not found.*
38:n5   *for* 1859 *read* 1858
39:n5   *add* For further discussion of Casaubon see John Sparrow, *Mark
          Pattison and the Idea of a University,*Cambridge, 1967; reviewed by G. S.
          Haight in *Notes and Queries*, 213 (May 1968), 191–194; Betty Askwith,
          Lady Dilke, 1969. Richard Ellmann revived the subject in "Doro-
          thea's Husbands," *TLS*, 16 February 1973, touching off a lively
          correspondence with letters from John Sparrow, S. A. Leavy, E. and

B. Jones, Margaret Maison, Miriam Allott, Leon Edel, Philip Collins, Barbara Hardy, and G. S. Haight, which ran until 22 June 1973.

41:n1   *delete* GE's letter is at Yale.

46:n8a   *delete last sentence*

67:24   *after* hostesses. *insert note* 1. "The farm was run by two brothers, Thomas (1839–1933) and James Steer (1843–1922), and their three sisters, Marian, Patience, and Hannah. (Information from James's daughter Miss Doris Steer of East Grinstead, 1969.)

72:14   *for* units *read* unites

74:3   *for* Huntington Library *read* Berg Collection, New York Public Library.

78:n8   *for* He was as *read* He was at

78:n8   *add* Now at Duke University. Published by P. F. Baum, *Duke University Library Notes*, No. 34 (June 1959), 18–19.

84:n2   *for* Journal *read* Diary

91:11   *for* mahlspeise *read* mehlspeise

100:10   *after* Haddington *insert* [Headington]

107:n8   *delete 1st sentence.*

115:n4   *after* lives, *add* including that of Commander Richard Sheepshanks.

139:20   *after* Ticknor *insert note* 7a. Mr. Simon Nowell-Smith informs me that when B. H. Ticknor joined Osgood, Ticknor & Co., the name became James R. Osgood & Co.

141:26   *for* 25 *read* 24

141:28   *for* 24 *read* 25

143:n1   *for* 1839 *read* 1838

152:28   *after* Algiers. *add note* 9a. During the insurrection, which was suppressed in August 1871.

161:n1   *add* Cf. Mirah in *Daniel Deronda*, ch. 17.

167:n1   *add* Blackwood means Fred Vincy.

170:29   *insert* MS: Sold at Sotheby's 29 October 1975, item 186.

174:12   *insert* MS: Princeton.

174:13   *Address is written, not printed.*

174:19   *after* Romŏla *insert* *There is a mountain named Romŏla in sight from Florence.

174:22   *delete* ('Romola')

174:27   *for* Shakspeare *read* Shakespeare

174:27   *after* glasses *add note* 4a. *The Vicar of Wakefield*, ch. 9.

174:28   *for* 'Romola' *read* Romola *and for* quack *read* Quack

175:4   *for* that *read* which

181:n7   *add* Mrs. Tennyson wrote to Hallam, 29 August 1871: "Papa will not walk with Lionel. I got him to take Mr. and Mrs. Barlow down the hill yesterday, and on Saturday [26th] he walked home with Mr. and Mrs. Lewes. . . . I called there and stayed some time and then left him and he read some of 'Maud.' Mrs. Lewes said that his reading ought to be taken down in notes recitative-wise, but that will not give his magnificent voice with its delicate intonations." (*Letters of Emily Lady Tennyson*, ed. J. O. Hoge, [1974], p. 277.)

199:18   *after* delay *add note* 2a. Cf. *Paradise Lost*, IV, 311.

217:n5   *after* birthday *add* and GE's 52d.

221:10   *for* 23 *read* 24
224:n6   *add* It was by R. H. Hutton.
228:25   *for* I *read* It
238:n2   *add* He is mentioned in *Middlemarch*, ch.38.
246:5   *after* belief *insert* [Blackwood's copyist may have missed a line here.]
247:n9   *add* Edith Simcox was the reviewer.
261:25   *after* experience *add note* 2a. Main wrote 26 March 1872 that Caleb Garth is "one of those characters which make one proud to be called a man.... It is Adam Bede, the strong British workman, returned upon us in spiritual guise." (NLS.)
264:10   *for* 6 APRIL 1872 *read* [6 MAY 1872] *and transpose to* v, 270.
268:9   *for* honour *read* honor
268:10   *after* contradiction *insert* or reply
268:15   *for* expectation *read* expectations
271:23   *for* If *read* Of
280:16   *for* sense by *read* sensory
284:n3   *for* eldest *read* younger. Cf. v, 296.
290:n7   *after* *Dorfgeschichten*, read Mannheim, 1848; reprinted in Vol. vii of the *Deutscher Novellenschatz*, 1872.
299:21   insert *MS:* McGill University.
299:22   *insert* Eversley | Red Hill | Surrey | 17th August 1872 | My dear Sir |
299:24   *after* works *read* that—being now away from home and from all chance of seeing Reviews—it is only
300:5   *after* much *add* and although we both desire all criticism, as all literature, to be kept as free as possible from personal influences, she feels with me that to leave unacknowledged so precious a token of sympathy as that of your article would be to do violence to our feelings. Accept then our gratitude for your kindly feeling, and its public expression! | I had already been arrested by writing of yours in the 'Fortnightly'[6a] and made some ineffectual inquiries as to 'who you were'—little suspecting how near your spirit moved to mine! | Ever yours faithfully | G. H. Lewes | Prof. E. Dowden.

        6a. Dowden had written five articles in the *Fortnightly* since January 1869 on Lamennais, Landor, Marlowe, Quinet, and de Laprade.
305:18   *for* [6 SEPTEMBER 1872] *read* [13 SEPTEMBER 1872] *and transpose letter to* v, 309.
310:n4   *for* sister *read* aunt
311:n5   *substitute* William Cyples's *Permutation of Ideas*, privately printed, 1868. GHL refers to it in *Mind as a Function of the Organism*, 1879, p. 142.
312:16   *after* vile." *insert note* 1a. Reginald Heber, "Missionary Hymn," stanza 2.
312:17   *after* mind to *insert note* 1b. Butler, *Hudibras*, i, i, 213–214.
314:n6   *after* 1872.) *substitute* Geraldine Amelia Leigh, daughter of Byron's nephew Henry Leigh and Mary Edgar Leigh, was born 26 October 1845. (Somerset House.)
338:15   *for* RODGERS read ROSLYN [pseud. of GEORGE BARNETT SMITH]. GHL misread the name in his reply, v, 339.
338:18   *for* Hill *read* Hall
338:n5   *add* In the 1874 reprint, however, she changed it from "the bright

	dilated eyes" to "the peculiar look in the eyes" (ch. 63).
339:5	*for* Rodgers *read* Roslyn.
339:24	*for* Hill *read* Hall
346:17	*for* also is enclosed *read* also to enclose
353:n5	*for* the Earl of Lytton *read* Bulwer Lytton
355:12	for *11* read *5*
357:n2	*substitute* Antonin Roche, Director of the Educational Institute, London, and Mrs. Roche.
362:n4	*for* Bruyn *read* Bruijn
367:3	insert *MS:* University of Texas.	**The Priory,**	**21. North Banks,**	**Regents Park.**	January 16.73	My dear Miss Wellington	
367:8	*after* Lewes *insert* does not let me read criticisms on my writings. He always reads them himself, and gives me occasional quotations, when he thinks that they show a spirit and mode of appreciation which will win my gratitude. He has
367:22	*after* obligation, *add* M. E. Lewes.
375:n1	*add* "Exquisite letters to Polly from Mrs. Stuart of Dinan, M. Ritter of Morges, and Mrs. [Caroline I.] Hill [of Brookline, Massachusetts], Grant & Anton Dohrn from Naples—all expressing their deep gratitude for 'Middlemarch.'" (GHL Diary, 13 February 1873.)
377:n5	*after* reprint *insert* and £50 for
378:n8	*substitute* Laurence W. M. Lockhart (1831–82), whose *Double and Quits*, 1869, and *Fair to See*, 1871, were published in a 6/ ed. after appearing in *Blackwood's*.
386:n6	*for* Tunbridge *read* Tonbridge
391:n5	*for* κιθαρα *read* κιθάρα.
398:n1	*add* Goldsmith's "Retaliation" accuses Burke of having given up to pity "what was meant for mankind." (line 32.)
405:n9	*add* See also Ethel Bassin, *The Old Songs of Skye. Frances Tolmie and Her Circle*, 1977.
428:35	*after* land. *insert note* 4a. She left for Algiers 15 September 1873, travelling overland via Marseilles with Miss Gertrude Jekyll (1843–1932).
434:20	*for* [11 SEPTEMBER 1873] read [18 SEPTEMBER 1873] *and transpose to* v, 439.
440:26	*after* he *insert* is
465:27	*after* letter *insert note* 6. Springhill Academy, Shawlands, Glasgow.

VOLUME VI

4:14	*for* Mr. J. H. Appleton. *read* Princeton.
6:n3	*for* at the Erasmus Darwins' *read* at Erasmus Darwin's *and add* Charles Darwin wrote: "I found it so hot and tiring that I went away before all these astounding miracles or jugglery took place." (*Life and Letters*, 3 vols., 1887, III, 187.)
23:11	*after* Magazine. *insert note* 8a. "John Stuart Mill: An Autobiography," *Blackwood's*, 115 (January 1874), 75–94.
23:n9	*add* The passage is copied in GE's Commonplace Book, p. 73. (Yale.)
25:2	*for* [3 MARCH 1865] *read* [3 MARCH 1874]

42:n10   *for* 7th *read* 8th

45:23   *for* Mrs. Michael Womersley *read* British Museum. *Envelope:* Mrs. Griffiths | Colmore Terrace | Summer Lane | Birmingham. *Postmarks:* ST. JOHNS-WOOD N.W | B 5 | MY 9 | 74; BIRMINGHAM | L | MY 9 | 74.

45:n4   *delete last sentence and add* The inscription is not in GE's hand. Another copy inscribed "To Charles and Gertrude Lewes from their ever loving Mutter. May 1874." was in Mrs. Ouvry's collection.

61:26   *for* 23 JUNE 1874 *read* 25 JUNE 1874 *and transpose letter to* VI, 63.

71:30   *for* health *read* breath

75:21   *after* whooping, *insert note* 6a. *As You Like It,* III, ii, 203.

84:n8   *after* Allingham *insert* , who became editor of *Fraser's Magazine* in June,

91:n1   *delete* GE's letter has not been found. *and read* Blackwood enclosed GE's letter of 11 November 1874 in a note to Langford, 20 November *etc.*; *delete* GE's letter was probably sent to Blackwood when *and read* They.

100:n4   *add* Or for Grandcourt's son Henleigh?

125:17   *after* liber *insert note* 3a. Martial, *Epigrammata,* I, 16.

126:26   *insert MS:* Yale. | **The Priory,** | **21. North Bank,** | **Regents Park.** | March 2. 75. | Dear Mr. Browning

127:11   *add* Always truly yours, | M. E. Lewes.

144:n9   *substitute* I, 104. (ch. 6.)

145:11   *for* as *read* a

145:19   *after* Miriam's *insert note* 3a. i.e. Mirah's.

148:10   *for* 149 *read* 139

148:22   *delete* It is required *through* get 40 years. (149:6)

156:n7   *for* C. E. *read* C. W.

159:19   *for* 'cockaloop' *read* 'cockahoop'

163:3   *insert MS:* Princeton. *Published: Harper's,* 64 (March 1882), 568–569.

163:5   *for* Madame *read* Madam

163:26   *for* Calvinists and Baptists *read* Calvinistic Anabaptists

164:4   *for* offense *read* offence

164:12   *for* us *read* me

164:14   for *Madame*' read *Madam*'

169:32   *after* frightened. *insert note* 7a. According to the coachman GE was very nervous of a carriage, always wanted to go on a smooth road, and seemed dreadful feared of being thrown out." *Bookman* (London), 77 (October 1929), 9–11.

176:30   *after* makes. *insert note* 8a. *Winter's Tale,* IV, iv, 90–92.

183:n7   *for* 13 *read* 7

207:26   for *24* read *22*

209:3   *for* The Countess of Iddesleigh. *read* Mr. Gordon N. Ray.

244:34   *after* this,' *insert note* 3a. Cf. Shakespeare, *Sonnets,* 66.

248:8   *for* [asks] *read* wishes

250:n1   *for* Albemarle *read* Arlington

256:24   *for* uncle *read* buck [i.e. Jack Blackwood]

260:29   *after* get it! *insert note* 2a. Cf. Barham *The Ingoldsby Legends,* "The Lay of St. Aloys."

275:18   *for* even *read* ever

285:26   *insert MS:* Girton College
287:31   *add* ... Mrs. Lewes said a good deal besides what I have put down. She thinks people who write regularly for the Press are almost sure to be spoiled by it. There is so much dishonesty, "bad people's books being praised because they belong to the confederacy." She spoke very strongly about the wickedness of not paying one's debts. She thinks it worse than drunkenness, not in its consequences, but in the character itself.
301:11   *after* thanks' *insert note* 6a. *Richard II,* ii, iii, 65.
302:n8   *add* Cross omits "at Rugby."
308   *transpose to* VI, 412:1.
333:26   insert *MS:* University College, London. *Envelope:* James Sully Esq. | 17 Nicoll Road | Willesden | N.W. *Postmark:* st johns-wood n.w | c 12 | ja 20 | 77. *Endorsed:* Mrs. G. H. Lewes (George Eliot) meliorist. *Mostly published.*
333:26   *insert* **The Priory, | 21. North Bank, | Regents Park.** | January 19.77 | Dear Mr. Sully |
334:3   *add* Always yours sincerely | M. E. Lewes.
337:n5   *for* 142 *read* 192; *for* 143 *read* 193
344:26   *for* buglewoman *read* fuglewoman
347:11   insert *MS:* The late Mr. W. B. Stockhausen.
348:35   *after* Blind. *insert note* 6a. The Princess Louise sketched GE on her program. (Mr. Reginald Allen. See Haight, *George Eliot,* facing p. 530.)
349:1   *for* Petre *read* Petri *and add note* 6a. Henri Willem Petri (1856–1914).
361:22   *for* Miss Mary Kirby. *read* Nuneaton Public Library. *Envelope:* Mrs. Cash | Rosehill | Coventry | *Postmark:* st. johns-wood n.w | c 5 | ap 10 | 77.
363:18   *after* Viardot, *insert note* 1a. Paul Viardot (1857–1941), violinist and conductor.
370:n7   *after* Neruda, *insert* later
378:20   insert *MS:* Akademie der Wissenschaften, East Berlin.
387:n4   *delete* Harrison's letter has not been found.
388:n5   *for* BM *read* Yale.
398:31   *for* solidarity *read* solidity
401:29   *for* Parrish Collection, Princeton. *read* Mr. Alexander W. Armour.
406:n7   *for* Malloch *read* Mallock
407:7   *after* good!" *insert note* 8a. *Cymbeline,* v, iv, 212.
424:n1   *delete last sentence.*
431:22   *for* folks *read* folk
433:3   *after* vessels. *insert note* 7a. ii Corinthians 4:7.
435:24   *after* Harris.' *insert note* 10. In contemporary keys to "Amos Barton" Mr. Harris is listed as the original of Mr. Brand, the Shepperton doctor.

VOLUME VII

18:n8   *for* Fraülein *read* Fräulein
19:1   *after* widow' *insert note* 8a. Luke 7:12

19:7	insert *MS:* Trinity College, Cambridge.
19:9	*read* **The Priory,** | **21. North Bank,** | **Regents Park.** | April 9. 1878.
20:n4	*delete* first
30:1	*for* knew *read* know
36:30	*after* come, *insert note* 5b. *Macbeth*, v, v, 2.
37:3	add *Envelope:* Mrs. Bray | 3 Barrs Hill Terrace | Coventry. *Postmark:* B | GODALMING | JY 9 | 78.
47:17	*for* [GHL] *read* GHL
47:19	insert *MS:* Tennyson Research Centre, Lincoln.
47:21	*address is printed*; 3 August 78
47:22	*for* My Dear Mr. Tennyson *read* My dear Tennyson
47:27	*for* it free and cosy. *read* us free and eager. *and add* With our kind regards to Mrs. Tennyson and Hallam | Ever yours truly | G. H. Lewes.
52:12	*for* forget *read* forgot
55:19	*for* at *read* after
60:16	*for* dies *read* dico; *for* oggie *read* oggi è
62:37	*after* duty. *insert note* 1a. Bishop Ken, "Morning Hymn." Cf. *Adam Bede*, ch. 1.
65:27	*for* Mrs. Carrington Ouvry. *read* Mr. Robert Nuttall.
73:n6	*add* See S. M. Petrov and V. G. Fridlyand, *I. S. Turgenev, v vospominiyakh sovremennikov*, 2 vols., Moscow, 1969, II, 141–143.
84:5–9	*delete*
91:6	for *March 5* read *February 23.*
104:11	*after* corrupt. *insert note* 4a. Cf. Tennyson, "Morte d'Arthur," line 242.
105:3	*for* Mrs. Michael Womersley. *read* British Museum.
114:n2	*add* Sidgwick wrote to GE, 2 March 1879, saying that he has talked with Francis Balfour about the Studentship. They were agreed that the London Society for Extension of University Teaching is not to be recommended; for serious physiological study a good laboratory is needed. Foster suggests a Studentship in Physiology at Cambridge worth £200 to £250 a year for three years.
119:12	*for* readings *read* headings
121:n3	for *Sud* read *Süd*
143:n6	*add* Robert R. Evans left a memorandum dated 18 June 1910: "A small Copyhold Property in Herefordshire was omitted from G. Eliot's will. My father was Heir at law. He gave up his claim thinking she meant all to go to C. Lewes. We thought afterwards that GE might have purposely made the omission, knowing as a good lawyer that it would come to I.P.E. and wishing in that way to say 'No ill will.' My Father had left GE £100 in his will with the same intention."
153:31	insert *MS:* University College, London. *Envelope:* James Sully Esq. | 1 Christ Church Road | Hampstead | London N.W. *Postmark:* GODALMING | 8 | MY 28 | 79.
153:32	*insert* **The Heights, Witley,** | **Nr. Godalming.** | 28 May. 79. | Dear Mr. Sully |
154:10	*for* Mesmerism *read* Materialism
154:22	*add* Yours always sincerely | M. E. Lewes.
163:n8	*add* Mrs. Pattison's excerpt from the *Livret du Salon*, 1879, at Yale.
172:27	insert *MS:* University of London.

173:5   *after* unshunnable. *insert note* 4a. *Othello*, iii, iii, 275.
183:19   *after* paradise. *insert note* 10. Cf. Gray, "Ode on the Pleasure Arising from Vicissitude," last stanza.
190:n9   *for* 7th ed., *read* 6th ed., ed. W. Sharpey and D. V. Ellis, 3 vols., 1856.
191:3   insert *MS:* University College, London. *Envelope:* James Sully Esq | care of Prof. Alexander Bain | Aberdeen N.B. *Postmarks:* GODALMING | c | AU 7 | 79; ABERDEEN | A | AU 9 | 79. *Endorsed:* On GHL's posthumous vol. | **The Heights, Witley,** | **Nr. Godalming.** | August 7.79. | Dear Mr. Sully |
191:16   *add* There has been a hitch in the printing (I think) because Prof. Foster had not returned four sheets, which are come only this morning.
191:17   *add* Yours very sincerely | M. E. Lewes.
205:n6   *after* married *insert* 21 August 1879
208:3   insert *MS:* University College, London. *Envelope:* James Sully Esq | Holyrood House | Windmill Hill | Hampstead | London N.W. *Postmarks:* GODALMING | c | oc 7 | 79; LONDON N.W | Y 7 | oc 8 | 79. *Endorsed:* Thanks for proof reading. | **The Heights, Witley,** | **Nr. Godalming.** | October 7.79. | Dear Mr. Sully
208:8   *add* Yours always truly | M. E. Lewes
210:20   *after* ills, *insert note* 1a. *Comus*, line 359.
215:3   *after* weak, *insert note* 6a. Romans 15:1.
222:16   *for* one whom *read* one [of] whom
225:12   *after* labours, *insert note* 8a. Cf. Revelation 14: 13.
234:20   *for* us *read* me
235:11   *for* honor *read* honour
241:3   insert *MS:* Brotherton Library, Leeds. *Published:* Pall Mall Gazette, 5 January 1886. | **The Priory,** | **21. North Bank,** | **Regents Park.** | January 4.80 | Dear Sir |
241:15   *add* Believe me | Yours faithfully | M. E. Lewes.
265:21   insert *MS:* University College, London. *Envelope:* James Sully Esq | Holyrood House | Windmill Hill | Hampstead | N.W. *Postmark:* ST JOHNS-WOOD N.W | AP 26 | 80. *Endorsed:* April 26 1880. On my review of last volumes of Problems. | **The Priory,** | **21. North Bank,** | **Regents Parks.** | April 26.80 | Dear Mr. Sully |
265:23   *for* volume *read* volumes
265:27   *after* me. *read* Always yours gratefully | M. E. Lewes.
266:3   *MS:* Mr. Ian Maclean. *Envelope:* Albert Druce, Esq. | Thornhill | Sevenoaks. *Postmark:* ST JOHNS WOOD N.W | cx | AP 27 | 80.
266:18   *for* liberal *read* literal
268:3   *insert* Berg Collection, New York Public Library.
268:30   *for* communicate with *read* communicate to
290:15   *after* letter *insert* was
291:21   *for* after *read* again ⟨when⟩
300:25   *after* Richetti *insert note* 6. Giacomo Richetti (1833–92). See *Lancet* (1892), p. 1538. For Cross's mental derangement during which he jumped from his balcony into the canal see Haight, *George Eliot*, p. 544.
307:3   insert *MS:* British Museum.
313:15   *for* Bilge" *read* Belge"
348:13   insert *MS:* University College, London. *Endorsed:* I believe this was

the last letter she wrote. I called the next afternoon (Sunday) and had a long pleasant talk with her—thought her looking worn, but she did not seem otherwise unwell. I little thought I should never see her more! She was taken ill that night and I heard nothing of it until, at Hastings, I saw it announced in the papers that she had died on Wednesday night. Alas! H.S.

348:15   *substitute* **4, Cheyne Walk,** | **Chelsea, S. W.** | December 18.80 | *and add* | Dear Friend

348:22   *after* welcome. *add* | Yours always sincerely | M. A. Cross.

349:20   insert *MS:* British Museum. *Published with facsimile: TLS*, 16 May 1969, p. 507. | **4, Cheyne Walk,** | **Chelsea, S. W.** | December 19.1880. | Dear Mrs. Strachey

365:18   *for* Koch *read* Kock

INDEX

I. SOURCES OF TEXT

MANUSCRIPT
(See VIII, xi)

Academy of Sciences, Leningrad, IX, 166

Allen, Percival R., VIII, 68

Angeli, Mrs. Helen Rossetti, V, 93

Appleton, J. H., V, 473, VI, 3, 4, IX, 10

Armour, Alexander W., VI, 401, IX, 356

Badgley, Mrs. Irene Reed, VII, 356

Balfour-Browne, V. E. C., IX, 31

Balliol College, Oxford, VII, 84, 86-7, IX, 239, 246-7, 249, 257

Barrett, Oliver R. VI, 30, IX, 264

Beauman, Christopher, IX, 288

Bennett, R. M., II, 201

Berg Collection, *see* New York Public Library

Bibliothèque Nationale, IX, 243

Birmingham Reference Library, IX, 83, 151

Blackwood Letter Books, MSS now in NLS

Bodleian Library, V, 408, VI, 175, 202, 204, 243, IX, 196, 199-324 *passim*

Boston Public Library, II, 133, V, 272, VII, 123, IX, 43, 51, 56

British Museum, I, 49, 333, II, 423, III, 230, V, 21, 38, 52, 65, 74, 77, 92, 95, 98, 116, 120, 141, 151, 215, 244, 246, 304, 343, 371, 374, 376, 408, 437, 442, 460, 462, 466, VI, 12, 35, 45, 66, 70, 78, 81, 84, 85, 86, 97, 107, 112, 120, 121, 127, 133, 176, 190, 200, 228, 230, 242, 248, 259, 260, 262, 284, 291, 306, 322, 327, 334, 338, 342, 355, 365, 377, 393, 399, 400, 403, 437, VII, 3, 17, 23, 34, 38, 53, 105, 154, 169, 198, 210,

232, 249, 258, 262, 271, 275, 281, 301, 303, 307, 315, 323, 330, 334, 345, 348, 350, 385, VIII, 42, 50, 56, 61, 142, 155, 221, 245, 247, 457, IX, 63, 65, 91, 172, 186, 278, 301, 307, 315, 320-2, 325, 330, 337, 355, 357, 359

Brotherton Library, Leeds, VII, 241, IX, 194, 279, 284, 358

Bryn Mawr College, IX, 28, 124

Buffalo Public Library, VII, 160

Bullett, Gerald, IV, 88, 145, 170, 181, VIII, 355

California, University of, Berkeley, VIII, 77, 132

California, University of, Los Angeles, IV, 384, 409-10, 446, V, 39, 73, 115, VIII, 254, 258, 272, 305-6, 320, 404, 447, 449, IX, 22, 91, 102, 125, 175-6, 233

Cambridge University Library, VIII, 418-20, 425-6, 436-8

Canberra National Library, IX, 240

Cash, Mrs. Peter (Ursula Ouvry), IV, 234

Chambers, W. & R., Ltd., VIII, 125, 311, 405, IX, 350

Clarke, C. E., VI, 150, 277

Cobbold, Lady Hermione, V, 32, VIII, 350, 365, 398, 406, 429, 448, 453, 472, 474, 477-9, 481, 485, 487, IX, 6, 14, 18, 20, 25, 44, 48, 59, 86, 112, 119, 120, 145-7, 150, 152, 295, 351

Colby College, VIII, 369

Colorado College, IX, 263

Columbia University, I, 341, 346, 363, 365, 371, 373, VII, 235, VIII, 339,

PRINTED

II. GENERAL INDEX

In addition to those listed in I, xxxvii–xxxix, the following abbreviations are used in the index:

Barbara	Barbara Leigh Smith Bodichon
Bertie	Herbert Arthur Lewes
Bessie	Bessie Rayner Parkes Belloc
Cara	Caroline Hennell Bray
CLL	Charles Lee Lewes
ES	Edith Simcox
JB	John Blackwood
Maga	*Blackwood's Edinburgh Magazine*
Sara	Sara Sophia Hennell
Thornie	Thornton Arnott Lewes
WB	William Blackwood (1836–1912)
WR	*Westminster Review*

The asterisk indicates that GE is reading or quoting from the work mentioned.

"American Wonder," the, II, 248

Americanisms, VIII, 226, 361, IX, 49–50, 59, 219

Americans, at Plongeon, I, 290–1, 293, II, 21; at 142 Strand, 30; GE loathes, 85; 148, at Hofwyl, III, 178; in Italy, 291–5; and Spencer, 329; G. Peabody, IV, 23; GE would rather be a Turk or Arab, 72; 194, at Granada, 346; V, 14, 22, 30, preacher on *Middlemarch*, 415; VI, 40, rumored about American life, 189; 266, VII, 22, 193, Bret Harte visits GE, 241–2; 285

Amesbury, VI, 69

Amiens, VI, 263; GE at (May 1880), VII, 273, VIII, 333

Amory, Blanche (*Pendennis*), II, 110

Amory, Lady (Henrietta Mary Unwin), VII, 35, IX, 230

Amsterdam, GE looks for Spinoza's synagogue, IV, 298

Amys family at Gorey, II, 369

Anabaptists, IX, 355

Analytical Catalogue of Mr. Chapman's Publications, I, 348, 349, 354, 368, II, 31, 39

Ancelot, Mme Marguerite Chardon, II, 98

Anders, Herr, II, 16

Anders, Henry Smith, and Liggins, III, 48, 50–1, 62, 65–6

Anders, John (surgeon), III, 48, 51

Anderson, Miss (governess), II, 170

Anderson, Charles, I, 184

Anderson, Mrs. Elizabeth Garrett, V, 209–10, 389, VI, 128, IX, 323–4

Anderson, J. G. S., V, 209

Anderson, J. P., V, 338

Andrews, E. A., II, 258

Andrieu, Jules, VI, 73, VII, 17, and Mrs. Burne Jones, 158, 174

Anecdotes, GHL's, VI, 391–2, 394, 429, VII, 22, 31, 33, 60

Angel, Frère (*Spiridion*), I, 270

Angelico, Fra, III, 295, 296, VIII, 455

Angelico, Padre, III, 422

Angelier, Émile l', II, 360

Animal World, VI, 118, 220

Ann (Barbara's maid), V, 126

Annual Register, GE studies floods for

Mill, III, 33; VIII, 188, IX, 322

Anstey, Henry, II, 511

Anstruther-Thomson, John, VI, 74, 80, VII, 45, 48

Antacus, VI, 189, IX, 168

Antichrist, Sara's essay on, II, 405

Anti-Corn Law League, I, xliv, II, 12, VI, 320, VIII, 111

"Antigone" (GHL, *For. Quarterly*, Apr. 1845), VII, 367

Antwerp, II, 108, 171, Passion Play at, IV, 270–2; VIII, 116

Apocryphal Gospels, II, 164

Apollo, I, 68

Appleton, Charles Edward, V, 247, 473–4, GE on *Academy*, VI, 3–4; 14, VII, 31, IX, 10–1

Appleton and Co., bid for *Mill*, III, 268; IV, 316, reprint *Physiology*, VIII, 268, *History of Philosophy*, 400–1

"Apprenticeship of Life" (GHL novel, *Leader*, Apr.–Sept. 1850), VII, 370

Aquarone, Bartolommeo, tr. *Romola*, VI, 316

Arabian Nights, II, 65*, 164, VIII, 239

Arbroath, Angus, 1, lxxiii, V, 200, 206, 310, 417, VII, 313

Arbroath *Herald*, V, 449

Arbury, Warks, I, lxv

Arbury Hall, II, 460, III, 221–4

Arbuthnot, William Urquhart, VI, 375

Archimedes, IV, 126

Archimedes, IX, 30

Architect, VI, 4

Arenberg. Prince Joseph, V, 90

Arenberg, Princess Francisca, smokes cigars, V, 90

Arezzo, VIII, 445

Argosy, VIII, 353, 369

Argyll, George Douglas Campbell, 8th Duke of, III, 326

Ariadne (yacht), II, 312

Ariel, I, 239

Aristophanes, VI, 407

Aristotle, I, 325, *Ethics*, II, 46*; GHL studies scientific works of, III, 468, 472–3; IV, 4, 8, 14, *Poetics*, 195*; *Politics*, V, 256*; VII, 162

Aristotle: A Chapter from the History of Science (1864), GHL begins, III, 468; IV, 4, 1st draft, 17, 19; rewritten, 24,

374

Baginton School, I, 79, 82, 84
Bagster, Samuel, *Polyglott Bible*, I, 31*
Bahlman, Dudley W. R., I, xx
Baiae, VIII, 25
Bailey, J., VIII, 347
Baille, Col., VII, 193
Baillie, George, prize essays, I, 343, II,
   259, 263, 268, 282, 290, 301; Sara
   wins 5th contest, III, 329; "a re-
   markably silly person," 304-5
Baillière, Hippolite (bookseller), I, 196,
   III, 196
Baily, Henry (draper), I, 362
Bain, Alexander, II, 126, GHL on, III,
   127, VI, 218; IV, 192, 266, 446, V, 45,
   VI, 142, VIII, 151, 171, IX, 271, 358
Bain, Mrs. A., IV, 446, V, 45, VI, 142
Bakeless, John, VIII, xv
Baker, Martha (Agnes Lewes's servant),
   III, 149, 150. *See also* Mrs. Bell
Baker, Thomas, I, 184
Balaklava, III, 183
Balbirnie, John, II, 158, 160, VIII, 122
Baldwin, Alfred, V, 57
Baldwin, Mrs. A. (Louisa Macdonald),
   V, 57
Baldwin of Bewdley, Stanley Baldwin,
   1st Earl, V, 57
Balfour, Arthur James Balfour, 1st Earl
   of, V, 409, VI, 380, VII, 16
Balfour, Lady Betty (Lady Elizabeth
   Edith Bulwer-Lytton), V, 88, VII,
   264
Balfour, Lady Blanche, IV, 282
Balfour, Eustace James Anthony, VI,
   380
Balfour, Francis Maitland, V, 409, VI,
   181, VII, 117, trustee of GHL
   Studentship, 177; 227, IX, 357
Balfour, Gerald William, V, 409, VII,
   31
Balfour, James Maitland, IV, 282
Balfour of Burley, John, VI, 223
Balfour-Brown, John Hutton, IX, 31
Ball, Mr. (surgeon), I, 58
Ball, Miss, I, 4
Ballantine, William, V, 243
Ballantyne, Thomas, I, 353, GE rev. his
   Carlyle (*Leader*, 27 Oct. 1855), VII,
   358
Ballantyne, Hanson and Co., print *Prob-*

lems, V, 416; VII, 166, 168, 179
Balliol College, V, 234, VI, 138, VII,
   155
Balmes, J. L., V, 150
Balmoral, VI, 137
Baltozzi, Alexander, VI, 292
Balzac, Honoré de, Agnes Lewes trans-
   lates, I, lxviii; GE quotes, II, 149, IV,
   464; colloquial style, III, 374; 475,
   VI, 57, *Correspondence*, 364; *Eugénie
   Grandet*, VII, 273*; GHL's arts. on
   (*Monthly Mag.*, May 1842, *Foreign
   Quarterly*, July 1844), VII, 365-6;
   VIII, 201, 483, IX, 47
Bamberger, Ludwig, CLL tr. *Count Bis-
   marck*, IV, 369; VI, 395
Bamborough Castle, V, 458
Bancroft, George, GE meets at Berlin,
   V, 83; 454, asked to get facts about
   GE for *New American Cyclopaedia*, VI,
   63-4; GE refuses, 67-9
Bancroft, Mrs. G., invites GE to dinner,
   V, 83; VI, 67, 69
Bandmann, VIII, 429
Bank of England, I, xlv, GE visits, VI,
   91; signs £1000 note, 93
Bánóczi, Dr. J., tr. GHL's *History of
   Philosophy*, VII, 137
Banstead, V, 412
Banting, William, IV, 170
Baptists, I, xliii, I, 243, II, 465, III, 328,
   VI, 163, 320
Baraldi, Neri, II, 370
Barbarus, Hermolaus, III, 471-2
Barbauld, Anna Letitia, "Against In-
   consistency in Our Expectations," II,
   227*
Barbauld, J. and A. L., *Evenings at Home*,
   VII, 186*
Barbier, M., VIII, 360
Barcelona, GE at (Feb. 1867), IV, 338-
   42, VIII, 396
Barclay, Ellen, I, 141
Barclay, Henry (dentist), II, 103, 105
Barclay, Henry (dentist at Cape Town
   1812-84), I, xlix
Barclay, Mrs. Henry (Martha Jackson),
   I, xlix-l
Barclay, Henry J., I, xx, xlix
Barclay, James, I, 38, 141
Barclay, Jessie, goes to New Zealand, I,

BLACKWOOD, JOHN (*continued*)
improving, 68–9; ill again, 147–8,
153, 163; 172, on the Zulu War,
181–2; ordered to quit desk, 203;
little hope of recovery, 217; dies,
219–20
Conventional propriety
    II, 297–8, 322, wants realism of
"Janet" softened, 344–5, 347–8, 360,
Arthur and Hetty, 445–6; fears effect
of GE's name on *Maga*, III, 112;
256–7, thinks GHL too "heathenish,"
VIII, 229–30; III, 259–60, refuses
to pub. *Physiology for Schools*, 363,
VIII, 273–4; III, 459–60, dislikes
GHL's Hugo rev., IV, 47–50; refuses
to pub. *Problems*, V, 410–11, IX, 80–
1, 88–90, 121, V, 449, VI, 17
Interest in sports
    curling, III, 237, 241–2, V, 236,
VI, 101; golf, passion for, I, lii, II,
324, 386, III, 29, 327; GE sees JB
play at Greenwich, 427, V, 298; III,
459, "a nasty enteecing gemm," IV,
400; 402, 427, 429, V, 20, 206, 230.
"May Meeting" at St. Andrews, 269,
297, 331, 353, VII, 68–9; Tom
Morris's match, V, 421; VI, 74–5,
before Duke of Connaught, 272; 282,
293; plays with Whyte-Melville, 305–
6; 361, 367, unable to play, VII, 203–
4; has 4 dogs, VIII, 240; 198, 212,
226, IX, 100, 138–9
GE and JB
    GE sends "Amos," II, 269; "a
Clergyman," 275–7; JB makes out
checks to GHL, 284; GE defends her
art, 291–2; deletes French phrases,
299; JB's doubts about the dagger in
"Janet," 308; agrees to incognito,
308; hopes next tale will be on
brighter theme, 322; warns against
huddling up stories, 324; GE defends
realism of "Janet," 347, 362, 376;
hopes to meet JB, 352; JB sends
Jones's note on "Amos," 374; GE
planning a novel, 381; retains copyright of *Scenes*, 388, 394; 407–9, motto
for *Scenes*, 413–4; presentation copies,
418–9; GE sends JB Dickens's letter,
424; JB meets GE, 435–6; JB finds

Vol. I of *Adam* all right, VIII, 197,
II, 444–6; "right sort of person to
deal with GE," 448; GE refuses to
sketch plot, VIII, 201–2; JB hesitates
to pub. in *Maga*, 202–3; JB on Vol.
II, 211; 214, 228, JB meets Newde-
gate, II, 457; GE explains Arbury,
459–60; JB on *Adam* Vol. II, 483–4;
cautions about dialect, 499, VIII,
214; GE accepts £800 for *Adam*, 4
years, II, 494; "keep your secret,"
508; JB advises against preface, 510;
GE's gratitude to JB, III, 6; JB on
GE's triumph, 33; has MS of *Adam*
bound, 38–9; JB gives £400 bonus
for *Adam*, 68; dines with GE, 73;
calls on GE, regrets they cannot
marry, 94; advises on Liggins affair,
q.v.; gives GE Pug, 113, 121–2, 125,
143; GE has "author's malady," 119;
JB's lapse of tact in offer for *The Mill*,
161; 192–4, 204–5, 215–9, 222–4,
232–6; JB disgusted with GE, 200;
206, opinion of GE's fine character
restored, 235–6; "By God, she is a
wonderful woman," 276; GE hints
vaguely about *Romola*, 305, tells
secret, 314–5; JB wants her photo,
305; buys Laurence portrait, 343,
VIII, 277; III, 351, gives GE dinner
at Greenwich, 427, IX, 347; GE
considers selling copyrights, VIII,
plan for 6/ ed. of novels, VIII, 290–3,
337–8; 289–90; 292; gives GE china
pug, IV, 3; 6–7, on adv. of 6/ ed.,
18; GE's defection, 34–6; *Romola* adv.
in *Maga*, 38; JB's interview with GE,
44; 62–3, 73–4, 76, hopes GE is
thinking of something new, 113; GE
returns to her old friend with *Felix*,
240–2, 244, VIII, 373; JB approves
politics of *Felix*, IV, 246; 250, gets
Alison to answer GE's queries, 251;
JB vies in generosity over American
rights, 251–3; his letters lighten her
depression, 258; 256, 284, his hair-
dresser admires *Felix*, 290, 294; 311,
on Cheap ed., 313; 318–9, buys
copyright for 10 years, 320–1, 327,
wants innovation for next novel, 352;
GE confesses her Spanish story is a

Blackwood, William *(continued)*
xiii. *See also* John Blackwood, *Blackwood's Magazine* and titles of works published by.
Blackwood's Ancient Classics, JB sends GE whole series, VI, 58, IX, 319
Blackwood's Educational series, VII, 236
Blackwood's Edinburgh Magazine (Maga), I, li–liii, lxi, lxx, GHL sends Tugwell's art., II, 274; sends "Amos," 269; each page of *Maga* makes 3 pp. of novel, 381; *Adam* intended for, 388; JB wants GE's Italian story for, 510; would welcome rev. or art. by GE, 510; 512, sales of, III, 8; on Carlyle's *Frederick*, 23; *Adam* rev. (Collins), 42; JB on contributors, 47; *Mill* would help *Maga*, 92; would cut sales of *Mill*, 151; JB wants to pub. anonymously, 160; travel arts. a speciality, 185; JB offers £3000 for anonymous pub. of *Mill*, 206; dropping of incognito will affect circ. in families, 221; GHL proposes art. on Darwin, 242; 269, sells 8000, 275; 341, 352, 381, may count on GHL's pen, 406; "A Month with the Rebels," 472–3; rejects poem by Mrs. Browning, IV, 22; 25, Mrs. Oliphant in, 25; Smith and Elder adv. *Romola* in, 38; GHL's last contribution to, 47; GE reads, 76; *Felix* rev. (Collins), 280, 294; 290, 370, Aytoun and, 391; 416, *Spanish Gypsy* rev. (E. Hamley), 450; 480; JB on believers in, V, 15; 18, on Byron, 55; 297, 310, *Middlemarch* rev. (Collins), 334; Lytton's, *Parisians*, 315; 452, VI, 20, 87, 92, 101, 205, 282, 335, 359, VII, 41, 68, 79, 83, GE suggests reprints from *Maga*, 171; 174, 220, GE's advice on, 228; 255, CLL in, 314; GE refuses to introduce contributors, VIII, 251; Mrs. Gaskell and *Maga*, 224–5; GHL introduces Kebbel, 348, and T.A. Trollope, 447
GE in *Maga*, "Amos" (Jan.–Feb. 1857), II, 283; "Mr. Gilfil" (Mar.–June 1857), II, 303; "Janet" (July–Nov. 1857), II, 359; "Address to

Working Men, By Felix Holt" (Jan. 1868), IV, 402, 405
GHL in *Maga*. For payments *see* VII, 366, 369, 374–7. "Lesurques" (Jan. 1843), VII, 43, "The Great Tragedian" (Sept. 1848), 43; "Metamorphoses" (May–July 1856), VIII, 152–4; reprinted in *Tales from Blackwood*, VII, 41, 43; "Sea-Side Studies" 1st ser., (Aug.–Oct. 1856); 2d ser., (June–Oct. 1857), II, 259, VIII, 168, 172–3, 181; "New Facts and Old Fancies about Sea Anemones" (Jan. 1857), II, 269, 273; Dr. Carlyle on, 295; "Phrenology in France" (Dec. 1857), VIII, 179, 181–4; "People I Have Never Met" (Jan. 1858), II, 410, "Food and Drink" (Mar.–May 1858), 429, 432, 435, 447–8, VIII, 187–9, 194, 197–8, 222; "Blood" (June 1858), II, 447; "Circulation of the Blood" (July 1858), 464, VIII, 198, 202–4; "Respiration and Suffocation" (Sept. 1858), II, 473; "Animal Heat" (Oct. 1858), 474, VIII, 211; "A Pleasant French Book" (Dec. 1858), II, 491, VIII, 212–4; "Falsely Accused" (Feb. 1859), III, 8, reprinted in *Tales from Blackwood*, VII, 41, 376, VIII, 221; "Only a Pond!" (May 1859), III, 28, 46, 52, VIII, 226, 229; "The Novels of Jane Austen" (July 1859), III, 10, 28, 46; "Voluntary and Involuntary Actions" (Sept. 1859), 127, 143; "Another Pleasant French Book" (Renan, Dec. 1859), 183, VIII, 397; "A Word About Tom Jones" (Mar. 1860), III, 242, 245, 248–52; "Great Wits, Mad Wits" (Sept. 1860), 322, 327, 332, 335; "Seeing is Believing" (Oct. 1860). 335–6, 345, 359; "Theories of Food" (Dec. 1860), 355; "Uncivilized Man" (Jan. 1861), 355, VIII, 273; "Spontaneous Generation" (Feb. 1861), III, 370, 375; "Recent Natural History Books" (Mar. 1861), 378, 380, VIII, 274; "Spontaneous Combustion" (Apr. 1861), III, 375, 393, VII, 355, IX,

Brescia, IV, 151

Breslau, VI, 316, 317

Breton, Jules Adolphe, VII, 281

Brett (parlormaid), comes to Witley, VII, 32; 130, 249, 277, 279, 286, 311, 318, IX, 235, 242, 256, 259, 261, 265, 267, 305

Brett, John (1831–1902), IX, 298

Brett, Reginald Baliol, *see* Viscount Esher

Brewitt, Bellamy, II, 35

Brewster, Sir David, I, 367, II, 158, 233, III, 254, and D. D. Home, 359; *Martyrs of Science*, IV, 416

Brewster, Margaret Maria, at 142 Strand, I, 306, 367, III, 254

Brezzi, Joseph Henry, I, 38, teaches GE German, 43, Italian, 53; attracts GE, 51; 69, 91, his charges, 117, IX, 333

Brick, Allan R., *The Leader: Organ of Radicalism*, VIII, 131, 206, IX, 93

Brickhill, Sr., Mr., IV, 141, IX, 102, 159

Brickhill, Jr., Mr., IV, 140

Bricolin (*Le Meunier d'Angibault*), I, 275

Bridewell Hospital, London, VII, 60

Bridges, Anna Maria, V, 138

Bridges, John Henry, GE meets at Congreves, III, 238; VIII, 243–4, IV, 111, 227, 474, tr. Comte's *System of Positive Polity*, VI, 126; 398, VII, 20, 260, 271, 326, IX, 194

Bridport, Alexander Hood, Viscount, VII, 29

Bright, Henry A., II, 111

Bright, John, IV, 245; *Speeches on Questions of Public Policy*, V, 6*; on Ireland, 12; VI, 394, takes GE down to dinner at Goschens', 372, 374, IX, 212

Brighton, I, 51, 239, 360, II, 12, 70, 79, 99, V, 249, 251, 259, 446, 467, VI, 81, 150–1, 278, VII, 76, 295, 326, VIII, 28, 200, IX, 151, 184, 262, 318, 334

Brinton, William, III, 446, 451, IV, 233, VIII, 321

Bristol, I, 160, II, 238

British Association, Owen reads GHL's paper at, II, 487; 479; GHL's papers

read at, III, 189, 195; IV, 306, VI, 79, 274, VIII, 429, 454

British and Foreign Medical Review, II, 132, III, 328–9, 355

British and Foreign Review, GHL's arts., "Hegel" (Mar. 1842), "Göthe" (Mar. 1843), "French Philosophy" (July 1843), "French Historians" (Oct. 1843), VII, 365–6, VIII, 77–8

British Medical Assn., GHL at meeting of, IV, 466

British Medical Journal, VII, 16, VIII, 404

British Museum, now British Library, VIII, xiv, IX, 329, 342, I, xi, xix, lxxvii, 225, 250, GE's 1st visit, III, 394; GHL goes for GE, 403; GE at, 472; reads for *Romola*, IV, 15; GE in print room, 34; 36, research for *Felix*, 248; 266, Deutsch shows GE recent accessions, 365; 478, V, 40, 116, 142, 155, 359, 371, GE sees bronzes, 408; 460, VI, 31, Ralston, IX, 224, resigns from, VI, 132; GE's MSS given to, VII, 245, Owen and Panizzi, VIII, 229

British Quarterly Review, I, 343, II, 48, 118, 219, IV, 452–3, VI, 15, GHL arts., "Reid" (May 1847), "Friends in Council" (July 1847), "Browning's Poems" (Nov. 1847), "Dumas" (Feb. 1848), "Lamb" (May 1848), "Goldsmith" (Aug. 1848), "Keats and Lamb" (Nov. 1848), "Macaulay" (Feb. 1849), "Bruno" (May 1849), "D'Israeli" (Nov. 1849), "Spanish Literature" (Feb. 1850), "History of 30 Years" (May 1850), "Sedgwick" (Oct. 1850), "French Literature" (May 1851), "French Historians" (Nov. 1851), VII, 368–71, VIII, 86, 88, IX, 272, 340

Brittany, I, lxviii, II, 295, VIII, 349–50

Broadhead, William (trades-unionist), IV, 378

Broadmoor Prison, VIII, 317

Broadstairs, II, 36, GE at (July–Aug. 1852), 40, 42, VIII, 48–61

Broadway, The, begins, IV, 371

Brock (gardener at Witley), VII, 32, 175, 258

411

D'Albert-Durade, Mme (*continued*)
 ill, 320; 321, 392–3, ill; GE wants
 to see again, 419; 426–8, 433, VI, 24,
 129–30, 173–4, 277, 427, VII, 28,
 46, 115, 226–7, 257, dies, 333
D'Albert-Durade, Alphonse, I, 312,
 330, III, 187, marries, 447; IV, 5,
 155, 359, V, 142, VI, 130, 427, VII,
 257, VIII, 18
D'Albert-Durade, Charles, I, 312, III,
 187, 348, 373, IV, 5, 155, V, 142,
 meets Mrs. Sartoris at Aix, 242; less
 prosperous, VII, 115, VIII, 18
D'Albert-Durade, Mme Charles (Marguerite Frisch), V, 242
Dale, Thomas, I, 6
Dalhousie, 12th Earl of, VI, 138
Dallas, Eneas Sweetland, rev. *Life of
 C. Brontë (Maga)*, II, 323, VIII, 225;
 III, 50, receives tracts, 58; 60, 305, at
 Priory housewarming, IV, 115; 122,
 124, V, 54, revs. in *Times*, *Adam*, III,
 24, *Mill*, 298, *Silas*, 397, *Felix*, IV,
 275, VIII, 379; IV, *Spanish Gypsy*,
 449, VIII, 316, 350
Dallas, Isabella Gearns, *see* Glyn, III,
 210, VIII, 316
Daly, Augustin, IV, 132
Damietta, VIII, 321
Daniel, Samuel, V, 213
Daniel Deronda (1876), GE sees Miss
 Leigh at Homburg, V, 314, IX, 353;
 V, goes to synagogues at Frankfurt,
 424, and Mainz, 427; buys books on
 Jewish subjects, 425; simmering toward a big book, 454; 461, despairs,
 VI, 11; 50, brewing, deep shafts
 sunk, 58; 62, 79, to Wiltshire for
 local color, 84, 86, 136; 91, consults
 Harrison on law, 100, 105, 110–1,
 126, 147–9, 151–3, IX, 155; VI, 109,
 116, Bks. I and III done, title secret,
 136; consults Stephen on Cambridge
 life, 140–1; 168, IV done, 172; anxiety
 about MS, 172, 178, 180; plans for
 pub., 177–9, 186; terms, 180; division of Bks., 181–2, 185–7, 189, 192–
 3; printing, 180, 184, 186, 195;
 stereotyped before 1st ed., 196; 199,
 motto for t.p., 201, 226; for ch. 17,
 232; ch. 29, Whitman, 241, 421; Bk.

v done, 201; VI goes slowly, 210; 215
 Bk. I pub., VI, 219; Bk. II subscribed, 222; Bk. VI printed, 233; Bk.
 VII done, 237; GE won't pad it, 240;
 242; Bk. VIII; 256, 259, 261; erratum
 in Bk. v, 259; last proof read, 264,
 IX, 179; VI, Bk. VI out, 266; proof
 bound, 211, 262; table of printings,
 279
 comments, JB on, VI, 143–5, psychological notation, 182–4; 195.
 203, 221–2, 225, at GHL's hint JB
 praises Mordecai, 227; 232, 239, 263,
 295, 305; GE on, 198, 200, 240–1,
 303–4, 314, IX, 227; GHL on, VI,
 210, 247, 268, 413, IX, 138; VI,
 Kaufmann's pamphlet, 378–9, 410,
 VII, 197; Koeckert, VI, 395; Leavis,
 290; E. S. Phelps, VII, 133; Reeve
 on "lay odds," VI 232; Mrs. Senior,
 270; Simcox, IX, 232; Simpson, VI,
 295; Mrs. Stowe, 246
 characters, Daniel, VI, 100, and
 Edmund Gurney, 140; 145, 185, 222,
 239, 253, 263, a prig, 337; 396–7;
 Grandcourt, 110, 126, 145, 150, 152–
 3, 182, 185, 195, 203, 221, 240–1,
 315; Gwendolen, 144–5, mental reflections a new device, 182; 183, 185,
 186–7, 195, 221, 232, 238–9, 240–1,
 262, 272, 303, 315, VII, 133, IX,
 275, 353; Klesmer, VI, 144, 193, 221,
 IX, 177; Lush, VI, 183, 233, 240–1;
 Meyricks, IX, 173, 184; Mirah, VI,
 145, 181, her songs, 184; 185, 221,
 235, 241, 285, IX, 352, 355; Mordecai, VI, 195, 196, 221–5, 227, 270,
 285, 318, a shadow, 337, VII, 95–6;
 Rex, VI, 183; others, 84, 100, 110,
 126, 140, 144–5, 148, 150–3, 183–6,
 195, 203, 221–2, 227, 263
 Jewish element in, I, xliii, VI, 250,
 316, 322–3; JB troubled by, 221–2;
 227, 303–4; Hebrew dictionary, 239;
 250, 305; GE on, 238, 259, separating
 from Gwendolen parts, 290; aim of,
 301, 304; GHL on, 196, 224, 247, 268,
 294; Adler, 275; Grove, IX, 173;
 Guedalla, VI, 288; Langford, 262;
 Leavis, 290
 reviews, *Contemporary* (Dowden),

416

Duncan, David (Spencer's biographer), VI, 311, VIII, 43, 76, 150

Duncker, Franz, II, 307, III, 425, offers £60 for new matter in *Goethe*, IV, 115, VIII, 147, IX, 65; takes GE to Reichstag, V, 84; begins an English series, 258; VII, 119; not prosperous, 126, 149

Duncker, Mrs. F., V, 84

Dunn, John and Joseph (booksellers), VIII, 307

Dunn, Robert (1799–1870, surgeon), II, 84, 100, 101, VIII, 55, 60

Dupin, and Bayard, *Alexandre chez Apelles*, VIII, 140

Duprez, Christian, VIII, 431

Du Quairo, Mme, VI, 363

Durade, Jeanne Sara, I, lxiv

Durand, Alice M. C. F. (Henry Gréville), VII, 6

Durban, IV, 141, 142, VIII, 321, 323, 344, 351, 376, 390–2

Dussek, III, 361

Dutch painting, II, 292

Dyer, John, V, 14

Dyer, William T. Thistleton, trustee of GHL Studentship, VII, 117; 177

Eade, Susan, VIII, xv

Earle, Charles Williams, V, 88

Earle, Mrs. C. W. (Maria Theresa Villiers), meets GE, V, 88; VI, 348, IX, 147

Earlswood Asylum for Idiots, GHL visits, VI, 66

Earlswood Common, GE at (June–Sept. 1874), VI, 52–83, IX, 125

East Lynne, Mrs. Norton on., V, 208

East Sheen, GE and GHL at 7 Clarence Row (May–Sept. 1855), II, 199, 202

Eastbourne, GE at, May 1865, IV, 192

Eastern Question, VI, 359, VII, 47

Eastlake, Sir Charles Lock, II, 6

Eastlake, Lady (Elisabeth Rigby), II, 6, V, 263

Easton, Reginald, I, 184

Eathorpe, I, 78

Eaton, Frederick A., IX, 94

Ebdell, Bernald Gilpin, orig. of Mr. Gilfil, I, 41; III, 21

Ebelites, V, 335

Ebenezer, VI, 258

Eberstatt, Herr, IX, 177

Eborall, Eliza, III, 142, VII, 356, VIII, 221, 250–1

Echo, VI, 341–2

Ecker, J. M. A., IV, 458–9

Eckermann, Johann Peter, GE and GHL call on, II, 178, 204–5; *Conversations with Goethe*, II, 204*, V, 123, IX, 140

Eckley, Mrs. Sophia Tuckerman, Browning's difficulty with, V, 41

Eclectic Review, III, 44, 47

Eclipse, VI, 426

Economist, Spencer subed. of, I, 352, II, 28, IV, 192, 195

Edda, Prose, VII, 259*

Edel, Leon, VIII, 449, IX, 352

Edgbaston, GE at, I, 68

Edger, Beatrice Blanche (Mrs. John Wyman), IV, 476, at Priory, V, 342

Edger, Henry (American Positivist), IV, 476, IX, 351

Edger, Sophie Clotilde (Mrs. Edward Nicholson), on GE's marriage to Cross, I, lxii; IV, 476, V, 163, at Priory, V, 342

Edgeworth, Maria, GE translates into French, I, 214*, VII, 197

Edinburgh, GE at (Oct. 1845), I, 200; visits George Combes at (Oct. 1852), II, 59–62; 117, VIII, 62; II, 183, Thornie at High School, III, 333, 347, 349, VIII, 222

Edinburgh Bee, VIII, 436

Edinburgh Courant, rev. *Adam*, III, 20, 25

Edinburgh News, VIII, 40

Edinburgh Review, I, lii, GHL art. on Strauss's *Julian der Abtrünnige* (July 1848), I, 270; GE proposes arts. for, 345, VIII, 44; circulation 9000, 58; 72, 89, 269, has £700 for each number, II, 95; 123, 189, GHL's art. on *Shirley* (Jan. 1850), 316; III, 10, rev. of *Adam*, 148; challenges law in *Felix*, IV, 342, 350, 353, Disraeli on, 394; VI, 157, other arts. by GHL, "Drama" (Oct. 1843), "Lessing" (Oct. 1845), "Algazzali" (Apr. 1847), "Strauss," (July 1848), "Shaks-

422

ELIOT, GEORGE (*continued*)
George Eliot, pseudonym (*continued*)
28, Mrs. Howther, 417; V. 171, 223,
402, VIII, 429; wants to be quoted
as GE in *OED*, IX, 279
Health
eyes, V, 451, long-sighted, VI, 276,
VII, 266
gastro-intestinal, I, 198, 205, 275,
281, 305, II, 53–4, 129, 273, 289,
292, 468–71, III, 382, 461, IV, 168–
70, 175, 234, 338, V, 47, gastric
attack, 191–7; 232, 234, 259, 310,
VI, 3, 205, VII, 57, VIII, 80, 334,
355, "congested liver," 448; 474,
IX, 20, 25–6, 30, 69, 234
headache, I, 5, 21, 70, 115–6,
185–7, 188, 206, nothing but subjective maladies, 207, 241, 253, 282,
295, 307, 328–9, 369, 376–7, II, 27,
53, 58, 67, 81, 90, 96, 126, 143, 148,
151–2, 161, 165, 237–8, 240, 255,
306, 329, 340, 354, 370, 403–4, III,
70, 271, 303, 420, 468, IV, 69, 87,
139, 147, 179, 240, 379, V, 161, 259,
261, 310, VI, 3, 11, 76, 364, VII,
57, 146, VIII, 62, 65, 93, 293, IX,
13, 21, 50, 295
hysterics, I, 41, II, 34, V, 28, 310,
IX, 258
kidney stone, 1st attack, VI, 13,
16; 127–9, 139, 142, 240, 248–9,
267, 285, 337, 344–5, 352, 369, 391,
VII, 100, 102, 151–2, 166, 170, 174,
326, IX, 116, 152–3, 186–90, 270,
317
medication, I, 89, 138, 146, 186,
376, chloroform, II, 105, 261; qui-
nine, 261; III, 357, 359, 363, VII,
328
neuralgia, I, 256, 294, 356, II, 84,
102, 155–8, III, 468, IV, 352, V,
132, 151, 268, VIII, 71, IX, 7, 20,
51, 69–70
palpitation, II, 149, IV, 413, VIII,
95–6
respiratory, I, 93, 196, 212, 356, II,
99–101, 104, 142, 209, 221, 452, III,
30, 37, 288, 412–3, 463, IV, 6, 86,
350, 360, V, 20, 86, 88–9, 273, 326,

VI, 159, 197, 258, 364, VII, 18, 320,
350, VIII, 111, 314, 475, IX, 218–9,
305, final illness, 320
seasickness, I, 262, 332, II, 193,
312
teeth, I, 160, 202, 255, 256, 258, II,
103, 105, 261, IV, 454, V, 150, 352,
357, 360, 362, 371, VI, 261, 306, VI,
159, VIII, 471, 488, IX, 71
vague illnesses, III, 254, IV, 84,
233, 408, 438, V, 105, 375, 445, VI,
230, 277, VIII, 31, 40, 56, 169, 273
excellent health, I, 62–3, 95, 117,
II, 63, 109, 113, 117, 123, 145, 170,
III, 148, 286, 294, 362, 428, 437,
441, 460, IV, 127, V, 218, 285–6,
VI, 50, 117, VII, 225, 229, 279, IX,
60, 280
Homage to GE
Mrs. Malleson, IV, 346; 458, V,
83–4, 86, 144, Mrs. Cowper-Temple
copies passages of *Romola* in her N.T.,
276; GHL calls GE Madonna, VI,
121, 169, 322, 389, IX, 188; ladies
kiss GE's hand, VI, 27, VII, 16;
touch her, 14; ES kisses feet, IX,
202; Elma Stuart's "relic," VI, 121,
243; GE stops GHL's talk about her,
381
Housekeeping
I, 18, 31, 52, 56, 82, 86, II, 145,
195, 203, 278, 314, III, 10, 79, 238,
304, 344–5, IV, 112, 116, 127, 152,
V, 104, 146–7, 436, 445, VI, 73,
327–8, 343, 377, VII, 28, 40, 232,
263–4
carriage, V, 469, IX, 238, 355
furniture, I, 79, II, 215, 339, III,
3–4, 364–5, IV, 298, V, 172, VI,
386, VII, 30, 33, 38–9, 232, 322
repairs, I, 44, 233, 235, II, 152,
VII, 5
servants, I, 9, III, 19, 26, 29, 32, 37,
53, IV, 152, V, 3, 184, 274, VI, 3,
52, 346, IX, 40, 124–5, 183, 236–7,
262
Literature
spelling, I, xxxv; beginning of ma-
ture style, 85; abandons Language
of Flowers, 116; 121, 185, 189, 199,

ELIOT, GEORGE (*continued*)
Literature (*continued*)
  Spencer's art. on "Style," II, 54;
  good style needs no italics, 155;
  criticizes Chapman's art., 205–9;
  slovenly writing a crime, 210, IX,
  55–6; "Miss So and Sos," II, 361;
  427, D'Albert finds later style more
  difficult, V, 300; scientific language,
  359; matter and form an inseparable
  truthfulness, 374; rhythm determined
  choice of "adust," IX, 278
  Fiction, GE on dangers of, I, 21–3;
  unfairness of using puppets, 45, 309;
  few writers use colloquial style, III,
  374; experience and faculty rarely go
  together, VI, 378; treatment of subject the essence of art, II, 447; GE
  refuses to outline plot of *Adam*, VIII,
  201–2; GE thought to be writing a
  novel, in 1846, I, 223; in 1858, II,
  442; GE on Browning's analysis of
  motive, II, 305; on *Jane Eyre*, I,
  268; *Villette*, II, 87, 91, 92; Mrs.
  Gaskell not content with the half
  tints of real life, 86; *Esmond*, 66–7, IV,
  90–1; *Vanity Fair*, II, 157; GE reads
  little contemporary, IV, 123, 377,
  VI, 75–6, 199, 418, VIII, 466, GE's
  influence, IX, 98, 220–1, Jowett on,
  284–6; every writer a teacher, 213–4
  GE on her own fiction, II, 299,
  realism, 308, 347–9; on use of observed materials, 376; "How I Came
  to Write Fiction," IX, 406–10, III,
  156; last vols. written fast, 249; cries
  writing *Mill*, 269; hears her characters talking, 427; integrity, IV, 20;
  insists on unity of structure, excluding
  didactic, V, 459; same principles in
  early and late novels, VI, 318; advice to aspiring author, VII, 178,
  GE "gestating," books like children,
  VIII, 384, IX, 149; needs even,
  quiet life to write, VIII, 209, 306;
  can't alter what is written under
  strong feeling, 415, or what she does
  not care about, 466
Love
  GE "of a most affectionate dis-

position, always requiring some one
to lean upon," I, 126; VIII, 131,
love for Isaac Evans, VII, 287; affair
with picture-restorer, I, 183–8, IX,
336–7; with Dr. Brabant, I, lvii,
163–8; with John Chapman, xiv, lx,
349, 354, II, 132; with Spencer, I,
lxxv–vi, II, 35, VIII, 42, 50, GE
will die if he forsakes her, 56–7;
remain friends, 61; GE and GHL, *see*
GHL and GE; GE and JWC, I,
lxiii–iv, needs his affection, VII, 101–
2, 138–40; likes "to be loved in this
faulty, frail (yet venerable) flesh,"
IX, 226;
  women attracted to GE, Mrs.
Linton, I, 337; Mrs. Congreve loved
GE "lover-wise," VIII, x; pained by
2nd marriage, VII, 227, 296; Mrs.
Burne-Jones, I, lix, VIII, 482–3,
IX, 101, VII, 299; Mrs. Ponsonby,
VIII, x; Mrs. Peirce, VIII, 461;
Elma Stuart, I, lxxvii, VII, 266, IX,
283, 323; Edith Simcox, VIII, xviii–
xix, GE tells she never cared much
for women, IX, 299
Melancholy
  horrible scepticism about all things,
  IV, 158; V, 225, 261, 296, James
  Thomson on, VI, 60–1; 70, has lost
  personal melancholy, 310
Meliorism
  IV, 499, VI, 287, 333–4, IX, 356
Metrics
  IV, 463–4, 467, V, 141, VI, 96
Money
  GE's income from trust fund, I,
  353, II, 178, 184, 252, 350; 97, not
  paid for ed. *WR*, 127–8; £50 for
  Feuerbach tr., 152; economy 1st law,
  180; 184, doles out sovereigns like a
  miser, 233; can't afford 3*d* tax to
  ascend Tors, 251; laughed at poverty,
  IX, 267; GHL opens bank account,
  II, 321; GE's money paid into it,
  336, 378; 339, 377, gold standard,
  414; 508, III, 69, 94, 118, important
  to GE, 151–2; 214, 219, offers to
  lend Bray £100, 325; buys Indian
  railway stock, 352; has enough to

ELIOT, GEORGE (*continued*)
Religion (*continued*)
Evangelical piety: I, 5–117 *passim*
heterodoxy: begins with Scott's
novels, 21; *Devereux*, 45; ecclesiastical
history, 46; Isaac Taylor, 64, 72;
effect of Hennell's *Inquiry*, 120–2;
Carlyle, 122; refuses to go to church,
124; the "holy war," 124–38; rejects
Calvinism, 143; heterodoxy, 309,
330, II, 3, 126, objects to theological
views in *WR*, VIII, 60; eternal
punishment, 69; Combe's *Relation
between Religion and Science*, 85
pantheism: I, 136, V, 31. *See also*
Feuerbach; Spinoza
morality and religion: I, 72, good
for its own sake, 143; good and evil,
146; GE's religion and conduct, IV,
104; modern civilization, 162, 472,
VI, 87; desire to ennoble human life,
89; debt to Judaism, 301–2; morality
not dependent on dogma, 338–9;
respectability only possible religion
for English masses, VIII, 465
conformity: GE loses antagonism,
I, 162, 228, 235, II, 403, 421, III,
230–1, IV, 95, VII, 241; no negative
propagandism, I, 231, IV, 64–5, VI,
65; disagrees with Mrs. Cash, IV,
437; conformity better than nega-
tion, V, 447–8; Mrs. Ponsonby consults on doubts, VI, 97–100, 120, 124,
VIII, 307, 456
future reward as motive: GE dis-
cards, I, 125; immortality of the soul,
VIII, 66, 70; the "new protestant-
ism," I, 315, highest calling to do
without opium, III, 366, IV, 491,
499, V, 69, VI, 216–7; look less to
personal consolation, more to sympathy with humanity, V, 31; IX, 201,
324, 333
See also Baptists: Calvinism; Church
of England; Dissenters; Evangeli-
calism; Free thinkers; Future life;
Independents; Jews; Lutherans;
Methodists; Positivism; Roman
Catholic Church; Russian Church;
Theology; Tractarian Movement;

Unitarians
Residences
South Farm, Arbury (1819–20) I,
xxiii; Griff House (1820–17 Mar.
1841), xxiii; Foleshill Road, Coventry
(17 Mar. 1841–12 June 1849), 89–
285; 142 Strand (8 Jan. 1851–8 Oct.
1853), 341–II, 119; 21 Cambridge
St. (18 Oct. 1853–20 July, 1854),
119–166, VIII, 85–6; 1 Sydney
Place, Dover (Mar.–Apr. 1855), II,
195; 8 Victoria Grove Terrace (Apr.–
May 1855), 198; 7 Clarence Row,
East Sheen (2 May–3 Oct. 1855),
200–217; 8 Park Shot, Richmond (3
Oct. 1855–5 Feb. 1859), 218–III, 5,
VIII, 146, Holly Lodge, South Fields,
Wandsworth (Feb. 1859–Sept. 1860),
III, 3–348; 10 Harewood Square
(24 Sept.–17 Dec. 1860), 348–364;
16 Blandford Square (17 Dec. 1860–
5 Nov. 1863), 364–IV, 111; The
Priory, 21 North Bank, Regent's
Park, (5 Nov. 1863–80), 111–VII,
270; The Heights, Witley (6 Dec.
1876–80), VI, 314–VII, 351; 4
Cheyne Walk, Chelsea (3 Dec.–22
Dec. 1880), 342–351
Resignation
I, 159, 359, II, 42, nobler than
hope without reason, 49; 127, 134,
156, 254, detests compensation, 258;
342, 360, IV, 128, 196, 201, counsels
Allbutt, 499; V, 53, happiness depends on "must do," 177; VI, 3, 17,
65, 165, 311, VII, 63, can live without
happiness, 113; adapt one's soul to
the irremediable, VIII, 358
Self-reproach
novel reading, I, 22; 40, dispute
with father, 134; Sara, 337; a wretched helpmate, II, 48; Chrissey, 97;
egoism, 101; 112, 215, 277–8, 342–3,
397, revealing incognito, III, 90;
Agnes's faults, 91; Mme D'Albert,
314; IV, 28, Spencer, 66; "my own
miserable imperfections," VIII, 61;
ideal of Romola: "my own books
scourge me," IV, 104; 182, 198, 268,
Cara, 421; past full of errors, 437;

ELIOT, GEORGE (*continued*)

Self-reproach (*continued*)

467, Pattison, V, 44–5, 46–7, faults of a friend, 123; egoism causes melancholy, 124–5; VII, 3, 235, may not have done best for Cross in marrying him, 278; VIII, 56–7, 131, 247, 330, 465–6

Sensitive to criticism

I, 129, 138, 227, 301, II, 152, 164, 182, 189, 198, letters addressed Miss Evans, 200, 201, 232; 212, 218, 224, 231, wishes not to be known as tr. of *Ethics*, 233; "unusually sensitive," 276; 295, 305, 339, 372, 384, 428, 448, 467, III, 15, 26, 99, reason enough for incognito, 103, 106; called Miss Evans, 121; 157, 162, 170, photo, 171; 179, 184, 194, reads no reviews of *Mill*, 214; forbids discussion of her work, VIII, 252; III, 254, 302, 324, GE reads praise, 351; 356, 405, GHL suppresses unfavorable comments, IV, 58–9; VIII, 313, 380, 382, 385, IX, 227, IV, 414, 438, 446, 481, V, 214–5, 228, 374, GHL warns WB against mentioning criticisms of *Deronda*, VI, 218; 230, 244–5, IX, 299, on puffing, 356; VI, 312, GE paralyzed by misunderstanding, 394; friends blame GE for not telling of plan to marry, VII, 289; made Cross tell CLL, IX, 308

Society

young ladies least attractive to GE, I, 91; aversion to society, 99; no visits to pay, II, 232; refuses to visit Brays, 279; invites no one who doesn't ask, 339; Bessie can't call, 384; III, 396, 436, 469, IV, 477, Norton on GE's position, V, 7; GE returns no calls, VIII, 446; IX, 266–7; V, 28, lords and ladies, poets, cabinet ministers at Priory, 275; 393, 454, 468, 474, VI, 274; Longfellow, VIII, 452; dines with Princess Louise, VI, 372, and Crown Princess of Germany, IX, 229

Studies

education: I, xlix, 47–8, 92, reputation for learning, 180; uses Arbury

Hall library, 40; lessons in Geneva, 312; at Bedford College, 343; learning without any ulterior purpose, IX, 223; inexhaustible craving for knowledge, 235

languages: I, 54, French, 117, 180, 212, 299, speaks with Lizst, II, 172; VII, 197; German, I, xliii, 43, 67, 69, 117, 148, 153, 166, 180, 211–2, 363, II, 142, 144, speaks badly, 171–2, 452, 475; Greek, I, 147, 168, 180–1, 185–6, 197, 199, 210, 225, Sibree teaches GE, VIII, 15; IX, 88; Hebrew, I, 195, 204, II, 164, V, 73, VII, 209, IX, 193; Italian, I, 53, 69, 117, III, 287, IV, 151, 431, V, 6; Latin, I, 29, Locke's method, 38; 47–8, 147, 180, 189, 208, 240, II, 129, 306; Sanscrit, VIII, 461; comparative grammar, 341; knows 7 languages, IX, 185; Spanish, IV, 165, 330, 332, 334

sciences: early interest in, I, 29, 110, II, 270, scientific allusions in *Scenes*, 291–4; anatomy, brain, GHL gives lesson on, V, 90, Rolleston dissects for, 100; astronomy, I, 29, 110, 147, III, 432, 437, IV, 210, 425, V, 6; botany, II, 46, 242–51, 369, 440; chemistry, I, 29, 123, 342, III, 353; entomology, I, 29; geology, 110, 144, VIII, 8; doing conic sections, IX, 293; mathematics, I, 29, at Geneva, 321, 343; fond of algebra, III, 216, VII, 209, paleontology, III, 373; physics, I, 325, 329, IV, 306, 334, VI, 4; physiology, II, 220, 470; zoology, 103, 242–4, 335, 440

Theater

I, 196, 376, II, 18, 98, 103–4, 131, 162, 185, 189, 263–4, 301, 370, 372, III, 149, 355, 422, 442, 463, 467, IV, 10, 24, 92, 132, 144, 151, 177, 181, 186, 341–2, V, 24, 318, VI, 25, 51, 58, 86, 142, 147, 194, 264, VII, 6, 13, 23, 162, 288, 345, VIII, 282, 445, IX, 175, 179, 195, 275, 288, IX, 321

Translator

offers to tr. Vinet for F. Watts, I, 136; Spinoza for Bray, 158; Strauss,

ELIOT, GEORGE (*continued*)
Translator (*continued*)
Leben Jesu and Feuerbach, *Wesen*,
q.v. VIII, 78
Union with GHL

I, xlv, liv, lviii, lxx, happier every
day, II, 173; defends GHL from
slanders, 178–9; Bray and Chapman
only persons GE spoke to about, 179;
Bray on, Agnes and GHL, VIII,
122–3; 131, no longer secret, II, 182,
364; 183, 186, writes Mrs. Bray on
union, 213–5; VIII, 119; GE has
"nothing to deny or conceal," 124,
128; Mrs. Taylor's sympathy, II, 254;
not legal, but a sacred bond, 349;
Bessie calls GE Miss Evans, 384,
GHL dines with Agnes, III, 195;
GHL's will, 212; divorce impossible,
366–7; saves GE from contact with
frivolous women, 367; Mrs. Willim
calls, 372; GE writes Mrs. Taylor on,
396; religious beliefs and, IV, 104;
both GE and GHL sign agreement
for *Romola*, VIII, 307

comments on: Woolner, II, 175–
6; Carlyle, 177; Mrs. Jameson, 231;
Chapman on, VIII, 125–6; Combe
on, 129–30; C. Kingsley on, 179; H.
Martineau, 127–8; JB, III, 94; no
other ladies at JB's dinner, 427; Mrs.
E. Chapman asks after Mrs. Evans
Lewes, 196; Mrs. Gaskell wishes
"you *were* Mrs. Lewes," 197; WB
fears GE may pub. in her own name,
221; Mudie invites GE to opening,
360; Langford, 377; D'Albert ad-
dresses letters Mistress Evans-Lewes,
IV, 5; Norton on, V, 7–9; Locker
heard GE was married in Germany,
227; GE on, VIII, 134, 140, 321, 456,
IX, 266–7; 313
War

"a necessary vent," I, 37; 254–5,
II, 150, Crimean, 197, VI, 123; III,
227–8, 247–8, GE sees Prussian
troops, IV, 278, 284; 283, 411,
Franco-Prussian, V, 110, lies worse
than bloodshed, 112; Goethe's contempt for, 123; 127, 132, 135, GE

hates war, loves discipline, VI, 123;
327, "The Battle of Dorking," 390;
"The New Ordeal,", VII, 68; 76,
132, JB on Kaffirs, 141
Will

GE signs (1858), II, 288, (1859),
III, 212–3; (1880), VII, 270; proves
GHL's will, 389; IX, 346; left Emily
Clarke £5,000, 306; Herefordshire
property, 357
Works of George Eliot

6/ ed., (3 vols. 1861–63), *Adam,
Mill, Scenes and Silas*, III, 453–4,
458, 463–4, IV, 6, 62, a failure, 113;
137, VIII, 289, 291, 293, 337–8

Cheap (or Illustrated) ed. (30 6*d*
nos., 4 vols. 3/6 each), *Adam, Mill,
Scenes and Silas* (from plates of 6/ eds.)
and *Felix*, IV, 63, JB leases, 320–3,
327; 353, 372, a failure in nos., 394;
VIII, 393, IV, 498, 500, V, 407,
VI, 22, 299, 331, VII, 252, 314

Author's Household ed. (5 vols.,
$1 each 1869), Boston, Fields, Os-
good and Co., V, 16, 36, 38, Library
ed., VIII, 451

Romantische Werken, Dutch tr. by
P. Bruijn, (5 vols., 1870–73), Sneek,
Van Druten and Bleeker, *Novellen,
Adam Bede, De Molen van Dorlcotc,
Romola*, and *Felix Holt, de Radikaal*,
V, 362

Cabinet ed., JB proposes to renew
lease, VI, 297; estimates of cost, 308;
312, format, 345, 349, 351, 357–9;
361, 366, 422–3; terms, 303, 405,
410, 422; "Lifted Veil" and "Brother Jacob" with *Silas*, 340–349, 351;
VII, 51, *Jubal* added, 55, 58, 69;
Theophrastus added, 196, 226, 243;
sales and payments, 25–6, 43–4, 98,
204, 252, 314, IX, 240

See also *Scenes of Clerical Life*; *Adam
Bede*; "The Lifted Veil"; *The Mill
on the Floss*; *Silas Marner*; "Brother
Jacob"; *Romola*; *Felix Holt*; *The Span-
ish Gypsy*; *Middlemarch*; *The Legend of
Jubal*; *Daniel Deronda*; *Impressions of
Theophrastus Such*; *Analytical Catalogue*;
Blackwood's; Coventry *Herald*; *Fort-*

442

444

450

Hill, Emily (*continued*)
C. E. Maurice), IV, 184, engaged, V, 284; 289
Hill, Florence, IV, 184, VII, 217, 284, 318
Hill, Gertrude, *see* Mrs. C. L. Lewes
Hill, James, IV, 156
Hill, (3) Mrs. James (Caroline Southwood Smith), IV, 156, V, 53, 61, at Witley with CLL family, VII, 303
Hill, Matthew Davenport, II, 225
Hill, Miranda, IV, 184
Hill, Octavia, I, lxxi, IV, 184, 213, V, 124, 161, 284, GE goes to tenants' party, 336; 371, tries to buy pub, 373; GE contributes to annuity for, VI, 31; 83, and Swiss Cottage fields, 153; nervous break-down, VII, 6, 38; VIII, 477, dines at Priory, IX, 71; 248
Hill, Sir Richard, I, 38
Hill, Rowland, I, 110, II, 442, IV, 186
Hill, T. W., I, xx, VI, 311, VIII, vii
Hillern, Wilhelmine Birch-Pfeiffer von, *Ein Arzt der Seele*, IV, 458, V, 11
Hilles, Frederick Whiley, I, xviii
Hilton, Jane, VIII, xv
Himalaya, VI, 92
Hincks, Miss, I, 360
Hind, Arthur Mayger, I, xxi
Hindhead, IX, 197
Hine, Joseph, I, 184
Hinton, James, III, 328, GHL meets, 329; 438, V, 436, VI, 142
Hinton, John H., III, 328
Hiphil and Hophal, forms of Hebrew verb to do, VII, 212
Hipparchus, IV, 126
Hippolytus, II, 98, VIII, 63
Hirn, G. A., V, 150
Hirshberg, Edgar W., II, 222, VIII, xv, IX, 341
Hirst, Leo, IX, 106
His, Wilhelm, IV, 459
Historical Register, GHL contributes to (Jan., Apr. 1845), VII, 366
Hitchcock, Ethan Allen (1835–1909), I, 321
Hitchcock, Samuel, tr. Spinoza's *Ethics*, I, 321
Hitchin, *see* Girton College

Hoare, Mr., VII, 22
Hoary Head, I, 192*
Hobbema, Meindert, V, 329
Hodgskin, Thomas, II, 4
Hodgson, David, VII, 343
Hodgson, Shadworth Hollway, VII, 21
Hodgson, Mrs. Stewart, VII, 12
Hodgson, William Ballantyne, mesmerizes GE, I, 180, 341, 342, 352, 360, 365, 366, 367, II, 101, 180, 187, 189, and *WR*, 206, 444, VIII, 23, 28, 65, 73, 80, 89, 115, 118, 125–6, 134
Hofer, Philip, I, xx, IV, 39, 63
Hoffmann, I, 174
Hoffmann von Fallersleben, August Heinrich, I, 174, II, 169–70
Hofmann, A. W., III, 353
Hofmeister, Friedrich, IV, 415–6
Hofwyl (Hofwil) School, GHL's sons at, I, lxi; lxxi, Sara tells GE of, II, 236; 253, 261, GHL delighted with, 262, 339, 377, 383, visits sons at, 466; III, 46, 69, 79, GHL at, 115–6; religious instruction at, 120; 123, 126, 187, CLL leaves, 242; GHL forbids sons' confirmation, 273–4; GE and GHL at, 306, 308, 311; 325, 347, 413, 425, 446, CLL returns for holiday, 466; CLL visits Bertie, IV, 37; GHL at, April 1863, 83; V, 328, CLL at, 424, VII, 64, VIII, 165–7, Thornie at, 170, 190–2, 233–4, 242, 252, 259–60, 267, Thornie Leaves, 270–1; 280, 446
Hogarth, Georgina, IX, 212
Hogarth, William, VIII, 205
Hoge, J. O., IX, 352
Hogg, Mr. (Chapman's assistant), I, 350, VII, 70
Hogg, Jabez, IX, 222, 233
Hohenlohe-Langenburg, Prince Ernest, GHL sees, V, 90
Hohenlohe-Langenburg, Princess Léopoldine, wants to see GE and GHL, V, 89; GHL calls, 90
Hohenlohe-Schillingsfürst, Prince Constantine Victor, II, 169
Holbeach, Henry, V, 131
Holbeche, Vincent (attorney), I, xlix, II, 178, asks details of marriage, 346; 349–50, sends I. Evans GE's letter,

460

Lamb (*continued*)
(May and Nov. 1848), VII, 369
Lambeth Pottery, GE visits, VII, 52, 53
Lambton, Lady, III, 255
Lamennais, Félicité de, IX, 353
Lampson, Sir Curtis Miranda, VI, 122
Lancashire, cotton famine, IV, 72; dialect, VI, 348
Lancashire Independent College, IX, 340
Lancashire Public School Assn., VIII, 74
Lancet, IX, 358
Landolphe, Mme F., plans to tr. *Middlemarch*, V, 256
Landon, Letitia Elizabeth (L.E.L.), I, 298
Landor, Robert Eyres, *Fawn of Sertorius*, I, 225*
Landor, Walter Savage, I, 225; praises Massey's poems, II, 146; GHL's art. on, *Lowe's Magazine* (Nov. 1846), VII, 368, IX, 353
Landsborough, David, *A Popular History of British Sea-Weeds*, II, 244*
Landseer, Sir Edwin Henry, I, 342
Lane, John, VI, 102
Lane-Fox, Charles, IX, 133
Lanfrey, Pierre, IV, 328
Lang, Cecil Y., I, xxi, VIII, xv
Langford, Joseph Munt (Blackwoods' London manager, 1809–84), I, liii, hears hint he dare not entertain as to GE's identity, II, 298; 386, 413, 418–9, VIII, 192–4, II, 424–5, 431, 434–5, 457, 461, 477, 491, 498–9, 506–9; inscribes presentation copies of *Adam*, III, 6, 8, 9, 10, 12, 24, 33, VIII, 226, 229, III, 39–41, 44, 51, VIII, 231–2, III, 65, 77, 84, 89, 92, 118, 121, brings Pug, 124; 127, 131, 137, 173, recommends lawyer to consult on *Mill*, 180; 182, 193–4, 200–1, letters from Simpson, 205, 209; 206–8, 212, 218, 250, 262, GHL calls on, 268; VIII, 259, inscribes *Mill* for Dickens, III, 279; 283, 289, 290, 296, 300, 314, 323, 339, reports on Laurence portrait of GE, 343; 352, 360, 390, looks up old costumes for GE, 393; brings GE box for opera, 397; VIII, 278;

III, 401, brings GE *Le Moyen Age*, 435; 443
IV, 7, on 6/ ed. of *Works*, 18; tells JB of GE's defection, 38; 121, 246–7, 251, 252, 255, sees change in book trade since 1860, 274; 293, on *Felix*, 2d ed., 307; 308, 311, on *Felix* and *Mill*, 318; 422, 441, 443, 445, 449, 453, and WB, 460; 462, 474, 480, 491, 492
on "Lisa," V, 23, 32; stern moralist, 99; on *Middlemarch*, 186–8; 190, 203, 207–8, 223, 240, 243, 245, 247, IX, 43, V, 254, 269, 294, 350, on Harry Trollope, 351; 361, 379, writes GE about advts., 381; 410, IX, 94
VI, 5, 44–5, 58, 62, 91, 136, enthusiasm for *Deronda*, 198; lunches at Priory, 214; 215, 217–8, 222–3, 225, 232, 237–8, has gout, 253; 273, 390, GE asks about Emma Gwyther, 435
VII, 7, 25, 27, 73, 82, 85, 111, 121, 163, 183, 219, IX, 276, too late to see JB, VII, 220; 229, 242, 244, 245, valuing JB's estate, 251; 253–5, 271, 314, IX, 318, 343
Langley, John Newport, VI, 181
Langsford, John Alfred, I, 354
Language of Flowers, The, I, xlix, 60, 67, 96
Lankester, Miss, IX, 298
Lankester, Edwin, II, 24; lectures at Coventry, 222; III, 352, IX, 298
Lankester, Mrs. Edwin (Phebe Pope), VII, 21, IX, 222, 298, 324
Lankester, Sir Edwin Ray, V, 88, VII, 21, IX, 298
Lansdowne, 3d Marquis of, I, 168, VI, 315
Lansdowne, 5th Marquis of, GE meets at Jowett's, VI, 138, IX, 152–3
Lansdowne, Marchioness of (Lady Maud Hamilton), VI, 138, IX, 152–3
Laon, VIII, 333
Laplace, Pierre Simon, Marquis de, II, 491
Lapland, VII, 110
Laprade, Victor Richard de, IX, 353
Larby, Mrs. (servant at Brookbank), V, 146, 172
Larken, Edmund Roberts (1810–95),

470

490

492

Opera (*continued*)
504, IV, 148
    Verdi, *Attila*, III, 412; VIII, 283; *Ernani*, II, 102; *Macbeth*, IX, 15; *Rigoletto*, IV, 34; VIII, 395, 476; IV, 92–3, 328; *La Traviata*, 92, *Il Trovatore*, III, 414; GHL likes Verdi, IV, 478; GE likes Italian opera, VIII, 92
    Wagner, *Fliegende Holländer*, IV, 388; *Lohengrin*, conducted by Wagner, II, 174; *Tannhäuser*, V, 84–5; Wagner not for GHL, 85; a language we do not understand, 317; GHL on Munich opera, VIII, 205–6
Opinione, VII, 257
Oppenheimer, Judith, VIII, xv
Opplinger, marries Miss Eborall, VII, 356
Opzoomer, C. W., V, 150
Oratorios, I, 9, 13, IX, 330. *See also* Handel, Haydn, Mendelssohn, Liszt
Oriel College, Oxford, V, 100
Origen, VIII, 63
Orléans, Duke of, VIII, 162
Orléans, Duchess of, II, 115, VIII, 162
Orléans, GE at (Jan. 1867), IV, 331, VIII, 395
Ormond, Leonée, IX, 41
Ormond, Richard, VIII, xv
"Orphic Fragments," GHL (*Leader*), III, 319
Orr, Mrs. Sutherland (Alexandra Leighton), V, 144, 333, 419, VI, 14, 43, 234, 364, 436, VII, 267, VIII, 457, IX, 76, 90
Orr and Co., VIII, 125
Orsini, Felice, GE rev. *Austrian Dungeons in Italy* (*Leader*, 30 Aug. 1856), VII, 359
Orton, Arthur, V, 237, 257, guilty of perjury, VI, 22
Osborne, Ralph Bernal, on *Deronda*, VI, 241
Osborne, Sidney Godolphin, on Liggins, III, 75, 104
Osgood, James Ripley, V, 94, accepts GHL's proposal for *Middlemarch*, 165–6; *Jubal* offered to, VI, 44, IX, 155–7, 352
Osgood, Ticknor and Co., V, 139, want *Middlemarch* for *Every Saturday*, 152,

IX, 22–4, V, 195, 198, transfer it to *Harper's*, 216–7, IX, 35
Ossoli, Marchioness, *see* Margaret Fuller
Ostend, IV, 291
Ostrovsky, A. N., IV, 478
Oswald, Mrs., IV, 486
Oswald (*Corinne*), I, 71
Otter, Francis, I, lxiii, V, 143, 216, 238, 286, going to Australia, 304–5; VI, 43, engaged to Emily Cross, 116, 117–8, VII, 312, 318–9, Cross visits, 234; GE's trustee, 268; 279, 321–2, at Witley, 335
Otter, Mrs. Francis (Emily Helen Cross), I, lxiii, V, 143, 171, 201, 215, 302, 310, 420, 435, 446, VI, 7, engaged to Francis Otter, 116, 117–8; 169, 233, 354, VII, 286, 299, 312, 318–320, 322, at Witley, 335, VIII, 28, IX, 20, 111, 312
Otter, Gwendolen, VI, 355
Otto, Dr., sells farm to Thornie, VIII, 391
Ouchy, I, 289
Ouvry, Mrs., II, 112
Ouvry, Mrs. E. Carrington, I, xi, xiii, xvii, V, 109, 156, VIII, xiii. *See also* Elinor Southwood Lewes
Ouvry, Jonathan, VIII, xiii
Ouvry, Norman Delamain, VII, viii
Overton, Ann (servant), III, 29, 32
Overton, John Henry, IX, 280
Overton, Mrs. J. H., IX, 281
Ovid, *Metamorphoses*, I, 38*
Ovsyannikov, Filipp, VIII, 453
Owen, Richard, I, xliv, II, 24, 56, and GHL, 281; likes "Amos," 295; commends *Sea-Side Studies*, 370; 470, 479, reads GHL's paper at British Association, 487; III, 6, on *Adam*, 20, 43, 55, art. on Johnston, 62; GHL proposes art. on, 117, 127; 334, gives GE *Memoir on the Megatherium*, 373, V, 158; GHL's art. on, *Fraser's* (Jan. 1856), VII, 374, VIII, ix, 90, 141–2, 179, 181, 203, 207, 222, 229–30, 240, 407, IX, 347
Owen, Mrs. Richard, thinks "Amos" clever, II, 295
Owen, Robert (socialist, 1771–1858), I, xliv, GE meets, 161; plans Anglo-

494

Pardy, Mr., IX, 160
Paris, I, 270, 301, 319, II, 216, V, 114, siege of, 118; 152–3
GE at (June 1849), I, 289; Mar. and June 1860), III, 285, 309; (April 1861), 407; (May and June 1864), IV, 148; (Jan. 1865), 176–7, VIII, 329, 333; (Dec. 1866), IV, 327–9, VIII, 395; (Mar. 1867), 349; (July 1868), 449; (May 1869), V, 26, (May 1870), 92, VIII, 475; (Oct. 1872), V, 317; (June 1873), 423; (Oct. 1874), VI, 86; (June 1876), 264, IX, 179; (May 1880), VII, 273–80; VIII, xviii, 451–2
Paris Salon, VII, 165
Parish Magazine, III, 146
Parizade, Princess, III, 172, VIII, 239
Park, W., I, xix
Park Shot, 8, Richmond, GE and GHL at (Oct. 1855–11 Feb. 1859), II, 216–III, 13
Park Village West, London, III, 342
Parker, Mr. (of Coventry), II, 26
Parker, J. H., GE rev. his *Antigone*, *Leader* (29 Mar. 1856), VII, 359
Parker, John William, II, 264, 419, 434, 512, IV, 316, VIII, 39, 149–50, 155, 401
Parker, John William, Jr., VIII, 148–9, 155
Parker, Theodore, II, 38, 57, 120, IV, 78
Parkes, Bessie Rayner, VIII, 46, 96, 241–2; *see also* Mme Louis Belloc
Parkes, Joseph, I, 1, II, 7, invites GE to meet Cobden, 9; 21, 37, GE dines with, 41, 91; unfaithful to wife, 342; VIII, 241, 307, 329
Strauss tr., initiates it, I, 171–2; contributes £150, 172; 175, 185, 187, 190–1, 196, II, 149
Parkes, Mrs. Joseph (Eliza Priestley), I, 1, calls on GE, II, 7; 9, 26–7, 129, invites GE to a ball, 138; 141, 342, dies, VI, 420; VIII, 241, 329
Parkes, Josiah, bequest to Bessie, V, 181
Parkes, Priestley, I, 1
Parkhurst, Rodie, VIII, 270
Parkinson, R. N., VII, viii, VIII, ix
Parkinson, S., III, 174
Parkinson-Fortescue, C. S., VIII, 313

Parrish, Morris Longstreth, I, xi, *Victorian Lady Novelists*, V, 155, VIII, xviii
Parry, R. St. John, V, 410
Parson, William (Witley surgeon). VII, 170, 174, 178, 180, 185, 326
Parthenon, II, 194–5
Parthey, Dr., II, 194
Partridge, Richard, V, 365
Partridge, Samuel William, V. 389, VI, 32, 220
Pascal, Blaise, *Pensées*, I, 7*, 25*, 34, 56, 186, VII, 11
Patagonian Missionaries, II, 48
Pater, Walter Horatio, V, 100, *Renaissance*, 455*, in *The New Republic*, VI, 406
Paterson, Mr. ("the bore"), VI, 142
Paterson, Alexander Henry, VI, 84
Paterson, Arthur, ed. *George Eliot's Family Life and Letters*, I, xii, III, 415, V, 317
Paton, Mr., IX, 177
Patrick, J. M., VI, 406
Patterson, Mr., V, 310
Patterson, Robert Hogarth, II, 420, JB introduces to GHL, III, 183; 208, 237, on *Spanish Gypsy*, IV, 452; 455, 458, VIII, 249, 417
Patti, Adelina, IV, 266, V, 144
Pattison, Mark, and *WR*, VIII, 133, 172, IX, 342; V, 6, 13, not orig. of Casaubon, 38–9, VII, 96, IX, 257; a "general writer," V, 44–5; 96, 98, GE and GHL visit at Oxford, 99–100, VIII, 476; V, 117, 124, 141, 216, 304, 344, 420, VI, 43, *Isaac Casaubon*, 66, 97, 108, 176, IX, 157; VI, 139, GE reads "Philosophy at Oxford," 202, IX, 171; rev. *Problems*, VI, 202; 204, 210, 229, 243, 343, GHL smokes with, 376; ES on his conversation, IX, 212; 217–8, GE meets at Hamilton & Co., 228; GE and GHL call on, VII, 31; writes GE on GHL's death, 155; sends Greek errata to Trübner, 160–2; Jowett on his *Milton*, IX, 284–5
Pattison, Mrs. Mark (Emilia Frances Strong, later Lady Dilke), V, 5–6, 13, not orig. of Dorothea, 38–9; sits

Powell, Baden (*continued*)
bach, 382
Powell, Henry, I, 258, VIII, 17
Powers, Mrs., IV, 424
Powerscourt, 6th Viscount, V, 247
Powick, Worcs., I, 315
Poynter, Sir Edward John, V, 57, VII, 23
Poynter, F. N. L., on Chapman, II, 238
Poysers at the Seaside, III, 89
Pozzuoli, VIII, 265
Prague, GE at (July 1858), II, 468–9, 476, VIII, 207–8, 472–3
Prater (agent), buys Heights, VI, 323
Preachings, the, Edinburgh, II, 393, VI, 41, 137, VII, 142, VIII, 415
Prefaces, GE on, V, 459
Pre-Raphaelites, II, 48, Ruskin's letter to *Times*, 156; VI, 252
Prescott, William Hickling, *Ferdinand and Isabella*, IV, 168*
Press, Patterson acquires, III, 183, 237, VIII, 249
Preston, I, 269, II, 374
Preston, John, VIII, xv
Prévost, Abbé, *Manon Lescaut*, IV, 386*
Prevost, Jean Louis (1796–1852), I, 294, 298, 305
Prevost-Martin, Alexandre Louis, I, 305
Preyer, Wilhelm Thierry, IV, 415–6, VI, 236
Price, Mrs. Lucy, I, 79
Priestley, Joseph, I, l, lvi, II, 7
Priestley, Mr. and Mrs. William Overend, V, 357, VII, 21
Primitive Methodists, *see* Methodists
Princeites, V, 335
Princess's Theatre, VIII, 144
Princeton University Library, I, xi, II, 80, VI, 414, VIII, 321
"Principles of Success in Literature," VIII, 340, IX, 62
Prinsep, Val, V, 386, IX, 81
Prior, Sir James, III, 196, IX, 345
Prior, Matthew, Johnson's *Life of*, V, 238*
Priory, The, 21 North Bank, Regent's Park, I, xlvi, IV, 93 GE buys, 103; moves into, 111; decorating, 106, 111–12, VIII, 314; CLL's party, IV,

115; GE describes, 117; alterations, V, 141–2, 144, 151, 156; recarpeted, IX, 131; ES describes drawing-room, 259; GE leaves, VII, 270; CLL attends to, 283, 340
Pritchett, Victor Sawdon, I, x
Problems of Life and Mind (5 vols., 1874–79), I, lxx, Vol. I, 1st ser., *The Foundations of a Creed* (1874), GHL studies nervous system for, IV, 405, V, 150, 261; fears it will be left to GE to finish, 291; 305, GE reads MS, 321, 324, 332, 344; GHL discusses printing with JB, 350, 364, 366; terms, 369; GHL feared it would shock JB, 371; 383, estimate of bulk and page, 386, 392, JB disconcerted by, 400; asks GHL to get another publisher, 410; Trübner takes over, 411; 413, 415–6, nearly printed, 431; 800 sold, 472; new ed. needed, VI, 8; GHL wants *Maga* to attack, 11; 2d ed., 31; GHL writes Druce on, 39; Bray on, 425
Vol. II (1875), GHL recasts, VI, 31; 50, 60, GHL wants *Maga* to attack, 62; rewriting, 72, 79, ready for press, 83; 89, 93, 95–6, nearly through press, 106, 108, 131, 138–9, cited by Ribot, 243; IX, 7, 10, 14, 17, 20, 23, 63, 80, 85–6, 88–9, 98–101, 120–1, 127–8
Vol. III, 2d ser., *The Physical Basis of Mind* (1877), VI, 113, 157, 174, gets on slowly, 210; illustrations, 211, 256, 261; 226, 233, 236, 254, printing, 291; GE reads proofs, 294; 297, 310, preface rewritten, 346; 362, VII, 154, IX, 139, 145, 189–90
Vol. IV, 3d ser., Problem I, *The Study of Psychology* (1879), GHL busy with, VII, 18, 20–4, 30, 60; GE intends to finish, 90; revises through ch. 3, 100; 107, 111, revising, not finishing, 115; 116, 128, 138, GE sends to Kaufmann, 156; 157, 350 sold, 161; errata in Greek, 162; 168, 170, 329, Sir Henry Maine on, 176; IX, 223, 260–1, 271
Vol. V, 3d ser. cont., Problems II–IV (1879), GE revises, VII, 116; Sully and Foster read proof, 154;

Raaff, VIII, 368

Rabelais, *Pantagruel*, IV, 85; ed. Walter Besant, VII, 190

Race, Sydney, I, lix, xxi, 334, II, 35

Rachel, Mme (medium), IV, 457

Rachel, Mlle (Élisa Félix, 1820–58, actress), GE sees, II, 103–4; GHL art., in *Fraser's*, (July 1846), VII, 367; IX, 166

Racine, Jean, *Phèdre*, II, 103–4*; *Britannicus*, V, 374

Raczynsky, Count Atanazy, II, 194

Radcliffe, Ann, III, 168

Radclyffe, E. (engraver), VIII, 309, IX, 70

Radford, distressed weavers at, IV, 169, V, 114, 329

Radipole, Dorset, III, 148–9

Radnor, Countess of, V, 85

Raff, Joseph Joachim, II, 169

Ragatz, GE at (July 1876), VI, 263, 265–74; 275, 283–4, 296

Raglan, F. J. H. Somerset, 1st Baron, VI, 123

Rahel, Antonie (Levin), Varnhagen von Ense, II, 205, VI, 293

Rajon, P., etches GE portrait (Burton), IV, 212

Ralph the Heir (Trollope), dramatized by Reade, V, 351

Ralston, William Ralston Shedden-, IV, 360, 364, 478, V, 116, *Songs of the Russian People*, 142*, IX, 45; V, 262; 385, 415, 463–4, VI, 14, sends GE Turgenev story; resigns from BM, 132; IX, 45, 95, 224

Ramsay, Edward Bannerman, *Reminiscences of Scottish Life*, IV, 305*, 308–9

Ramsay, John William, Lord, VI, 138–9, 254

Ramsgate, II, 36, 40, 42, 45, 465

Ranby Hall, Lincs., VI, 116, GE visits Otters at, VII, 318–9

Rand, Mr., III, 143

Randolph Crescent, 3, JB's Edinburgh house, IV, 403

Rands, William Brighty, essays in *Tait's*, II, 382, V, 131

Rank, J. Arthur, II, 360

Ranke, Johannes, III, 448

Ranke, Leopold von, writes for *Fort-*

nightly, IV, 194

Ranson, W. H., IV, 179

Ranthorpe, 1847, GHL's novel, VII, 368, VIII, 168–9, IX, 62

Raphael, I, 188, II, 451, *Sistine Madonna*, 471–2, 494, III, 295, IV; 182, GE dislikes, VIII, 455

Raphall, Morris, IX, 193

Rassam, Hormuzd, IV, 405

Ratchford, Fannie E., I, xxi, IX, 329

Ratcliffe, F. W., VIII, xv

Ratcliff Highway, IV, 360

Rathbone, Richard (1788–1860), I, 179–80, 200

Rathbone, Mrs. Richard (1798–1878), ed. *Diary of Lady Willoughby*, I, 179–80

Rathbone, William, I, 179

Rauch, Christian Daniel, II, 193, VI, 48

Ravel, Pierre A., VIII, 180

Ravené Collection, Berlin, II, 194

Ravenna, IV, 154, GE at, Apr. 1869, V, 26–7, VIII, 451–2

Ravensbourne (Bonham Carter house nr Keston, Kent), II, 257, III, 364, V, 217, 226, 232, VI, 35

Ravenscroft, Amberleys' house nr Trelleck, VIII, 484

Rawlins, Sarah, *see* Mrs. I. P. Evans

Rawlinson, George, V, 99

Ray, Gordon N., I, xxi, II, 291, III, 308, IV, 24, VIII, xiv, 139

Reade, Charles, *White Lies*, "inflated plagiarisms," II, 422; 467, IV, 257, and *Felix*, 281, 282, *Griffith Gaunt*, V, 18, VIII, 380; quarrels with Trollope, V, 351; GE has tea with, 420; *A Woman Hater* (*Maga*), VI, 253, 389–91*; *A Terrible Temptation*, 253–4, *The Courier of Lyons*, VII, 43

Reader, The, IV, 170, GHL refuses editorship of, 172

Reading, Berks., I, 164

Realism, Ruskin's influence on GE's, II, 228, 422; art of the commonplace, 269, 292, 299, 309, 347–9; real and concrete, 362; GE on originals, 375, 459; III, 356, 382, 427, IV, 43, 97, VI, 223, needed for tragedy, VIII, 466

JB wants GE to soften, II, 291,

Senior, Mrs. Nassau John (Jane Elisabeth Hughes), offers GE house in Spain, IV 317; 365, 403–4, sings to GE, 422; 436, V, 14, sends grapes to Thornie, 55; 57, 82–3, 249, sister of Thomas Hughes, 285; 286, 383, becomes inspector of workhouses, 372; visits Girton, VIII, 469; *Report on Pauper Schools*, VI, 46–7; IX, 138, 151, CLL on, VI, 87, 157; attacked, 65, 70; ill, 90; moves to Chelsea, 269–71; dies, 359; 393, VIII, 469, IX, 5–6
Senior, Nassau William, IV, 317
Serbia, VI, 266
Sestri, III, 412, VIII, 284, 448
Seth Bede, "The Methody," III, 226
Sevenoaks, IV, 481, VII, 263, 266, GE at, Aug. 1880, 311; GE plans Christmas at, 347
Sevigné, Mme de, VIII, 67
Seville, GE at (Feb. 1867), IV, 339; 348–50
Seville cathedral, justifies western civilization, IV, 351
Sèvres, VIII, 333
Seward, Anna, "female pedant," I, 55
Seward, William H., VIII, 339
Seymour, Lord Edward Percy, VIII, 359
Seymour, Edward (Scribner's), VIII, 486
Seymour, Frederick Beauchamp Paget, 1st Baron Alcester, VI, 373
Seymour, Henry Danby, IV, 172, 195, VIII, 330–2, 387
Seymour, Mrs. Laura Alison, VI, 253
Shacklewell, II, 27
Shaen, Miss, III, 324
Shakers, V, 335
Shakespear, Emily, VI, 423
Shakespare, works mentioned, *Antony and Cleopatra*, III, 53*, *As You Like It*, I, 15*, 44, 71, 92, 203, 259, 266, 326, II, 283, 330, IV, 29, 181, 186, VI, 274, VII, 290, VIII, 14, IX, 335, 340; *Coriolanus*, V, 145*, VIII, 401; *Cymbeline*, IX, 356*; *Hamlet*, I, 116*, 325, II, 117, 461, III, 374, VII, 325, VIII, 6, 293, IX, 128, 166, 175, 335, 339, 350; *I Henry IV*, I,

36*, 194, III, 127, VII, 52, IX, 20, 341; *II Henry IV*, IX, 41*, I, 194, VII, 52; *Henry V*, I, 100*, 211, II, 245, VIII, 240; *II Henry VI*, III, 68*; *Henry VIII*, V, 304*; *Julius Caesar*, III, 110*; *King John*, I, 148–9*, IV, 195, IX, 348; *King Lear*, II, 366*, IV, 484, IX, 279, 330; *Love's Labour's Lost*, VI, 96*; *Macbeth*, I, 324*, II, 358, III, 324, 470, V, 472, VII, 262, VIII, 198, IX, 99, 218, 348, 357; *Measure for Measure*, IX, 348–50; *Merchant of Venice*, I, 156*, II, 186, VIII, 306; *Merry Wives of Windsor*, I, 245*, IX, 14, 54, 272; *Mid-summer Night's Dream*, I, 91*, V, 132, VIII, 6, IX, 332; *Much Ado about Nothing*, I, 122*, 250, II, 340, IV, 174, VI, 25, IX, 139; *Othello*, III, 18*, IV, 400, (Salvini), VI, 142, 183, VIII, 144, 175, 219, 270, 293, 350, 385; *Pericles*, IV, 386*; *Richard II*, IX, 356*; *Richard III*, I, 100*, VIII, 111, III, 443; *Romeo and Juliet*, I, 228*, II, 336, IV, 186, IX, 310, 343; *Sonnets*, VI, 399*, VII, 10, 158, IX, 346, 355; *Tempest*, I, 239*; *Troilus and Cressida*, I, 130*, III, 382; *Twelfth Night*, I, 275*, II, 358, IX, 350; *Two Gentlemen of Verona*, III, 66*, VIII, 11; *Venus and Adonis*, IV, 386*, IX, 54; *Winter's Tale*, I, 89*, 177, IV, 364, 469; VII, 385–6, 389, VIII, 402, IX, 92, 336, 355
GE on, I, 22, 29, at Stratford, 271; II, 25, 114–5, 165, moves one through worst actor, 301; 319, IV, 143, 174, VI, 113, refuses to write life for EML ser. 416; reads aloud to Cross, VII, 140; discussed, IX, 228
GE compared with I, xlviii, III, 42, 163, 351, V, 176, 206, 465, VI, 49, 146, VII, 108, 313, IX, 55, 225
GHL on, I, 377, plays Shylock, II, 488; III, 420, IV, 386, VI, 337; "Shakspeare," *WR* (Mar. 1845), "Shakspeare's Dramatic Art," (lecture, Dec. 1848), "Shakspeare's Critics," *Edinburgh Rev.*, (July 1849), "Shakspeare in France," *Cornhill* (Jan. 1865), VII, 366, 369, 379;

514

518

Snow, Lord, VIII, xvi
Social Science Association, IV, 468
Socialism, I, xliv, 375
Society of Antiquaries, IV, 24
Society for the Conversion of the Jews, II, 102
Society for the Prevention of Cruelty to Animals, VI, 33, 52, 94
Society for Promoting Christian Knowledge, V, 443, 471, VI, 16, 18–9
Society for Promoting the Employment of Women, VI, 347
Society for Psychical Research, VI, 6, IX, 286
Socinianism, I, 90, IX, 333
Socrates, II, 59, VI, 99, 338, 407
Soissons, VI, 83
Sola, D. A. de, IX, 193
Solmar, Fräulein von, II, 184–5
Solomon, I, 108, V, 437
Solon, V, 240
Somerville, Mary Fairfax, *On the Connection of the Physical Sciences*, I, 56*, VI, 5
Sommaia, Count della, III, 457
Somnophilus, I, 96
Sophia Frederika, Queen of the Netherlands, IV, 453
"Sophie Arnould" (Agnes Lewes's art., *WR*, Sept. 1844), VII, 366
Sophocles, *Oedipus Coloneus, Oedipus Rex*, II, 319*, 358*, *Electra, Philoctetes*, III, 357*; *Felix* motto from *Ajax*, V, 325*; *Philoctetes*, VIII, 201*
Soret, Frédéric, IV, 359, V, 123
Sorosis, New York, GE declines membership in, V, 14
Sorrento, III, 292, 311, VIII, 265
Sotheby, Mrs. Hans William, VII, 243
Sotheran, Henry, II, 24
South Fields, Wandsworth, GE at Holly Lodge (Jan. 1859—Sept. 1860), III, 3—349
South Kensington Museum, IV, 144, GE at, VI, 93
Southborough, II, 110
Southcote (or Southcott), Joanna, I, 11
Southey, Robert, poetical romances, I, 21*; *The Doctor*, 48*; *Thalaba*, III, 48*; *Madoc in Wales*, 412, VIII, 282
Souvestre, M., III, 274

Soyer (confectioner), VIII, 168
Spa, GHL at (July–Aug. 1862), III, 443, IV, 52, VII, 389
Spain, GE's journey to (Jan.–Mar. 1867), IV, 338–49; GE on, V, 227; VIII, 366, 395–7
Spalding, Douglas A., V, 405, consumptive, 467
Spanish Drama, Lope de Vega and Calderon, 1846, VII, 367
Spanish Gypsy, The (1868), orig. *Fidalma*, IV, 370; GE reads for, 163, 301, 316, V, 32; begun as play; prologue and Act I written, IV, 165; reads Act II to GHL, 167; settles 3d and 5th acts, 168; at p. 33 of Act III 169; GHL takes it away, 179; idea predominated; needs complete recasting, 301; mentioned to JB, 347; plot entirely GE's, 355; *Fidalma*, 372; GE says unsuitable for *Cornhill*, 377; 392, JB suggests trying in type, 394–8; GE sends Bk. I, 399; 403, 404, has 6 proofs, 406, 412, VIII, 415; GE cannot hurry revision, IV, 422; 2d revise, 426; title 1st given, 427–8; Fidalma, or Fedalma, 428, 429, 433, 435; at p. 4 of Bk. V, 429; GHL advises return to less tragic ending, 430–1; GE sends end, 432, and notes, 433, 434; terms, 435, 442, 444; binding, 443, 445; Lytton indicates false accent Zincálo, 432, V, 32, VI, 22; readings from by Mrs. Dallas, V, 54; printer's errors in, VI, 39; paper, 42
  1st ed. (1868, 10/6), IV, 434, pub., 441, 475
  2d ed. (1868, 10/6), 460, 462–3, 474
  3d ed. (1868, 7/6), 475, 479–81, 487, 491, each 1000 to be called an ed., 495, 497; stereotyped, VI, 22; paper, 42
  4th ed. (1868, 7/6), IV, 497
  5th ed. (1875, 7/6), VI, 14, 22, 75, pub. 116; 123, IX, 115
  6th ed. (1878, 7/6), VI, 330
  Cabinet ed., (1878, 5/), VII, 51, 55, 57–8, GE sees no proof, 70
  reprints, American (Ticknor and Fields), IV, 440, 480–1, V, 37, 46;